50% OFF!

HiSET Online Test Prep Course

We consider it an honor and a privilege that you chose our HiSET Study Guide. As a way of showing our appreciation and to help us better serve you, we have partnered with Mometrix Test Preparation to offer you 50% off their online HiSET Prep Course.

Mometrix has structured their online course to perfectly complement your printed study guide. Many HiSET courses are needlessly expensive and don't deliver enough value. With their course, you get access to the best HiSET prep material, and you only pay half price.

WHAT'S IN THE HISET TEST PREP COURSE?

- **HiSET Study Guide**: Get access to content that complements your study guide.
- **Progress Tracker**: Their customized course allows you to check off content you have studied or feel confident with.
- **1,950+ Practice Questions**: With 1,950+ practice questions and lesson reviews, you can test yourself again and again to build confidence.
- **HiSET Flashcards**: Their course includes a flashcard mode consisting of over 1,230 content cards to help you study.

TO RECEIVE THIS DISCOUNT, VISIT THE WEBSITE AT

link.mometrix.com/hiset

USE THE DISCOUNT CODE:
STARTSTUDYING

IF YOU HAVE ANY QUESTIONS OR CONCERNS, PLEASE CONTACT MOMETRIX AT SUPPORT@MOMETRIX.COM

HiSET Prep Book 2025-2026
2 Practice Tests and HiSET Study Guide for All Subjects [4th Edition]

G. T. McDivitt

Copyright ©2025 Accepted, Inc.

ISBN-13: 9781637989166

ALL RIGHTS RESERVED. By purchase of this book, you have been licensed on copy for personal use only. No part of this work may be reproduced, redistributed, or used in any form or by any means without prior written permission of the publisher and copyright owner. Trivium Test Prep; Accepted, Inc.; Cirrus Test Prep; and Ascencia Test Prep are all imprints of Trivium Test Prep, LLC.

TABLE OF CONTENTS

1. Reading 7
- The Main Idea 7
- Supporting Details 10
- The Author's Purpose 11
- Organization and Text Structures 12
- The Audience 13
- Evaluating Arguments 14
- Drawing Conclusions 15
- Tone and Mood 17
- Meaning of Words and Phrases 19
- Figurative Language 20
- Graphic Sources of Information 22
- Elements of Fiction 23
- Answer Key 25

2. Grammar and Sentence Structure 26
- Parts of Speech 26
- Constructing Sentences 34
- Common Language Errors 38
- Answer Key 45

3. The Essay 47
- Writing a Thesis Statement 47
- Structuring the Essay 48
- Providing Supporting Evidence 50
- Writing Well 51

4. Numbers and Operations 53

Types of Numbers 53
Scientific Notation 55
Positive and Negative Numbers 56
Order of Operations 58
Units of Measurement 58
Decimals and Fractions 60
Rounding and Estimation 63
Ratios 63
Proportions 64
Percentages 64
Comparison of Rational Numbers 65
Exponents and Radicals 66
Factorials 68
Sequences and Series 68
Answer Key 72

5. Algebraic Concepts 85
Algebraic Expressions 85
Operations with Expressions 86
Linear Equations 88
Linear Inequalities 92
Quadratic Equations 96
Functions 99
Answer Key 105

6. Measurement and Geometry 121
Properties of Shapes 121
Three-Dimensional Shapes 133
Answer Key 135

7. Data Analysis, Probability, and Statistics 139

Describing Sets of Data 139
Graphs, Charts, and Tables 141
Probability 148
Answer Key 151

8. Scientific Practices 158
Scientific Inquiry 158
Designing Experiments 159
Facts, Theories, and Laws 160
Answer Key 161

9. Life Science 162
Biological Molecules 162
Nucleic Acids 163
Structure and Function of Cells 165
Cellular Respiration 166
Photosynthesis 168
Cell Division 169
Genetics 170
Evolution 171
Ecology 172
Human Anatomy and Physiology 174
Answer Key 182

10. Physical Science 183
The Structure of the Atom 183
The Periodic Table of the Elements 184
Chemical Bonds 186
Properties of Matter 187
States of Matter 188
Chemical Reactions 189

Mixtures 191

Acids and Bases 192

Motion 193

Forces 194

Work 195

Energy 195

Waves 197

Electricity and Magnetism 199

Answer Key 201

11. Earth and Space Science 203

Astronomy 203

Geology 204

Hydrology 206

Meteorology 208

Answer Key 210

12. United States History 211

North America Before European Contact 211

Colonial North America 211

Civil War and Westward Expansion 217

Industrialization and the Progressive Era 220

The United States Becomes a Global Power 221

Postwar and Contemporary United States 223

Answer Key 227

13. Civics and Government 228

The Constitution 228

Organization of the Federal Government 232

Civil Liberties and Rights 245

Political Parties 247

Other Groups 249

Answer Key 252

14. Economics 253

Types of Economic Systems 253

Functions of the Market 254

Government Intervention 258

Answer Key 262

15. Geography and World History 263

Geography 263

World History 267

Twentieth Century 282

Answer Key 292

Practice Test #1 293

Language Arts: Reading Comprehension 293

Language Arts: Writing 306

Mathematics 320

Science 332

Social Studies 353

Answer Explanations 369

Language Arts: Reading Comprehension 369

Language Arts: Writing 372

Mathematics 376

Science 386

Social Studies 390

Practice Test #2 395

ONLINE RESOURCES

Accepted, Inc. includes online resources with the purchase of this study guide to help you fully prepare for the exam.

To help you fully prepare for your HiSET, Accepted, Inc. includes online resources with the purchase of this study guide.

Practice Tests

In addition to the practice test included in this book, we also offer another online test. Since many exams today are computer based, getting to practice your test-taking skills on the computer is a great way to prepare.

Flash Cards

A convenient supplement to this study guide, Accepted Inc.'s flash cards enable you to review important terms easily on your computer or smartphone.

From Stress to Success

Watch "From Stress to Success," a brief but insightful YouTube video that offers the tips, tricks, and secrets experts use to score higher on the exam.

Access these materials at: **acceptedinc.com/hiset-online-resources**

INTRODUCTION

Congratulations on choosing to take the HiSET exam! By purchasing this book, you've taken an important step on your path to earning your high school-equivalency credential.

This guide will provide you with a detailed overview of the HiSET exam so that you know exactly what to expect on test day. We'll take you through all the concepts covered on the exam and give you the opportunity to test your knowledge with practice questions. Even if it's been a while since you last took a major test, don't worry; we'll make sure you're more than ready!

What is the HiSET?

The High School Equivalency Test—HiSET—exam is offered by ETS (Educational Testing Services). As its name suggests, the HiSET is a high school equivalency test; successful candidates will receive their High School Equivalency, or HSE. Twenty-three states and five US territories currently offer the HiSET. You may take the HiSET in English or in Spanish; this book prepares candidates for the English version.

The HiSET is an exam composed of five subject tests. It certifies that the test-taker has high school level academic skills in reading, writing, math, science, and social studies. The five subject tests can be taken together or separately, but you must pass all five tests in order to pass the exam overall. Once a test-taker passes the exam, then that person becomes eligible to receive their HSE, which can be used in job applications or in applying to colleges or universities. The HiSET is specifically designed for individuals who did not complete high school, no matter the reason.

What's on the HiSET?

The HiSET gauges high school level content knowledge and skills in five areas: Language Arts—Reading, Language Arts—Writing, Mathematics, Science, and Social Studies. On the English-language version of the test, candidates are expected to be able to read closely, write clearly, edit and understand standard written English as it is used in context, and solve quantitative and algebraic problems. You must also demonstrate strong comprehension and analysis of sources from life science, physical science, and Earth and space science as well as civics and government, history, geography, and economics. All questions are multiple choice; the Language Arts—Writing test includes an additional essay question.

Each subject test is taken separately. You must complete one subject test before moving on to the next. You will have 65 minutes for the Language Arts—Reading test, 120 minutes for the Language Arts—Writing test, 90 minutes for the Mathematics test, 80 minutes for the Science test, and 70 minutes for the Social Studies test. Bear in mind that the time may be different for the Spanish version of the HiSET.

Language Arts—Reading Test

The Language Arts—Reading test assesses your ability to understand a range of texts that can be found in both academic and workplace settings. The test includes literary and informational texts varying in length from 400 to 600 words. You will be asked to identify details and make logical inferences from—as well as valid claims about—the texts. You also will be asked to define key vocabulary and use textual evidence to analyze the texts in your own words in the form of a written response.

Language Arts—Reading Test		
Topics	Percentage of Test	Skills Assessed
Informational texts	60% of reading test	• Read closely • Understand key concepts • Distinguish main idea, supporting ideas, inferences • Understand vocabulary in context
Literary texts	40% of reading test	
Total	50 multiple-choice questions	65 minutes

Language Arts—Writing Test

The Language Arts—Writing test will ask you to revise excerpts of text. The multiple-choice questions will test your ability to recognize mechanical and grammatical errors such as those in subject-verb agreement, pronoun agreement, sentence structure, and punctuation. Anticipate questions about reorganizing paragraphs and choosing words for optimal coherence and clarity. For the essay question, you will read two written excerpts about an issue, develop a position on it, and argue your point of view. The essay is a chance for you to demonstrate your ability to form and present your ideas in an organized piece of writing.

Language Arts—Writing Test		
Topics	Percentage of Test	Skills Assessed
Language facility	43% of writing test	• Write with precision and organization • Use appropriate style, tone, and idioms • Recognize and use correct grammar, mechanics, and sentence structure
Conventions of writing	35% of writing test	
Organization of ideas	22% of writing test	
Total	60 multiple-choice questions 1 essay question	120 minutes

Mathematics Test

The Mathematics test assesses mastery of key fundamental math concepts. The test focuses on reasoning skills and modes of thinking that can be used in a variety of mathematical content areas, specifically algebra, data analysis, geometry, and number sense. Questions will assess your ability to make sense of complex problems, use logical thinking to find solutions, recognize structure, and look for and express regularity in repeated reasoning. You also will be evaluated on the precision of your mathematics. The test center will provide a calculator.

Mathematics Test		
Topics	Percentage of Test	Skills Assessed
Algebraic concepts	45% of math test	• Understand key mathematical concepts • Demonstrate skill and fluency with key math procedures • Apply concepts to realistic situations
Numbers and operations	19% of math test	
Measurement and geometry	18% of math test	
Data analysis, probability, and statistics	18% of math test	
Total	55 multiple-choice questions	90 minutes

Science Test

The Science test assesses your mastery of scientific content in life science, physical science and Earth and space science, as well as your ability to apply scientific reasoning. Questions will ask you to interpret materials like charts, graphs, tables, and short textual excerpts. Material covered may include biology, chemistry, physics, health, astronomy, ecology, zoology, and botany. Prepare to evaluate the quality of research design, research questions, procedures, and conclusions. You may also be asked to analyze assumptions, hypotheses, and observations or distinguish among them.

Science Test		
Topics	Percentage of Test	Skills Assessed
Life science	49% of science test	• Use scientific reasoning (textually and quantitatively) • Apply scientific reasoning to realistic situations
Physical science	28% of science test	
Earth and space science	23% of science test	
Total	60 multiple-choice questions	80 minutes

Social Studies Test

The Social Studies test assesses your mastery of social studies concepts and skills. The primary focus of the test is on history—primarily US history—and American civics and government. Geography and economics are supplementary. As on the Science test, questions will ask you to interpret short textual excerpts, maps, graphs, tables, pictures, and other materials. You don't need to worry about memorizing dates and names. Instead, prepare to analyze sources and judge their validity, understand the difference between fact and opinion, and gauge the reliability of conclusions. Be familiar with historical trends and economic and geographic terminology.

Social Studies Test		
Topics	Percentage of Test	Skills Assessed
History	35% of social studies test	• Textual analysis
Civics/Government	35% of social studies test	• Data representation
Economics	20% of social studies test	• Inference skills
Geography	10% of social studies test	• Problem-solving using social studies content
Total	60 multiple-choice questions	70 minutes

How is the HiSET Scored?

Passing the Exam

Different states have different criteria for passing the HiSET. The most common criteria are found below:

- A candidate must score 8 out of 20 on each subtest AND
- a candidate must score 2 out of 6 AND
- a candidate must achieve on all five subtests a total scaled score of 45 out of 100.

Your raw score is simply the number of questions you answer correctly. The number of questions varies among subtests. There are 50 raw score points on the Language Arts—Reading subtest, 60 on the Language Arts—Writing subtest (excluding the essay), 55 on the Mathematics subtest, 60 on the Science subtest, and 60 on the Social Studies exam. A candidate who answers 50 questions correctly on the Social Studies subtest, for instance, will have a raw score of 50 on that subtest.

For each subtest, the total number of raw points earned is then scaled to a score between 1 and 20. You must earn at least 8 on each subtest scaled score points to qualify for your high school equivalency.

The essay on the Language Arts—Writing subtest is scored on four traits: development of ideas or position, organization and structure, conventions of writing (grammar and mechanics), and language facility (word choice and expression). Essays receive a score from 1 to 6 based on these traits.

Each test is scored independently, and points from one test cannot affect the point value of another. You must pass each subject test in order to qualify for your high school equivalency credential.

There is no guessing penalty on the HiSET exam, so you should always guess if you do not know the answer to a question. You might get the answer right!

Receiving Your Scores

If you take the computer-administered version of the HiSET, you will receive your *unofficial* scores immediately after completing the exam for all subtests except for the Language Arts—Writing test. You can expect to receive your *official* scores within three business days except for the essay. The essay score is generally available within five business days. If you take the pencil-and-paper version of the HiSET, you will wait longer to receive your scores, depending on how long it takes your test center to contact ETS. You can view your official scores through your HiSET account; you will not receive them by mail.

How is the HiSET Administered?

The HiSET exam is offered in both computer-based and pencil-and-paper formats. To find a test center near you, check with ETS.

You will need to print your registration ticket from your online account and bring it, along with photo identification, to the testing site on test day. Some test centers will require other forms or documentation, so make sure to check with your test center in advance. No pens, pencils, erasers, printed or written materials, electronic devices or calculators are allowed. An on-screen calculator will be provided to you at the time of the test (or a handheld one if you are taking the test in a paper format). You will also receive scratch paper. Check in advance with your testing center for specific testing guidelines, including restrictions on dress and accessories.

You may take all the tests that compose the HiSET on the same day or individually on separate days. You will have scheduled breaks if you take more than one test on the same day. There is no required order for completing the tests. Certain jurisdictions may apply limits to the amount of time available for completing all five tests.

You may retake a test up to three times in a year. If you do not pass one test, you are not required to retake all the tests—only the one you failed.

About This Guide

This guide will help you to master the most important test topics and also develop critical test-taking skills. We have built features into our books to prepare you for your tests and increase your score. Along with a detailed summary of the format, content, and scoring of the HiSET, we offer an in-depth overview of the content knowledge required to pass the exam. In the review you'll find sidebars that provide interesting information, highlight key concepts, and review content so that you can solidify your understanding of the exam's concepts. You can also test your knowledge with sample questions throughout the text and practice questions that reflect the content and format of the HiSET. We're pleased you've chosen Accepted, Inc. to be a part of your journey!

1. Reading

To do well on reading comprehension questions on the HiSET, you should be able to identify explicit details in a text, draw inferences about the text, grasp the author's intent, and understand the main idea of a text. On the Reading test, 60 percent of the questions ask about informational sources; the other 40 percent ask about literary sources.

The Main Idea

The main idea of a text describes the author's main topic and general concept; it also generalizes the author's point of view about a subject. It is contained within and throughout the text. The reader can find the main idea by considering how the main topic is addressed throughout a passage. On reading questions, you are expected not only to identify the main idea but also to be able to differentiate it from a text's theme and to summarize the main idea clearly and concisely. For instance, you might be asked to pick an answer choice that best summarizes the main idea of a passage.

The main idea is closely connected to topic sentences and how they are supported in a text. Questions may deal with finding topic sentences, summarizing a text's ideas, or locating supporting details. The sections and practice examples that follow detail the distinctions between these aspects of text.

> **Did You Know?**
>
> The author's perspective on the subject of the text and how he or she has framed the argument or story hints at the main idea. For example, if the author framed the story with a description, image, or short anecdote, he or she is hinting at a particular idea or point of view.

Identifying the Main Idea

To identify the main idea, first identify the topic. The difference between these two things is simple: the **topic** is the overall subject matter of a passage; the **main idea** is what the author wants to say about that topic. The main idea covers the author's direct perspective about a topic, as distinct from the **theme**, which is a generally true idea that the reader might derive from a text. Most of the time, fiction has a theme, whereas non-fiction has a main idea. This is the case because in a nonfiction text, the author speaks more directly to the audience about a topic—his or her perspective is more visible. For example, the following passage conveys the topic as well as what the author wants to communicate about that topic.

The "shark mania" of recent years can be largely pinned on the sensationalistic media surrounding the animals: from the release of *Jaws* in 1975 to the week of ultra-hyped shark feeding frenzies and "worst shark attacks" countdowns known as *Shark Week*, popular culture both demonizes and fetishizes sharks until the public cannot get enough. Swimmers and beachgoers may look nervously for the telltale fin skimming the surface, but the reality is that shark bites are extremely rare and they are almost never unprovoked. Sharks attack people at very predictable times and for very predictable reasons. Rough surf, poor visibility, or a swimmer sending visual and physical signals that mimic a shark's normal prey are just a few examples.

Of course, some places are just more dangerous to swim. Shark attack "hot spots," such as the coasts of Florida, South Africa, and New Zealand try a variety of solutions to protect tourists and surfers. Some beaches employ "shark nets," meant to keep sharks away from the beach, though these are controversial because they frequently trap other forms of marine life as well. Other beaches use spotters in helicopters and boats to alert beach officials when there are sharks in the area. In addition, there is an array of products that claim to offer personal protection from sharks, ranging from wetsuits in different colors to devices that broadcast electrical signals in an attempt to confuse the sharks' sensory organs. At the end of the day, though, beaches like these remain dangerous, and swimmers must assume the risk every time they paddle out from shore.

The author of this passage has a clear topic: sharks and their relationship with humans. In order to identify the main idea of the passage, the reader must ask, What does the author want to say about this topic? What is the reader meant to think or understand?

The author makes sure to provide information about several different aspects of the relationship between sharks and humans, and points out that humans must respect sharks as dangerous marine animals, without sensationalizing the risk of attack. The reader can figure this out by looking at the various pieces of information the author includes as well as the similarities between them. The passage describes sensationalistic media, then talks about how officials and governments try to protect beaches, and ends with the observation that people must take personal responsibility. These details clarify what the author's main idea is: thanks to safety precautions and their natural behavior, sharks are not as dangerous as they are portrayed to be. Summarizing that main idea by focusing on the connection between the different details helps the reader draw a conclusion.

> **Did You Know?**
>
> Readers should identify the topic of a text and pay attention to how the details about it relate to one another. A passage may discuss, for example, topic similarities, characteristics, causes, and/ or effects.

Practice Question

The art of the twentieth and twenty-first centuries demonstrates several aspects of modern social advancement. A primary example is the advent of technology: new technologies have developed new avenues for art making, and the globalization brought about by the internet has both diversified the art world and brought it together simultaneously. Even as artists are able to engage in a global conversation about the categories and characteristics of art, creating a more uniform understanding, they can now express themselves in a diversity of ways for a diversity of audiences. The result has been a rapid change in how art is made and consumed.

1. This passage is primarily concerned with
    A) the importance of art in the twenty-first century.
    B) the use of art to communicate overarching ideals to diverse communities.
    C) the importance of technology to art criticism.
    D) the change in understanding and creation of art in the modern period.

2. Which of the following best describes the main idea of the passage?
   A) Modern advances in technology have diversified art making and connected artists to distant places and ideas.
   B) Diversity in modern art is making it harder for art viewers to understand and talk about that art.
   C) The use of technology to discuss art allows us to create standards for what art should be.
   D) Art-making before the invention of technology such as the internet was disorganized and poorly understood.

Topic and Summary Sentences

Identifying the main idea requires understanding the structure of a piece of writing. In a short passage of one or two paragraphs, the topic and summary sentences quickly relate what the paragraphs are about and what conclusions the author wants the reader to draw. These sentences function as bookends to a paragraph or passage, telling readers what to think and keeping the passage tied tightly together.

Generally, the **topic sentence** is the first, or very near the first, sentence in a paragraph. It is a general statement that introduces the topic, clearly and specifically directing the reader to access any previous experience with that topic.

Did You Know?

A summary is a very brief restatement of the most important parts of an argument or text. Building a summary begins with the most important idea in a text. A longer summary also includes supporting details. The text of a summary should be much shorter than the original.

The **summary sentence**, on the other hand, frequently—but not always!—comes at the end of a paragraph or passage, because it wraps up all the ideas presented. This sentence provides an understanding of what the author wants to say about the topic and what conclusions to draw about it. While a topic sentence acts as an introduction to a topic, allowing the reader to activate his or her own ideas and experiences, the summary statement asks the reader to accept the author's ideas about that topic. Because of this, a summary sentence helps the reader quickly identify a piece's main idea.

Practice Question

There is nowhere more beautiful and interesting than California. With glimmering azure seas, fertile green plains, endless deserts, and majestic mountains, California offers every landscape. Hikers can explore the wilderness in Yosemite National Park, where a variety of plants and animals make their home. Farmers grow almonds, apricots, cotton, tomatoes, and more in the Central Valley that winds through the middle of the state. Skiers enjoy the slopes and backcountry of the Sierra Nevada and Lake Tahoe area. In the desert of Death Valley, temperatures rise well over one hundred degrees Fahrenheit.

And of course, California's famous beaches stretch from the Mexican border to Oregon. Furthermore, California features some of America's most important cities. In the south, Los Angeles is home to the movie industry and Hollywood. Farther north, the San Francisco Bay Area includes Silicon Valley, where the US tech industry is based. Both places are centers of commercial activity. In fact, California is the most populous state in the country. There is no shortage of things to do or sights to see!

3. Which of the following best explains the general idea and focus indicated by the topic sentence?
   A) The diversity of California's landscape allows agriculture to flourish, and the most important crops will be detailed.
   B) California is beautiful and diverse; the reader will read on to find out what makes it so interesting.
   C) California is a peaceful place; its people live with a sense of predictability and the state is prosperous.
   D) The incredible geography of California is the reason it is a rural state, and the reader can expect a discussion of the countryside.

4. Which of the following best states what the author wants the reader to understand after reading the summary sentence?
   A) Tourists should see everything in California when they visit.
   B) The cities of California are interesting, but the rural parts are better.
   C) The resources of California are nearly exhausted.
   D) California is an inspiring and exciting place.

Supporting Details

Between a topic sentence and a summary sentence, the rest of a paragraph is built with **supporting details**. Supporting details come in many forms; the purpose of the passage dictates the type of details that will support the main idea. A persuasive passage may use facts and data or detail specific reasons for the author's opinion. An informative passage will primarily use facts about the topic to support the main idea. Even a narrative passage will have supporting details—specific things the author says to develop the story and characters.

The most important aspect of supporting details is exactly what it sounds like: they support the main idea. Examining the various supporting details and how they work with one another will reveal how the author views a topic and what the main idea of the passage is. Supporting details are key to understanding a passage.

Supporting details can often be found in texts by looking for **signal words**—transitions that explain to the reader how one sentence or idea is connected to another. Signal words can add information, provide counterarguments, create organization in a passage, or draw conclusions. Some common signal words and phrases include *in particular, in addition, besides, contrastingly, therefore*, and *because*.

Practice Question

Increasingly, companies are turning to subcontracting services rather than hiring full-time employees. This provides companies with advantages like greater flexibility, reduced legal responsibility to employees, and lower possibility of unionization within the company. However, this has led to increasing confusion and uncertainty over the legal definition of employment. Courts have grappled with questions about the hiring company's responsibility in maintaining fair labor practices. Companies argue that they delegate that authority to subcontractors, while unions and other worker advocate groups argue that companies still have a legal obligation to the workers who contribute to their business.

5. According to the passage, why do companies use subcontractors? Hiring subcontractors
    A) costs less money than hiring full-time employees.
    B) increases the need for unionization of employees.
    C) reduces the company's legal responsibilities.
    D) gives the company greater control over worker's hours.

The Author's Purpose

The author of a passage sets out with a specific goal in mind: to communicate a particular idea to an audience. The **author's purpose** is determined by asking why the author wants the reader to understand the passage's main idea. There are four basic purposes to which an author can write: narrative, expository, technical, and persuasive. Within each of these general purposes, the author may direct the audience to take a clear action or respond in a certain way.

The purpose for which an author writes a passage is also connected to the structure of that text. In a **narrative**, the author seeks to tell a story, often to illustrate a theme or idea the reader needs to consider. In a narrative, the author uses characteristics of storytelling, such as chronological order, characters, and a defined setting, and these characteristics communicate the author's theme or main idea.

In an **expository** passage, on the other hand, the author simply seeks to explain an idea or topic to the reader. The main idea will probably be a factual statement or a direct assertion of a broadly held opinion. Expository writing can come in many forms, but one essential feature is a fair and balanced representation of a topic. The author may explore one detailed aspect or a broad range of characteristics, but he or she mainly seeks to prompt a decision from the reader.

> **Did You Know?**
>
> Reading persuasive text requires an awareness of what the author believes about the topic.

Similarly, in **technical** writing, the author's purpose is to explain specific processes, techniques, or equipment in order for the reader to use that process or equipment to obtain a desired result. Writing like this employs chronological or spatial structures, specialized vocabulary, and imperative or directive language.

In **persuasive** writing, the author actively seeks to convince the reader to accept an opinion or belief. Much like expository writing, persuasive writing is presented in many organizational forms.

Practice Question

University of California, Berkeley, researchers decided to tackle an age-old problem: why shoelaces come untied. They recorded the shoelaces of a volunteer walking on a treadmill by attaching devices to record the acceleration, or g-force, experienced by the knot. The results were surprising. A shoelace knot experiences more g-force from a person walking than any rollercoaster can generate. However, if the person simply stomped or swung their feet—the two movements that make up a walker's stride—the g-force was not enough to undo the knots.

6. What is the purpose of this passage?
    A) to confirm if shoelaces always come undone
    B) to compare the force of treadmills and rollercoasters
    C) to persuade readers to tie their shoes tighter
    D) to describe the results of an experiment on shoelaces

Organization and Text Structures

It's important to analyze the organization and structure of informational texts, as these details can provide valuable insight into the author's purpose and the overall meaning of a text. Several common structures are used in informative texts, and understanding these structures will help readers quickly make sense of new texts. Texts may be organized in one of the following ways:

- **Chronological** texts describe events in the order they occurred.
- **Problem-solution** texts begin by describing a problem and then offer a possible solution to the issue.
- **Cause-effect** is a text structure that shows a causal chain of events or ideas.
- **General-to-specific** is a text structure that describes a general topic then provides details about a specific aspect of that topic.
- **Compare-contrast** texts give the similarities and differences between two things.

Authors choose the organizational structure of their text according to their purpose. For example, an author who hopes to convince people to begin recycling might begin by talking about the problems that are caused by excessive waste and end by offering recycling as a reasonable solution. On the other hand, the author might choose to use a chronological structure for an article whose purpose is to give an impartial history of recycling.

Practice Question

For thirteen years, a spacecraft called *Cassini* was on an exploratory mission to Saturn. The spacecraft was designed not to return but to end its journey by diving into Saturn's atmosphere. This dramatic ending provided scientists with unprecedented information about Saturn's atmosphere and its magnetic and gravitational fields. First, however, *Cassini* passed Saturn's largest moon, Titan, where it recorded data on Titan's curious methane lakes, gathering information about potential seasons on the planet-sized moon. Then it passed through the unexplored region between Saturn itself and its famous rings. Scientists hope to learn how old the rings are and to directly examine the particles that make them up. *Cassini*'s mission ended in 2017, but researchers have new questions for future exploration.

7. Which of the following best describes the organization of this passage?
   A) general-to-specific
   B) compare-contrast
   C) chronological
   D) problem-solution

The Audience

The structure, purpose, main idea, and language of a text all converge on one target: the intended **audience**. An author makes decisions about every aspect of a piece of writing based on that audience, and readers can evaluate the writing by considering who the author is writing for. By considering the probable reactions of an intended audience, readers can determine many things:

- whether they are part of that intended audience
- the author's purpose for using specific techniques or devices
- the biases of the author and how they appear in the writing
- how the author uses rhetorical strategies

> **Did You Know?**
>
> When reading a persuasive text, students should maintain awareness of what the author believes about the topic.

The audience for a text can be identified by careful analysis of the text. First, the reader considers who most likely cares about the topic and main idea of the text: who would want or need to know about this topic? The audience may be **specific** (e.g., biologists who study sharks) or more **general** (e.g., people with an interest in marine life).

Next, consider the language of the text. The author tailors language to appeal to the intended audience, so the reader can determine from the language who the author is speaking to. A **formal** style is used in business and academic settings and can make the author seem more credible. Characteristics of a formal style include:

- third person perspective (i.e., no use of *I* or *you*)
- no use of slang or clichés
- follows a clear structure (e.g., an introduction, a body, and a conclusion)
- technically correct grammar and sentence structure
- objective language

An **informal** style is used to appeal to readers in a more casual setting, such as a magazine or blog. Using an informal style may make the author seem less credible, but it can help create an emotional connection with the audience. Characteristics of informal writing include:

- use of first or second person (e.g., *I* or *you*)
- use of slang or casual language

- follows an unusual or flexible structure
- bends the rules of grammar
- appeals to audience's emotions

Practice Question

What do you do with plastic bottles? Do you throw them away, or do you recycle or reuse them? As landfills continue to fill up, there will eventually be no place to put our trash. If you recycle or reuse bottles, you will help reduce waste and turn something old into a creative masterpiece!

8. Which of the following BEST describes the intended audience for this passage?
    A) a formal audience of engineering professionals
    B) an audience of English language learners
    C) a general audience that includes children
    D) a group of scientists at an environmental conference

Evaluating Arguments

An author selects details to help support the main idea. The reader must then evaluate these details for relevance and consistency. Though the author generally includes details that support the text's main idea, it's up to the reader to decide whether those details are convincing.

Readers should be able to differentiate between facts and opinions in order to more effectively analyze supporting details. **Facts** are based in truth and can usually be proven. They are pieces of information that have been confirmed or validated. An opinion is a judgment, belief, or viewpoint that is not based on evidence. **Opinions** are often stated in descriptive, subjective language that is difficult to define or prove. While opinions can be included in informative texts, they are often of little impact unless they are supported by some kind of evidence.

> **Quick Review**
>
> Which of the following phrases would be associated with opinions?
>
> *for example, studies have shown, I believe, in fact, it's possible that*

Sometimes, the author's **bias**—an inclination towards a particular belief—causes the author to leave out details that do not directly support the main idea or that support an opposite idea. The reader has to be able to notice not only what the author says but also what the author leaves out. Discovering the author's bias and how the supporting details reveal that bias is also key to understanding a text.

Writers will often use specific techniques, or **rhetorical strategies**, to build an argument. Readers can identify these strategies in order to clearly understand what an author wants them to believe, how the author's perspective and purpose may lead to bias, and whether the passage includes any logical fallacies.

Common rhetorical strategies include the appeals to ethos, logos, and pathos. An author uses these to build trust with the reader, explain the logical points of his or her argument, and convince the reader that his or her opinion is the best option.

An **ethos (ethical) appeal** uses balanced, fair language and seeks to build a trusting relationship between the author and the reader. An author might explain her or his credentials, include the reader in an argument, or offer concessions to an opposing argument.

> **Quick Review**
>
> Consider how different audiences would react to the same text.

A **logos (logical) appeal** builds on that trust by providing facts and support for the author's opinion, explaining the argument with clear connections and reasoning. At this point, the reader should beware of logical fallacies that connect unconnected ideas and build arguments on incorrect premises. With a logical appeal, an author strives to convince the reader to accept an opinion or belief by demonstrating that not only is it the most logical option but that it also satisfies her or his emotional reaction to a topic.

A **pathos (emotional) appeal** does not depend on reasonable connections between ideas; rather, it seeks to remind the reader, through imagery, strong language, and personal connections, that the author's argument aligns with her or his best interests.

Practice Question

Exercise is critical for healthy development in children. Today in the United States, there is an epidemic of poor childhood health; many of these children will face further illnesses in adulthood that are due to poor diet and lack of exercise now. This is a problem for all Americans, especially with the rising cost of health care.

It is vital that school systems and parents encourage children to engage in a minimum of thirty minutes of cardiovascular exercise each day, mildly increasing their heart rate for a sustained period. This is proven to decrease the likelihood of developmental diabetes, obesity, and a multitude of other health problems. Also, children need a proper diet, rich in fruits and vegetables, so they can develop physically and learn healthy eating habits early on.

9. Which of the following statements from the passage is a fact, not an opinion?
    A) Fruits and vegetables are the best way to help children be healthy.
    B) Children today are lazier than they were in previous generations.
    C) The risk of diabetes in children is reduced by physical activity.
    D) Children should engage in thirty minutes of exercise a day.

Drawing Conclusions

Reading text begins with making sense of the explicit meanings of information or a narrative. Understanding occurs as the reader draws conclusions and makes logical inferences. First, the reader considers the details or facts. He or she then comes to a **conclusion**—the next logical point in the thought sequence. For example, in a Hemingway story, an old man sits alone in a cafe. A young waiter says that the cafe is closing, but the old man continues to drink. The waiter starts closing up, and the old man signals for a refill. Based on these details, the reader might conclude that the old man has not understood the young waiter's desire for him to leave.

An inference is distinguished from a conclusion drawn. An **inference** is an assumption the reader makes based on details in the text as well as his or her own knowledge. It is more of an educated guess that extends the literal meaning of a text. Inferences begin with the given details; however, the reader uses the facts to determine additional information. What the reader already knows informs what is being suggested by the details of decisions or situations in the text. Returning to the example of the Hemingway story, the reader might *infer* that the old man is lonely, enjoys being in the cafe, and therefore is reluctant to leave.

> **Did You Know?**
>
> When considering a character's motivations, the reader should ask what the character wants to achieve, what the character will get by accomplishing this, and what the character seems to value the most.

When reading fictional text, inferring character motivations is essential. The actions of the characters move the plot forward; a series of events is understood by making sense of why the characters did what they did. Hemingway includes contrasting details as the young waiter and an older waiter discuss the old man. The older waiter sympathizes with the old man; both men have no one at home and experience a sense of emptiness in life, which motivates them to seek the cafe.

> **Did You Know?**
>
> Conclusions are drawn by thinking about how the author wants the reader to feel. A group of carefully selected facts can cause the reader to feel a certain way.

Another aspect of understanding text is connecting it to other texts. Readers may connect the Hemingway story about the old man in the cafe to other Hemingway stories about individuals struggling to deal with loss and loneliness in a dignified way.

They can extend their initial connections to people they know or their personal experiences. When readers read a persuasive text, they often connect the arguments made to counterarguments and opposing evidence of which they are aware. They use these connections to infer meaning.

Practice Question

After World War I, political and social forces pushed for a return to normalcy in the United States. The result was disengagement from the larger world and increased focus on American economic growth and personal enjoyment.

Caught in the middle were American writers, raised on the values of the prewar world and frustrated with what they viewed as the superficiality and materialism of postwar American culture. Many of them fled to Paris, where they became known as the "lost generation," creating a trove of literary works criticizing their home culture and delving into their own feelings of alienation.

10. Which conclusion about the effects of war is most likely true, according to the passage?
    A) War served as an inspiration for literary works.
    B) It was difficult to stabilize countries after war occurred.
    C) Writers were torn between supporting war and their own ideals.
    D) Individual responsibility and global awareness declined after the war.

Tone and Mood

The **tone** of a passage describes the author's attitude toward the topic. In general, the author's tone can be described as positive, negative, or neutral. The **mood** is the pervasive feeling or atmosphere in a passage that provokes specific emotions in the reader. Put simply, tone is how the author feels about the topic. Mood is how the reader feels about the text.

Diction, or word choice, helps determine mood and tone in a passage. Many readers make the mistake using the author's ideas alone to determine tone; a much better practice is to look at specific words and try to identify a pattern in the emotion they evoke. Does the writer choose positive words like *ambitious* and *confident*? Or does he describe those concepts with negative words like *greedy* and *overbearing*? The first writer's tone might be described as admiring, while the more negative tone would be disapproving.

> **Did You Know?**
>
> To decide the connotation of a word, the reader examines whether the word conveys a positive or negative association in the mind. Adjectives are often used to influence the feelings of the reader, such as in the phrase *an ambitious attempt to achieve*.

When looking at tone, it's important to examine not just the literal definition of words. Every word has not only a literal meaning but also a **connotative meaning**, which relies on the common emotions and experiences an audience might associate with that word. The following words are all synonyms: *dog, puppy, cur, mutt, canine, pet*. Two of these words—*dog* and *canine*—are neutral words, without strong associations or emotions. Two others—*pet* and *puppy*—have positive associations. The last two—*cur* and *mutt*—have negative associations. A passage that uses one pair of these words versus another pair activates the positive or negative reactions of the audience.

Table 1.1. Words That Describe Tone

Positive	Neutral	Negative
admiring	casual	angry
approving	detached	annoyed
celebratory	formal	belligerent
earnest	impartial	bitter
encouraging	informal	condescending
excited	objective	confused
funny	questioning	cynical
hopeful	unconcerned	depressed
humorous		disrespectful
nostalgic		embarrassed
optimistic		fearful
playful		gloomy

Table 1.1. Words That Describe Tone		
Positive	**Neutral**	**Negative**
poignant		melancholy
proud		mournful
relaxed		pessimistic
respectful		skeptical
sentimental		solemn
silly		suspicious
sympathetic		unsympathetic

Practice Question

Day had broken cold and grey, exceedingly cold and grey, when the man turned aside from the main Yukon trail and climbed the high earth-bank, where a dim and little-travelled trail led eastward through the fat spruce timberland.

It was a steep bank, and he paused for breath at the top, excusing the act to himself by looking at his watch. It was nine o'clock. There was no sun nor hint of sun, though there was not a cloud in the sky. It was a clear day, and yet there seemed an intangible pall over the face of things, a subtle gloom that made the day dark, and that was due to the absence of sun. This fact did not worry the man. He was used to the lack of sun. It had been days since he had seen the sun, and he knew that a few more days must pass before that cheerful orb, due south, would just peep above the sky-line and dip immediately from view.

—from "To Build a Fire" by Jack London

11. Which of the following best describes the mood of the passage?
    A) exciting and adventurous
    B) unhappy and anxious
    C) bleak but accepting
    D) grim yet hopeful

12. The connotation of the words *intangible pall* is
    A) a death-like covering.
    B) a sense of familiarity.
    C) a feeling of communal strength.
    D) an understanding of the struggle ahead.

Meaning of Words and Phrases

The HiSET does not specifically ask you to define words, but it is good to know strategies to determine the meaning of unfamiliar words you may encounter when analyzing reading passages and improving paragraphs.

When confronted with unfamiliar words, the passage itself can help clarify their meaning. Often, identifying the tone or main idea of the passage can help eliminate answer choices. For example, if the tone of the passage is generally positive, try eliminating the answer choices with a negative connotation. Or, if the passage is about a particular occupation, rule out words unrelated to that topic.

Passages may also provide specific context clues that can help determine the meaning of a word. One type of context clue is a **definition**, or **description**, **clue**. Sometimes, authors use a difficult word, then include *that is* or *which is* to signal that they are providing a definition. An author also may provide a synonym or restate the idea in more familiar words:

> Teachers often prefer teaching students with intrinsic motivation; these students have an internal desire to learn.

The meaning of *intrinsic* is restated as *an internal desire*.

Similarly, authors may include an **example clue**, providing an example phrase that clarifies the meaning of the word:

> Teachers may view extrinsic rewards as efficacious; however, an individual student may not be interested in what the teacher offers. For example, a student who does not like sweets may not feel any incentive to work when offered a sugary reward.

Efficacious is explained with an example that demonstrates how an extrinsic reward may not be effective.

Another commonly used context clue is the **contrast**, or **antonym**, **clue**. In this case, authors indicate that the unfamiliar word is the opposite of a familiar word:

> In contrast to intrinsic motivation, extrinsic motivation is contingent on teachers offering rewards that are appealing.

The phrase *in contrast* tells the reader that extrinsic is the opposite of intrinsic.

Practice Question

13. Which of the following is the meaning of *incentivize* as used in the sentence?

One challenge of teaching is finding ways to incentivize, or to motivate, learning.
- A) encourage
- B) determine
- C) challenge
- D) improve

14. Which of the following is the meaning of *apprehensive* as used in the sentence?

If an extrinsic reward is extremely desirable, a student may become so apprehensive he or she cannot focus. The student may experience such intense pressure to perform that the reward undermines its intent.
- A) uncertain
- B) distracted
- C) anxious
- D) forgetful

Figurative Language

Figures of speech are expressions that are understood to have a nonliteral meaning. Rather than stating their ideas directly, authors use **figurative language** to suggest meaning by speaking of a subject as if it were something else. For example, when Shakespeare says, "All the world's a stage,/ And all men and women merely players," he is speaking of the world as if it is a stage. Since the world is not literally a stage, the reader has to ask how the two are similar and what Shakespeare might be implying about the world through this comparison. Figures of speech extend the meaning of words by engaging the reader's imagination and adding emphasis to different aspects of their subject.

A **metaphor** is a type of figurative language that describes something that may be unfamiliar to the reader (the topic) by referring to it as though it were something else that is more familiar to the reader (the vehicle). A metaphor stands in as a synonym, interchangeable with its corresponding topic. As the reader reflects on the similarities between the topic and the vehicle, he or she forms a clearer understanding of the topic. For example, in Shakespeare's *Romeo and Juliet*, Romeo says that "Juliet is the sun." By making this comparison, Romeo is comparing Juliet's energy to the brightness of the sun, which is familiar to readers.

A **simile** is a type of figurative language that directly points to similarities between two things. As with a metaphor, the author uses a familiar vehicle to express an idea about a less familiar topic. Unlike a metaphor, however, a simile does not replace the object with a figurative description; it compares the vehicle and topic using "like," "as," or similar words. For example, in his poem "The Rime of the Ancient Mariner," Coleridge describes his ship as "idle as a painted ship/ Upon a painted ocean." He speaks about the boat as if it were painted (unlike Romeo above, who says explicitly that Juliet is the sun itself). The reader understands that paintings do not move, so Coleridge uses this comparison to show the reader that the ship in the poem is completely motionless.

Imagery is vivid description that appeals to the reader's sense of sight, sound, smell, taste, or touch. This type of figurative language allows readers to experience through their senses what is being described; as readers use their imaginations to visualize or recall sensory experience, they are drawn into the scene of the story or poem.

Hyperbole is an overstatement, an exaggeration intended to achieve a particular effect. Hyperbole can create humor or add emphasis to a text by drawing the reader's attention to a particular idea. For example, a character might say he or she is "so hungry, [he or she] could eat a horse." Though the character probably cannot literally eat a horse, the reader understands that he or she is extremely hungry.

Personification is a type of figurative language in which human characteristics are attributed to objects, abstract ideas, natural forces, or animals. For example, if a writer refers to "murmuring pine trees," he or she is attributing to the pine trees the human ability of murmuring. The writer is using the familiar vehicle of the sound of murmuring to help the reader understand the sound pine trees make in the wind.

Symbolism is a literary device in which the author uses a concrete object, action, or character to represent an abstract idea. The significance of the symbol reaches beyond the object's ordinary meaning. Familiar symbols are roses representing beauty, light representing truth, and darkness representing evil. As readers notice an author's use of symbolism, they begin to make connections and to formulate ideas about what the author is suggesting.

An **allusion**, not to be confused with illusion, is a reference to a historical person or event, a fictional character or event, a mythological or religious character or event, or an artist or artistic work. When a reader recognizes an allusion, he or she may make associations that contribute to his or her understanding of the text. For example, if a character is described as having a "Mona Lisa smile," an instant image will arise in the minds of most readers. Because allusions can be difficult to recognize, especially for young readers whose experiences are limited, teachers must provide instruction in how to recognize, research, and interpret unfamiliar references.

Clichés are common sayings that lack originality but are familiar and relatable to an audience. Though clichés are not necessarily beneficial to the author who is trying to write a wholly original work, they can be helpful for a writer who is attempting to show that he or she can relate to the audience.

Dialect and **Slang** are linguistic qualities that an author might incorporate into his or her writing in order to develop characters or setting. A character's dialect may reveal where he or she is from, while the slang he or she uses may be an indication of social, economic, and educational status.

Irony comes in different forms. **Verbal irony** is used when a character or narrator says something that is the opposite of what he or she means. **Situational irony** occurs when something happens that contradicts what the audience expected to happen. **Dramatic irony** occurs when the audience knows about something of which a character or characters are not aware.

Practice Question

Alfie closed his eyes and took several deep breaths. He was trying to ignore the sounds of the crowd, but even he had to admit that it was hard not to notice the tension in the stadium. He could feel 50,000 sets of eyes burning through his skin—this crowd expected perfection from him. He took another breath and opened his eyes, setting his sights on the soccer ball resting peacefully in the grass. One shot, just one last shot, between his team and the championship.

He didn't look up at the goalie, who was jumping nervously on the goal line just a few yards away. Afterward, he would swear he didn't remember anything between the referee's whistle and the thunderous roar of the crowd.

15. Which of the following best describes the meaning of the phrase "he could feel 50,000 sets of eyes burning through his skin"?
    A) The 50,000 people in the stadium were trying to hurt Alfie.
    B) Alfie felt uncomfortable and exposed in front of so many people.
    C) Alfie felt immense pressure from the 50,000 people watching him.
    D) The people in the stadium are warning Alfie that the field is on fire.

Graphic Sources of Information

Informational texts on the HiSET may be accompanied by graphic sources of information, including graphs, diagrams, or photographs. There's no simple set of rules for handling these questions, but many of the same strategies that are used for other figures and for text passages are applicable.

Always start with the title of a figure—it will provide information that is likely crucial to understanding the figure. An anatomical diagram might have a title such as *Lobes of the Brain* that tells the viewer that the diagram will likely show the names and locations of the brain's lobes. Similarly, a graph may have a title like *Number of Customers per Month*, which describes the information in the graph.

Also make sure to examine any **labels**, legends, or scales provided with the figure. Graphs, for example, should always include labels on the axes that describe what's shown on each axis, and a flowchart will have arrows indicating an ordered sequence.

Many of the strategies needed to interpret traditional reading passages can also be used for graphic representations of information, particularly those that may be text heavy. When looking at a photograph or advertisement, it will help to identify:

- the purpose of the author
- the intended audience
- rhetorical strategies designed to influence the viewer
- the main idea of the image

A flyer for a local bake sale, for example, may be designed to appeal to the viewer's emotions by including pictures of local schoolchildren. Similarly, a computer advertisement meant to appeal to corporate buyers would probably use more formal language than one aimed at teenagers.

Practice Question

As you can see from the graph, my babysitting business has been really successful. The year started with a busy couple of months—several snows combined with a large number of requests for Valentine's Day services boosted our sales quite a bit. The spring months have admittedly been a bit slow, but we're hoping for a big summer once school gets out. Several clients have already put in requests for our services!

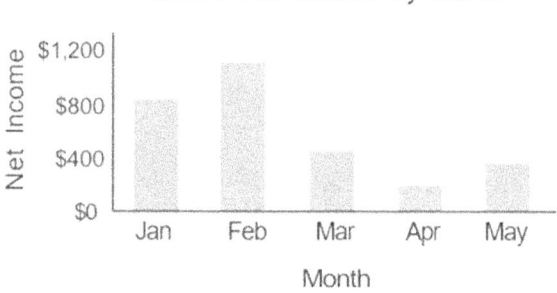

16. Based on the information in the graph, how much more did Sam's Babysitting Service bring in during February than during April?
    A) $200
    B) $900
    C) $1100
    D) $1300

Elements of Fiction

Fiction is a prose genre, made up of narratives whose details are not based in truth but are instead the creation of the author. Just as artists have the tools of color and shape to communicate ideas, so have writers their literary tools. These tools include point of view, plot, setting, character, tone, and figurative language. Each of these elements contributes to the overall idea that is developed in the text and, as such, can provide valuable insight into the theme of the work.

Point of view is the perspective from which the action in a story is told. By carefully selecting a particular point of view, writers are able to control what their readers know. Most literature is written in either first person or third person point of view. With the **first-person point of view**, the action is narrated by a character within the story, which can make it feel more believable and authentic to the reader. However, as a result of the first-person point of view, the reader's knowledge and understanding are constrained by what the narrator notices and influenced by what the narrator thinks and values.

An author may, on the other hand, choose to tell the story from the **third-person point of view**. A third-person narrator is a voice outside the action of the story, an observer who shares what he or she knows, sees, or hears with the reader. A third person narrator might be **fully omniscient** (able to see into the minds of the characters and share what they are thinking and feeling), **partially omniscient** (able to see into the minds of just one or a few characters), or **limited** (unable to see into the minds of any of the characters and only able to share what can be seen and heard).

Plot structure is the way the author arranges the events of a narrative. In a conventional plot line, the story is structured around a central conflict, a struggle between two opposing forces. Conflicts in literature can be categorized in general terms as either internal or external, though most stories have a combination of both. Internal conflicts take place inside the main character's mind; he or she might be making a difficult decision, struggling with change, or sorting out priorities. External conflicts, on the other hand, occur when a character is in conflict with something or someone in the external world—the elements of nature, another character, supernatural forces, destiny, or society.

In a traditional plot structure, the author begins with **exposition**: important background information about the setting, the characters, and the current state of the world. Following the exposition, an **inciting incident** introduces the antagonist and establishes the conflict. As the story progresses, the conflict becomes more complicated and tension increases, moving the story toward a **climax** or turning point, in which the conflict reaches a crisis point. Finally, there is a **resolution** to the conflict, followed by falling actions, events that move the characters away from the conflict and into a new life.

Setting is the geographical and chronological location of events in a story. When considering setting, readers should examine how characters interact with their surroundings, how they are influenced by the societal expectations of that time and place, and how the location and time period impact the development of the story. Often, setting can seem inseparable from plot; therefore, a helpful question for beginning the discussion of setting is, How would this story change if it were set in a different time or place?

Character development is the process an author uses to create characters that are complex and, to some degree, believable. One way authors develop their characters is directly: they tell the reader explicitly what the character is like by describing traits and assigning values. Sometimes, authors might include the thoughts and feelings of the characters themselves, offering readers even more insight. Authors can also develop their characters indirectly by revealing their actions and interactions with others, sometimes including what one character says or thinks about another and allowing the reader to draw his or her own conclusions. Most authors use a combination of direct and indirect characterization; this ensures that readers know what they need to know while also providing opportunities for reflection and interpretation.

Practice Question

17. Which passage below from *A Mystery of Heroism* by Stephen Crane best demonstrates the third person omniscient point of view?
    A) In the midst of it all Smith and Ferguson, two privates of A Company, were engaged in a heated discussion, which involved the greatest questions of the national existence.
    B) An officer screamed out an order so violently that his voice broke and ended the sentence in a falsetto shriek.
    C) The officer's face was grimy and perspiring, and his uniform was tousled as if he had been in direct grapple with an enemy. He smiled grimly when the men stared at him.
    D) No, it could not be true. He was not a hero. Heroes had no shames in their lives, and, as for him, he remembered borrowing fifteen dollars from a friend and promising to pay it back the next day, and then avoiding that friend for ten months.

Answer Key

1. D: The art of the modern period reflects the new technologies and globalization possible through the internet.

2. A: According to the text, technology and the internet have "diversified the art world and brought it together simultaneously."

3. B: This option indicates both the main idea and what the reader will focus on while reading.

4. D: The phrase "no shortage of things to do or sights to see" suggests the writer is enthusiastic about the many interesting activities possible in California. There is no indication that the writer should do everything, though, or that one part is better than another.

5. C: The passage states that hiring subcontractors provides the advantage of "reduced legal responsibility to employees."

6. D: The text provides details on the experiment as well as its results.

7. C: The passage describes the journey of Cassini in chronological order: it passed by Titan, went through the region between Saturn and its rings, and ended its mission in 2017.

8. C: The informal tone and direct address of this passage suggest that the author is writing for a general audience that may include children. For instance, turning bottles into an art project could be a good activity for children.

9. C: Choice C is a simple fact stated by the author. It is introduced by the word *proven* to indicate that it is supported by evidence.

10. D: After the war, in the US there was a lack of focus on the world and greater focus on personal comforts, which writers viewed as superficiality and materialism.

11. C: The day is described as "cold and grey" with an "intangible pall," which creates a bleak mood. However, the man himself "did not worry" and knew that only "a few more days must pass" before he would see the sun again, suggesting he has accepted his circumstances.

12. A: Within the context of the sentence "It was a clear day, and yet there seemed an intangible pall over the face of things, a subtle gloom that made the day dark," the words *gloom* and *dark* are suggestive of death; the phrase *over the face* suggests a covering.

13. A: The word *incentivize* is defined immediately with the synonym *motivate*, or *encourage*.

14. C: The reader can infer that the *pressure to perform* is making the student anxious.

15. C: The metaphor implies that Alfie felt pressure from the people watching him to perform well. There is no indication that he is threatened physically.

16. B: In February the service earned $1100, and in April it earned $200. The difference between the two months is $900.

17. D: The narrator is reporting the thoughts of the character, as the character's memory about not acting heroic in the past is revealed. The other choices only include descriptions of the characters words or actions.

1. Reading

2. Grammar and Sentence Structure

The Writing test of the HiSET will test your understanding of the basic rules of grammar. You will be asked to improve paragraphs by choosing the best way to complete sentences. To do so correctly, you must know the basic rules of grammar, mechanics, and sentence structure.

Parts of Speech

The **parts of speech** are the building blocks of sentences, paragraphs, and entire texts. Grammarians have typically defined eight parts of speech—nouns, pronouns, verbs, adverbs, adjectives, conjunctions, prepositions, and interjections—all of which play unique roles in the context of a sentence. Thus, a fundamental understanding of the parts of speech is necessary for comprehending basic sentence construction.

Though some words fall easily into one category or another, many words can function as different parts of speech based on their usage within a sentence.

Nouns and Pronouns

Nouns are the words that describe people, places, things, and ideas. Most often, nouns fill the position of subject or object within a sentence. Nouns have several subcategories: common nouns (*chair, car, house*), proper nouns (*Julie, David*), noncountable nouns (*money, water*), and countable nouns (*dollars, cubes*), among others. There is much crossover among these subcategories (for example, *chair* is common and countable), and other subcategories do exist.

Pronouns replace nouns in a sentence or paragraph, allowing a writer to achieve a smooth flow throughout a text by avoiding unnecessary repetition. While there are countless nouns in the English language, there are only a few types of pronouns. The ones important for the HiSET follow:

- **Personal pronouns** act as subjects or objects in a sentence.

    She received a letter; I gave the letter to her.

- **Possessive pronouns** indicate possession.

    The apartment is hers, but the furniture is mine.

- **Reflexive or Intensive pronouns** intensify a noun or reflect back on a noun.

    I made the dessert myself.

- **Indefinite pronouns** simply replace nouns to avoid unnecessary repetition.

    Several came to the party to see both.

Table 2.1. Personal, Possessive, and Reflexive Pronouns						
Case	First Person		Second Person		Third Person	
	Singular	Plural	Singular	Plural	Singular	Plural
Subject	I	we	you	you (all)	he, she, it	they
Object	me	us	you	you (all)	him, her, it	them
Possessive	mine	ours	yours	yours	his, hers, its	theirs
Reflexive/Intensive	myself	ourselves	yourself	yourselves	himself, herself, itself	themselves

Practice Question

1. What purpose do nouns usually serve in a sentence?
    A) They indicate possession.
    B) They act as subject or object.
    C) They intensify other nouns.
    D) They clarify when an action occurs.

2. Which pronoun best completes the sentence?

    _____ baked the cookies ourselves and ate most of them.
    A) She
    B) Her
    C) I
    D) We

Verbs

Verbs express action (*run, jump, play*) or state of being (*is, seems*). Verbs that describe action are **action verbs**, and those that describe being are **linking verbs**.

- **Action:** My brother <u>plays</u> tennis.
- **Linking:** He <u>is</u> the best player on the team.

Verbs are conjugated to indicate **person**, which refers to the point of view of the sentence. First-person is the speaker (*I, we*); second-person is the person being addressed (*you*); and third-person is outside the conversation (*they, them*). Verbs are also conjugated to match the **number** (singular or plural) of their subject. **Helping verbs** (*to be, to have, to do*) are used to conjugate verbs. An unconjugated verb is called an **infinitive** and includes the word *to* in front (*to be, to break*).

Participles are verb forms lacking number and person. The **past participle** is usually formed by adding the suffix *–ed* to the verb stem (*type* becomes *typed*; *drop* becomes *dropped*). The **present participle** is always formed by adding the suffix *–ing* to the verb stem (*typing, dropping*). Participles are used in verb conjugation to indicate the state of an action (*she is going*; *we had waited*).

Participles also act in *participial phrases* that act as descriptors in sentences:

<u>Seated</u> politely, Ron listened to his friend's boring story.

Maya petted the <u>sleeping</u> cat.

When a present participle acts as a noun, it is called a **gerund**. In the following sentence, *running* is a noun and serving as the subject of the sentence:

<u>Running</u> is my favorite form of exercise.

A common error in sentence structure is the *dangling participle*: when a participial phrase is disconnected from the word or phrase it modifies.

Incorrect: <u>Discussing the state of the nation</u>, I listened to the president's speech.

Here, the president, not the narrator, is discussing the state of the nation; the narrator is simply *listening*. However, the participial phrase "Discussing the state of the nation" is disconnected from the word it modifies, *president*. Thus, it is *dangling* in the sentence—a dangling participle.

To fix a dangling particle, rearrange the sentence so that the modifying phrase is next to the word it modifies.

Correct: I listened to the president's speech <u>discussing the state of the nation</u>.

Table 2.2. Verb Conjugation (Present Tense)		
Person	**Singular**	**Plural**
First person	I give	we give
Second person	you give	you (all) give
Third person	he/she/it gives	they give

Verbs are also conjugated to indicate **tense**, or when the action has happened. Actions can happen in the past, present, or future. Tense also describes over how long a period the action took place:

- **Simple** verbs describe something that happened once or general truths.
- **Continuous** verbs describe an ongoing action.
- **Perfect** verbs describe repeated actions or actions that started in the past and have been completed.
- **Perfect continuous** verbs describe actions that started in the past and are continuing.

Table 2.3. Verb Tenses			
Tense	**Past**	**Present**	**Future**
Simple	I <u>gave</u> her a gift yesterday.	I <u>give</u> her a gift every day.	I <u>will give</u> her a gift on her birthday.
Continuous	I <u>was giving</u> her a gift when you got here.	I <u>am giving</u> her a gift; come in!	I <u>will be giving</u> her a gift at dinner.
Perfect	I <u>had given</u> her a gift before you got there.	I <u>have given</u> her a gift already.	I <u>will have given</u> her a gift by midnight.

Table 2.3. Verb Tenses

Tense	Past	Present	Future
Perfect continuous	Her friends <u>had been giving</u> her gifts all night when I arrived.	I <u>have been giving</u> her gifts every year for nine years.	I <u>will have been giving</u> her gifts on holidays for ten years next year.

Verbs that follow the standard rules of conjugation are called **regular** verbs. **Irregular verbs** do not follow these rules, and their conjugations must be memorized. Some examples of irregular verbs are given in Table 2.4.

Table 2.4. Irregular Verbs

Present	Past	Has/Have/Had
am	was	been
do	did	done
see	saw	Seen
write	wrote	written
break	broke	broken
grow	grew	grown
speak	spoke	spoken
begin	began	begun
run	ran	run
buy	bought	bought

Transitive verbs take a **direct object**, which receives the action of the verb. **Intransitive verbs** have no object. The person or thing that receives the direct object is the **indirect object**.

> **Transitive:** Alex <u>gave</u> the ball to his brother.
>
> (The *ball* is the direct object; *his* brother is the indirect object.)
>
> **Intransitive:** She <u>jumped</u> over the fence.

Practice Question

3. Which verb phrase best completes the sentence?

By this time tomorrow, we _____ in New York.
  A) will have arrived
  B) have arrived
  C) arrive
  D) was arriving

4. Identify the direct object in the following sentence:

My friends brought me a package of souvenirs from their trip to Spain.
- A) friends
- B) me
- C) package
- D) trip

Adjectives and Adverbs

Adjectives modify or describe nouns and pronouns. In English, adjectives are usually placed before the word being modified, although they can also appear after a linking verb such as *is* or *smells*.

The <u>beautiful blue jade</u> necklace will go perfectly with my dress.

I think that lasagna smells <u>delicious</u>.

When multiple adjectives are used, they should be listed in the following order:

- Determiners: articles (*a*, *an*, and *the*), possessive adjectives (e.g., *my*, *her*), and descriptors of quantity (e.g., *three*, *several*)
- Opinions: modifiers that imply a value (e.g., *beautiful*, *perfect*, *ugly*)
- Size: descriptions of size (e.g., *small*, *massive*)
- Age: descriptions of age (e.g., *young*, *five-year-old*)
- Shape: descriptions of appearance or character (e.g., *smooth*, *loud*)
- Color: descriptions of color (e.g., *blue*, *dark*)
- Origin: modifiers that describe where something came from (e.g., *American*, *homemade*)
- Material: modifiers that describe what something is made from (e.g., *cotton*, *metallic*)
- Purpose: adjectives that function as part of the noun to describe its purpose (e.g., <u>sewing</u> *machine*, <u>rocking</u> *chair*)

> **Did You Know?**
>
> Adjectives answer the questions *what kind*, *how many*, or *which one*?
>
> Adverbs answer the questions *how*, *when*, *where*, *why*, or *to what extent*?

Adverbs, which are often formed by adding the suffix *–ly*, modify any word or set of words that is not a noun or pronoun. They can modify verbs, adjectives, other adverbs, phrases, or clauses.

He <u>quickly</u> ran to the house next door. (*Quickly* modifies the verb *ran*.) Her <u>very</u> effective speech earned her a promotion. (*Very* modifies the adjective *effective*.)

<u>Finally</u>, the table was set and dinner was ready. (*Finally* modifies the clause *the table was set and dinner was ready*.)

Comparative adjectives and adverbs compare two items. For most one- or two-syllable words, the suffix *–er* is added to make it comparative; the word may be followed by *than*.

Superlative adjectives and adverbs compare three or more items. Most one- or two-syllable words are made superlative by adding a suffix, *–est*.

Comparative: My brother is <u>taller</u> than my sister.

Superlative: My brother is the <u>tallest</u> of my five siblings.

Longer adjectives and adverbs must be preceded by *more* to form the comparative and *most* to form the superlative.

Comparative: My bed at home is <u>more comfortable</u> than the one at the hotel.

Superlative: The bed in your guestroom is the <u>most comfortable</u> bed I've ever slept in!

Some adjectives and adverbs form irregular comparatives and superlatives (see Table 2.5.).

Comparative: The weather is bad today, but it was <u>worse</u> yesterday.

Superlative: The <u>worst</u> day this week was Monday, when it rained.

Table 2.5. Irregular Comparative and Superlative Adjectives and Adverbs		
Adjective/Adverb	Comparative	Superlative
much	more	most
bad	worse	worst
good	better	best
little	less	least
fat	further/farther	furthest/farthest

Practice Question

5. Which of the following sentences is CORRECTLY constructed?
    A) Between my mom and dad, my father is the oldest.
    B) I ran less than usual today.
    C) Henry's cat is more fatter than mine.
    D) After taking medicine, she felt worser.

6. Which is the adverb in the following sentence?

He carelessly sped around the flashing yellow light.
    A) flashing
    B) yellow
    C) around
    D) carelessly

Conjunctions

Conjunctions join words into phrases, clauses, and sentences. The *coordinating conjunctions* (FANBOYS) join two independent clauses: **F**or, **A**nd, **N**or, **B**ut, **O**r, **Y**et, **S**o.

Marta went to the pool, <u>and</u> Alex decided to go shopping.

Aisha didn't want to eat tacos for dinner, <u>so</u> she picked up a pizza on her way home.

Subordinating conjunctions join dependent clauses to the independent clauses to which they are related.

We chose that restaurant <u>because</u> Juan loves pizza.

Table 2.6. Subordinating Conjunctions	
Time	after, as, as long as, as soon as, before, since, until, when, whenever, while
Manner	as, as if, as though
Cause	because
Condition	although, as long as, even if, even though, if, provided that, though, unless, while
Purpose	in order that, so that, that
Comparison	as, than

Practice Question

7. The following sentence contains an error. How should it be rewritten?

He liked to cook and baking was his specialty.
    A) He liked to cook, and baking was his specialty.
    B) He liked to cook so baking was his specialty.
    C) He liked to cook; and baking was his specialty.
    D) He liked to cook, baking was his specialty.

8. Identify the underlined part of speech in the following sentence:

Anne and Peter drank their coffee languidly <u>while</u> they read the paper.
    A) subordinating conjunction
    B) coordinating conjunction
    C) irregular verb
    D) adverb

Prepositions

Prepositions set up relationships in time (*after* the party) or space (*under* the cushions) within a sentence. A preposition will always function as part of a prepositional phrase— the preposition along with the object of the preposition.

Table 2.7. Common Prepositions			
Prepositions			
about	by	off	toward
among	despite	on	under
around	down	onto	underneath

Table 2.7. Common Prepositions			
at	during	out	until
before	except	outside	up
behind	for	over	upon
below	from	past	with
beneath	in	since	within
beside	into	through	
between	near	till	
beyond	of	to	
Compound Prepositions			
according to	because of	in place of	on account of
as of	by means of	in respect to	out of
as well as	in addition to	in spite of	prior to
aside from	in front of	instead of	with regard to

Practice Question

9. Identify the prepositional phrase in the following sentence.

John and Carol must drive through the tunnel, but Carol is claustrophobic.
- A) must drive
- B) through the tunnel
- C) drive through
- D) but Carol is

Interjections

Interjections have no grammatical attachment to the sentence itself other than to add expressions of emotion. These parts of speech may be punctuated with commas or exclamation points and may fall anywhere within the sentence.

<u>Ouch!</u> He stepped on my toe.

Practice Question

10. Identify the interjection in the following sentence. "Come here! Look! Our team won the Super Bowl! Yay!"
- A) Come here!
- B) Our team won
- C) Look!
- D) Yay!

2. Grammar and Sentence Structure

Constructing Sentences

Phrases

A **phrase** is a group of words that communicates a partial idea and lacks either a subject or a predicate. Several phrases may be strung together, one after another, to add detail and interest to a sentence.

Phrases are categorized based on the main word in the phrase. A **prepositional** phrase begins with a preposition and ends with an object of the preposition; a **verb phrase** is composed of the main verb along with its helping verbs; and a **noun phrase** consists of a noun and its modifiers.

   Prepositional phrase: The dog is hiding under the porch.

   Verb phrase: The chef wanted to cook a different dish.

   Noun phrase: The big, red barn rests beside the vacant chicken house.

An **appositive phrase** is a particular type of noun phrase that renames the word or group of words that precedes it. Appositive phrases usually follow the noun they describe and are set apart by commas.

   Appositive phrase: My dad, a clock maker, loved antiques.

Verbal phrases begin with a word that would normally act as a verb but is instead filling another role within the sentence. These phrases can act as nouns, adjectives, or adverbs.

   Noun: To become a doctor had always been her goal.

   Adjective: Enjoying the stars that filled the sky, Ben lingered outside for quite a while.

Practice Question

11. Identify the type of phrase underlined in the following sentence:

Dodging traffic, Rachel drove to work on back roads.
   A) prepositional phrase
   B) noun phrase
   C) verb phrase
   D) verbal phrase

Clauses and Types of Sentences

Clauses contain both a subject and a predicate. They can be either independent or dependent. An **independent** (or main) clause can stand alone as its own sentence:

   The dog ate her homework.

Dependent (or subordinate) clauses cannot stand alone as their own sentences. They start with a subordinating conjunction, relative pronoun, or relative adjective, which will make them sound incomplete:

   Because the dog ate her homework

Table 2.8. Words That Begin Dependent Clauses	
Subordinating Conjunctions	**Relative Pronouns and Adjectives**
after, before, once, since, until, when, whenever, while, as, because, in order that, so, so that, that, if, even if, provided that, unless, although, even though, though, whereas, where, wherever, than, whether	who, whoever, whom, whomever, whose, which, that, when, where, why, how

Sentences can be classified based on the number and type of clauses they contain. A **simple sentence** will have only one independent clause and no dependent clauses. The sentence may contain phrases, complements, and modifiers, but it will comprise only one independent clause, one complete idea.

The cat ran under the porch.

A **compound sentence** has two or more independent clauses and no dependent clauses.

The cat ran under the porch, and the dog ran after him.

A **complex sentence** has only one independent clause and one or more dependent clauses.

The cat, who is scared of the dog, ran under the porch.

A **compound-complex sentence** has two or more independent clauses and one or more dependent clauses.

The cat, who is scared of the dog, ran under the porch, and the dog ran after him.

Table 2.9. Sentence Structure and Clauses		
Sentence Structure	**Independent Clauses**	**Dependent Clauses**
Simple	1	0
Compound	2+	0
Complex	1	1+
Compound-complex	2+	1+

Practice Question

12. Which of the following is a compound sentence?
    A) The turtle swam slowly around the pond.
    B) Alligators generally lie still, but they can move with lightning speed.
    C) Mice are most likely to come out at night after other animals have gone to sleep.
    D) Squirrels, to prepare for winter, gather and hide seeds and nuts underground.

Punctuation

Terminal punctuation marks are used to end sentences. The **period** (.) ends declarative (statement) and imperative (command) sentences. The **question mark** (?) terminates interrogative sentences (questions). Lastly, **exclamation points** end exclamatory sentences, in which the writer or speaker is exhibiting intense emotion or energy.

Sarah and I are attending a concert**.**

How many people are attending the concert**?**

What a great show that was**!**

The colon and the semicolon, though often confused, each have a unique set of rules for their use. While both punctuation marks are used to join clauses, the construction of the clauses and the relationship between them is different. The **semicolon** (;) is used to join two independent clauses (IC; IC) that are closely related.

I need to buy a new car soon**;** my old car broke down last month.

The **colon** (:) is used to introduce a list, definition, or clarification. The clause preceding the colon has to be independent, but what follows the colon can be an independent clause, a dependent clause, or a phrase.

The buffet offers three choices**:** ham, turkey, or roast beef.

He decided to drive instead of taking the train**:** he didn't think the train would arrive in time.

Commas show pauses in the text or set information apart from the main text. There are lots of rules for comma usage, so only the most common are summarized below.

- Commas separate two independent clauses along with a coordinating conjunction.

  George ordered the steak, <u>but</u> Bruce preferred the ham.

- Commas separate coordinate adjectives.

  She made herself a big bowl of <u>cold, delicious</u> ice cream.

- Commas separate items in a series.

  The list of groceries included <u>cream, coffee, donuts, and tea</u>.

- Commas separate introductory words and phrases from the rest of the sentence.

  <u>For example</u>, we have thirty students who demand a change.

- Commas set off non-essential information and appositives.

  Estelle, <u>our newly elected chairperson</u>, will be in attendance.

- Commas set off the day and month of a date within a text.

  I was born on February <u>16, 1988</u>.

- Commas set up numbers in a text of more than four digits.

  We expect <u>25,000</u> visitors to the new museum.

- Commas set off the names of cities from their states, territories, or provinces.

    She lives in Houston, Texas.

Quotation marks have a number of different purposes. They enclose titles of short, or relatively short, literary works such as short stories, chapters, and poems. (The titles of longer works, like novels and anthologies, are italicized.) Additionally, quotation marks are used to enclose direct quotations within the text of a document where the quotation is integrated into the text. Writers also use quotation marks to set off dialogue.

We will be reading the poem "Bright Star" in class today.

The poem opens with the line "Bright star, would I were steadfast as thou art."

Apostrophes, sometimes referred to as single quotation marks, have several different purposes.

- They show possession.

    boy's watch, Ronald and Maria's house

- They replace missing letters, numerals, and signs.

    do not = don't, 1989 = '89

- They form plurals of letters, numerals, and signs.

    A's, 10's

Less commonly used punctuation marks include:

- **en dash (–):** indicates a range
- **em dash (—):** shows an abrupt break in a sentence and emphasizes the words within the em dashes
- **parentheses ( ):** enclose nonessential information
- **brackets [ ]:** enclose added words to a quotation and add insignificant information within parentheses
- **slash (/):** separates lines of poetry within a text or indicates interchangeable terminology
- **ellipses (…):** indicates that information has been removed from a quotation or creates a reflective pause

Practice Question

13. Which sentence includes an improperly placed comma?
    A) Ella, Cassie, and Cameron drove to South Carolina together.
    B) Trying to impress his friends, Carl ended up totaling his car.
    C) Ice cream is my favorite food, it is so cold and creamy.
    D) Mowing the lawn, Navid discovered a family of baby rabbits.

14. The following sentence contains an error. How should it be rewritten?

Oak trees—with proper care—can grow taller than thirty feet; providing shade for people, shelter for animals, and perches for birds.
- A) replace the em dashes with commas
- B) remove the comma after *people*
- C) insert an apostrophe at the end of *animals*
- D) replace the semicolon with a comma

Capitalization

Capitalization is writing the first letter of a word in uppercase and the remaining letters in lowercase. Capitalization is used in three main contexts. The first, and most common, is in the first word after a period or the first word of a text. For example, the first word in each sentence of this paragraph is capitalized.

The second most common usage of capitalization is for proper nouns or adjectives derived from proper nouns. For instance, *France*—as the name of a country—is capitalized. Similarly, *French*, the adjective derived from the proper noun *France*, is also capitalized. There is an exception to this rule: when the adjective has taken on a meaning independent of the original proper noun. For example, the term *french fries* is not capitalized.

The third usage of capitalization is in a title or honorific that appears before a name: "**P**resident George Washington never lived in the capital." If, however, that same title is used *instead* of the name, or if the name and title are separated by a comma, it remains lowercase. For example, "The first **p**resident, George Washington, never lived in the capital" or "The **p**resident did not originally live in the capital."

Practice Question

15. Which sentence CORRECTLY uses capitalization?
    - A) Robert and Kelly raced across the River in their small boats.
    - B) ducks flying in a V-formation cross the Midwest in the fall.
    - C) The chairwoman of the board, Keisha Johnson, will lead today's meeting.
    - D) The Senators from Virginia and Louisiana strongly favor the bill.

Common Language Errors

Subject-Verb Agreement

Verbs must agree in number with their subjects. Common rules for subject/verb agreement are given below.

- Single subjects agree with single verbs; plural subjects agree with plural verbs.

    The <u>girl walks</u> her dog. The <u>girls walk</u> their dogs.

- Ignore words between the subject and the verb: agreement must exist between the subject and verb.

The new library ~~with its many books and rooms~~ fills a long-felt need.

- Compound subjects joined by *and* typically take a plural verb unless considered one item.

  Correctness and precision are required for all good writing. Macaroni and cheese makes a great snack for children.

- The linking verbs agree with the subject and not the subject complement (predicate nominative).

  My favorite is strawberries and apples. My favorites are strawberries and apples.

- When a relative pronoun (*who, whom, which, that*) is used as the subject of the clause, the verb will agree with the antecedent of the relative pronoun.

  This is the student who is receiving an award.

  These are the students who are receiving awards.

- All single, indefinite pronouns agree with single verbs.

  Neither of the students is happy about the play.

  Each of the many cars is on the grass.

  Every one of the administrators speaks highly of Trevor.

Practice Question

16. Which sentence in the following list is CORRECT in its subject and verb agreement?
    A) My sister and my best friend lives in Chicago.
    B) My parents or my brother is going to pick me up from the airport.
    C) Neither of the students refuse to take the exam.
    D) The team were playing a great game until the rain started.

Pronoun-Antecedent Agreement

Similarly, pronouns must agree with their antecedents (the words they replaced) in number; however, some pronouns also require gender agreement (*him, her*). **Pronoun/antecedent agreement** rules can be found below:

- Antecedents joined by *and* typically require a plural pronoun.

  The children and their dogs enjoyed their day at the beach.

  If the two nouns refer to the same person, a singular pronoun is preferable.

  My best friend and confidant still lives in her log cabin.

- For compound antecedents joined by *or*, the pronoun agrees with the nearer or nearest antecedent.

  Either the resident mice or the manager's cat gets itself a meal of good leftovers.

- When indefinite pronouns function in a sentence, the pronoun must agree with the number of the indefinite pronoun.

  Neither student finished his or her assignment. Both students finished their assignments.

2. Grammar and Sentence Structure

39

- When collective nouns function as antecedents, the pronoun choice will be singular or plural depending on the function of the collective.

    The <u>audience</u> was cheering as <u>it</u> rose to its feet in unison.

    Our <u>family</u> are spending <u>their</u> vacations in Maine, Hawaii, and Rome.

- When *each* and *every* precede the antecedent, the pronoun agreement will be singular.

    <u>Each and every man, woman, and child</u> brings unique qualities to <u>his or her</u> family.

    <u>Every creative writer, technical writer, and research writer</u> is attending <u>his or her</u> assigned lecture.

How would you complete the following sentence? "Every boy and girl should check _____ homework before turning it in." Many people would use the pronoun *their*. But since the antecedent is "every boy and girl," technically, the correct answer would be *his* or *her*. Using *they* or *their* in similar situations is increasingly accepted in formal speech, however. It is unlikely that you will see questions like this appear on the HiSET, but if you do, it is safest to use the technically correct response.

Practice Question

17. Which sentence in the following list is CORRECT in its pronoun and antecedent agreement?
    A) The grandchildren and their cousins enjoyed their day at the park.
    B) Most of the grass has lost their deep color.
    C) The jury was relieved as their commitment came to a close.
    D) Every boy and girl must learn to behave themselves in school.

18. Which sentence in the following list is CORRECT in its pronoun and antecedent agreement?
    A) Either my brother or my dad will bring their van to pick us up.
    B) The university is having their tenth fundraiser tonight.
    C) Alyssa and Jacqueline bought herself a big lunch today.
    D) Each dog, cat, and rabbit has its own bowl and blanket.

Verb-Tense Agreement

In any passage, verb tense should be consistent and make sense in context of other verbs, adverbs, and general meaning. Verb tense questions appear frequently on the HiSET, so pay attention to the context of the entire passage.

Incorrect: Deborah <u>was speaking</u> with her colleague when her boss <u>will appear</u>, demanding a meeting.

In this sentence, the subject, *Deborah*, is acting in an ongoing event in the past, so the verb describing this action, *speaking*, is conjugated in the continuous past tense. In the context of the sentence, the appearance of her boss is a completed event that happens during the conversation. The verb describing the boss' appearance should be conjugated in the simple past tense. The corrected sentence reads as follows:

Correct: Deborah <u>was speaking</u> with her colleague when her boss <u>appeared</u>, demanding a meeting.

One clue to the correct conjugation of the verb *appeared* is the adverb *when*, which implies that a completed event occurred to interrupt the ongoing event (in this case, Deborah's talk with her colleague).

Pay attention to how verbs are conjugated in the beginning of a sentence or passage, and look for clues to spot any errors in verb tense agreement.

Practice Question

19. The following sentence contains an error. How should it be rewritten? Veronica attended cooking classes, and she goes to yoga classes too.
    A) Veronica attends cooking classes, and she went to yoga classes too.
    B) Veronica attended cooking classes, and she went to yoga classes too.
    C) Veronica attended cooking classes; she goes to yoga classes too.
    D) Veronica attended cooking classes. She goes to yoga classes too.

Parallelism

Errors in **parallelism** prevent a writer from creating a smooth flow, or coherence, from word to word and sentence to sentence. Writers should create parallel structure in words, phrases, and clauses wherever two or more similar and equally important ideas exist next to each other in a sentence. Errors in parallel structure frequently appear in sentences with verb phrases, prepositional phrases, and correlative conjunctions like *either…or*, *neither…nor*, and *not only…but also*.

  Incorrect: Adia could program computers, repair cars, and knew how to make croissants.

  Correct: Adia could program computers, repair cars, and bake croissants.

In the corrected sentence, the verbs are aligned in parallel structure. Furthermore, the first sentence contains a verb error. By omitting "program computers, repair cars," the sentence reads "Adia could…knew how to make croissants" Rewriting the sentence in parallel structure corrects the verb error.

In sentences with multiple prepositional phrases in a parallel series, the preposition must be repeated unless the same preposition begins each phrase.

  Incorrect: You can park your car in the garage, the carport, or on the street.

  Correct: You can park your car in the garage, in the carport, or on the street.

Practice Question

20. The following sentence contains an error. How should it be rewritten?

Shelly achieved more at nursing school because she was going to bed earlier, eating healthy food, and she started to stay home and study more.
- A) Shelly achieved more at nursing school. She was going to bed earlier, eating healthy food, and she started to stay home and study more.
- B) Shelly achieved more at nursing school because she was going to bed earlier, eating healthy food, and studying more.
- C) Shelly achieved more at nursing school; she was going to bed earlier, eating healthy food, and she started to stay home and study more.
- D) Shelly achieved more at nursing school; she was going to bed earlier, and she started to eat healthy food and studying more.

Sentence Construction Errors

Sentence errors fall into three categories: fragments, comma splices (comma fault), and fused sentences (run-on). A **fragment** occurs when a group of words is not a complete sentence but is punctuated like one. The fragment might be a phrase or a dependent clause. To fix a fragment, an independent clause needs to be created.

Fragment (phrase): The girl in my class who asks a lot of questions.

Correct: The girl in my class who asks a lot of questions sits in the back row.

Fragment (dependent clause): Because of the big storm we had last weekend.

Correct: Because of the big storm we had last weekend, the park will be closed.

A **comma splice** (comma fault) occurs when two independent clauses are joined together in a paragraph with only a comma to "splice" them together. **Fused** (run-on) sentences occur when two independent clauses are joined with no punctuation what- soever. To fix a comma splice or fused sentence, add the correct punctuation and/or conjunction.

Comma splice: My family eats turkey at Thanksgiving, we eat ham at Christmas.

Correct: My family eats turkey at Thanksgiving, and we eat ham at Christmas.

Correct: My family eats turkey at Thanksgiving. We eat ham at Christmas.

Correct: My family eats turkey at Thanksgiving; we eat ham at Christmas.

Fused sentence: I bought a chocolate pie from the bakery it was delicious.

Correct: I bought a chocolate pie from the bakery. It was delicious.

Correct: I bought a chocolate pie from the bakery, and it was delicious.

Correct: I bought a chocolate pie from the bakery; it was delicious.

Practice Question

21. Which of the following is CORRECTLY punctuated?
    A) Since she went to the store.
    B) The football game ended in a tie, the underdog caught up in the fourth quarter.
    C) The mall is closing early today so we'll have to go shopping tomorrow.
    D) When the players dropped their gloves, a fight broke out on the ice hockey rink floor.

Easily Confused Words

- **a, an:** *a* precedes words beginning with consonants or consonant sounds; *an* precedes words beginning with vowels or vowel sounds.

- **affect, effect:** *affect* is most often a verb; *effect* is usually a noun. (*The experience affected me significantly* OR *The experience had a significant effect on me.*)

- **among, amongst, between:** *among* is used for a group of more than two people or items; *amongst* is an uncommon, archaic term; *between* distinguishes two people or items.

- **amount, number:** *amount* is used for noncountable sums; *number* is used with countable nouns.

- **cite, site:** the verb *cite* credits an author of a quotation, paraphrase, or summary; the noun *site* is a location.

- **every day, everyday:** *every day* is an indefinite adjective modifying a noun; *everyday* is a one-word adjective implying frequent occurrence. (*Our visit to the Minnesota State Fair is an everyday activity during August.*)

- **fewer, less:** *fewer* is used with a countable noun; *less* is used with a noncountable noun. (*Fewer parents are experiencing stress since the new teacher was hired; parents are experiencing less stress since the new teacher was hired.*)

- **good, well:** *good* is always the adjective; *well* is always the adverb except in cases of health. (*He writes well. She felt well after the surgery.*)

- **implied, inferred:** *implied* is something a speaker does; *inferred* is something the listener does after assessing the speaker's message. (*The speaker implied something mysterious, but I inferred the wrong thing.*)

- **irregardless, regardless:** *irregardless* is nonstandard usage and should be avoided; *regardless* is the proper usage of the transitional statement.

- **its, it's:** *its* is a possessive pronoun; *it's* is a contraction for *it is*.

- **principal, principle:** as a noun, *principal* is an authority figure, often the head of a school; as an adjective, *principal* means *main*; the noun *principle* means idea or belief. (*The principal of the school spoke on the principal meaning of the main principles of the school.*)

- **quote, quotation:** *quote* is a verb; *quotation* is a noun.

- **should of, should have:** *should of* is improper usage—*of* is not a helping verb and therefore cannot complete the verb phrase; *should have* is the proper usage. (*He should have driven.*)

2. Grammar and Sentence Structure

- **than, then:** *than* sets up a comparison; *then* indicates a reference to a point in time. (*When I said that I liked the hat better than the gloves, my sister laughed; then she bought both for me.*)

- **their, there, they're:** *their* is the possessive case of the pronoun *they*. *There* is the demonstrative pronoun indicating location or place. *They're* is a contraction of the words *they are*.

- **to lie (to recline), to lay (to place):** *to lie* is the intransitive verb meaning *to recline*; *to lay* is the transitive verb meaning *to place something*. (*I lie out in the sun; I lay my towel on the beach.*)

- **who, whom:** *who* is the subject relative pronoun. (*My son, who is a good student, studies hard.*) Here, the son is carrying out the action of studying, so the pronoun is a subject pronoun (*who*). *Whom* is the object relative pronoun. (*My son, whom the other students admire, studies hard.*) Here, *son* is the object of the other students' admiration, so the pronoun standing in for him, *whom*, is an object pronoun.

- **your, you're:** *your* is the possessive case of the pronoun *you*. *You're* is a contraction of the words *you are*.

Practice Question

22. Which of the following sentences contains an error?
    A) I invited fewer people to my birthday party this year.
    B) The students asked the principle to postpone the meeting.
    C) My sister baked cookies then asked me to help clean the kitchen.
    D) She paints well even though she has no formal training.

Answer Key

1. B: Nouns are people, places, things, or ideas; they usually act as the subject or object in a sentence.

2. D: The reflexive pronoun *ourselves* refers back to the subject of the sentence. Because it is in the first person plural, the subject should also be in the first person plural (*we*).

3. A: The phrase *by this time tomorrow* describes as action that will take place and be completed in the future, so the future perfect tense (*will have arrived*) should be used.

4. C: *Package* is the direct object of the verb *brought*.

5. B: The speaker is comparing today's run to the norm, not to any additional instances, so the comparative is acceptable here. Furthermore, the word *than* appears, a clue that the comparative is appropriate. *Less* is the irregular comparative form of *little*.

6. D: *Carelessly* is an adverb modifying *sped* and explaining *how* the driving occurred. The subject was not mindful as he drove; he raced through a yellow light when he should have exercised caution.

7. A: This sentence includes two independent clauses: "He liked to cook" and "baking was his specialty." They can be connected with a comma and coordinating conjunction (the conjunction *and* is appropriate here). The sentence could also be written with a semicolon and no conjunction.

8. A: "While they read the paper" is a dependent clause; the subordinating conjunction *while* connects it to the independent clause "Anne and Peter drank their coffee languidly."

9. B: "Through the tunnel" is a prepositional phrase explaining the relationship between the subjects and the tunnel using the preposition *through* and the object *the tunnel*.

10. D: *Yay* is an expression of emotion and has no other grammatical purpose in the sentence.

11. D: The phrase is a verbal phrase modifying the noun *Rachel*. It begins with the word *dodging*, derived from the verb to *dodge*.

12. B: "Alligators...still" and "they...speed" are two independent clauses connected by a comma and the coordinating conjunction *but*.

13. C: "Ice cream... food" and "it...creamy" are two independent clauses. The writer should include a coordinating conjunction like *for* or separate the clauses with a semicolon.

14. D: "Providing shade..." is not an independent clause; therefore it cannot be preceded by a semicolon.

15. C: *Keisha Johnson*, as a proper noun, should be capitalized, but "chairwoman of

the board" should not be because it is separated from the name by a comma.

16. B: The verb agrees with the closest subject—in this case, the singular *brother*.

17. A: The plural antecedents *grandchildren* and *cousins* match the plural possessive pronoun *their*.

18. D: When *each* precedes the antecedent, the pronoun agreement is singular. The pronoun *its* therefore agrees with the antecedents *Each dog, cat, and rabbit*.

19. B: In this sentence, the verbs *attended* and *went* are both correctly conjugated in the simple past tense.

20. B: In this sentence, three related clauses are written in parallel structure using the participles *going*, *eating*, and *studying*.

21. D: This is a complete sentence that is punctuated properly with a comma between the dependent and independent clauses.

22. B: A principle is a belief; a principal is the head of a school.

3. The Essay

The HiSET requires an essay as part of the Writing test. You will be provided with two written excerpts about an issue and asked to take a position on that issue. To do well on the essay, take a clear side on the topic put forth in the prompt. Support your perspective with strong arguments and specific examples. An effective essay is clearly organized and structured, displays strong vocabulary, and features complex sentences.

There are two common types of essays:

- an expository essay explains an issue without taking sides or promoting a perspective
- a persuasive essay argues in favor of or against an issue or perspective

For the HiSET, you'll be writing a persuasive essay.

Writing a Thesis Statement

A **thesis statement** articulates the main argument of the essay. No essay is complete without it: the structure and organization of the essay revolves around the thesis statement. The thesis statement is simply the writer's main idea or argument. It usually appears at the end of the introduction.

In a good thesis statement, the author states his or her idea or argument and why it is correct or true.

Example
Take a position on the following topic in your essay. You can choose to write about either of the two viewpoints discussed in the prompt, or you may argue for a third point of view.

Many scientists argue that recent unusual weather patterns, such as powerful hurricanes and droughts, are due to climate change triggered by human activity. They argue that automobiles, oil and gas production, and manufacturing generate carbon emissions that artificially heat the atmosphere, resulting in extreme weather patterns. Others disagree. Some researchers and media pundits argue that climate change is natural, and that extreme weather has always been a feature of Earth's atmosphere.

Around the world more people than ever before are driving cars, and industrial production is at an all-time high: it is obvious that human activity is affecting the atmosphere and causing extreme weather events.

I believe that temperatures and storms are more extreme than ever because of the environmental impact of human activity; not only do scientists have overwhelming evidence that climate change is unnatural, but I can also personally remember when there were fewer storms and variations in temperature.

Society needs cars and manufacturing, but governments should restrict harmful emissions released into the atmosphere so we can slow down climate change and save lives.

Structuring the Essay

On the HiSET, a strong essay will have an introduction, a body, and a conclusion. While there are many ways to organize an essay, on this exam it is most important that the essay is clearly structured. There is no need to get too complicated: this simple structure will do.

Introductions

Some writers struggle with the introduction, but it is actually an opportunity to present your idea or argument. On the HiSET, the introduction can be one paragraph that ends with the thesis statement. In the rest of the paragraph, the writer provides some context for his or her argument. This context might include counterarguments, a preview of specific examples to be discussed later on, acknowledgement of the complexities of the issue, or even a reference to personal experience. The writer can reexamine some of these issues in the conclusion.

> **Did You Know?**
>
> If you're not sure what to include in your introduction, start your essay with just the thesis statement. You can go back and complete the introduction once the rest of the essay is finished.

Example
In the example below, the writer has written an introduction that includes context for her argument: background information, a counterargument, and personal experience. As a result, the reader has a better idea of how complex the issue is and why the writer feels the way she does. The thesis statement appears at the end of the paragraph; as a result of the introduction as a whole, the thesis statement has more impact.

A century ago, there were barely any cars on the road. Oil had just been discovered in a few parts of the world. Industrial production existed but had not yet exploded with the introduction of the assembly line. Refineries and factories were not yet churning out the chemical emissions they are today. Certainly, hurricanes and droughts occurred, but the populations and infrastructure affected were far smaller. Now, scientists have evidence that human activity— like pollution from industry and cars—is affecting the atmosphere and making weather more extreme. In 2017, millions of people were affected by hurricanes and wildfires. It is true that some researchers disagree that human activity

has caused these and other extreme weather events. But why take the risk? If we can limit destruction now and in the future, we should. Extreme weather events are a danger to people all around the world. Society needs cars and manufacturing, but governments should restrict harmful emissions released into the atmosphere so we can slow down climate change and save lives.

The Body Paragraphs

Most writers find the body of the essay the easiest part to write. The body of the essay is simply several paragraphs, each beginning with a topic sentence. Each paragraph usually addresses an example that supports the argument made in the thesis statement or, in the case of an expository essay, explains the writer's reasoning. On the HiSET, you may use specific examples or personal anecdotes, present problems and solutions, or compare and contrast ideas. You do not need to refer to any outside literature or documentation.

To strengthen the body of the essay, writers will maintain consistency in paragraphs, always beginning with a topic sentence, which introduces the main idea of each paragraph. Each paragraph deals with its own main topic, but writers should use transition words and phrases to link paragraphs with each other. A good essay maintains readability and flow.

Example

This example body paragraph is related to the introduction provided above. It provides reasoning and historical evidence for the author's argument that human activity is impacting the earth and causing climate change.

Human industrial activity has been growing exponentially, putting more pollution into the atmosphere than ever. Over the past forty years, large countries like China and India have become industrialized and manufacture many of the world's products. As their populations become more prosperous, demand for automobiles also rises, putting more cars on the road—and exhaust in the air. While industrial development has benefited Asia and other areas, carbon emissions that cause climate change have multiplied. Meanwhile, previously industrialized countries in Europe and North America continue to produce carbon emissions. In the nineteenth century, only a few countries had industrial sectors; today, global industry strains the environment like never before. The past 150 years have seen unprecedented industrial growth. Even if

the climate changes naturally over time, it cannot be denied that recent human activity has suddenly generated enormous amounts of carbon emissions that have impacted the atmosphere. Scientists say that the earth is warming as a result.

Conclusions

The conclusion does not need to be long. Its purpose is to wrap up the essay, reminding the reader why the topic and the writer's argument is important. It is an opportunity for the writer to reexamine the thesis statement and ideas in the introduction. It is a time to reinforce the argument, not just to repeat the introduction.

Example

This example is taken from the same essay as the introduction and body paragraph above. It reinforces the writer's argument without simply repeating what she said in the introduction. The writer does address the topics she spoke about in the introduction (climate change and protecting people from extreme weather) but she does not simply rewrite the thesis: she calls for action.

No doubt, scientists, pundits, and politicians will continue to argue over the reasons for extreme weather. Meanwhile, Mother Nature will continue to wreak havoc on vulnerable areas regardless of what we think. Because we have proof that climate change is related to extreme weather and we know that extreme weather threatens people's lives, the time to act is now. We can take steps

to mitigate pollution without lowering quality of life. Doing anything else is irresponsible—and for some, deadly.

Providing Supporting Evidence

As discussed above, a good essay should have specific evidence or examples that support the thesis statement. On the HiSET, a specific example should be something related to the idea of the paragraph and the essay, not a new idea. A specific example can be from your general knowledge; you do not need to know about specific academic issues to do well on the essay. Remember, you are being tested on your reasoning and argumentative skills.

The following are some examples of general statements and specific statements that provide more detailed support:

General: Human industrial activity has been growing exponentially, putting more pollution into the atmosphere than ever.

Specific: Over the past forty years, large countries like China and India have become industrialized and manufacture many of the world's products. As their populations become more prosperous, demand for automobiles also rises, putting more cars on the road—and exhaust in the air.

Specific: Meanwhile, previously industrialized countries in Europe and North America continue to produce carbon emissions. In the nineteenth century, only a few countries had industrial sectors; today, global industry strains the environment like never before.

General: More people than ever are affected by extreme weather.

Specific: In 2017, several hurricanes affected the United States and the Caribbean. In Texas, Hurricane Harvey led to historic flooding in Houston and the Texas Coast. Millions of people were affected; thousands lost their homes, jobs, and livelihoods.

Specific: Hurricane Irma damaged the US Virgin Islands and neighboring Caribbean nations. Soon after, Hurricane Maria catastrophically devastated Puerto Rico. Months later, Puerto Ricans were still without power and basic necessities. It is still not clear how many have died due to the storm and related damage.

Example

In the example below, the paragraph is structured with a topic sentence and specific supporting ideas. This paragraph supports the introduction in the example above.

More people than ever are affected by extreme weather. In 2017, several hurricanes affected the United States and the Caribbean. In Texas, Hurricane Harvey led to historic flooding in Houston and the Texas Coast. Millions of people were affected; thousands lost their homes, jobs, and livelihoods.

Hurricane Irma damaged Florida, the US Virgin Islands, and neighboring Caribbean nations. Soon after, Hurricane Maria catastrophically devastated Puerto Rico. Months later, Puerto Ricans were still without power and basic necessities. It is still not clear how many have died due to the storm and related damage. In California, severe droughts led to exceptionally large wildfires that threatened Los Angeles and destroyed neighboring communities. Meanwhile, those same areas—Southern California, the Texas Coast, and Florida—continue to grow, putting more people at risk when the next hurricane or fire strikes.

Writing Well

Using transitions, complex sentences, and certain words can turn a good essay into a great one. Transitions, syntax, word choice, and tone all help clarify and amplify a writer's argument or point and improve the flow of an essay.

Transitions

An essay consists of several paragraphs. **Transitions** are words and phrases that help connect the paragraphs and ideas of the text. Most commonly, transitions would appear at the beginning of a paragraph, but writers should also use them throughout a text to connect ideas. Common transitions are words like *also*, *next*, *still*, *although*, *in addition to*, and *in other words*. A transition shows a relationship between ideas, so writers should pay close attention to the transition words and phrases they choose. Transitions may show connections or contrasts between words and ideas.

Table 3.1. Common Transitions

Transition Type	Examples
addition	additionally, also, as well, further, furthermore, in addition, moreover
cause and effect	as a result, because, consequently, due to, if/then, so, therefore, thus
concluding	briefly, finally, in conclusion, in summary, thus, to conclude
contrast	but, however, in contrast, on the other hand, nevertheless, on the contrary, yet
examples	in other words, for example, for instance
similarity	also, likewise, similarly
time	after, before, currently, later, recently, subsequently, since, then, while

Syntax

Syntax refers to how words and phrases are arranged in writing or speech. Writing varied sentences is essential to capturing and keeping a reader's interest. A good essay features different types of sentences: simple, complex, compound, and compound-complex. Sentences need not always begin with the subject; they might start with a transition word or phrase, for instance. Variety is key.

Still, writers should keep in mind that the point of an essay is to get an idea across to the reader, so it is most important that writing be clear. They should not sacrifice clarity for the sake of flowery, overly wordy language or confusing syntax.

Word Choice and Tone

Like syntax, word choice makes an impression on readers. The HiSET does not test on specific vocabulary or require writers to use specific words on the essay. However, the essay is a good opportunity to use strong vocabulary pertaining to the prompt or issue under discussion. Writers should be careful, though, that they understand the words they are using. Writers should also avoid vague, imprecise, or generalizing language like *good*, *bad*, *a lot*, *a little*, *very*, *normal*, and so on.

Editing, Revising, and Proofreading

On the HiSET, the writer has a limited amount of time to complete the essay. If there is time for editing or proofreading, writers should hunt for grammar, spelling, or punctuation mistakes that could change the meaning of the text or make it difficult to understand. These include sentence fragments, run-on sentences, subject-verb disagreement, and pronoun-antecedent disagreement.

4. Numbers and Operations

This chapter provides a review of the basic yet critical components of mathematics such as manipulating fractions, comparing numbers, and using units. These concepts will provide the foundation for more complex mathematical operations in later chapters.

Types of Numbers

Numbers are placed in categories based on their properties.

A **natural number** is greater than 0 and has no decimal or fraction attached. These are also sometimes called counting numbers: $\{1, 2, 3, 4, \ldots\}$.

Whole numbers are natural numbers and the number 0: $\{0, 1, 2, 3, 4, \ldots\}$.

Integers include positive and negative natural numbers and 0: $\{\ldots, -4, -3, -2, -1, 0, 1, 2, 3, 4, \ldots\}$.

A **rational number** can be represented as a fraction. Any decimal part must terminate or resolve into a repeating pattern. Examples include -12, $-\frac{4}{5}$, 0.36, 7.7, $26\frac{1}{2}$, etc.

An **irrational number** cannot be represented as a fraction. An irrational decimal number never ends and never resolves into a repeating pattern. Examples include $-\sqrt{7}$, π, and $0.34567989135\ldots$

A **real number** is a number that can be represented by a point on a number line. Real numbers include all the rational and irrational numbers.

An **imaginary number** includes the imaginary unit i, where $i = \sqrt{-1}$. Because $i^2 = -1$, imaginary numbers produce a negative value when squared. Examples of imaginary numbers include $-4i$, $0.75i$, $i\sqrt{2}$, $\frac{8}{3}i$.

A **complex number** is in the form $a + bi$, where a and b are real numbers.

Examples of complex numbers include $3 + 2i$, $-4 + i$, $\sqrt{3} - i^3\sqrt{5}$, and $\frac{5}{8} - \frac{7i}{8}$.

All imaginary numbers are also complex.

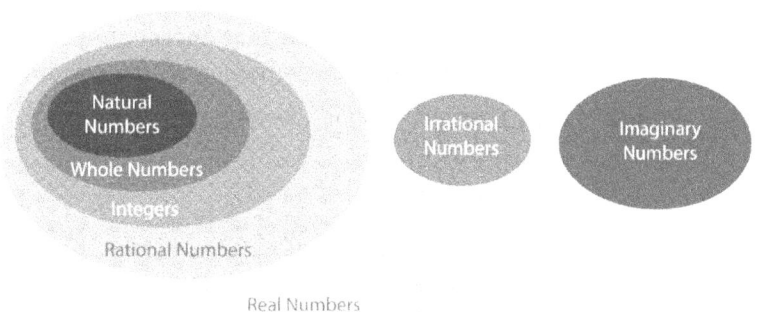

Figure 4.1. Types of Numbers

> **Did You Know?**
>
> If a real number is a natural number (e.g., 50), then it is also a whole number, an integer, and a rational number.

The **factors** of a natural number are all the numbers that can multiply together to make the number. For example, the factors of 24 are 1, 2, 3, 4, 6, 8, 12, and 24. Every natural number is either prime or composite. A **prime number** is a number that is only divisible by itself and 1. (The number 1 is not considered prime.) Examples of prime numbers are 2, 3, 7, and 29. The number 2 is the only even prime number. A **composite number** has more than two factors. For example, 6 is composite because its factors are 1, 6, 2, and 3. Every composite number can be written as a unique product of prime numbers, called the **prime factorization** of the number. For example, the prime factorization of 90 is $90 = 2 \times 3^2 \times 5$. All integers are either even or odd. An even number is divisible by 2; an odd number is not.

Properties of Number Systems

A system is **closed** under an operation if performing that operation on two elements of the system results in another element of that system. For example, the integers are closed under the operations of addition, subtraction, and multiplication but not division. Adding, subtracting, or multiplying two integers results in another integer. However, dividing two integers could result in a rational number that is not an integer: $-2 \div 3 = \frac{-2}{3}$.

The rational numbers are closed under all four operations (except for division by 0).

The real numbers are closed under all four operations.

The complex numbers are closed under all four operations.

The irrational numbers are NOT closed under ANY of the four operations.

The **commutative property** holds for an operation if order does not matter when performing the operation. For example, multiplication is commutative for integers: $(-2)(3) = (3)(-2)$.

The **associative property** holds for an operation if elements can be regrouped without changing the result. For example, addition is associative for real numbers: $-3 + (-5 + 4) = (-3 + -5) + 4$.

The **distributive property** of multiplication over addition allows a product of sums to be written as a sum of products: $a(b + c) = ab + ac$. The value a is distributed over the sum $(b + c)$. The acronym FOIL (First, Outer, Inner, Last) is a useful way to remember the distributive property.

When an operation is performed with an **identity element** and another element a, the result is a. The identity element for multiplication on real numbers is 1 ($a \times 1 = a$), and for addition is 0 ($a + 0 = a$).

An operation of a system has an **inverse element** if applying that operation with the inverse element results in the identity element. For example, the inverse element of a for addition is $-a$ because $a + (-a) = 0$. The inverse element of a for multiplication is $\frac{1}{a}$ because $a \times \frac{1}{a} = 1$.

Practice Question

1. Classify the following numbers as natural, whole, integer, rational, or irrational. (The numbers may have more than one classification.)
   [A] 72
   [B] $-\frac{2}{3}$
   [C] $\sqrt{5}$

2. Determine the real and imaginary parts of the following complex numbers.
   [A] 20
   [B] $10 - i$
   [C] $15i$

3. Answer True or False for each statement:
   [A] The natural numbers are closed under subtraction.
   [B] The sum of two irrational numbers is irrational.
   [C] The sum of a rational number and an irrational number is irrational.

4. Answer true or false for each statement:
   [A] The associative property applies for multiplication in the real numbers.
   [B] The commutative property applies to all real numbers and all operations.

Operations with Complex Numbers

Operations with complex numbers are similar to operations with real numbers in that complex numbers can be added, subtracted, multiplied, and divided. When adding or subtracting, the imaginary parts and real parts are combined separately. When multiplying, the distributive property (FOIL) can be applied. Note that multiplying complex numbers often creates the value i^2 which can be simplified to –1.

To divide complex numbers, multiply both the top and bottom of the fraction by the **complex conjugate** of the divisor (bottom number). The complex conjugate is the complex number with the sign of the imaginary part changed. For example, the complex conjugate of $3 + 4i$ would be $3 - 4i$. Since both the top and the bottom of the fraction are multiplied by the same number, the fraction is really just being multiplied by 1. When simplified, the denominator of the fraction will now be a real number.

Practice Question

5. Simplify: $(3 - 2i) - (-2 + 8i)$

6. Simplify: $\frac{4i}{5-2i}$

Scientific Notation

Scientific notation is a method of representing very large and small numbers in the form $a \times 10^n$, where a is a value between 1 and 10, and n is a nonzero integer. For example, the number 927,000,000 is written in scientific notation as 9.27×10^8. Multiplying 9.27 by 10 eight times gives 927,000,000. When performing operations with scientific notation, the final answer should be in the form $a \times 10^n$.

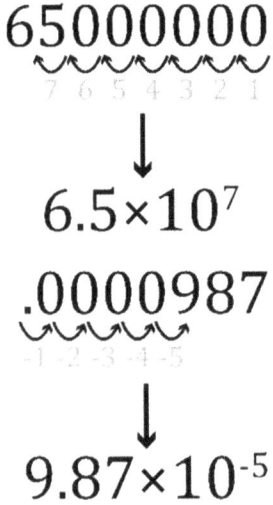

Figure 4.2. Scientific Notation

When adding and subtracting numbers in scientific notation, the power of 10 must be the same for all numbers. This results in like terms in which the a terms are added or subtracted and the 10^n remains unchanged. When multiplying numbers in scientific notation, multiply the a factors, and then multiply that answer by 10 to the sum of the exponents. For division, divide the a factors and subtract the exponents.

Did You Know?

When multiplying numbers in scientific notation, add the exponents. When dividing, subtract the exponents.

Practice Question

7. Simplify: $(3.8 \times 10^3) + (4.7 \times 10^2)$

8. Simplify: $(8.1 \times 10^{-5})(1.4 \times 10^7)$

Positive and Negative Numbers

Positive numbers are greater than 0, and **negative numbers** are less than 0. Both positive and negative numbers can be shown on a **number line**.

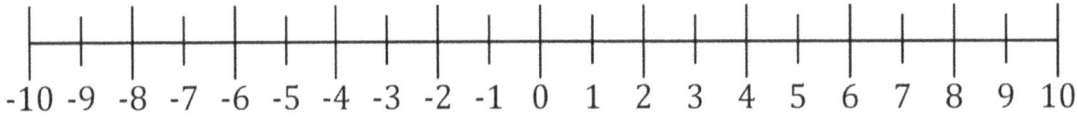

Figure 4.3. Number Line

The **absolute value** of a number is the distance the number is from 0. Since distance is always positive, the absolute value of a number is always positive. The absolute value of a is denoted $|a|$. For example, $|-2| = 2$ since -2 is two units away from 0.

Positive and negative numbers can be added, subtracted, multiplied, and divided. The sign of the resulting number is governed by a specific set of rules shown in the table below.

Table 4.1. Operations with Positive and Negative Numbers			
Adding Real Numbers		**Subtracting Real Numbers**	
Positive + Positive = Positive	$7 + 8 = 15$	Negative − Positive = Negative	$-7 - 8 = -7 + (-8) = -15$
Negative + Negative = Negative	$-7 + (-8) = -15$	Positive − Negative = Positive	$7 - (-8) = 7 + 8 = 15$
Negative + Positive OR Positive + Negative = Keep the sign of the number with larger absolute value	$-7 + 8 = 1$ $7 + -8 = -1$	Negative − Negative = Change the subtraction to addition and change the sign of the second number; then use addition rules.	$-7 - (-8) = -7 + 8 = 1$ $-8 - (-7) = -8 + 7 = -1$
Multiplying Real Numbers		**Dividing Real Numbers**	
Positive × Positive = Positive	$8 \times 4 = 32$	Positive ÷ Positive = Positive	$8 \div 4 = 2$
Negative × Negative = Positive	$-8 \times (-4) = 32$	Negative ÷ Negative = Positive	$-8 \div (-4) = 2$
Positive × Negative OR Negative × Positive = Negative	$8 \times (-4) = -32$ $-8 \times 4 = -32$	Positive ÷ Negative OR Negative ÷ Positive = Negative	$8 \div (-4) = -2$ $-8 \div 4 = -2$

Practice Question

9. Add or subtract the following real numbers:
   [A] $-18 + 12$
   [B] $-3.64 + (-2.18)$
   [C] $9.37 - 4.25$
   [D] $86 - (-20)$

10. Multiply or divide the following real numbers:
    [A] $\frac{10}{3} - \frac{9}{5}$
    [B] $\frac{-64}{-10}$
    [C] $(2.2)(3.3)$
    [D] $-52 \div 13$

Order of Operations

The **order of operations** is simply the order in which operations are performed. Multiplication and division, and addition and subtraction, are performed together from left to right. So, performing multiple operations on a set of numbers is a four-step process. **PEMDAS** is a common way to remember the order of operations:

Parentheses: Calculate expressions inside parentheses, brackets, braces, etc.

Exponents: Calculate exponents and square roots.

Multiplication: Calculate any remaining multiplication and division in order from left to right.

Division: Calculate any remaining multiplication and division in order from left to right.

Addition: Calculate any remaining addition and subtraction in order from left to right.

Subtraction: Calculate any remaining addition and subtraction in order from left to right.

Always work from left to right within each step when simplifying expressions.

Practice Question

11. Simplify: $2(21 - 14) + 6 \div (-2) \times 3 - 10$

12. Simplify: $-(3)2 + 4(5) + (5 - 6)2 - 8$

13. Simplify: $\frac{(7-9)^3 + 8(10-12)}{4^2 - 5^2}$

Units of Measurement

The standard units for the metric and American systems are shown below, along with the prefixes used to express metric units.

Table 4.2. Units and Conversion Factors

Dimension	American	SI
length	inch/foot/yard/mile	meter
mass	ounce/pound/ton	gram
volume	cup/pint/quart/gallon	liter
force	pound-force	newton
pressure	pound-force per square inch	pascal
work and energy	cal/British thermal unit	joule
temperature	Fahrenheit	kelvin
charge	faraday	coulomb

Table 4.3. Metric Prefixes

Prefix	Symbol	Multiplication Factor
tera	T	1,000,000,000,000
giga	G	1,000,000,000
mega	M	1,000,000
kilo	k	1,000
hecto	h	100
deca	da	10
base unit	--	--
deci	d	0.1
centi	c	0.01
milli	m	0.001
micro	μ	0.000001
nano	n	0.000000001
pico	p	0.000000000001

Units can be converted within a single system or between systems. When converting from one unit to another unit, a conversion factor (a numeric multiplier used to convert a value with a unit to another unit) is used. The process of converting between units using a conversion factor is sometimes known as dimensional analysis.

Table 4.4. Conversion Factors

1 in. = 2.54 cm	1 lb. = 0.454 kg
1 yd. = 0.914 m	1 cal = 4.19 J
1 mi. = 1.61 km	$1°F = \frac{9}{5}°C + 32°C$
1 gal. = 3.785 L	$1 cm^3 = 1 mL$
1 oz. = 28.35 g	1 hr = 3600 s

Practice Question

14. Convert the following measurements in the metric system.
    [A] 4.25 kilometers to meters
    [B] $8 m^2$ to mm^2

15. Convert the following measurements in the American system.
    [A] 12 feet to inches
    [B] 7 yd² to ft²

16. Convert the following measurements in the metric system to the American system.
    [A] 23 meters to feet
    [B] 10 m² to yd²

17. Convert the following measurements in the American system to the metric system.
    [A] 8 in³ to milliliters
    [B] 16 kilograms to pounds

Decimals and Fractions

Decimals

A **decimal** is a number that contains a decimal point. A decimal number is an alternative way of writing a fraction. The place value for a decimal includes **tenths** (one place after the decimal), **hundredths** (two places after the decimal), **thousandths** (three places after the decimal), etc.

Table 4.5. Place Values		
1,000,000	10^6	millions
100,000	10^5	hundred thousands
10,000	10^4	ten thousands
1,000	10^3	thousands
100	10^2	hundreds
10	10^1	tens
1	10^0	ones
.		decimal
$\frac{1}{10}$	10^{-1}	tenths
$\frac{1}{100}$	10^{-2}	hundredths
$\frac{1}{1000}$	10^{-3}	thousandths

Decimals can be added, subtracted, multiplied, and divided:

To add or subtract decimals, line up the decimal point and perform the operation, keeping the decimal point in the same place in the answer.

> **Did You Know?**
> To determine which way to move the decimal after multiplying, remember that changing the decimal should always make the final answer smaller.

To multiply decimals, first multiply the numbers without the decimal points. Then, sum the number of decimal places to the right of the decimal point in the original numbers and place the decimal point in the answer so that there are that many places to the right of the decimal.

When dividing decimals move the decimal point to the right in order to make the divisor a whole number and move the decimal the same number of places in the dividend. Divide the numbers without regard to the decimal. Then, place the decimal point of the quotient directly above the decimal point of the dividend.

$$2.5 \overline{)10.5} = 4.2$$

quotient: 4.2
dividend: 10.5
divisor: 2.5

Figure 4.4. Division Terms

Practice Question

18. Simplify: $24.38 + 16.51 - 29.87$

19. Simplify: $(10.4)(18.2)$

20. Simplify: $80 \div 2.5$

Fractions

A **fraction** is a number that can be written in the form $\frac{a}{b}$, where b is not equal to 0.

The a part of the fraction is the **numerator** (top number) and the b part of the fraction is the **denominator** (bottom number).

If the denominator of a fraction is greater than the numerator, the value of the fraction is less than 1 and it is called a **proper fraction** (for example, $\frac{3}{5}$ is a proper fraction). In an **improper fraction**, the denominator is less than the numerator and the value of the fraction is greater than 1 ($\frac{8}{3}$ is an improper fraction). An improper fraction can be written as a mixed number, which has a whole number part and a proper fraction part. Improper fractions can be converted to **mixed numbers** by dividing the numerator by the denominator, which gives the whole number part, and the remainder becomes the numerator of the proper fraction part. (For example, the improper fraction $\frac{25}{9}$ is equal to mixed number $2\frac{7}{9}$ because 9 divides into 25 two times, with a remainder of 7.)

Conversely, mixed numbers can be converted to improper fractions. To do so, determine the numerator of the improper fraction by multiplying the denominator by the whole number, and then adding the numerator. The final number is written as the (now larger) numerator over the original denominator.

> **Did You Know?**
> To convert mixed numbers to improper fractions:
> $$a\frac{m}{n} = \frac{n \times a + m}{n}$$

Fractions with the same denominator can be added or subtracted by simply adding or subtracting the numerators; the denominator will remain unchanged. To add or subtract fractions with different denominators, find the **least common denominator (LCD)** of all the fractions. The LCD is the smallest number exactly divisible by each denominator. (For example, the least common denominator of the numbers 2, 3, and 8 is 24.) Once the LCD has been found, each fraction should be written in an equivalent form with the LCD as the denominator.

To multiply fractions, the numerators are multiplied together and denominators are multiplied together. If there are any mixed numbers, they should first be changed to improper fractions. Then, the numerators are multiplied together and the denominators are multiplied together. The fraction can then be reduced if necessary. To divide fractions, multiply the first fraction by the reciprocal of the second.

Any common denominator can be used to add or subtract fractions. The quickest way to find a common denominator of a set of values is simply to multiply all the values together. The result might not be the least common denominator, but it will allow the problem to be worked.

Practice Question

21. Simplify: $2\frac{3}{5} + 3\frac{1}{4} - 1\frac{1}{2}$

22. Simplify: $\frac{7}{8} \times 3\frac{1}{3}$

23. Simplify: $4\frac{1}{2} \div \frac{2}{3}$

Converting between Fractions and Decimals

A fraction is converted to a decimal by using long division until there is no remainder and no pattern of repeating numbers occurs.

A decimal is converted to a fraction using the following steps:

Place the decimal value as the numerator in a fraction with a denominator of 1.

Multiply the fraction by $\frac{10}{10}$ for every digit in the decimal value, so that there is no longer a decimal in the numerator.

Reduce the fraction.

Practice Question

24. Write the fraction $\frac{7}{8}$ as a decimal.

25. Write the fraction $\frac{5}{11}$ as a decimal.

26. Write the decimal 0.125 as a fraction.

Rounding and Estimation

Rounding is a way of simplifying a complicated number. The result of rounding will be a less precise value with which it is easier to write or perform operations. Rounding is performed to a specific place value, for example the thousands or tenths place.

The rules for rounding are as follows:

First, underline the place value being rounded to.

Then locate the digit one place value to the right of the underlined value. If this value is less than 5, then keep the underlined value and replace all digits to the right of the underlined value with 0. If the value to the right of the underlined digit is greater than or equal to 5, then increase the underlined digit by one and replace all digits to the right of it with 0.

> **Did You Know?**
>
> Estimation can often be used to eliminate answer choices on multiple-choice tests without having to work the problem to completion.

Estimation is when numbers are rounded and then an operation is performed. This process can be used when working with large numbers to find a close, but not exact, answer.

Practice Question

27. Round the number 138,472 to the nearest thousands.

28. The populations of five local towns are 12,341, 8975, 9431, 10,521, and 11,427. Estimate the total population to the nearest 1000 people.

Ratios

A **ratio** is a comparison of two numbers and can be represented as $\frac{a}{b}$, $a:b$, or a to b. The two numbers represent a constant relationship, not a specific value: for every a number of items in the first group, there will be b number of items in the second. For example, if the ratio of blue to red candies in a bag is $3:5$, the bag will contain 3 blue candies for every 5 red candies. So, the bag might contain 3 blue candies and 5 red candies, or it might contain 30 blue candies and 50 red candies, or 36 blue candies and 60 red candies. All of these values are representative of the ratio 3:5 (which is the ratio in its lowest, or simplest, terms).

To find the "whole" when working with ratios, simply add the values in the ratio. For example, if the ratio of boys to girls in a class is $2:3$, the "whole" is five: 2 out of every 5 students are boys, and 3 out of every 5 students are girls.

Practice Question

29. There are 10 boys and 12 girls in a first-grade class. What is the ratio of boys to the total number of students? What is the ratio of girls to boys?

30. A family spends $600 a month on rent, $400 on utilities, $750 on groceries, and $550 on miscellaneous expenses. What is the ratio of the family's rent to their total expenses?

Proportions

A **proportion** is an equation which states that two ratios are equal. A proportion is given in the form $\frac{a}{b} = \frac{c}{d}$ where the a and d terms are the extremes and the b and c terms are the means. A proportion is solved using cross-multiplication ($ad = bc$) to create an equation with no fractional components. A proportion must have the same units in both numerators and both denominators.

Practice Question

31. Solve the proportion for x: $\frac{3x-5}{2} = \frac{x-8}{3}$

32. A map is drawn such that 2.5 inches on the map equates to an actual distance of 40 miles. If the distance measured on the map between two cities is 17.25 inches, what is the actual distance between them in miles?

33. A factory knows that 4 out of 1000 parts made will be defective. If in a month there are 125,000 parts made, how many of these parts will be defective?

Percentages

A percent (or percentage) means per hundred and is expressed with a percent symbol (%). For example, 54% means 54 out of every 100. A percent can be converted to a decimal by removing the % symbol and moving the decimal point two places to the left, while a decimal can be converted to a percent by moving the decimal point two places to the right and attaching the % sign. A percent can be converted to a fraction by writing the percent as a fraction with 100 as the denominator and reducing. A fraction can be converted to a percent by performing the indicated division, multiplying the result by 100, and attaching the % sign.

The equation for finding percentages has three variables: the part, the whole, and the percent (which is expressed in the equation as a decimal). The equation, as shown below, can be rearranged to solve for any of these variables.

$$part = whole \times percent$$
$$percent = \frac{part}{whole}$$
$$whole = \frac{part}{percent}$$

This set of equations can be used to solve percent word problems. All that's needed is to identify the part, whole, and/or percent, and then to plug those values into the appropriate equation and solve.

Practice Question

34. Change the following values to the indicated form:

[A] 18% to a fraction

[B] $\frac{3}{5}$ to a percent

[C] 1.125 to a percent

[D] 84% to a decimal

35. In a school of 650 students, 54% of the students are boys. How many students are girls?

Percent change

Percent change problems involve a change from an original amount. Often percent change problems appear as word problems that include discounts, growth, or markups. In order to solve percent change problems, it's necessary to identify the percent change (as a decimal), the amount of change, and the original amount. (Keep in mind that one of these will be the value being solved for.) These values can then be plugged into the equations below:

> **Did You Know?**
> Key terms associated with percent change problems include discount, sales tax, and markup.

$$amount\ of\ change = original\ amount \times percent\ change$$

$$percent\ change = \frac{amount\ of\ change}{original\ amount}$$

$$original\ amount = \frac{amount\ of\ change}{percent\ change}$$

Practice Question

36. An HDTV that originally cost $1,500 is on sale for 45% off. What is the sale price for the item?

37. A house was bought in 2000 for $100,000 and sold in 2015 for $120,000. What was the percent growth in the value of the house from 2000 to 2015?

Comparison of Rational Numbers

Rational numbers can be ordered from least to greatest (or greatest to least) by placing them in the order in which they fall on a number line. When comparing a set of fractions, it's often easiest to convert each value to a common denominator. Then, it's only necessary to compare the numerators of each fraction.

> **Did You Know?**
> Drawing a number line can help when comparing numbers: the final list should go in order from left to right (least to greatest) or right to left (greatest to least) on the line.

When working with numbers in multiple forms (for example, a group of fractions and decimals), convert the values so that the set contains only fractions or only decimals. When ordering negative numbers, remember that the negative numbers with the largest absolute values are farthest from 0 and are therefore the smallest numbers. (For example, –75 is smaller than –25.)

Practice Question

38. Order the following numbers from greatest to least: $-\frac{2}{3}, 1.2, 0, -2.1, \frac{5}{4}, -1, \frac{1}{8}$.

39. Order the following numbers from least to greatest: $\frac{1}{3}, -\frac{5}{6}, 1\frac{1}{8}, \frac{7}{12}, -\frac{3}{4}, -\frac{3}{2}$.

Exponents and Radicals

Exponents

An expression in the form b^n is in an exponential notation where b is the base and n is an **exponent**. To perform the operation, multiply the base by itself the number of times indicated by the exponent. For example, 2^3 is equal to $2 \times 2 \times 2$ or 8.

Table 4.6. Operations with Exponents

Rule	Example	Explanation
$a^0 = 1$	$5^0 = 1$	Any base (except 0) to the 0 power is 1.
$a^{-n} = \frac{1}{a^n}$	$5^{-3} = \frac{1}{5^3}$	A negative exponent becomes positive when moved from numerator to denominator (or vice versa).
$a^m a^n = a^{m+n}$	$5^3 5^4 = 5^{3+4} = 5^7$	Add the exponents to multiply two powers with the same base.
$(a^m)^n = a^{m \times n}$	$(5^3)^4 = 5^{3(4)} = 5^{12}$	Multiply the exponents to raise a power to a power.
$\frac{a^m}{a^n} = a^{m-n}$	$\frac{5^4}{5^3} = 5^{4-3} = 5^1$	Subtract the exponents to divide two powers with the same base.
$(ab)^n = a^n b^n$	$(5 \times 6)^3 = 5^3 6^3$	Apply the exponent to each base to raise a product to a power.
$\left(\frac{a}{b}\right)^n = \frac{a^n}{b^n}$	$\left(\frac{5}{6}\right)^3 = \frac{5^3}{6^3}$	Apply the exponent to each base to raise a quotient to a power.
$\left(\frac{a}{b}\right)^{-n} = \left(\frac{b}{a}\right)^n$	$\left(\frac{5}{6}\right)^{-3} = \left(\frac{6}{5}\right)^3$	Invert the fraction and change the sign of the exponent to raise a fraction to a negative power.
$\frac{a^m}{b^n} = \frac{b^{-n}}{a^{-m}}$	$\frac{5^3}{6^4} = \frac{6^{-4}}{5^{-3}}$	Change the sign of the exponent when moving a number from the numerator to denominator (or vice versa).

Practice Question

40. Simplify: $\dfrac{(10^2)^3}{(10^2)^2}$

41. Simplify: $\dfrac{(x^{-2}y^2)^2}{x^3y}$

Radicals

Radicals are expressed as $\sqrt[b]{a}$, where b is called the **index** and a is the **radicand**. A radical is used to indicate the inverse operation of an exponent: finding the base which can be raised to b to yield a. For example, $\sqrt{125}$ is equal to 5 because $5 \times 5 \times 5$ equals 125.

The same operation can be expressed using a fraction exponent, so $\sqrt{a} = a^b$. Note that when no value is indicated for b, it is assumed to be 2 (square root).

When b is even and a is positive, $\sqrt[b]{a}$ is defined to be the positive real value n such that $nb = a$ (example: $\sqrt{16} = 4$ only, and not -4, even though $(-4)(-4) = 16$). If b is even and a is negative, $\sqrt[b]{a}$ will be a complex number (example: $\sqrt{-9} = 3i$). Finally, if b is odd, $\sqrt[b]{a}$ will always be a real number regardless of the sign of a. If a is negative, $\sqrt[b]{a}$ will be negative since a number to an odd power is negative (example: $\sqrt{-32} = -2$ since $(-2)5 = -32$).

$\sqrt{x}$ is referred to as the nth root of x.

$n = 2$ is the square root

$n = 3$ is the cube root

$n = 4$ is the fourth root

$n = 5$ is the fifth root

The following table of operations with radicals holds for all cases EXCEPT the case where b is even and a is negative (the complex case).

Table 4.7. Operations with Radicals		
Rule	Example	Explanation
$\sqrt[b]{ac} = \sqrt[b]{a}\sqrt[b]{c}$	$\sqrt[3]{81} = \sqrt[3]{27}\sqrt[3]{3} = 3\sqrt[3]{3}$	The values under the radical sign can be separated into values that multiply to the original value.
$\sqrt[b]{\dfrac{a}{c}} = \dfrac{\sqrt[b]{a}}{\sqrt[b]{c}}$	$\sqrt{\dfrac{81}{4}} = \dfrac{\sqrt{81}}{\sqrt{4}} = \dfrac{9}{2}$	The b-root of the numerator and denominator can be calculated when there is a fraction under a radical sign.
$\sqrt[b]{a^c} = \left(\sqrt[b]{a}\right)^c = a^{\frac{c}{b}}$	$\sqrt[3]{6^2} = \left(\sqrt[3]{6}\right)^2 = 6^{\frac{2}{3}}$	The b-root can be written as a fractional exponent. If there is a power under the

Table 4.7. Operations with Radicals

Rule	Example	Explanation
		radical sign, it will be the numerator of the fraction.
$\dfrac{c}{\sqrt[b]{a}} \times \dfrac{\sqrt[b]{a}}{\sqrt[b]{a}} = \dfrac{c\sqrt[b]{a}}{a}$	$\dfrac{5}{\sqrt{2}} \times \dfrac{\sqrt{2}}{\sqrt{2}} = \dfrac{5\sqrt{2}}{2}$	To rationalize the denominator, multiply the numerator and denominator by the radical in the denominator until the radical has been canceled out.
$\dfrac{c}{b - \sqrt{a}} \times \dfrac{b + \sqrt{a}}{b + \sqrt{a}}$ $= \dfrac{c(b + \sqrt{a})}{b^2 - a}$	$\dfrac{4}{3 - \sqrt{2}} \times \dfrac{3 + \sqrt{2}}{3 + \sqrt{2}} = \dfrac{4(3 + \sqrt{2})}{9 - 2}$ $= \dfrac{12 + 4\sqrt{2}}{7}$	To rationalize the denominator, the numerator and denominator are multiplied by the conjugate of the denominator.

Practice Question

42. Simplify: $\sqrt{48}$

43. Simplify: $\dfrac{6}{\sqrt{8}}$

Factorials

A **factorial** of a number n is denoted by $n!$ and is equal to $1 \times 2 \times 3 \times 4 \times \ldots \times n$. Both $0!$ and $1!$ are equal to 1 by definition. Fractions containing factorials can often be simplified by crossing out the portions of the factorials that occur in both the numerator and denominator.

Practice Question

44. Simplify: $8!$

45. Simplify: $\dfrac{10!}{7!3!}$

Sequences and Series

Sequences can be thought of as a set of numbers (called **terms**) with a rule that explains the particular pattern between the terms. The terms of a sequence are separated by commas. There are two types of sequences that will be examined, arithmetic and geometric. The sum of an arithmetic sequence is known as an **arithmetic series**; similarly the sum of a geometric sequence is known as a **geometric series**.

Arithmetic Sequences

Arithmetic growth is constant growth, meaning that the difference between any one term in the series and the next consecutive term will be the same constant. This constant is called the **common difference**. Thus, to list the terms in the sequence, one can just add (or subtract) the same number repeatedly. For example, the series {20, 30, 40, 50} is arithmetic since 10 is added each time to get from one term to the next. One way to represent this sequence is using a **recursive** definition, which basically says: $next\ term = current\ term + common\ difference$. For this example, the recursive definition would be $a_{n+1} = a_n + 10$ because the *next* term $a_n + 1$ in the sequence is the current term a_n plus 10. In general, the recursive definition of a series is:

$$a_{n+1} = a_n + d, \text{ where } d \text{ is the common difference.}$$

Often, the objective of arithmetic sequence questions is to find a specific term in the sequence or the sum of a certain series of terms. The formulas to use are:

Table 4.8. Formulas for Arithmetic Sequences and Series	
Finding the nth term . . .	
$a_n = a_1 + d(n-1)$ $a_n = a_m + d(n-m)$	d = the common difference of the sequence a_n = the nth term in the sequence n = the number of the term a_m = the mth term in the sequence m = the number of the term a_1 = the first term in the sequence
Finding the partial sum . . .	
$S_n = \dfrac{n(a_1 + a_n)}{2}$	S_n = sum of the terms through the nth term a_n = the nth term in the sequence n = the number of the term a_1 = the first term in the sequence

Practice Question

46. Find the ninth term of the sequence: $-57, -40, -23, -6$ ...

47. If the 23rd term in an arithmetic sequence is 820, and the 5th term is 200, find the common difference between each term.

48. Evaluate $\sum_{n=14}^{45} 2n + 10$.

Geometric Sequences

While an arithmetic sequence has an additive pattern, a **geometric sequence** has a multiplicative pattern. This means that to get from any one term in the sequence to the next term in the sequence, the term is multiplied by a fixed number (called the **common ratio**). The following sequence is a geometric sequence: {8, 4, 2, 1, .5, .25, .125}. In this case, the multiplier (or common ratio) is $\frac{1}{2}$. The multiplier can be any real number other than 0 or 1. To find the common ratio, simply choose any term in the sequence and divide it by the previous term (this is the ratio of two consecutive terms—thus the name common *ratio*). In the above example, the ratio between the second and third terms is $\frac{2}{4} = \frac{1}{2}$.

Geometric sequences require their own formulas to find the next term and a sum of a specific series.

Table 4.9. Geometric Sequences: Formulas

Finding the nth term ...	
$a_n = a_1 \times r_{n-1}$ $a_n = a_m \times r_{n-m}$	r = the common ratio of the sequence a_n = the nth term in the sequence n = the number of the term a_m = the mth term in the sequence m = the number of the term a_1 = the first term in the sequence
Finding the partial sum ...	
$S_n = \dfrac{a_1(1-r^n)}{1-r}$	S_n = sum of the terms through the nth term r = the common ratio of the sequence a_n = the nth term in the sequence n = the number of the term a_1 = the first term in the sequence
Finding the sum of an infinite series ...	
$S_\infty = \dfrac{a}{1-r}$ $(|r| < 1)$	S_∞ = sum of all terms r = the common ratio of the sequence a = the fifth term in the sequence

The finite sum formula works similarly to the arithmetic sequence sum. However, sometimes the **infinite sum** of the sequence must be found. The sum of an infinite number of terms of a sequence is called a **series**. If the infinite terms of the sequence add up to a finite number, the series is said to **converge** to that number. If the sum of the terms is infinite, then the series **diverges**. Another way to say this is to ask: is there a limit to the finite sum S_n as n goes to infinity? For geometric series in the form $\sum_{n=1}^{\infty} a \times r^n$, the series converges only when $|r| < 1$ (or $-1 < r < 1$). If r is greater than 1, the sum will approach infinity, so the series diverges.

Practice Question

49. Find the 8th term in the sequence: $\{13, 39, 117, 351 \ldots\}$

50. Find the sum of the first 10 terms of this sequence: $\{-4, 16, -64, 256 \ldots\}$

Answer Key

1. [A] The number is natural, whole, an integer, and rational.

[B] The fraction is rational.

[C] The number is irrational. (It cannot be written as a fraction, and written as a decimal is approximately 2.2360679...)

2. A complex number is in the form of $a + bi$, where a is the real part and bi is the imaginary part.

[A] $20 = 20 + 0i$

The real part is 20, and there is no imaginary part.

[B] $10 - i = 10 - 1i$

The real part is 10, and $-1i$ is the imaginary part.

[C] $15i = 0 + 15i$

The real part is 0, and the imaginary part is $15i$.

3. [A] is false. Subtracting the natural number 7 from 2 results in $2 - 7 = -5$, which is an integer, but not a natural number.

[B] is false. For example, $(5 - 2\sqrt{3}) + (2 + 2\sqrt{3}) = 7$. The sum of two irrational numbers in this example is a whole number, which is not irrational. The sum of a rational number and an irrational number is sometimes rational and sometimes irrational.

[C] is true. Because irrational numbers have decimal parts that are unending and with no pattern, adding a repeating or terminating decimal will still result in an unending decimal without a pattern.

4. [A] is true. For all real numbers, $a \times (b \times c) = (a \times b) \times c$. Order of multiplication does not change the result.

[B] is false. The commutative property does not work for subtraction or division on real numbers. For example, $12 - 5 = 7$, but $5 - 12 = -7$, and $10 \div 2 = 5$, but $2 \div 10 = \frac{1}{5}$.

5. $(3 - 2i) - (-2 + 8i)$

Distribute the –1.

$$(3 - 2i) - 1(-2 + 8i)$$
$$3 - 2i + 2 - 8i$$

Combine like terms.

$$\mathbf{5 - 10i}$$

6. $\dfrac{4i}{5-2i}$

Multiply the top and bottom of the fraction by the complex conjugate of $5 + 2i$.

$$\dfrac{4i}{5-2i} \times \dfrac{5+2i}{(5+2i)}$$

$$\dfrac{20i + 8i^2}{25 + 10i - 10i - 4i^2}$$

Simplify the result using the identity $i^2 = -1$.

$$\dfrac{20i + 8(-1)}{25 + 10i - 10i - 4(-1)}$$

$$\dfrac{20i - 8}{25 + 10i - 10i + 4}$$

Combine like terms.

$$\dfrac{20i - 8}{29}$$

Write the answer in the form $a + bi$.

$$-\dfrac{8}{29} + \dfrac{20i}{29}$$

7. $(3.8 \times 10^3) + (4.7 \times 10^2)$

To add, the exponents of 10 must be the same.

$$3.8 \times 10^3 = 3.8 \times 10 \times 10^2 = 38 \times 10^2$$

Add the a terms together.

$$38 \times 10^2 + 4.7 \times 10^2 = 42.7 \times 10^2$$

Write the number in proper scientific notation.

$$\mathbf{4.27 \times 10^3}$$

8. $(8.1 \times 10^{-5})(1.4 \times 10^7)$

Multiply the a factors and add the exponents on the base of 10.

$$8.1 \times 1.4 = 11.34$$
$$10^{-5+7} = 10^2$$
$$= 11.34 \times 10^2$$

Write the number in proper scientific notation.

$$\mathbf{1.134 \times 10^3}$$

9. [A] Since $|-18| > |12|$, the answer is negative: $|-18| - |12| = 6$. So the answer is **–6**.

[B] Adding two negative numbers results in a negative number. Add the values: **–5.82**.

4. Numbers and Operations

[C] The first number is larger than the second, so the final answer is positive: **5.12**.

[D] Change the subtraction to addition, change the sign of the second number, and then add: $86 - (-20) = 86 + (+20) = $ **106**.

10. [A] Multiply the numerators, multiply the denominators, and simplify: $-\frac{90}{15} = $ **−6**.

[B] A negative divided by a negative is a positive number: **6.4**.

[C] Multiplying positive numbers gives a positive answer: **7.26**.

[D] Dividing a negative by a positive number gives a negative answer: **–4**.

11. $2(21 - 14) + 6 \div (-2) \times 3 - 10$

Calculate expressions inside parentheses.

$$2(7) + 6 \div (-2) \times 3 - 10$$

There are no exponents or radicals, so perform multiplication and division from left to right.

$$14 + 6 \div (-2) \times 3 - 10$$
$$14 + (-3) \times 3 - 10$$
$$14 + (-9) - 10$$

Perform addition and subtraction from left to right.

$$5 - 10 = \mathbf{-5}$$

12. $-(3)^2 + 4(5) + (5 - 6)^2 - 8$

Calculate expressions inside parentheses.

$$-(3)^2 + 4(5) + (-1)^2 - 8$$

Simplify exponents and radicals.

$$-9 + 4(5) + 1 - 8$$

Perform multiplication and division from left to right.

$$-9 + 20 + 1 - 8$$

Perform addition and subtraction from left to right.

$$11 + 1 - 8$$
$$12 - 8 = \mathbf{4}$$

13. Simplify: $\frac{(7-9)^3 + 8(10-12)}{4^2 - 5^2}$

Calculate expressions inside parentheses.

$$\frac{(-2)^3 + 8(-2)}{4^2 - 5^2}$$

Simplify exponents and radicals.

$$\frac{-8+(-16)}{16-25}$$

Perform addition and subtraction from left to right.

$$\frac{-24}{-9}$$

Simplify.

$$\frac{8}{3}$$

14. [A] $4.25 \text{ km} \left(\frac{1000 \text{ m}}{1 \text{ km}}\right) = \mathbf{4250 \text{ m}}$

[B] $8 \text{ m}^2 \times \frac{1000 \text{ mm}}{1 \text{ m}} \times \frac{1000 \text{ mm}}{1 \text{ m}} = \mathbf{8{,}000{,}000 \text{ mm}^2}$

Since the units are square units (m²), multiply by the conversion factor twice, so that both meters cancel.

15. [A] $12 \text{ ft} \left(\frac{12 \text{ in}}{1 \text{ ft}}\right) = \mathbf{144 \text{ in}}$

[B] $7 \text{ yd}^2 \times \frac{3 \text{ ft}}{1 \text{ yd}} \times \frac{3 \text{ ft}}{1 \text{ yd}} = \mathbf{63 \text{ ft}^2}$

Since the units are square units (ft²), multiply by the conversion factor twice.

16. [A] $23 \text{ m} \times \frac{3.28 \text{ ft}}{1 \text{ m}} = \mathbf{75.44 \text{ ft}}$

[B] $10 \text{m}^2 \times \frac{1.094 \text{ yd}}{1 \text{ m}} \times \frac{1.094 \text{ yd}}{1 \text{ m}} = \mathbf{11.97 \text{ yd}^2}$

17. [A] $8 \text{ in}^3 \times \frac{16.39 \text{ mL}}{1 \text{ in}^3} = \mathbf{131.12 \text{ mL}}$

[B] $16 \text{ kg} \times \frac{2.2 \text{ lb}}{1 \text{ kg}} = \mathbf{35.2 \text{ lb}}$

18. $24.38 + 16.51 - 29.87$

Align the decimals and apply the order of operations left to right.

```
  24.38         40.89
+ 16.51        -29.87
= 40.89       = 11.02
```

19. $(10.4)(18.2)$

Multiply the numbers ignoring the decimals.

$$104 \times 182 = 18{,}928$$

The original problem includes two decimal places (one in each number), so move the decimal point in the answer so that there

$$18{,}928 \rightarrow \mathbf{189.28}$$

Estimating is a good way to check the answer: $10.4 \approx 10$, $18.2 \approx 18$, and $10 \times 18 = 180$.

20. $80 \div 2.5$

Move both decimals one place to the right (multiply by 10) so that the divisor is a whole number.

$$80 \rightarrow 800$$
$$2.5 \rightarrow 25$$

Divide normally.

$$800 \div 25 = \mathbf{32}$$

21. $2\frac{3}{5} + 3\frac{1}{4} - 1\frac{1}{2}$

Change each fraction so it has a denominator of 20, which is the LCD of 5, 4, and 2.

$$2 + 3 - 1 = 4$$
$$\frac{12}{20} + \frac{5}{20} - \frac{10}{20} = \frac{7}{20}$$

Combine to get the final answer (a mixed number).

$$4\frac{7}{20}$$

22. $\frac{7}{8} \times 3\frac{1}{3}$

Change the mixed number to an improper fraction.

$$3\frac{1}{3} = \frac{10}{3}$$

Multiply the numerators together and the denominators together.

$$\frac{7}{8} \times \frac{10}{3} = \frac{7 \times 10}{8 \times 3} = \frac{70}{24}$$

Reduce the fraction.

$$\frac{35}{12} = \mathbf{2\frac{11}{12}}$$

23. $4\frac{1}{2} \div \frac{2}{3}$

Change the mixed number to an improper fraction.

$$4\frac{1}{2} = \frac{9}{2}$$

Multiply the first fraction by the reciprocal of the second fraction.

$$\frac{9}{2} \div \frac{2}{3} = \frac{9}{2} \times \frac{3}{2} = \frac{27}{4}$$

Simplify.

$$6\frac{3}{4}$$

24. Divide the denominator into the numerator using long division.

$$\begin{array}{r} 0.875 \\ 8\overline{)7000} \\ \underline{-64}\downarrow \\ 60 \\ \underline{-56}\downarrow \\ 40 \end{array}$$

25. Dividing using long division yields a repeating decimal.

$$\begin{array}{r} 0.4545 \\ 11\overline{)50000} \\ \underline{-44}\downarrow \\ 60 \\ \underline{-55}\downarrow \\ 50 \\ \underline{44}\downarrow \\ 60 \end{array}$$

26. Create a fraction with 0.125 as the numerator and 1 as the denominator.

$$\frac{0.125}{1}$$

Multiple by $\frac{10}{10}$ three times (one for each numeral after the decimal).

$$\frac{0.125}{1} \times \frac{10}{10} \times \frac{10}{10} \times \frac{10}{10} = \frac{125}{1000}$$

Simplify.

$$\frac{1}{8}$$

Alternatively, recognize that 0.125 is read "one hundred twenty-five thousandths" and can therefore be written in fraction form as $\frac{125}{1000}$.

27. The 8 is in the thousands place, and the number to its right is 4. Because 4 is less than 5, the 8 remains all numbers to the right become 0.

$$138,472 \approx \mathbf{138,000}$$

28. Round each value to the thousands place.

$$12{,}341 \approx 12{,}000$$
$$8975 \approx 9000$$
$$9431 \approx 9000$$
$$10{,}521 \approx 11{,}000$$
$$11{,}427 \approx 11{,}000$$

Add.

$$12{,}000 + 9000 + 9000 + 11{,}000 + 11{,}000 = \mathbf{52{,}000}$$

29. Identify the variables.

Number of boys: 10

Number of girls: 12

Number of students: 22

Write out and simplify the ratio of boys to total students.

$$\text{number of boys} : \text{number of students} = 10 : 22 = \frac{10}{22} = \mathbf{\frac{5}{11}}$$

Write out and simplify the ratio of girls to boys.

$$\text{number of girls} : \text{number of boys} = 12 : 10 = \frac{12}{10} = \mathbf{\frac{6}{5}}$$

30. Identify the variables.

$$\text{rent} = 600$$
$$\text{utilities} = 400$$
$$\text{groceries} = 750$$
$$\text{miscellaneous} = 550$$
$$\text{total expenses} = 600 + 400 + 750 + 550 = 2300$$

Write out and simplify the ratio of rent to total expenses.

$$\text{rent} : \text{total expenses} = 600 : 2300 = \frac{600}{2300} = \mathbf{\frac{6}{23}}$$

31. $\frac{3x-5}{2} = \frac{x-8}{3}$

Cross-multiply.

$$3(3x - 5) = 2(x - 8)$$

Solve the equation for x.

$$9x - 15 = 2x - 16$$
$$7x - 15 = -16$$
$$7x = -1$$
$$x = -\frac{1}{7}$$

32. Write a proportion where x equals the actual distance and each ratio is written as inches : miles.

$$\frac{2.5}{40} = \frac{17.25}{x}$$

Cross-multiply and divide to solve for x.

$$2.5x = 690$$
$$x = 276$$

The two cities are **276 miles apart**.

33. Write a proportion where x is the number of defective parts made and both ratios are written as defective : total.

$$\frac{4}{1000} = \frac{x}{125,000}$$

Cross-multiply and divide to solve for x.

$$1000x = 500,000$$
$$x = 500$$

There are **500 defective parts** for the month.

34. [A] The percent is written as a fraction over 100 and reduced:

$$\frac{18}{100} = \frac{9}{50}$$

[B] Dividing 5 by 3 gives the value 0.6, which is then multiplied by 100: **60%**.

[C] The decimal point is moved two places to the right: $1.125 \times 100 =$ **112.5%**.

[D] The decimal point is moved two places to the left: 84 ÷ 100 = **0.84**.

35. Identify the variables.

$$\text{Percent of students who are girls} = 100\% - 54\% = 46\%$$
$$percent = 46\% = 0.46$$
$$whole = 650 \text{ students}$$
$$part = ?$$

4. Numbers and Operations

Plug the variables into the appropriate equation.
$$part = whole \times percent$$
$$= 0.46 \times 650 = 299$$

There are 299 girls.

36. Identify the variables.
$$original\ amount = \$1{,}500$$
$$percent\ change = 45\% = 0.45$$
$$amount\ of\ change = ?$$

Plug the variables into the appropriate equation.
$$amount\ of\ change = original\ amount \times percent\ change$$
$$1500 \times 0.45 = 675$$

To find the new price, subtract the amount of change from the original price.
$$1500 - 675 = 825$$

The final price is $825.

37. Identify the variables.
$$original\ amount = \$100{,}000$$
$$amount\ of\ change = 120{,}000 - 100{,}000 = 20{,}000$$
$$percent\ change = ?$$

Plug the variables into the appropriate equation.
$$percent\ change = \frac{amount\ of\ change}{original\ amount}$$
$$= \frac{20{,}000}{100{,}000} = 0.20$$

To find the percent growth, multiply by 100.
$$0.20 \times 100 = \mathbf{20\%}$$

38. Change each fraction to a decimal.
$$-\frac{2}{3} = -0.66$$
$$\frac{5}{4} = 1.25$$
$$\frac{1}{8} = 0.125$$

Place the decimals in order from greatest to least.

1.25, 1.2, 0.125, 0, -0.66, -1, -2.1

Convert back to fractions if the problem requires it.

$$\frac{5}{4}, 1.2, \frac{1}{8}, 0, -\frac{2}{3}, -1, -2.1$$

39. Convert each value using the least common denominator of 24.

$$\frac{1}{3} = \frac{8}{24}$$

$$-\frac{5}{6} = -\frac{20}{24}$$

$$1\frac{1}{8} = \frac{9}{8} = \frac{27}{24}$$

$$\frac{7}{12} = \frac{14}{24}$$

$$-\frac{3}{4} = -\frac{18}{24}$$

$$-\frac{3}{2} = -\frac{36}{24}$$

Arrange the fractions in order from least to greatest by comparing the numerators.

$$-\frac{36}{24}, -\frac{20}{24}, -\frac{18}{24}, \frac{8}{24}, \frac{14}{24}, \frac{27}{24}$$

Put the fractions back in their original form if the problem requires it.

$$-\frac{3}{2}, -\frac{5}{6}, -\frac{3}{4}, \frac{1}{3}, \frac{7}{12}, 1\frac{1}{8}$$

40. $\frac{(10^2)^3}{(10^2)^2}$

Multiply the exponents raised to a power.

$$\frac{10^6}{10^{-4}}$$

Subtract the exponent in the denominator from the one in the numerator.

$$10^{6-(-4)}$$

Simplify.

$$10^{10} = 10,000,000,000$$

41. $\frac{(x^{-2}y^2)^2}{x^3 y}$

4. Numbers and Operations

Multiply the exponents raised to a power.

$$\frac{x^{-4}y^4}{x^3 y}$$

Subtract the exponent in the denominator from the one in the numerator.

$$x^{-4-3}y^{4-1} = x^{-7}y^3$$

Move negative exponents to the denominator.

$$\frac{y^3}{x^7}$$

42. $\sqrt{48}$

Determine the largest square number that is a factor of the radicand (48) and write the radicand as a product using that square number as a factor.

$$\sqrt{16 \times 3}$$

Apply the rules of radicals to simplify.

$$\sqrt{16} \times \sqrt{3} = \mathbf{4\sqrt{3}}$$

43. $\frac{6}{\sqrt{8}}$

Apply the rules of radicals to simplify.

$$\frac{6}{\sqrt{4}\sqrt{2}} = \frac{6}{2\sqrt{2}}$$

Multiply by $\frac{\sqrt{2}}{\sqrt{2}}$ to rationalize the denominator.

$$\frac{6}{2\sqrt{2}} \times \frac{\sqrt{2}}{\sqrt{2}} = \frac{6\sqrt{2}}{4} = \mathbf{\frac{3\sqrt{2}}{2}}$$

44. 8!

Expand the factorial and multiply.

$$= 8 \times 7 \times 6 \times 5 \times 4 \times 3 \times 2 \times 1$$

$$= \mathbf{40,320}$$

45. $\frac{10!}{7!3!}$

Expand the factorial.

$$\frac{10 \times 9 \times 8 \times 7!}{7! \times 3 \times 2 \times 1}$$

Cross out values that occur in both the numerator and denominator.

$$\frac{10 \times 9 \times 8}{3 \times 2 \times 1}$$

Multiply and simplify.

$$\frac{720}{6} = \mathbf{120}$$

46. Identify the variables given.

$$a_1 = -57$$
$$d = -57 - (-40) = 17$$
$$n = 9$$

Plug these values into the formula for the specific term of an arithmetic sequence.

$$a_9 = -57 + 17(9 - 1)$$

Solve for a_9.

$$a_9 = -57 + 17(8)$$
$$a_9 = -57 + 136$$
$$\mathbf{a_9 = 79}$$

47. Identify the variables given.

$$a_5 = 200$$
$$a_{23} = 820$$
$$n = 23$$
$$m = 5$$
$$d = ?$$

Plug these values into the equation for using one term to find another in an arithmetic sequence.

$$a_n = a_m + d(n - m)$$
$$820 = 200 + d(23 - 5)$$
$$620 = d(18)$$
$$\mathbf{d = 34.44}$$

48. $\sum_{n=14}^{45} 2n + 10$.

Find the partial sum of the first 45 terms.

$$a_1 = 2(1) + 10 = 12$$
$$n = 45$$
$$a_n = 2(45) + 10 = 100$$
$$S_n = \frac{n(a_1 + a_n)}{2} = \frac{45(12 + 100)}{2} = 2520$$

Find the partial sum of the first 13 terms.

$$a_1 = 2(1) + 10 = 12$$

$$n = 13$$

$$a_n = 2(13) + 10 = 36$$

$$S_n = \frac{n(a_1 + a_n)}{2} = \frac{13(12 + 36)}{2} = 312$$

The sum of the terms between 14 and 45 will be the difference between S_{45} and S_{13}.

$$S_{45} - S_{13} = 2520 - 312 = \mathbf{2208}$$

49. Identify the variables given.

$$a_1 = 13$$

$$n = 8$$

$$r = \frac{39}{13} = 3$$

Plug these values into the equation to find a specific term in a geometric sequence.

$$a_8 = 13 \times 3^{8-1}$$

$$a_8 = 13 \times 2187 = 28{,}431$$

The eighth term of the given sequence is **28,431**.

50. Identify the variables given.

$$a_1 = -4$$

$$n = 10$$

$$r = \frac{16}{-4} = -4$$

Plug these values into the equation for the partial sum of a geometric sequence.

$$S_{10} = \frac{-4(1 - (-4)^{10})}{1 - (-4)}$$

$$\frac{-4(1 - 1{,}048{,}576)}{5} = \frac{4{,}194{,}300}{5} = \mathbf{838{,}860}$$

5. Algebraic Concepts

Algebra, meaning "restoration" in Arabic, is the mathematical method of finding the unknown. The first algebraic book in Egypt was used to figure out complex inheritances that were to be split among many individuals. Today, algebra is just as necessary when dealing with unknown amounts.

Algebraic Expressions

The foundation of algebra is the **variable**, an unknown number represented by a symbol (usually a letter such as x or a). Variables can be preceded by a **coefficient**, which is a constant (i.e., a real number) in front of the variable, such as $4x$ or $-2a$. An **algebraic expression** is any sum, difference, product, or quotient of variables and numbers (for example $3x^2$, $2x + 7y - 1$, and $\frac{5}{x}$ are algebraic expressions).

Terms are any quantities that are added or subtracted (for example, the terms of the expression $x^2 - 3x + 5$ are x^2, $3x$, and 5). A **polynomial expression** is an algebraic expression where all the exponents on the variables are whole numbers. A polynomial with only two terms is known as a **binomial**, and one with three terms is a **trinomial**. A **monomial** has only one term.

> **Did You Know?**
>
> Simplified expressions are ordered by variable terms alphabetically with highest exponent first then down to constants.

Evaluating expressions is another way of saying "find the numeric value of an expression if the variable is equal to a certain number." To evaluate the expression, simply plug the given value(s) for the variable(s) into the equation and simplify. Remember to use the order of operations when simplifying:

- Parentheses
- Exponents
- Multiplication
- Division
- Addition
- Subtraction

Practice Question

1. If $m = 4$, find the value of the following expression: $5(m - 2)^3 + 3m^2 - \frac{m}{4} - 1$

Operations with Expressions

Adding and Subtracting

Expressions can be added or subtracted by simply adding and subtracting **like terms**, which are terms with the same variable part (the variables must be the same, with the same exponents on each variable). For example, in the expressions $2x + 3xy - 2z$ and $6y + 2xy$, the like terms are $3xy$ and $2xy$. Adding the two expressions yields the new expression $2x + 6xy - 2z + 6y$. Note that the other terms did not change; they cannot be combined because they have different variables.

Practice Question

2. If $a = 12x + 7xy - 9y$ and $b = 8x - 9xz + 7z$, what is $a + b$?

Distributing and Factoring

Distributing and factoring can be seen as two sides of the same coin. **Distribution** multiplies each term in the first factor by each term in the second factor to get rid of parentheses. **Factoring** reverses this process, taking a polynomial in standard form and writing it as a product of two or more factors.

When distributing a monomial through a polynomial, the expression outside the parentheses is multiplied by each term inside the parentheses. Using the rules of exponents, coefficients are multiplied and exponents are added.

When simplifying two polynomials, each term in the first polynomial must multiply each term in the second polynomial. A binomial (two terms) multiplied by a binomial, will require 2 × 2 or 4 multiplications. For the binomial × binomial case, this process is sometimes called **foil**, which stands for first, outside, inside, and last. These terms refer to the placement of each term of the expression: multiply the first term in each expression, then the outside terms, then the inside terms, and finally the last terms. A binomial (two terms) multiplied by a trinomial (three terms), will require 2 × 3 or 6 products to simplify. The first term in the first polynomial multiplies each of the three terms in the second polynomial, then the second term in the first polynomial multiplies each of the three terms in the second polynomial. A trinomial (three terms) by a trinomial will require 3 × 3 or 9 products, and so on.

> **Did You Know?**
>
> Operations with polynomials can always be checked by evaluating equivalent expressions for the same value.

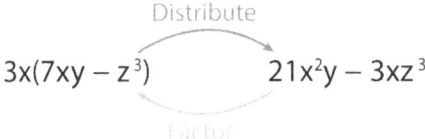

Figure 5.1 Distribution and Factoring

Factoring is the reverse of distributing: the first step is always to remove ("undistribute") the GCF of all the terms, if there is a GCF (besides 1). The GCF is the product of any constants and/or variables that every term shares. (For example, the GCF of $12x^3$, $15x^2$ and $6xy^2$ is $3x$ because $3x$ evenly divides all three terms.) This shared factor can be taken out of each term and moved to the outside of the parentheses, leaving behind a polynomial where each term is the original term divided by the GCF. (The remaining terms for the terms in the example would be $4x^2$, $5x$, and $2xy$.) It may be possible to factor the polynomial in the parentheses further, depending on the problem.

Practice Question

3. Expand the following expression: $5x(x^2 - 2c + 10)$

4. Expand the following expression: $(x^2 - 5)(2x - x^3)$

5. Factor the expression: $16z^2 + 48z$

6. Factor the expression: $6m^3 + 12m^3n - 9m^2$

Factoring Trinomials

If the leading coefficient is $a = 1$, the trinomial is in the form $x^2 + bx + c$ and can often be rewritten in the factored form, as a product of two binomials: $(x + m)(x + n)$. Recall that the product of two binomials can be written in expanded form $x^2 + mx + nx + mn$. Equating this expression with $x^2 + bx + c$, the constant term c would have to equal the product mn. Thus, to work backward from the trinomial to the factored form, consider all the numbers m and n that multiply to make c. For example, to factor $x^2 + 8x + 12$, consider all the pairs that multiply to be 12 ($12 = 1 \times 12$ or 2×6 or 3×4). Choose the pair that will make the coefficient of the middle term (8) when added. In this example 2 and 6 add to 8, so making $m = 2$ and $n = 6$ in the expanded form gives:

$$x^2 + 8x + 12 = x^2 + 2x + 6x + 12$$

Group the first two terms and the last two terms.	$(x^2 + 2x) + (6x + 12)$
Factor the GCF out of each set of parentheses.	$x(x + 6) + 2(x + 6)$
The two terms now have the common factor ($x + 6$), which can be removed, leaving ($x + 2$) and the original polynomial is factored.	$(x + 6)(x + 2)$

In general:

$$x^2 + bx + c = x^2 + mx + nx + mn, \text{ where } c = mn \text{ and } b = m + n$$

Group.	$(x^2 + mx) + (nx + mn)$
Factor each group.	$x(x + m) + n(x + m)$
Factor out the common binomial.	$(x + m)(x + n)$

Note that if none of the factors of c add to the value b, then the trinomial cannot be factored, and is called **prime**.

If the leading coefficient is not 1 ($a \neq 1$), first make sure that any common factors among the three terms are factored out. If the a-value is negative, factor out −1 first as well. If the a-value of the new polynomial in the parentheses is still not 1, follow this rule: Identify two values r and s that multiply to be ac and add to be b. Then write the polynomial in this form: $ax^2 + bx + c = ax^2 + rx + sx + c$, and proceed by grouping, factoring, and removing the common binomial as above.

5. Algebraic Concepts

There are a few special factoring cases worth memorizing: difference of squares, binomial squared, and the sum and difference of cubes.

Difference of squares (each term is a square and they are subtracted):
$$a^2 - b^2 = (a + b)(a - b)$$
Note that a SUM of squares is never factorable.

Binomial squared: $a^2 + 2ab + b^2 = (a + b)(a + b) = (a + b)^2$

Sum and Difference of cubes:
$$a^3 + b^3 = (a + b)(a^2 - ab + b^2)$$
$$a^3 - b^3 = (a - b)(a^2 + ab + b^2)$$
Note that the second factor in these factorizations will never be able to be factored further.

Practice Question

7. Factor: $16x^2 + 52x + 30$

8. Factor: $-21x^2 - x + 10$

Linear Equations

An **equation** states that two expressions are equal to each other. Polynomial equations are categorized by the highest power of the variables they contain: the highest power of any exponent of a linear equation is 1, a quadratic equation has a variable raised to the second power, a cubic equation has a variable raised to the third power, and so on.

Solving Linear Equations

Solving an equation means finding the value or values of the variable that make the equation true. To solve a linear equation, it is necessary to manipulate the terms so that the variable being solved for appears alone on one side of the equal sign while everything else in the equation is on the other side.

The way to solve linear equations is to "undo" all the operations that connect numbers to the variable of interest. Follow these steps:

- Eliminate fractions by multiplying each side by the least common multiple of any denominators.
- Distribute to eliminate parentheses, braces, and brackets.
- Combine like terms.
- Use addition or subtraction to collect all terms containing the variable of interest to one side, and all terms not containing the variable to the other side.
- Use multiplication or division to remove coefficients from the variable of interest.

> **Did You Know?**
>
> On multiple choice tests, it is often easier to plug the possible values into the equation and determine which solution makes the equation true than to solve the equation.

Sometimes there are no numeric values in the equation or there are a mix of numerous variables and constants. The goal is to solve the equation for one of the variables in terms of the other variables. In this case, the answer will be an expression involving numbers and letters instead of a numeric value.

Practice Question

9. Solve for x: $\frac{100(x+5)}{20} = 1$

10. Solve for x: $2(x+2)^2 - 2x^2 + 10 = 42$

11. Solve the equation for D: $\frac{A(3B+2D)}{2N} = 5M - 6$

Graphs of Linear Equations

The most common way to write a linear equation is **slope-intercept form**, $y = mx + b$. In this equation, m is the slope, which describes how steep the line is, and b is the intercept. Slope is often described as "rise over run" because it is calculated as the difference in y-values (rise) over the difference in x-values (run). The slope of the line is also the rate of change of the dependent variable y with respect to the independent variable x. The y-intercept is the point where the line crosses the y-axis, or where x equals zero.

> **Did You Know?**
>
> Use the phrase "Begin, Move" to remember that b is the y-intercept (where to begin) and m is the slope (how the line moves).

To graph a linear equation, identify the y-intercept and place that point on the y-axis. If the slope is not written as a fraction, make it a fraction by writing it over $1\frac{m}{(1)}$. Then use the slope to count up (or down, if negative) the "rise" part of the slope and over the "run" part of the slope to find a second point. These points can then be connected to draw the line.

To find the equation of a line, identify the y-intercept, if possible, on the graph and use two easily identifiable points to find the slope. If the y-intercept is not easily identified, identify the slope by choosing easily identifiable points; then choose one point on the graph, plug the point and the slope values into the equation, and solve for the missing value b.

> **Did You Know?**
>
> slope-intercept form: $y = mx + b$
>
> slope: $m = \frac{y_2 - y_1}{x_2 - x_1}$

Standard form: $Ax + By = C$

$$m = -\frac{A}{B}$$

$$x - \text{intercept} = \frac{C}{A}$$

$$y - \text{intercept} = \frac{C}{B}$$

Another way to express a linear equation is standard form: $Ax + By = C$. In order to graph equations in this form, it is often easiest to convert them to point-slope form. Alternately, it is easy to find the x- or y-intercept from this form, and once these two points are known, a line can be drawn through them. To find the x-intercept, simply make $y = 0$ and solve for x. Similarly, to find the y-intercept, make $x = 0$ and solve for y.

Practice Question

12. What is the equation of the following line?

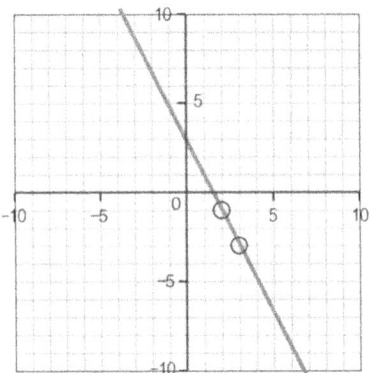

13. What is the slope of the line whose equation is $6x - 2y - 8 = 0$?

14. Write the equation of the line which passes through the points $(-2, 5)$ and $(-5, 3)$.

15. What is the equation of the following graph?

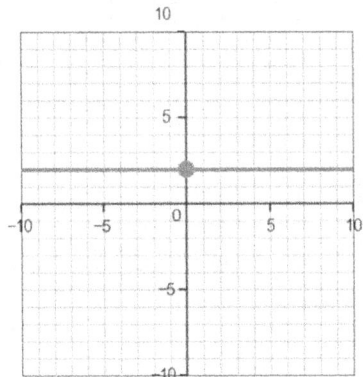

Systems of Linear Equations

Did You Know?

Plug answers back into both equations to ensure the system has been solved properly.

Systems of equations are sets of equations that include two or more variables. These systems can only be solved when there are at least as many equations as there are variables. Systems involve working with more than one equation to solve for more than one variable. For a system of linear equations, the solution to the system is the set of values for the variables that satisfies every equation in the system. Graphically, this will be the point where every line meets. If the lines are parallel (and hence do not intersect), the system will have no solution. If the lines are multiples of each other, meaning they share all coordinates, then the system has infinitely many solutions (because every point on the line is a solution).

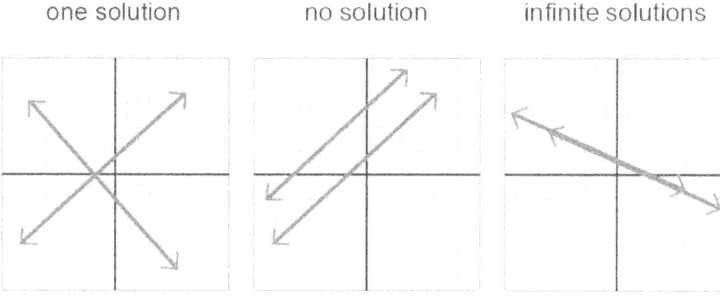

Figure 5.2. Systems of Equations

There are three common methods for solving systems of equations. To perform **substitution**, solve one equation for one variable, and then plug in the resulting expression for that variable in the second equation. This process works best for systems of two equations with two variables where the coefficient of one or more of the variables is 1.

To solve using **elimination**, add or subtract two equations so that one or more variables are eliminated. It's often necessary to multiply one or both of the equations by a scalar (constant) in order to make the variables cancel. Equations can be added or subtracted as many times as necessary to find each variable.

Yet another way to solve a system of linear equations is to use a **matrix equation**. In the matrix equation $AX = B$, A contains the system's coefficients, X contains the variables, and B contains the constants (as shown below). The matrix equation can then be solved by multiplying B by the inverse of A: $X = A^{-1}B$

$$\begin{matrix} ax + by = e \\ cx + dy = f \end{matrix} \rightarrow A = \begin{bmatrix} a & b \\ c & d \end{bmatrix} \quad X = \begin{bmatrix} x \\ y \end{bmatrix} \quad B = \begin{bmatrix} e \\ f \end{bmatrix} \rightarrow AX = B$$

This method can be extended to equations with three or more variables. Technology (such as a graphing calculator) is often employed when solving using this method if more than two variables are involved.

Practice Questions

16. Solve for x and y:

$$2x - 4y = 28$$
$$4x - 12y = 36$$

17. Solve for the system for x and y:

$$3 = -4x + y$$
$$16x = 4y + 2$$

Practice Questions

18. Solve the system of equations:
$$6x + 10y = 18$$
$$4x + 15y = 37$$

19. Solve the following systems of equations using matrix arithmetic:
$$2x - 3y = -5$$
$$3x - 4y = -8$$

Building Equations

In word problems, it is often necessary to translate a verbal description of a relationship into a mathematical equation. No matter the problem, this process can be done using the same steps:

- Read the problem carefully and identify what value needs to be solved for.
- Identify the known and unknown quantities in the problem, and assign the unknown quantities a variable.
- Create equations using the variables and known quantities.
- Solve the equations.
- Check the solution: Does it answer the question asked in the problem? Does it make sense?

> **Did You Know?**
>
> Use the acronym STAR to remember word-problem strategies: <u>S</u>earch the problem, <u>T</u>ranslate into an expression or equation, <u>A</u>nswer, and <u>R</u>eview.

Practice Question

20. A school is holding a raffle to raise money. There is a $3 entry fee, and each ticket costs $5. If a student paid $28, how many tickets did he buy?

21. Kelly is selling shirts for her school swim team. There are two prices: a student price and a nonstudent price. During the first week of the sale, Kelly raised $84 by selling 10 shirts to students and 4 shirts to nonstudents. She earned $185 in the second week by selling 20 shirts to students and 10 shirts to nonstudents. What is the student price for a shirt?

Linear Inequalities

Solving linear inequalities

An inequality shows the relationship between two expressions, much like an equation. However, the equal sign is replaced with an inequality symbol that expresses the following relationships:

- $<$ less than

- $>$ greater than
- $\leq$ less than or equal to
- $\geq$ greater than or equal to

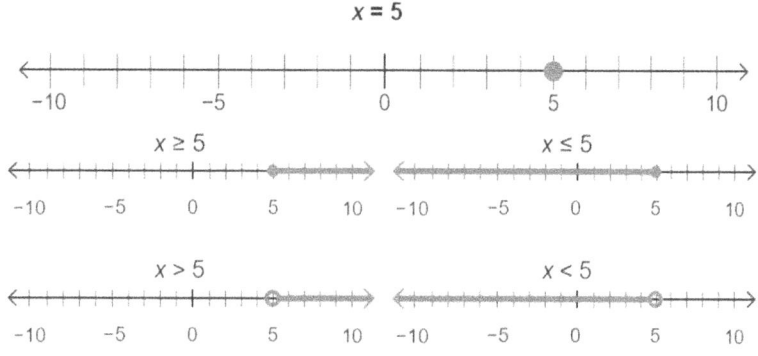

Figure 5.3. Inequalities on a Number Line

Inequalities are read from left to right. For example, the inequality $x < 8$ would be read as "x is less than or equal to 8," meaning x has a value smaller than or equal to 8. The set of solutions of an inequality can be expressed using a number line. The shaded region on the number line represents the set of all the numbers that make an inequality true. One major difference between equations and inequalities is that equations generally have a finite number of solutions, while inequalities generally have infinitely many solutions (an entire interval on the number line containing infinitely many values).

Linear inequalities can be solved in the same way as linear equations, with one exception. When multiplying or dividing both sides of an inequality by a negative number, the direction of the inequality sign must reverse—"greater than" becomes "less than" and "less than" becomes "greater than."

Practice Question

22. Solve for z: $3z + 10 < -z$

23. Solve for x: $2x - 3 > 5(x - 4) - (x - 4)$

Compound Inequalities

Compound inequalities have more than one inequality expression. Solutions of compound inequalities are the sets of all numbers that make *all* the inequalities true. Some compound inequalities may not have any solutions, some will have solutions that contain some part of the number line, and some will have solutions that include the entire number line.

Table 5.1. Unions and Intersections		
Inequality	**Meaning in Words**	**Number Line**
$a < x < b$	All values x that are greater than a and less than b	←—○———○—→ a b

5. Algebraic Concepts

Table 5.1. Unions and Intersections		
Inequality	Meaning in Words	Number Line
$a \leq x \leq b$	All values x that are greater than or equal to a and less than or equal to b	●————● a b
$x < a$ or $x > b$	All values of x that are less than a or greater than b	○————○ a b
$x \leq a$ or $x \geq b$	All values of x that are less than or equal to a or greater than or equal to b	●————● a b

Compound inequalities can be written, solved, and graphed as two separate inequalities. For compound inequalities in which the word *and* is used, the solution to the compound inequality will be the set of numbers on the number line where both inequalities have solutions (where both are shaded). For compound inequalities where *or* is used, the solution to the compound inequality will be *all* the shaded regions for *either* inequality.

Practice Question

24. Solve the compound inequalities: $2x + 4 < -18$ or $4(x + 2) > 18$

25. Solve the inequality: $-1 \leq 3(x + 2) - 1 \leq x + 3$

Graphing Linear Inequalities in Two Variables

Linear inequalities in two variables can be graphed in much the same way as linear equations. Start by graphing the corresponding equation of a line (temporarily replace the inequality with an equal sign, and then graph). This line creates a boundary line of two half-planes. If the inequality is a "greater/ less than," the boundary should not be included and a dotted line is used. A solid line is used to indicate that the boundary should be included in the solution when the inequality is "greater/less than or equal to."

> **Did You Know?**
>
> A dotted line is used for "greater/less than" because the solution may approach that line, but the coordinates on the line can never be a solution.

One side of the boundary is the set of all points (x, y) that make the inequality true. This side is shaded to indicate that all these values are solutions. If y is greater than the expression containing x, shade above the line; if it is less than, shade below. A point can also be used to check which side of the line to shade.

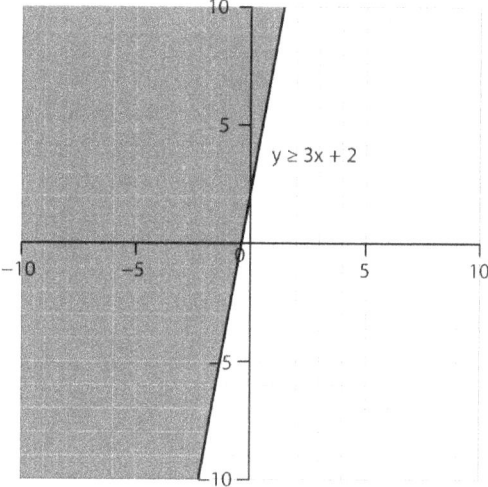

Figure 5.4. Graphing Inequalities

A set of two or more linear inequalities is a **system of inequalities**. Solutions to the system are all the values of the variables that make every inequality in the system true. Systems of inequalities are solved graphically by graphing all the inequalities in the same plane. The region where all the shaded solutions overlap is the solution to the system.

Practice Question

26. Graph the following inequality: $3x + 6y \leq 12$.

27. Graph the system of inequalities: $-x + y \leq 1, x \geq -1, y > 2x - 4$

28. What is the inequality represented on the graph below?

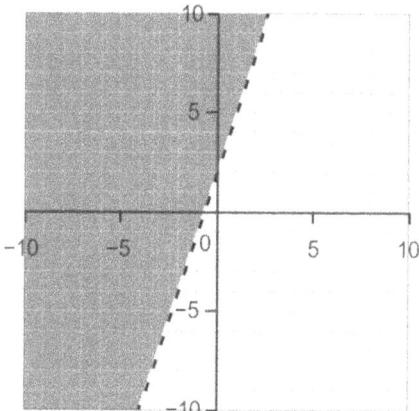

Quadratic Equations

Quadratic equations are degree 2 polynomials; the highest power on the dependent variable is two. While linear functions are represented graphically as lines, the graph of a quadratic function is a **parabola**. The graph of a parabola has three important components. The **vertex** is where the graph changes direction. In the parent graph $y = x^2$, the origin $(0, 0)$ is the vertex. The **axis of symmetry** is the vertical line that cuts the graph into two equal halves. The line of symmetry always passes through the vertex. On the parent graph, the y-axis is the axis of symmetry. The **zeros** or **roots** of the quadratic are the x-intercepts of the graph.

Forms of Quadratic Equations

Quadratic equations can be expressed in two forms:

- Standard form: $y + ax^2 + bx + c$

Axis of symmetry: $x = \frac{b}{a}$

Vertex: $(-\frac{b}{2a}, f(-\frac{b}{2a}))$

- Vertex form: $y = a(x - h)^2 + k$

Vertex: (h, k)

Axis of symmetry: $x = h$

In both equations, the sign of a determines which direction the parabola opens: if a is positive, then it opens upward; if a is negative, then it opens downward. The wideness or narrowness is also determined by a. If the absolute value of a is less than one (a proper fraction), then the parabola will get wider the closer $|a|$ is to zero. If the absolute value of a is greater than one, then the larger $|a|$ becomes, the narrower the parabola will be.

Equations in vertex form can be converted to standard form by squaring out the $(x - h)^2$ part (using FOIL), distributing the a, adding k, and simplifying the result.

Figure 5.5. Parabola

Equations can be converted from standard form to vertex form by **completing the square**. Take an equation in standard form, $y = ax^2 + bc + c$.

- Move c to the left side of the equation.
- Divide the entire equation through by a (to make the coefficient of x^2 be 1).
- Take half of the coefficient of x, square that number, and then add the result to both sides of the equation.
- Convert the right side of the equation to a perfect binomial squared, $(x + m)^2$.
- Isolate y to put the equation in proper vertex form.

Practice Question

29. What is the line of symmetry for $y = -2(x + 3)^2 + 2$?

30. What is the vertex of the parabola $y = -3x^2 + 24x - 27$?

31. Write $y = -3x^2 + 24x - 27$ in vertex form by completing the square.

Solving Quadratic Equations

Solving the quadratic equation $ax^2 + bx + c = 0$ finds x-intercepts of the parabola (by making $y = 0$). These are also called the roots or zeros of the quadratic function. A quadratic equation may have zero, one, or two real solutions. There are several ways of finding the zeros. One way is to factor the quadratic into a product of two binomials, and then use the zero product property. (If $m \times n = 0$, then either $m = 0$ or $n = 0$.) Another way is to complete the square and square root both sides. One way that works every time is to memorize and use the **quadratic formula**:

$$x = \frac{-b \pm \sqrt{b^2 - 4ac}}{2a}$$

The a, b, and c come from the standard form of quadratic equations above. (Note that to use the quadratic equation, the right-hand side of the equation must be equal to zero.)

> **Did You Know?**
>
> With all graphing problems, putting the function into the $y =$ window of a graphing calculator will aid the process of elimination when graphs are examined and compared to answer choices with a focus on properties like axis of symmetry, vertices, and roots of formulas.

The part of the formula under the square root radical ($b^2 - 4ac$) is known as the **discriminant**. The discriminant tells how many and what type of roots will result without actually calculating the roots.

Table 5.2. Discriminants		
If $b^2 - 4ac$ is	there will be	and the parabola
zero	only 1 real root	has its vertex on the x-axis
positive	2 real roots	has two x-intercepts
negative	0 real roots 2 complex roots	has no x-intercepts

Practice Question

32. Find the zeros of the quadratic equation: $y = -(x + 3)2 + 1$.

33. Find the root(s) for: $z^2 - 4z + 4 = 0$

34. Write a quadratic function that has zeros at $x = -3$ and $x = 2$ that passes through the point $(-2, 8)$.

Graphing Quadratic Equations

The final expected quadratic skills are graphing a quadratic function given its equation and determining the equation of a quadratic function from its graph. The equation's form determines which quantities are easiest to obtain:

Table 5.3. Obtaining Quantities from Quadratic Functions

Name of Form	Equation of Quadratic	Easiest Quantity to Find	How to Find Other Quantities
vertex form	$y = a(x - h)^2 + k$	vertex at (h, k) and axis of symmetry $x = h$	Find zeros by making $y = 0$ and solving for x.
factored form	$y = a(x - m)(x - n)$	x-intercepts at $x = m$ and $x = n$	Find axis of symmetry by averaging m and n: $x = \frac{m + n}{2}$ This is also the x-value of the vertex.
standard form	$y = ax^2 + bx + c$	y-intercept at $(0, c)$	Find axis of symmetry and x-value of the vertex using $x = \frac{-b}{2a}$. Find zeros using quadratic formula.

To graph a quadratic function, first determine if the graph opens up or down by examining the a-value. Then determine the quantity that is easiest to find based on the form given, and find the vertex. Then other values can be found, if necessary, by choosing x-values and finding the corresponding y-values. Using symmetry instantly doubles the number of points that are known.

Given the graph of a parabola, the easiest way to write a quadratic equation is to identify the vertex and insert the h- and k-values into the vertex form of the equation. The a-value can be determined by finding another point the graph goes through, plugging these values in for x and y, and solving for a.

Practice Question

35. Graph the quadratic $y = 2(x - 3)^2 + 4$.

Practice Question

36. What is the vertex form of the equation shown on the following graph?

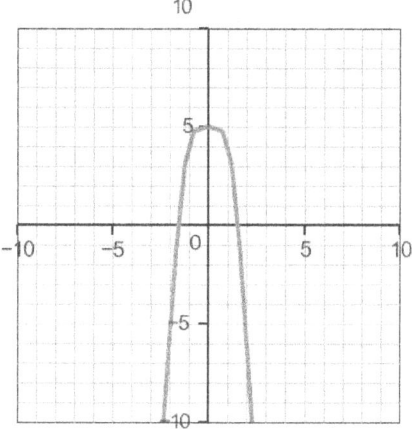

Functions

Working with Functions

Functions can be thought of as a process: when something is put in, an action (or operation) is performed, and something different comes out. A **function** is a relationship between two quantities (for example x and y) in which, for every value of the independent variable (usually x), there is exactly one value of the dependent variable (usually y). Briefly, each input has *exactly one* output. Graphically this means the graph passes the **vertical line test**: anywhere a vertical line is drawn on the graph, the line hits the curve at exactly one point.

The notation $f(x)$ or $g(t)$, etc., is often used when a function is being considered. This is **function notation**. The input value is x and the output value y is written as $y = f(x)$. Thus, $f(2)$ represents the output value (or y value) when $x = 2$, and $f(2) = 5$ means that when $x = 2$ is plugged into the $f(x)$ function, the output (y value) is 5. In other words, $f(2) = 5$ represents the point $(2, 5)$ on the graph of $f(x)$.

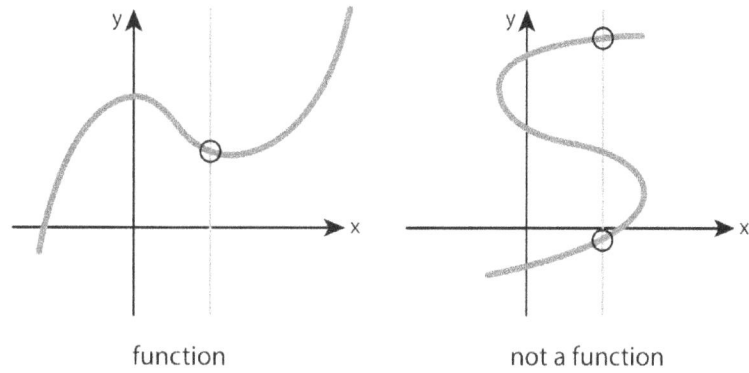

Figure 5.6. Vertical Line Test

Every function has an input Domain and output range. The domain is the set of all the possible x values that can be used as input values (these are found along the horizontal axis on the graph), and the range includes all the y values or output values that result from applying $f(x)$ (these are found along the vertical axis on the graph). Domain and range are usually intervals of numbers and are often expressed as inequalities, such as $x < 2$ (the domain is all values less than 2) or $3 < x < 15$ (all values between 3 and 15).

A function $f(x)$ is even if $f(-x) = f(x)$. Even functions have symmetry across the y-axis. An example of an even function is the parent quadratic $y = x^2$, because any value of x (for example, 3) and its opposite $-x$ (for example, –3) have the same y value (for example, $3^2 = 9$ and $(-3)^2 = 9$). A function is **odd** if $f(-x) = -f(x)$. Odd functions have symmetry about the origin. For example, $f(x) = x^3$ is an odd function because $f(3) = 27$, and $f(-3) = -27$. A function may be even, odd, or neither.

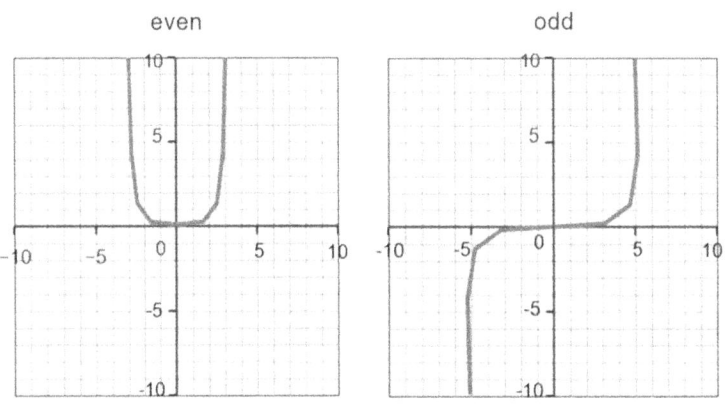

Figure 5.7. Even and Odd Functions

Practice Question

37. Evaluate: $f(4)$ if $f(x) = x^3 - 2x + \sqrt{x}$

38. What are the domain and range of the following function?

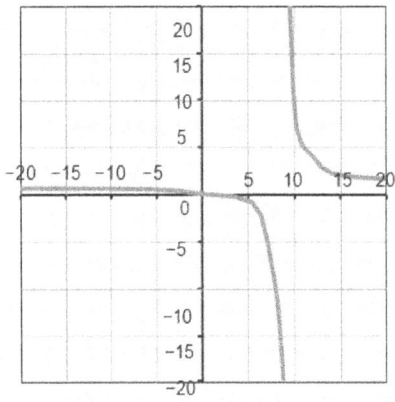

39. What is the domain and the range of the following graph?

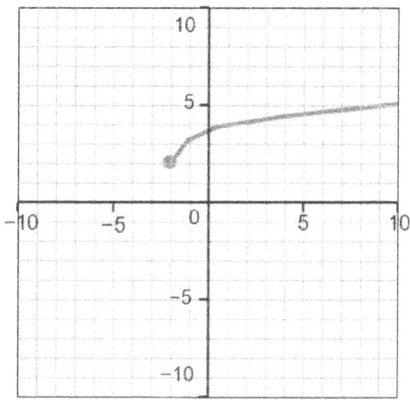

40. Which of the following represents a function?

A)

x	g(x)
0	0
1	1
2	2
1	3

B)

x	f(x)
0	1
0	2
0	3
0	4

C)

t	f(t)
1	1
2	2
3	3
4	4

D)

x	f(x)
0	0
5	1
0	2
5	3

Inverse Functions

Inverse functions switch the inputs and the outputs of a function. If $f(x) = k$ then the inverse of that function would read $f^{-1}(k) = x$. The domain of $f^{-1}(x)$ is the range of $f(x)$, and the range of $f^{-1}(x)$ is the domain of $f(x)$. If point (a, b) is on the graph of $f(x)$, then point (b, a) will be on the graph of $f^{-1}(x)$.

Because of this fact, the graph of $f^{-1}(x)$ is a reflection of the graph of $f(x)$ across the line $y = x$. Inverse functions "undo" all the operations of the original function.

The steps for finding an inverse function are:

- Replace $f(x)$ with y to make it easier manipulate the equation.
- Switch the x and y.

> **Did You Know?**
>
> Inverse graphs can be tested by taking any point on one graph and flipping coordinates to see if that new point is on the other curve. For example, the coordinate point $(5, -2)$ is on the function and $(-2, 5)$ is a point on its inverse.

- Solve for y.
- Label the inverse function as $f^{-1}(x) =$.

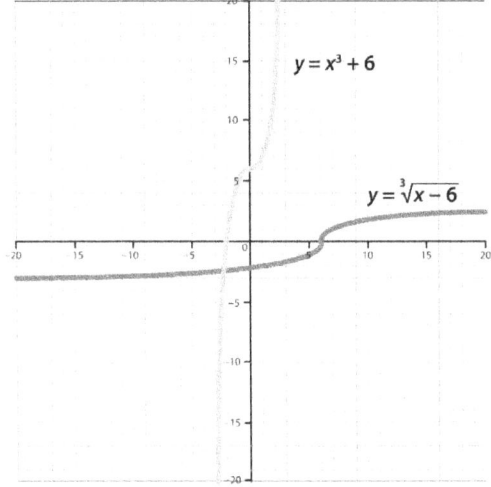

Figure 5.8. Inverse Functions

Practice Question

41. What is the inverse of function of $f(x) = 5x + 5$?

42. Find the inverse of the graph of $f(x) = -1 - \frac{1}{5}x$.

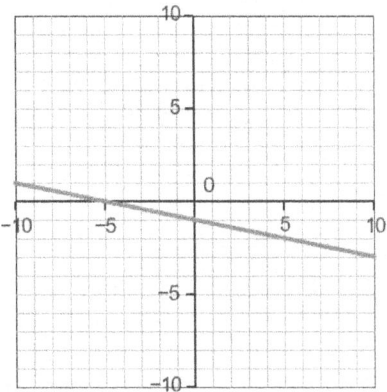

Compound Functions

Compound functions take two or more functions and combine them using operations or composition. Functions can be combined using addition, subtraction, multiplication, or division:

- Addition: $(f + g)(x) = f(x) + g(x)$
- Subtraction: $(f - g)(x) = f(x) - g(x)$
- Multiplication: $(fg)(x) = f(x)g(x)$
- Division: $\frac{f}{g}(x) = \frac{f(x)}{g(x)}$ (note that $g(x) \neq 0$)

Functions can also be combined using **composition**. Composition of functions is indicated by the notation $(f \circ g)(x)$. Note that the $\circ$ symbol does NOT mean multiply. It means take the output of $g(x)$ and make it the input of $f(x)$:

$$(f \circ g)(x) = f(g(x))$$

This equation is read f of g of x, and will be a new function of x. Note that order is important. In general, $f(g(x)) \neq g(f(x))$. They *will* be equal when $f(x)$ and $g(x)$ are inverses of each other, however, as both will simplify to the original input x. This is because performing a function on a value and then using that output as the input to the inverse function should bring you back to the original value.

The domain of a composition function is the set of x values that are in the domain of the "inside" function $g(x)$ such that $g(x)$ is in the domain of the outside function $f(x)$. For example, if $f(x) = \frac{1}{x}$ and $g(x) = \sqrt{x}$, $f(g(x))$ has a domain of $x > 0$ because $g(x)$ has a domain of $x \geq 0$. But when $f(x)$ is applied to the $\sqrt{x}$ function, the composition function becomes $\frac{1}{\sqrt{x}}$ and the value $x = 0$ is no longer allowed because it would result in 0 in the denominator, so the domain must be further restricted.

Practice Question

43. If $z(x) = 3x - 3$ and $y(x) = 2x - 1$, find $(y \circ z)(-4)$.

44. Find $(k \circ t)(x)$ if $k(x) = \frac{1}{2}x - 3$ and $t(x) = \frac{1}{2}x - 2$.

45. The wait (W) (in minutes) to get on a ride at an amusement park depends on the number of people (N) in the park. The number of people in the park depends on the number of hours, t, that the park has been open. Suppose $N(t) = 400t$ and $W(N) = 5(1.2)^{\frac{N}{100}}$. What is the value and the meaning in context of $N(4)$ and $W(N(4))$?

Transforming Functions

Many functions can be graphed using simple transformation of parent functions. Transformations include reflections across axes, vertical and horizontal translations (or shifts), and vertical or horizontal stretches or compressions. The table gives the effect of each transformation to the graph of any function $y = f(x)$.

Table 5.4. Effects of Transformations

Equation	Effect on Graph
$y = -f(x)$	reflection across the x-axis (vertical reflection)
$y = f(x) + k$	vertical shift up k units ($k > 0$) or down k units ($k < 0$)
$y = kf(x)$	vertical stretch (if $k > 1$) or compression (if $k < 1$)
$y = f(-x)$	reflection across the y-axis (horizontal reflection)
$y = f(x + k)$	horizontal shift right k units ($k < 0$) or left k units ($k > 0$)
$y = f(kx)$	horizontal stretch ($k < 1$) or compression ($k > 1$)

Note that the first three equations have an operation applied to the *outside* of the function $f(x)$ and these all cause *vertical changes* to the graph of the function that are **intuitive** (for example, adding a value moves it up). The last three equations have an operation applied to the *inside* of the function $f(x)$ and these all cause **horizontal changes** to the graph of the function that are **counterintuitive** (for example, multiplying the x's by a fraction results in stretch, not compression, which would seem more intuitive). It is helpful to group these patterns together to remember how each transformation affects the graph.

Practice Question

46. Graph: $y = |x + 1| + 4$

47. Graph: $y = -3|x - 2| + 2$

Answer Key

1. $5(m-2)^3 + 3m^2 - \frac{m}{4} - 1$

Plug the value 4 in for m in the expression.

$$5(4-2)^3 + 3(4)^2 - \frac{4}{4} - 1$$

Calculate all the expressions inside the parentheses.

$$5(2)^3 + 3(4)^2 - \frac{4}{4} - 1$$

Simplify all exponents.

$$5(8) + 3(16) - 4 - 1$$

Perform multiplication and division from left to right.

$$40 + 48 - 1 - 1$$

Perform addition and subtraction from left to right.

$$= \mathbf{86}$$

2. The only like terms in both expressions are $12x$ and $8x$, so these two terms will be added, and all other terms will remain the same.

$$a + b = (12x + 8x) + 7xy - 9y - 9xz + 7z = \mathbf{20x + 7xy - 9y - 9xz + 7z}$$

3. $5x(x^2 - 2c + 10)$

Distribute and multiply the term outside the parentheses to all three terms inside the parentheses.

$$(5x)(x^2) = 5x^3$$
$$(5x)(-2c) = -10xc$$
$$(5x)(10) = 50x$$
$$\mathbf{5x^3 - 10xc + 50x}$$

4. $(x^2 - 5)(2x - x^3)$

Apply FOIL: first, outside, inside, and last.

$$(x^2)(2x) = 2x^3$$
$$(x^2)(-x^3) = -x^5$$
$$(-5)(2x) = -10x$$
$$(-5)(-x^3) = 5x^3$$

5. Algebraic Concepts

Combine like terms and put them in order.

$$2x^3 - x^5 - 10x + 5x^3$$

$$\mathbf{-x^5 + 7x^3 - 10x}$$

5. $16z^2 + 48z$

Both terms have a z, and 16 is a common factor of both 16 and 48. So the greatest common factor is $16z$. Factor out the GCF.

$$16z^2 + 48z = \mathbf{16z(z+3)}$$

6. $6m^3 + 12m^3n - 9m^2$

All the terms share the factor m^2, and 3 is the greatest common factor of 6, 12, and 9. So, the GCF is $3m^2$.

$$\mathbf{3m^2(2m + 4mn - 3)}$$

7. $16x^2 + 52x + 30$

Remove the GCF of 2.

$$2(8x^2 + 26x + 15)$$

To factor the polynomial in the parentheses, calculate $ac = (8)(15) = 120$, and consider all the pairs of numbers that multiply to be 120: 1×120, 2×60, 3×40, 4×30, 5×24, 6×20, 8×15, and 10×12. Of these pairs, choose the pair that adds to be the b-value 26 (6 and 20).

$$2(8x^2 + 6x + 20x + 15)$$

Group.

$$2[(8x^2 + 6x) + (20x + 15)]$$

Factor out the GCF of each group.

$$2[2x(4x + 3) + 5(4x + 3)]$$

Factor out the common binomial.

$$2[(4x + 3)(2x + 5)]$$

$$\mathbf{2(4x + 3)(2x + 5)}$$

If there are no values r and s that multiply to be ac and add to be b, then the polynomial is prime and cannot be factored.

8. $-21x^2 - x + 10$

Factor out the negative.

$$-(21x^2 + x - 10)$$

Factor the polynomial in the parentheses.

$ac = 210$ and $b = 1$

The numbers 15 and −14 can be multiplied to get 210 and subtracted to get 1.

$$-(21x^2 - 14x + 15x - 10)$$

Group.

$$-[(21x^2 - 14x) + (15x - 10)]$$

Factor out the GCF of each group.

$$-[7x(3x - 2) + 5(3x - 2)]$$

Factor out the common binomial.

$$-(3x - 2)(7x + 5)$$

9. $\frac{100(x+5)}{20} = 1$

Multiply both sides by 20 to cancel out the denominator.

$$(20)\frac{100(x+5)}{20} = (1)(20)$$

$$100(x+5) = 20$$

Distribute 100 through the parentheses.

$$100x + 500 = 20$$

"Undo" the +500 by subtracting 500 on both sides of the equation to isolate the variable term.

$$100x = -480$$

"Undo" the multiplication by 100 by dividing by 100 on both sides to solve for x.

$$x = \frac{-480}{100}$$

$$x = -4.8$$

10. $2(x+2)^2 - 2x^2 + 10 = 42$

Eliminate the exponents on the left side.

$$2(x+2)(x+2) - 2x^2 + 10 = 42$$

Apply FOIL.

$$2(x^2 + 4x + 4) - 2x^2 + 10 = 42$$

Distribute the 2.

$$2x^2 + 8x + 8 - 2x^2 + 10 = 42$$

Combine like terms on the left-hand side.

$$8x + 18 = 42$$

Isolate the variable. "Undo" +18 by subtracting 18 on both sides.

$$8x = 24$$

5. Algebraic Concepts

"Undo" multiplication by 8 by dividing both sides by 8.

$$x = 3$$

11. $\frac{A(3B+2D)}{2N} = 5M - 6$

Multiply both sides by $2N$ to clear the fraction, and distribute the A through the parentheses.

$$3AB + 2AD = 10MN - 12N$$

Isolate the term with the D in it by moving $3AB$ to the other side of the equation.

$$2AD = 10MN - 12N - 3AB$$

Divide both sides by $2A$ to get D alone on the right-hand side.

$$D = \frac{(10MN - 12N - 3AB)}{2A}$$

12. The y-intercept can be identified on the graph as $(0, 3)$.

$$b = 3$$

To find the slope, choose any two points and plug the values into the slope equation. The two points chosen here are $(2, -1)$ and $(3, -3)$.

$$m = \frac{(-3) - (-1)}{3 - 2}$$

$$m = \frac{-2}{1} = -2$$

Replace m with −2 and b with 3 in

$$y = mx + b$$

$$y = -2x + 3$$

13. $6x - 2y - 8 = 0$

Rearrange the equation into slope-intercept form by solving the equation for y.

$$-2y = -6x + 8$$

$$y = \frac{-6x + 8}{-2}$$

$$y = 3x - 4$$

The slope is 3, the value attached to x.

$$m = 3$$

14. $(-2, 5)$ and $(-5, 3)$

Calculate the slope.

$$m = \frac{3 - 5}{(-5) - (-2)} = \frac{-2}{-3} = \frac{2}{3}$$

To find b, plug into the equation $y = mx + b$ the slope for m and a set of points for x and y.

$$5 = \frac{2}{3}(-2) + b$$

$$5 = \frac{-4}{3} + b$$

$$b = \frac{19}{3}$$

Replace m and b to find the equation of the line.

$$y = \frac{2}{3}x + \frac{19}{3}$$

15. The line has a rise of 0 and a run of 1, so the slope is $\frac{0}{1} = 0$. There is no x-intercept. The y-intercept is $(0, 2)$, meaning that the b-value in the slope-intercept form is 2.

$y = 0x + 2$, or $y = 2$

16. Solve the system with substitution. Solve one equation for one variable.

$$2x - 4y = 28$$

$$x = 2y + 14$$

Plug in the resulting expression for x in the second equation and simplify.

$$4x - 12y = 36$$

$$4(2y + 14) - 12y = 36$$

$$8y + 56 - 12y = 36$$

$$-4y = -20$$

$$y = 5$$

Plug the solved variable into either equation to find the second variable.

$$2x - 4y = 28$$

$$2x - 4(5) = 28$$

$$2x - 20 = 28$$

$$2x = 48$$

$$x = 24$$

The answer is $y = 5$ and $x = 24$ or $(\mathbf{24, 5})$.

17. Isolate the variable in one equation.

$$3 = -4x + y$$

$$y = 4x + 3$$

Plug the expression into the second equation.

Both equations have slope 4. This means the graphs of the equations are parallel lines, so no intersection (solution) exists.

$$16x = 4y + 2$$
$$16x = 4(4x + 3) + 2$$
$$16x = 16x + 12 + 2$$
$$0 = 14$$

No solution exists.

18. Because solving for x or y in either equation will result in messy fractions, this problem is best solved using elimination. The goal is to eliminate one of the variables by making the coefficients in front of one set of variables the same, but with different signs, and then adding both equations.

To eliminate the x's in this problem, find the least common multiple of coefficients 6 and 4. The smallest number that both 6 and 4 divide into evenly is 12.

Multiply the top equation by −2, and the bottom equation by 3.

$$(6x + 10y = 18)(-2) = -12x - 20y = -36$$
$$(4x + 15y = 37)(3) = 12x + 45y = 111$$

Add the two equations to eliminate the x's.

$$25y = 75$$

Solve for y.

$$y = \frac{75}{25}$$
$$y = 3$$

Replace y with 3 in either of the original equations.

$$6x + 10(3) = 18$$
$$6x + 30 = 18$$
$$6x = 18 - 30$$
$$x = \frac{-12}{6}$$
$$x = -2$$

The solution is $(-2, 3)$.

19. Write the system in matrix form, $AX = B$.

$$\begin{bmatrix} 2 & -3 \\ 3 & -4 \end{bmatrix} \begin{bmatrix} x \\ y \end{bmatrix} = \begin{bmatrix} -5 \\ -8 \end{bmatrix}$$

Calculate the inverse of Matrix A.

$$\begin{bmatrix} 2 & -3 \\ 3 & -4 \end{bmatrix}^{-1} = \frac{1}{(2)(-4) - (-3)(3)} \begin{bmatrix} -4 & 3 \\ -3 & 2 \end{bmatrix}$$

Multiply B by the inverse of A.

$$\begin{matrix} x \\ y \end{matrix} = \begin{bmatrix} -4 & 3 \\ -3 & 2 \end{bmatrix} \begin{matrix} -5 \\ -8 \end{matrix} = \begin{matrix} -4 \\ -1 \end{matrix}$$

Match up the 2×1 matrices to identify x and y.

$$x = -4$$
$$y = -1$$

20. Identify the quantities.

$$\text{Number of tickets} = x$$
$$\text{Cost per ticket} = 5$$
$$\text{Cost for } x \text{ tickets} = 5x$$
$$\text{Total cost} = 28$$
$$\text{Entry fee} = 3$$

Set up equations. The total cost for x tickets will be equal to the cost for x tickets plus the $3 flat fee.

$$5x + 3 = 28$$

Solve the equation for x.

$$5x + 3 = 28$$
$$5x = 25$$
$$x = 5$$

The student bought **5 tickets**.

21. Assign variables.

$$\text{Student price} = s$$
$$\text{Nonstudent price} = n$$

Create two equations using the number of shirts Kelly sold and the money she earned.

$$10s + 4n = 84$$
$$20s + 10n = 185$$

Solve the system of equations using substitution.

$$10s + 4n = 84$$
$$10n = -20s + 185$$
$$n = \frac{-20s + 185}{10}$$
$$n = \frac{-20s}{10} + \frac{185}{10} = -2s + 18.5$$
$$10s + 4(-2s + 18.5) = 84$$
$$10s - 8s + 74 = 84$$
$$2s + 74 = 84$$
$$2s = 10$$
$$s = 5$$

The student cost for shirts is **$5**.

22. $3z + 10 < -z$

Collect non variable terms to one side.

$$3z < -z - 10$$

Collect variable terms to the other side.

$$4z < -10$$

Isolate the variable.

$$z < -2.5$$
$$-2.5$$

23. $2x - 3 > 5(x - 4) - (x - 4)$

Distribute 5 through the parentheses and –1 through the parentheses.

$$2x - 3 > 5x - 20 - x + 4$$

Combine like terms.

$$2x - 3 > 4x - 16$$

Collect x-terms to one side, and constant terms to the other side.

$$-2x > -13$$

Divide both sides by –2; since dividing by a negative, reverse the direction of the inequality.

$$x < 6.5$$
$$6.5$$

24. $2x + 4 < -18$ or $4(x + 2) > 18$

Solve each inequality independently.

$$2x < -14$$
$$x < -7$$
$$4x + 8 > 18$$
$$4x > 10$$
$$x > 2.5$$

The solution to the original compound inequality is **the set of all x for which $x < -7$ or $x > 2.5$**.

25. $-1 \leq 3(x + 2) - 1 \leq x + 3$

Break up the compound inequality into two inequalities.

$-1 \leq 3(x + 2) - 1$ and $3(x + 2) - 1 \leq x + 3$

Solve separately.

$$-1 \leq 3x + 6 - 1$$
$$-6 \leq 3x$$
$$-2 \leq x$$
$$3x + 6 - 1 \leq x + 3$$
$$2x \leq -2$$
$$x \leq -1$$

The only values of x that satisfy *both* inequalities are the values between –2 and –1 (inclusive).

$$\mathbf{-2 \leq x \leq -1}$$

26. Find the x- and y-intercepts.

$$3x + 6y \leq 12$$
$$3(0) + 6y = 12$$
$$y = 2$$

y-intercept: $(0, 2)$

$$3x + 6(0) \leq 12$$
$$x = 4$$

x-intercept: $(4, 0)$

Graph the line using the intercepts, and shade below the line.

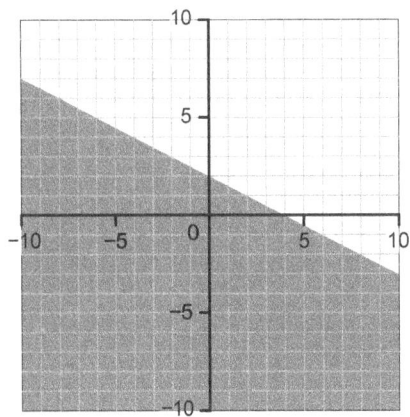

27. To solve the system, graph all three inequalities in the same plane; then identify the area where the three solutions overlap. All points (x, y) in this area will be solutions to the system since they satisfy all three inequalities.

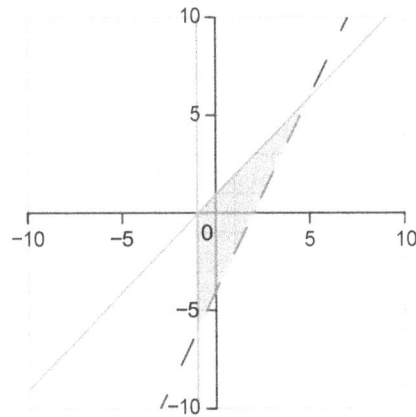

28. Determine the equation of the boundary line.

y-intercept: $(0, 2)$

slope: 3

$$y = 3x + 2$$

Replace the equal sign with the appropriate inequality: the line is dotted and the shading is above the line, indicating that the symbol should be "greater than." Check a point: for example, $(1, 5)$ is a solution since $5 > 3(-1) + 2$.

$$y > 3x + 2$$

29. This quadratic is given in vertex form, with $h = -3$ and $k = 2$. The vertex of this equation is $(-3, 2)$. The line of symmetry is the vertical line that passes through this point. Since the x-value of the point is -3, the line of symmetry is $x = -3$.

30. $y = -3x^2 + 24x - 27$

This quadratic equation is in standard form. Use the formula for finding the x-value of the vertex.

$x = -\frac{b}{2a}$ where $a = -3, b = 24$

$$x = -\frac{24}{2(-3)} = 4$$

Plug $x = 4$ into the original equation to find the corresponding y-value.

$$y = -3(4)^2 + 24(4) - 27 = 21$$

The vertex is at $(\mathbf{4, 21})$.

31. $y = -3x^2 + 24x - 27$

Move c to the other side of the equation.

$$y + 27 = -3x^2 + 24x$$

Divide through by a (–3 in this example).

$$\frac{y}{-3} - 9 = x^2 - 8x$$

Take half of the new b, square it, and add that quantity to both sides: $\frac{1}{2}(-8) = -4$. Squaring it gives $(-4)2 = 16$.

$$\frac{y}{-3} - 9 + 16 = x^2 - 8x + 16$$

Simplify the left side, and write the right side as a binomial squared.

$$\frac{y}{-3} + 7 = (x - 4)^2$$

Subtract 7, and then multiply through by –3 to isolate y.

$$\mathbf{y = -3(x - 4)^2 + 21}$$

32. Method 1: Make $y = 0$; isolate x by square rooting both sides:

Make $y = 0$.

$$0 = -(x + 3)^2 + 1$$

Subtract 1 from both sides.

$$-1 = -(x + 3)^2$$

Divide by –1 on both sides.

$$1 = (x + 3)^2$$

Square root both sides. Don't forget to write plus OR minus 1.

$$(x + 3) = \pm 1$$

Write two equations using +1 and −1.

$(x + 3) = 1$ or $(x + 3) = -1$

Solve both equations. These are the zeros.

$x = -2$ or $x = -4$

Method 2: Convert vertex form to standard form, and then use the quadratic formula.

Put the equation in standard form by distributing and combining like terms.

$$y = -(x+3)^2 + 1$$
$$y = -(x^2 + 6x + 9) + 1$$
$$y = -x^2 - 6x - 8$$

Find the zeros using the quadratic formula.

$$x = \frac{-b \pm \sqrt{(b^2 - 4ac)}}{2a}$$

$$x = \frac{-(-6) \pm \sqrt{(-6)^2 - 4(-1)(-8)}}{2(-1)}$$

$$x = \frac{6 \pm \sqrt{36 - 32}}{-2}$$

$$x = \frac{6 \pm \sqrt{4}}{-2}$$

$$\boldsymbol{x = -4, -2}$$

33. This polynomial can be factored in the form $(z - 2)(z - 2) = 0$, so the only root is $z = 2$. There is only one x-intercept, and the vertex of the graph is *on* the x-axis.

34. If the quadratic has zeros at $x = -3$ and $x = 2$, then it has factors of $(x + 3)$ and $(x - 2)$. The quadratic function can be written in the factored form $y = a(x + 3)(x - 2)$. To find the a-value, plug in the point $(-2, 8)$ for x and y:

$$8 = a(-2 + 3)(-2 - 2)$$
$$8 = a(-4)$$
$$a = -2$$

The quadratic function is:

$$\boldsymbol{y = -2(x + 3)(x - 2)}$$

35. Start by marking the vertex at $(3, 4)$ and recognizing this parabola opens upward. The line of symmetry is $x = 3$. Now, plug in an easy value for x to get one point on the curve; then use symmetry to find another point. In this case, choose $x = 2$ (one unit to the left of the line of symmetry) and solve for y:

$$y = 2(2-3)2 + 4$$
$$y = 2(1) + 4$$
$$y = 6$$

Thus the point $(2, 6)$ is on the curve. Then use symmetry to find the corresponding point one unit to the right of the line of symmetry, which must also have a y value of 6. This point is $(4, 6)$. Draw a parabola through the points.

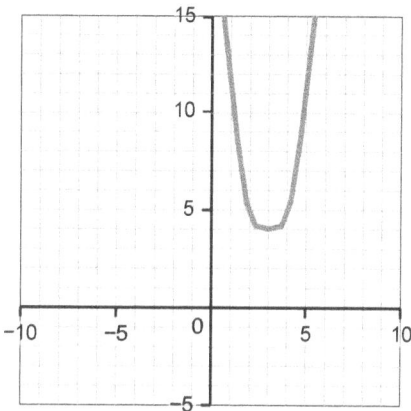

36. Locate the vertex and plug values for h and k into the vertex form of the quadratic equation.

$$(h, k) = (0, 5)$$
$$y = a(x - h)^2 + k$$
$$y = a(x - 0)^2 + 5$$
$$y = ax^2 + 5$$

Choose another point on the graph to plug into this equation to solve for a.

$$(x, y) = (1, 2)$$
$$y = ax^2 + 5$$
$$2 = a(1)^2 + 5$$
$$a = -3$$

Plug a into the vertex form of the equation.

$$\boldsymbol{y = -3x^2 + 5}$$

37. $f(4)$ if $f(x) = x^3 - 2x + \sqrt{x}$

Plug in 4.

$$f(4) = (4)^3 - 2(4) + \sqrt{(4)}$$

Follow the PEMDAS order of operations.

$$64 - 8 + 2 = \boldsymbol{58}$$

38. This function has an asymptote at $x = 9$, so is not defined there.

Otherwise, the function is defined for all other values of x.

D: $-\infty < x < 9$ or $9 < x < \infty$

Interval notation can also be used to show domain and range. Round brackets indicate that an end value is not included, and square brackets show that it is.

The symbol ∪ means or, and the symbol ∩ means and. For example, the statement (−infinity, 4) ∪ (4, infinity) describes the set of all real numbers except 4.

Since the function has a horizontal asymptote at $y = 1$ that it never crosses, the function never takes the value 1, so the range is all real numbers except 1:

R: $-\infty < y < 1$ or $1 < y < \infty$

39. For the domain, this graph goes on to the right to positive infinity. Its leftmost point, however, is $x = -2$. Therefore, its domain is all real numbers equal to or greater than –2, **D:** $-2 \leq x < \infty$, or $[-2, \infty)$.

The lowest range value is $y = 2$. Although it has a decreasing slope, this function continues to rise.

Therefore, the domain is all real numbers greater than 2, **R: $2 \leq y < \infty$** or $[2, \infty)$.

40. For a set of numbers to represent a function, every input must generate a unique output. Therefore, if the same input (x) appears more than once in the table, determine if that input has two different outputs. If so, then the table does not represent a function.

- A) This table is not a function because input value 1 has two different outputs (1 and 3).
- B) Table B is not function because 0 is the only input and results in four different values.
- C) This table shows a function because each input has one output.
- D) This table also has one input going to two different values, so it is not a function.

41. Replace $f(x)$ with y.

$$y = 5x + 5$$

Switch the places of y and x.

$$x = 5y + 5$$

Solve for y.

$$x = 5y + 5x - 5 = 5y$$

$$y = \frac{x}{5} - 1$$

$$f^{-1}(x) = \frac{x}{5} - 1$$

42. This is a linear graph with some clear coordinates: $(-5, 0)$, $(0, -1)$, $(5, -2)$, and $(10, -3)$. This means the inverse function will have coordinate $(0, -5)$, $(-1, 0)$, $(-2, 5)$, and $(-3, 10)$. The inverse function is reflected over the line $y = x$ and is the line $f^{-1}(x) = -5(x + 1)$ below.

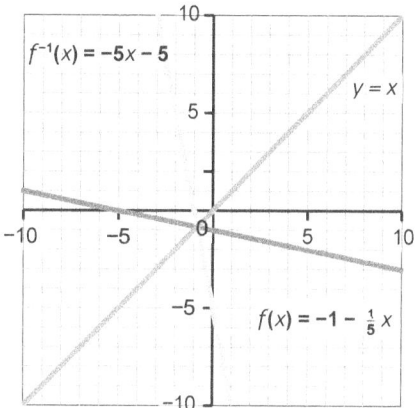

43. $(y \circ z)(-4) = y(z(-4))$

Starting on the inside, evaluate z.

$$z(-4) = 3(-4) - 3 = -12 - 3 = -15$$

Replace $z(-4)$ with -15, and simplify.

$$y(z(-4)) = y(-15) = 2(-15) - 1 = -30 - 1 = \mathbf{-31}$$

44. Replace x in the $k(x)$ function with $\frac{1}{2}x - 2$.

$$(k \circ t)(x) = k(t(x)) = k\left(\frac{1}{2}x - 2\right)$$

$$k(x) = \frac{1}{2}x - 3 = \frac{1}{2}\left(\frac{1}{2}x - 2\right) - 3$$

Simplify.

$$\frac{1}{4}x - 1 - 3 = \frac{1}{4}x - 4$$

$$(k \circ t)(x) = \mathbf{\frac{1}{4}x - 4}$$

45. $N(4) = 400(4) = 1600$ and means that 4 hours after the park opens there are 1600 people in the park. $W(N(4)) = W(1600) = 96$ and means that 4 hours after the park opens the wait time is about **96 minutes** for the ride.

46. This function is the absolute value function with a vertical shift up of 4 units (since the 4 is outside the absolute value bars), and a horizontal shift left of 1 unit (since it is inside the bars). The vertex of the graph is at $(-1, 4)$ and the line $x = -1$ is an axis of symmetry.

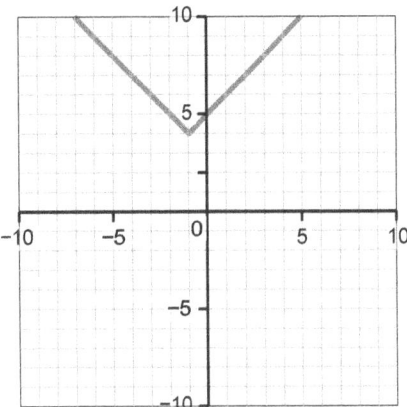

47. The negative sign in front of the absolute value means the graph will be reflected across the x-axis, so it will open down. The 3 causes a vertical stretch of the function, which results in a narrower graph. The basic curve is shifted 2 units right (since the −2 is an inside change) and 2 units up (since the +2 is an outside change), so the vertex is at $(2, 2)$.

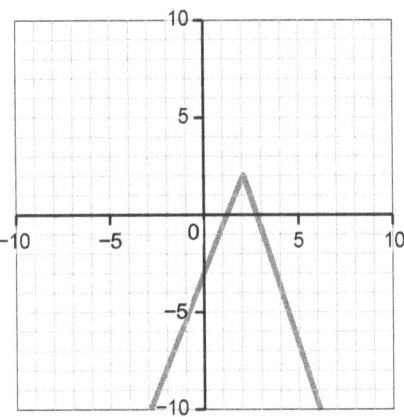

6. Measurement and Geometry

Properties of Shapes

Basic Definitions

The basic figures from which many other geometric shapes are built are points, lines, and planes. A **point** is a location in a plane. It has no size or shape, but is represented by a dot. It is labeled using a capital letter.

A **line** is a one-dimensional collection of points that extends infinitely in both directions. At least two points are needed to define a line, and any points that lie on the same line are **colinear**. Lines are represented by two points, such as **A** and **B**, and the line symbol: ($\overleftrightarrow{AB}$). Two lines on the same plane will intersect unless they are **parallel**, meaning they have the same slope. Lines that intersect at a 90 degree angle are **perpendicular**.

A **line segment** has two endpoints and a finite length. The length of a segment, called the measure of the segment, is the distance from **A** to **B**. A line segment is a subset of a line, and is also denoted with two points, but with a segment symbol: ($\overline{AB}$). The **midpoint** of a line segment is the point at which the segment is divided into two equal parts. A line, segment, or plane that passes through the midpoint of a segment is called a **bisector** of the segment, since it cuts the segment into two equal segments.

A **ray** has one endpoint and extends indefinitely in one direction. It is defined by its endpoint, followed by any other point on the ray: $\overrightarrow{AB}$. It is important that the first letter represents the endpoint. A ray is sometimes called a half line.

A **plane** is a flat sheet that extends indefinitely in two directions (like an infinite sheet of paper). A plane is a two-dimensional (2D) figure. A plane can always be defined through any three noncollinear points in three-dimensional (3D) space. A plane is named using any three points that are in the plane (for example, plane **ABC**). Any points lying in the same plane are said to be **coplanar**. When two planes intersect, the intersection is a line.

Table 6.1. Basic Geometric Figures			
Term	Dimensions	Graphic	Symbol
point	zero	●	· A
line segment	one	A————B	$\overline{AB}$
ray	one	A————B→	$\overrightarrow{AB}$

Table 6.1. Basic Geometric Figures			
Term	Dimensions	Graphic	Symbol
line	one		$\overleftrightarrow{AB}$
plane	two		Plane M

Practice Question

1. Which points and lines are not contained in plane M in the diagram below?

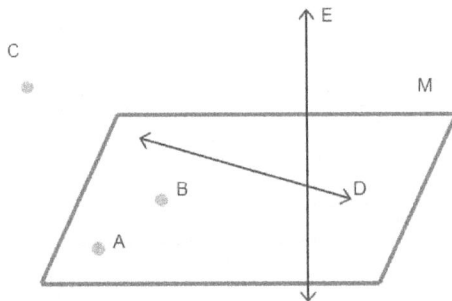

Angles

Angles are formed when two rays share a common endpoint. They are named using three letters, with the vertex point in the middle (for example $\angle ABC$, where B is the vertex). They can also be labeled with a number or named by their vertex alone (if it is clear to do so). Angles are also classified based on their angle measure. A **right angle** has a measure of exactly 90°. **Acute angles** have measures that are less than 90°, and **obtuse angles** have measures that are greater than 90°.

Any two angles that add to make 90° are called **complementary angles**. A 30° angle would be complementary to a 60° angle.

Did You Know?

Angles can be measured in degrees or radian. Use the conversion factor 1 rad = 57.3 degrees to convert between them.

Supplementary angles add up to 180°. A supplementary angle to a 60° angle would be a 120° angle; likewise, 60° is the **supplement** of 120°. The complement and supplement of any angle must always be positive. For example, a 140 degree has no complement. Angles that are next to each other and share a common ray are called **adjacent angles**. Angles that are adjacent and supplementary are called a **linear pair** of angles. Their nonshared rays form a line (thus the *linear* pair). Note that angles that are supplementary do not need to be adjacent; their measures simply need to add to 180°.

Vertical angles are formed when two lines intersect. Four angles will be formed; the vertex of each angle is at the intersection point of the lines. The vertical angles across from each other will be equal in measure. The angles adjacent to each other will be linear pairs and therefore supplementary.

122   6. Measurement and Geometry

A ray, line, or segment that divides an angle into two equal angles is called an **angle bisector**.

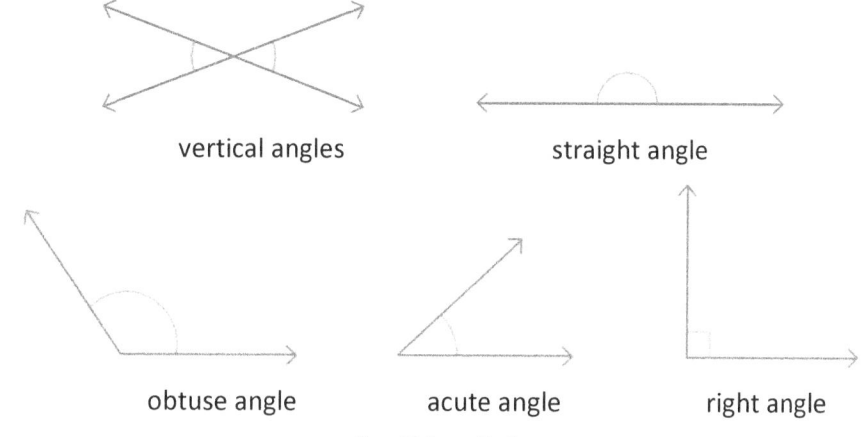

Figure 6.1. Types of Angles

Practice Question

2. How many linear pairs of angles are there in the following figure?

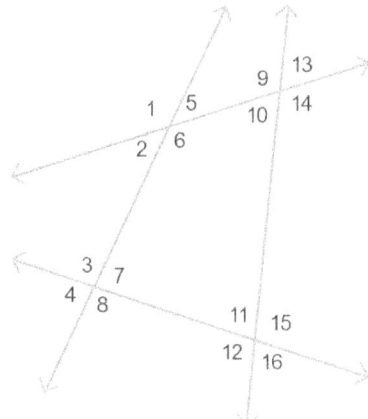

3. If angles *M* and *N* are supplementary and ∠M is 30° less than twice ∠N, what is the degree measurement of each angle?

Circles

A **circle** is the set of all the points in a plane that are the same distance from a fixed point called the **center**. The distance from the center to any point on the circle is the **radius** of the circle. The distance around the circle (the perimeter) is called the **circumference**.

The ratio of a circle's circumference to its diameter is a constant value called pi (π), an irrational number which is commonly rounded to 3.14. The formula to find a circle's circumference is $C = 2\pi r$. The formula to find the enclosed area of a circle is $A = \pi r^2$.

Circles have a number of unique parts and properties:

The **diameter** is the largest measurement across a circle. It passes through the circle's center, extending from one side of the circle to the other. The measure of the diameter is twice the measure of the radius.

A line that cuts across a circle and touches it twice is called a **secant** line. The part of a secant line that lies within a circle is called a **chord**. Two chords within a circle are of equal length if they are the same distance from the center.

> **Did You Know?**
>
> Trying to square a circle means attempting to create a square that has the same area as a circle. Because the area of a circle depends on π, which is an irrational number, this task is impossible. The phrase is often used to describe trying to do something that can't be done.

A line that touches a circle or any curve at one point is **tangent** to the circle or the curve. These lines are always exterior to the circle. A line tangent to a circle and a radius drawn to the point of tangency meet at a right angle (90°).

An **arc** is any portion of a circle between two points on the circle. The **measure** of an arc is in degrees, whereas the **length of the arc** will be in linear measurement (such as centimeters or inches). A **minor arc** is the small arc between the two points (it measures less than 180°), whereas a **major arc** is the large arc between the two points (it measures greater than 180°).

An angle with its vertex at the center of a circle is called a **central angle**. For a central angle, the measure of the arc intercepted by the sides of the angle (in degrees) is the same as the measure of the angle.

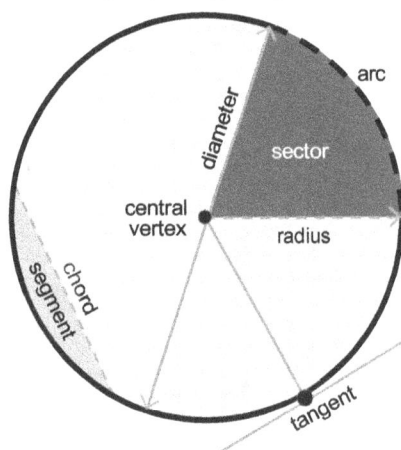

Figure 6.2. Parts of a Circle

A **sector** is the part of a circle *and* its interior that is inside the rays of a central angle (its shape is like a slice of pie).

	Area of Sector	Length of an Arc
Degrees	$A = \dfrac{\theta}{360°} \times \pi r^2$	$s = \dfrac{\theta}{360°} \times 2\pi r$
Radians	$A = \dfrac{1}{2}\pi^2\theta$	$s = r\theta$

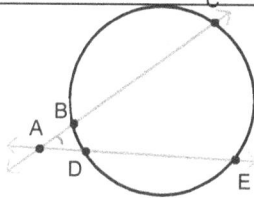

$$m\angle ACE = \frac{1}{2}(\widehat{CE} + \widehat{BD})$$

Figure 6.3. Angles Outside a Circle

An **inscribed angle** has a vertex on the circle and is formed by two chords that share that vertex point. The angle measure of an inscribed angle is one-half the angle measure of the central angle with the same endpoints on the circle.

A **circumscribed angle** has rays tangent to the circle. The angle lies outside of the circle.

Any angle outside the circle, whether formed by two tangent lines, two secant lines, or a tangent line and a secant line, is equal to half the difference of the intercepted arcs.

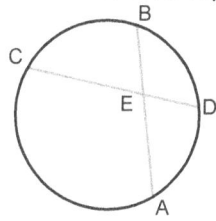

$$m\angle E = \frac{1}{2}(\widehat{AC} + \widehat{BD})$$

Figure 6.4. Intersecting Chords

Angles are formed within a circle when two chords intersect in the circle. The measure of the smaller angle formed is half the sum of the two smaller arc measures (in degrees).

Likewise, the larger angle is half the sum of the two larger arc measures.

If a chord intersects a line tangent to the circle, the angle formed by this intersection measures one half the measurement of the intercepted arc (in degrees).

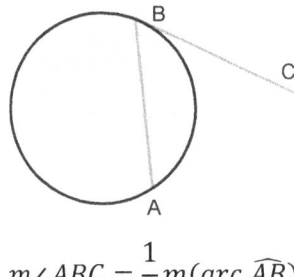

$$m\angle ABC = \frac{1}{2}m(arc\ \widehat{AB})$$

Figure 6.5. Intersecting Chord and Tangent

Practice Question

4. Find the area of the sector NHS of the circle below with center at H:

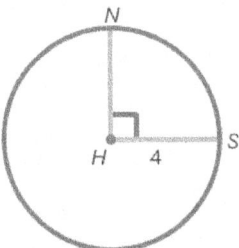

5. In the circle below with center O, the minor arc ACB measures 5 feet. What is the measurement of $m\angle AOB$?

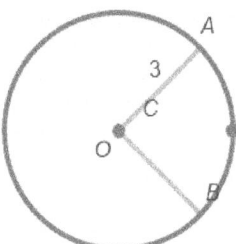

Triangles

Much of geometry is concerned with triangles as they are commonly used shapes. A good understanding of triangles allows decomposition of other shapes (specifically polygons) into triangles for study.

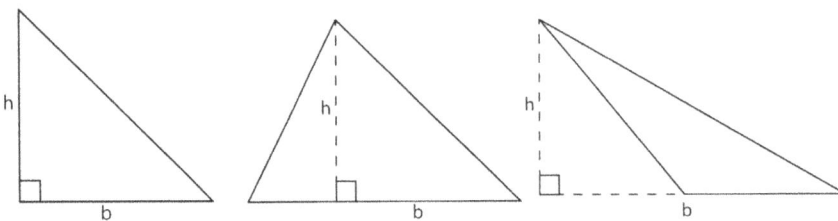

Figure 6.6. Finding the Base and Height of Triangles

Triangles have three sides, and the three interior angles always sum to 180°. The formula for the area of a triangle is $A = \frac{1}{2}bh$ or one-half the product of the base and height (or altitude) of the triangle.

Some important segments in a triangle include the angle bisector, the altitude, and the median. The **angle bisector** extends from the side opposite an angle to bisect that angle. The **altitude** is the shortest distance from a vertex of the triangle to the line containing the base side opposite that vertex. It is perpendicular to that line and can occur on the outside of the triangle. The **median** extends from an angle to bisect the opposite side.

Angel Bisector
Divides angle in half

Altitude
Shortest distance to side

Median
Divides opposite side in half

Figure 6.7. Critical Segments in a Triangle

Triangles have two "centers." The **orthocenter** is formed by the intersection of a triangle's three altitudes. The **centroid** is where a triangle's three medians meet.

Triangles can be classified in two ways: by sides and by angles.

A **scalene triangle** has no equal sides or angles. An **isosceles triangle** has two equal sides and two equal angles, often called **base angles**. In an **equilateral triangle**, all three sides are equal as are all three angles. Moreover, because the sum of the angles of a triangle is always 180°, each angle of an equilateral triangle must be 60°.

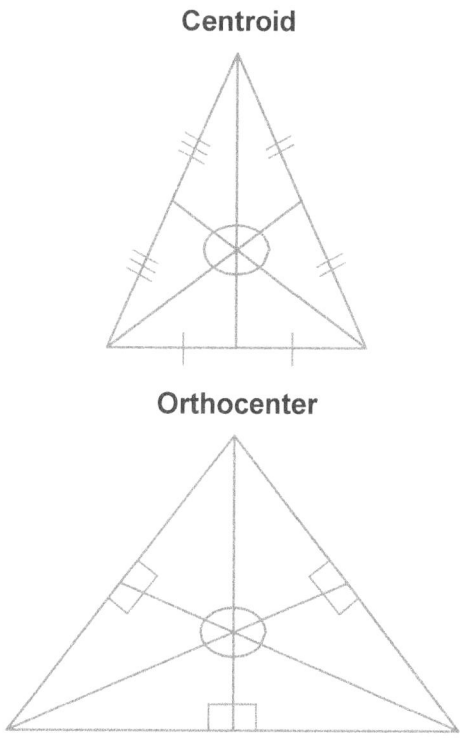

Figure 6.8. Centroid and Orthocenter of a Triangle

6. Measurement and Geometry

A **right triangle** has one right angle (90°) and two acute angles. An acute triangle has three acute angles (all angles are less than 90°). An obtuse triangle has one obtuse angle (more than 90°) and two acute angles.

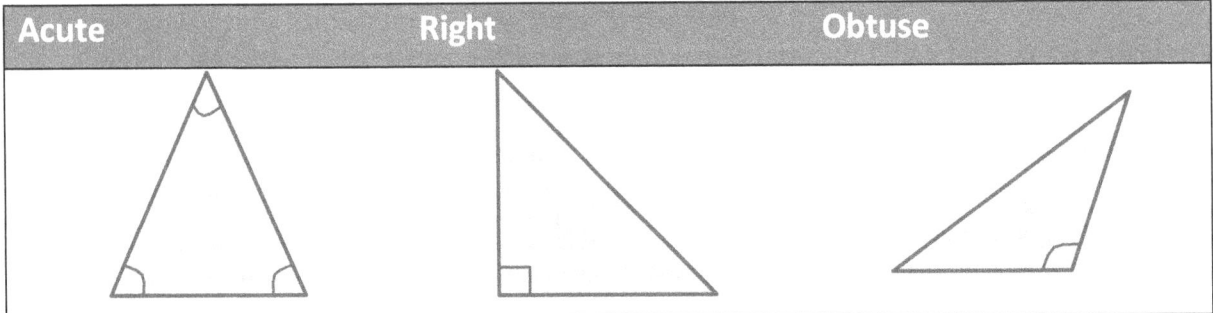

Figure 6.9. Types of Triangles

For any triangle, the side opposite the largest angle will have the longest length, while the side opposite the smallest angle will have the shortest length. The **triangle inequality theorem** states that the sum of any two sides of a triangle must be greater than the third side. If this inequality does not hold, then a triangle cannot be formed. A consequence of this theorem is the **third-side rule**: if b and c are two sides of a triangle, then the measure of the third side a must be between the sum of the other two sides and the difference of the other two sides: $c - b < a < c + b$.

> **Did You Know?**
>
> Trigonometric functions can be employed to find missing sides and angles of a triangle.

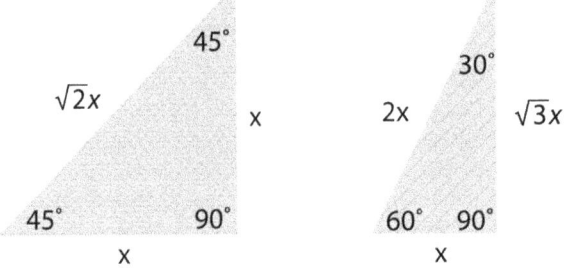

Figure 6.10. Special Right Triangles

Solving for missing angles or sides of a triangle is a common type of triangle problem. Often a right triangle will come up on its own or within another triangle. The relationship among a right triangle's sides is known as the **Pythagorean theorem**: $a^2 + b^2 = c^2$, where c is the hypotenuse and is across from the 90° angle. Right triangles with angle measurements of 90° – 45° – 45° and 90° – 60° – 30° are known as "special" right triangles and have specific relationships between their sides and angles.

Practice Question

6. What are the minimum and maximum values of x to the nearest hundredth?

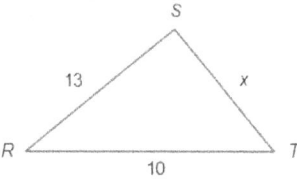

7. Given the diagram, if $XZ = 100$, $WZ = 80$, and $XU = 70$, then $WY = ?$

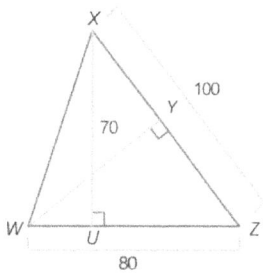

8. Examine and classify each of the following triangles:

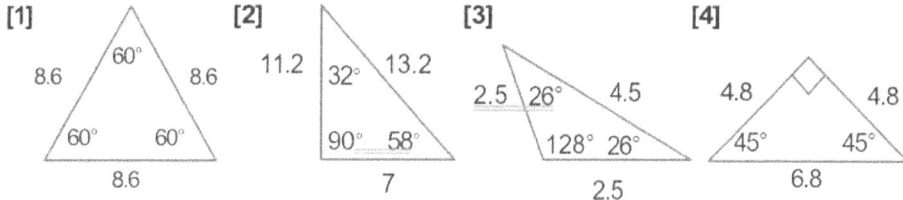

Quadrilaterals

All closed, four-sided shapes are **quadrilaterals**. The sum of all internal angles in a quadrilateral is always 360°. (Think of drawing a diagonal to create two triangles. Since each triangle contains 180°, two triangles, and therefore the quadrilateral, must contain 360°.) The **area of any quadrilateral** is $A = bh$, where b is the base and h is the height (or altitude).

> **Did You Know?**
>
> All squares are rectangles and all rectangles are parallelograms; however, not all parallelograms are rectangles and not all rectangles are squares.

A **parallelogram** is a quadrilateral with two pairs of parallel sides. A rectangle is a parallelogram with two pairs of equal sides and four right angles. A **kite** also has two pairs of equal sides, but its equal sides are consecutive. Both a **square** and a **rhombus** have four equal sides. A square has four right angles, while a rhombus has a pair of acute opposite angles and a pair of obtuse opposite angles. A **trapezoid** has exactly one pair of parallel sides.

6. Measurement and Geometry

Table 6.2 Properties of Parallelograms

Term	Shape	Properties
Parallelogram		Opposite sides are parallel. Consecutive angles are supplementary. Opposite angles are equal. Opposite sides are equal. Diagonals bisect each other.
Rectangle		All parallelogram properties hold. Diagonals are congruent *and* bisect each other. All angles are right angles.
Square		All rectangle properties hold. All four sides are equal. Diagonals bisect angles. Diagonals intersect at right angles and bisect each other.
Kite		One pair of opposite angles is equal. Two pairs of consecutive sides are equal. Diagonals meet at right angles.
Rhombus		All four sides are equal. Diagonals bisect angles. Diagonals intersect at right angles and bisect each other.
Trapezoid		One pair of sides is parallel. Bases have different lengths. Isosceles trapezoids have a pair of equal sides (and base angles).

Practice Question

9. In parallelogram $ABCD$, the measure of angle m is $m° = 260°$. What is the measure of $n°$?

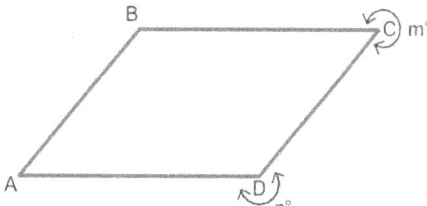

10. A rectangular section of a football field has dimensions of x and y and an area of 1000 square feet. Three additional lines drawn vertically divide the section into four smaller rectangular areas as seen in the diagram below. If all the lines shown need to be painted, calculate the total number of linear feet, in terms of x, to be painted.

Polygons

Any closed shape made up of three or more line segments is a polygon. In addition to triangles and quadrilaterals, **hexagons** and **octagons** are two common polygons.

The two polygons depicted in Figure 6.11 are **regular polygons**, meaning that they are equilateral (all sides having equal lengths) and equiangular (all angles having equal measurements). Angles inside a polygon are **interior angles**, whereas those formed by one side of the polygon and a line extending outside the polygon are **exterior angles**:

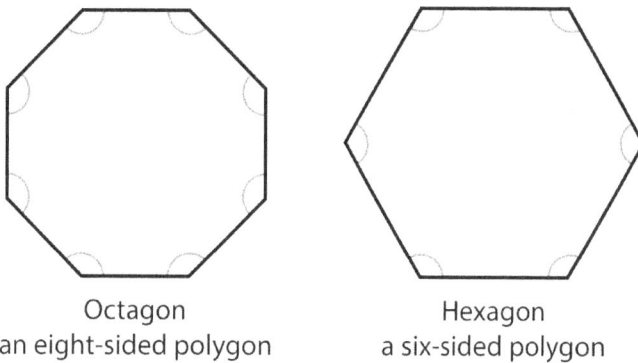

Octagon
an eight-sided polygon

Hexagon
a six-sided polygon

Figure 6.11. Common Polygons

The sum of the all the exterior angles of a polygon is always 360°. Dividing 360° by the number of a polygon's sides finds the measure of the polygon's exterior angles.

To determine the sum of a polygon's interior angles, choose one vertex and draw diagonals from that vertex to each of the other vertices, decomposing the polygon into multiple triangles. For example, an octagon has six triangles within it, and therefore the sum of the interior angles is $6 \times 180° = 1080°$. In general, the formula for finding the sum of the angles in a polygon is $sum\ of\ angles = (n - 2) \times 180°$, where n is the number of sides of the polygon.

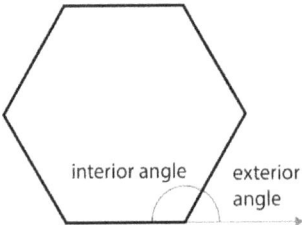

Figure 6.12. Interior and Exterior Angles

To find the measure of a single interior angle in a regular polygon, simply divide the sum of the interior angles by the number of angles (which is the same as the number of sides). So, in the octagon example, each angle is $\frac{1080}{8} = 135°$.

In general, the formula to find the measure of a regular polygon's interior angles is:

$$interior\ angle = \frac{n-2}{n} \times 180°$$

where n is the number of sides of the polygon.

To find the area of a polygon, it is helpful to know the perimeter of the polygon (p), and the apothem (a). The apothem is the shortest (perpendicular) distance from the polygon's center to one of the sides of the polygon. The formula for the area is: $area = \frac{ap}{2}$.

Figure 6.13. Apothem in a Hexagon

Finally, there is no universal way to find the perimeter of a polygon (when the side length is not given). Often, breaking the polygon down into triangles and adding the base of each triangle all the way around the polygon is the easiest way to calculate the perimeter.

Practice Question

11. What is the measure of an exterior angle and an interior angle of a regular 400-gon?

12. The circle and hexagon below both share center point T. The hexagon is entirely inscribed in the circle. The circle's radius is 5. What is the area of the shaded area?

Three-Dimensional Shapes

Three-dimensional shapes have depth in addition to width and length. **Volume** is expressed as the number of cubic units any solid can hold—that is, what it takes to fill it up. **Surface area** is the sum of the areas of the two-dimensional figures that are found on its surface. Some three-dimensional shapes also have a unique property called a slant height (ℓ), which is the distance from the base to the apex along a lateral face.

Finding the surface area of a three-dimensional solid can be made easier by using a **net**. This two-dimensional "flattened" version of a three-dimensional shape shows the component parts that comprise the surface of the solid.

Table 6.3. Three-Dimensional Shapes and Formulas		
Term	**Shape**	**Formula**
Prism		$V = bh$ $SA = 2lw + 2wh + 2lh$ $d^2 = a^2 + b^2 + c^2$	b = area of base h = height l = length w = width d = longest diagonal
Cube	s	$V = s3$ $SA = 6s^2$	s = cube edge

6. Measurement and Geometry

Table 6.3. Three-Dimensional Shapes and Formulas			
Term	Shape	Formula	
Sphere		$V = \frac{4}{3}\pi r^3$ $SA = 4\pi r^2$	r = radius
Cylinder		$V = bh = \pi r^2 h$ $SA = 2\pi r^2 + 2\pi rh$	b = area of base h = height r = radius
Cone		$V = \frac{1}{3}\pi r^2 h$ $SA = \pi r^2 + \pi rl$	r = radius h = height l = slant height
Pyramid		$V = \frac{1}{3}bh$	b = area of base h = height p = perimeter l = slant height

Practice Question

13. A sphere has a radius z. If that radius is increased by t, by how much is the surface area increased? Write the answer in terms of z and t.

14. A cube with volume 27 cubic meters is inscribed within a sphere such that all of the cube's vertices touch the sphere. What is the length of the sphere's radius?

Answer Key

1. Points A and B and line D are all on plane M. Point C is above the plane, and line E cuts through the plane and thus does not lie on plane M. The point at which line E intersects plane M is on plane M but the line as a whole is not.

2. Any two adjacent angles that are supplementary are linear pairs, so there are 16 linear pairs in the figure (∠1 and ∠5, ∠2 and ∠6, ∠5 and ∠6, ∠2 and ∠1, and so on).

3. Set up a system of equations.

$$\angle M + \angle N = 180°$$
$$\angle M = 2\angle N - 30°$$

Use substitution to solve for ∠N.

$$\angle M + \angle N = 180°$$
$$(2\angle N - 30°) + \angle N = 180°$$
$$3\angle N - 30° = 180°$$
$$3\angle N = 210°$$
$$\angle N = \mathbf{70°}$$

Solve for ∠M using the original equation.

$$\angle M + \angle N = 180°$$
$$\angle M + 70° = 180°$$
$$\angle M = \mathbf{110°}$$

4. Identify the important parts of the circle.

$$r = 4$$
$$\angle NHS = 90°$$

Plug these values into the formula for the area of a sector.

$$A = \frac{\theta}{360°} \times \pi r^2$$

$$A = \frac{90}{360} \times \pi(4)^2 = \frac{1}{4} \times 16\pi = \mathbf{4\pi}$$

5. Identify the important parts of the circle.

$$r = 3$$
$$length\ of\ ACB = 5$$

6. Measurement and Geometry

Plug these values into the formula for the length of an arc and solve for θ.

$$s = \frac{\theta}{360°} \times 2\pi r$$

$$5 = \frac{\theta}{360°} \times 2\pi(3)$$

$$\frac{5}{6\pi} = \frac{\theta}{360°}$$

$$\theta = 95.5°$$

$$m\angle AOB = 95.5°$$

6. The sum of two sides is 23 and their difference is 3. To connect the two other sides and enclose a space, x must be less than the sum and greater than the difference (that is, $3 < x < 23$). Therefore, x's minimum value to the nearest hundredth is 3.01 and its maximum value is 22.99.

7. $WZ = b_1 = 80$

$$XU = h_1 = 70$$
$$XZ = b_2 = 100$$
$$WY = h_2 = ?$$

The given values can be used to write two equation for the area of $\triangle WXZ$ with two sets of bases and heights.

$$A = \frac{1}{2}bh$$

$$A_1 = \frac{1}{2}(80)(70) = 2800$$

$$A_2 = \frac{1}{2}(100)(h_2)$$

Set the two equations equal to each other and solve for WY.

$$2800 = \frac{1}{2}(100)(h_2)$$

$$h_2 = 56$$

$$WY = 56$$

8. Triangle 1 is an equilateral triangle (all 3 sides are equal, and all 3 angles are equal)

Triangle 2 is a scalene, right triangle (all 3 sides are different, and there is a 90° angle)

Triangle 3 is an obtuse, isosceles triangle (there are 2 equal sides and, consequently, 2 equal angles)

Triangle 4 is a right, isosceles triangle (there are 2 equal sides and a 90° angle)

9. Find $\angle C$ using the fact that the sum of $\angle C$ and m is 360°.

$$260° + m\angle C = 360°$$

$$m\angle C = 100°$$

Solve for ∠D using the fact that consecutive interior angles in a quadrilateral are supplementary.

$$m\angle C + m\angle D = 180°$$
$$100° + m\angle D = 180°$$
$$m\angle D = 80°$$

Solve for n by subtracting $m\angle D$ from 360°.

$$m\angle D + n = 360°$$
$$\boldsymbol{n = 280°}$$

10. Find equations for the area of the field and length of the lines to be painted (L) in terms of x and y.

$$A = 1000 = xy$$
$$L = 2x + 5y$$

Substitute to find L in terms of x.

$$y = \frac{1000}{x}$$
$$L = 2x + 5y$$
$$L = 2x + 5\left(\frac{1000}{x}\right)$$
$$\boldsymbol{L = 2x + \frac{5000}{x}}$$

11. The sum of the exterior angles is 360°. Dividing this sum by 400 gives $\frac{360°}{400} = \boldsymbol{0.9°}$. Since an interior angle is supplementary to an exterior angle, all the interior angles have measure $180 - 0.9 = \boldsymbol{179.1°}$. Alternately, using the formula for calculating the interior angle gives the same result:

$$interior\ angle = \frac{400 - 2}{400} \times 180° = 179.1°$$

12. The area of the shaded region will be the area of the circle minus the area of the hexagon. Use the radius to find the area of the circle.

$$A_C = \pi r^2 = \pi(5)^2 = 25\pi$$

To find the area of the hexagon, draw a right triangle from the vertex, and use special right triangles to find the hexagon's apothem. Then, use the apothem to calculate the area.

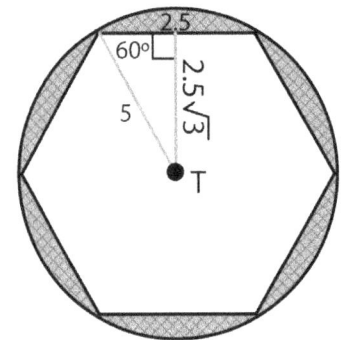

$$a = 2.5\sqrt{3}$$

$$A_H = \frac{ap}{2} = \frac{(2.5\sqrt{3})(30)}{2} = 64.95$$

Subtract the area of the hexagon from the circle to find the area of the shaded region.

$$x = A_C - A_H$$

$$x = 25\pi - 64.95$$

$$\mathbf{x \approx 13.59}$$

13. Write the equation for the area of the original sphere.

$$SA_1 = 4\pi z^2$$

Write the equation for the area of the new sphere.

$$SA_2 = 4\pi(z + t)^2$$

$$4\pi(z^2 + 2zt + t^2)$$

$$4\pi z^2 + 8\pi zt + 4\pi t^2$$

To find the difference between the two, subtract the original from the increased surface area:

$$A_2 - A_1 = 4\pi z^2 + 8\pi zt + 4\pi t^2 - 4\pi z^2$$

$$\mathbf{4\pi t^2 + 8\pi zt}$$

14. Since the cube's volume is 27, each side length is equal to $\sqrt[3]{27} = 3$. The long diagonal distance from one of the cube's vertices to its opposite vertex will provide the sphere's diameter:

$$d = \sqrt{3^2 + 3^2 + 3^2} = \sqrt{27} = 5.2$$

Half of this length is the radius, which is **2.6 meters**.

7. Data Analysis, Probability, and Statistics

Describing Sets of Data

Measures of Central Tendency

Measures of central tendency help identify the center, or most typical, value within a data set. There are three such central tendencies that describe the "center" of the data in different ways. The **mean** is the arithmetic average and is found by dividing the sum of all measurements by the number of measurements. The mean of a population is written as µ and the mean of a sample is written as x.

The data points are represented by x's with subscripts; the sum is denoted using the Greek letter sigma ($\sum$); N is the number of data points in the entire population; and n is the number of data points in a sample set.

> **Did You Know?**
>
> When the same value is added to each term in a set, the mean increases by that value and the standard deviation is unchanged.
>
> When each term in a set is multiplied by the same value, both the mean and standard deviation will also be multiplied by that value.

$$population\ mean = \mu = \frac{x_1 + x_2 + \cdots xN}{N} = \sum \frac{x}{N}$$
$$sample\ mean = \bar{x} = \frac{x_1 + x_2 + \cdots xn}{n} = \sum \frac{x}{n}$$

The **median** divides the measurements into two equal halves. The median is the measurement right in the middle of an odd set of measurements or the average of the two middle numbers in an even data set. When calculating the median, it is important to order the data values from least to greatest before attempting to locate the middle value. The **mode** is simply the measurement that occurs most often. There can be many modes in a data set, or no mode. Since measures of central tendency describe a *center* of the data, all three of these measures will be between the lowest and highest data values (inclusive).

Unusually large or small values, called **outliers**, will affect the mean of a sample more than the mode. If there is a high outlier, the mean will be greater than the median; if there is a low outlier, the mean will be lower than the median. When outliers are present, the median is a better measure of the data's center than the mean because the median will be closer to the terms in the data set.

Practice Question

1. What is the mean of the following data set? {1000, 0.1, 10, 1}

2. What is the median of the following data set? {1000, 10, 1, 0.1}

3. Josey has an average of 81 on four equally weighted tests she has taken in her statistics class. She wants to determine what grade she must receive on her fifth test so that her mean is 83, which will give her a B in the course, but she does not remember her other scores. What grade must she receive on her fifth test?

Measures of Variation

The values in a data set can be very close together (close to the mean), or very spread out. This is called the **spread** or **dispersion** of the data. There are a few **measures of variation** (or **measures of dispersion**) that quantify the spread within a data set. **Range** is the difference between the largest and smallest data points in a set:

$$R = largest\ data\ point - smallest\ data\ point$$

Notice range depends on only two data points (the two extremes). Sometimes these data points are outliers; regardless, for a large data set, relying on only two data points is not an exact tool.

The understanding of the data set can be improved by calculating **quartiles**. To calculate quartiles, first arrange the data in ascending order and find the set's median (also called quartile 2 or Q2). Then find the median of the lower half of the data, called quartile 1 (Q1), and the median of the upper half of the data, called quartile 3 (Q3). These three points divide the data into four equal groups of data (thus the word *quartile*). Each quartile contains 25% of the data.

Interquartile range (IQR) provides a more reliable range that is not as affected by extremes. IQR is the difference between the third quartile data point and the first quartile data point and gives the spread of the middle 50% of the data:

$$IQR = Q_3 - Q_1$$

The **variance** of a data set is simply the square of the standard variation:

$$V = \sigma^2 = \frac{1}{N}\sum_{i=1}^{N}(x_i - \mu)^2$$

Variance measures how narrowly or widely the data points are distributed. A variance of zero means every data point is the same; a large variance means the data is widely spread out.

Practice Question

4. What are the range and interquartile range of the following set?
{3, 9, 49, 64, 81, 100, 121, 144, 169}

Graphs, Charts, and Tables

Pie Charts

A pie chart simply states the proportion of each category within the whole. To construct a pie chart, the categories of a data set must be determined. The frequency of each category must be found and that frequency converted to a percent of the total. To draw the pie chart, determine the angle of each slice by multiplying the percentage by 360°.

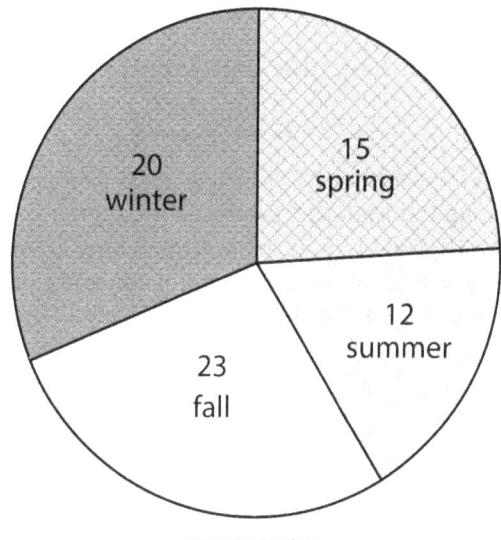

Figure 7.1. Pie Chart

Practice Question

5. A firm is screening applicants for a job by education-level attainment. There are 125 individuals in the pool: 5 have a doctorate, 20 have a master's degree, 40 have a bachelor's degree, 30 have an associate degree, and 30 have a high school degree. Construct a pie chart showing the highest level of education attained by the applicants.

Scatter Plots

A scatter plot is displayed in the first quadrant of the xy-plane where all numbers are positive. Data points are plotted as ordered pairs, with one variable along the horizontal axis and the other along the vertical axis. Scatter plots can show if there is a correlation between two variables. There is a **positive correlation** (expressed as a positive slope) if increasing one variable appears to result in an increase in the other variable. A **negative correlation** (expressed as a negative slope) occurs when an increase in one variable causes a decrease in the other. If the scatter plot shows no discernible pattern, then there is no correlation (a zero, mixed, or indiscernible slope).

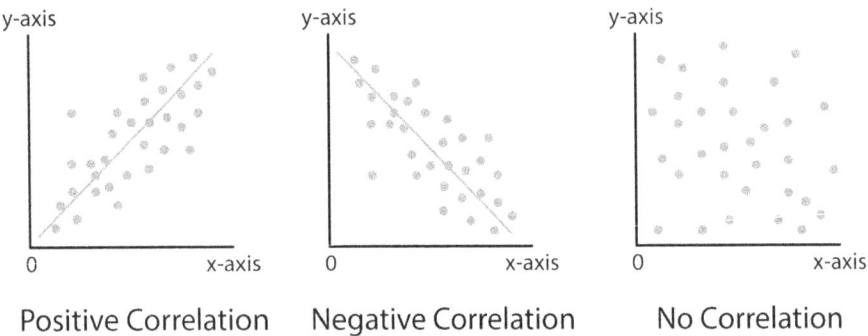

Figure 7.2. Scatter Plots and Correlation

Calculators or other software can be used to find the linear regression equation, which describes the general shape of the data. Graphing this equation produces the regression line, or line of best fit. The equation's **correlation coefficient** (r) can be used to determine how closely the equation fits the data. The value of r is between −1 and 1. The closer r is to 1 (if the line has a positive slope) or −1 (if the line has a negative slope), the better the regression line fits the data. The closer the r value is to 0, the weaker the correlation between the line and the data. Generally, if the absolute value of the correlation coefficient is 0.8 or higher, then it is considered to be a strong correlation, while an $|r|$ value of less than 0.5 is considered a weak correlation.

To determine which curve is the "best fit" for a set of data, residuals are calculated. The calculator automatically calculates and saves these values to a list called RESID. These values are all the differences between the actual y-value of data points and the y-value calculated by the best-fit line or curve for that x-value. These values can be plotted on an xy-plane to produce a **residual plot**. The residual plot helps determine if a line is the best model for the data. Residual points that are randomly dispersed above and below the horizontal indicate that a linear model is appropriate, while a u shape or upside-down u shape indicate a nonlinear model would be more appropriate.

Once a best-fit line is established, it can be used to estimate output values given an input value within the domain of the data. For a short extension outside that domain, reasonable predictions may be possible. However, the further from the domain of the data the line is extended, the greater the reduction in the accuracy of the prediction.

Figure 7.3. Residual Plots

Did You Know?

A graphing calculator can provide the regression line, r value, and residuals list.

It is important to note here that just because two variables have a strong positive or negative correlation, it cannot necessarily be inferred that those two quantities have a *causal* relationship—that is, that one variable changing *causes* the other quantity to change. There are often other factors that play into their relationship. For example, a positive correlation can be found between the number of ice cream sales and the number of shark attacks at a beach. It would be incorrect to say that selling more ice cream causes an increase in shark attacks. It is much more likely that on hot days more ice cream is sold, and many more people are swimming, so one of them is more likely to get attacked by a shark. Confusing correlation and causation is one of the most common statistical errors people make.

Practice Question

6. Based on the scatter plot on the following page, where the x-axis represents hours spent studying per week and the y-axis represents the average percent grade on exams during the school year, is there a correlation between the amount of studying for a test and test results?

Line Graphs

Line graphs are used to display a relationship between two variables, such as change over time. Like scatter plots, line graphs exist in quadrant I of the xy-plane. Line graphs are constructed by graphing each point and connecting each point to the next consecutive point by a line. To create a line graph, it may be necessary to consolidate data into single bivariate data points. Thus, a line graph is a function,

7. Data Analysis, Probability, and Statistics

with each *x*-value having exactly one *y*-value, whereas a scatter plot may have multiple *y*-values for one *x*-value.

Figure 7.4. Line Graph

Practice Question

7. Create a line graph based on the following survey values, where the first column represents an individual's age and the other represents that individual's reported happiness level on a 20-point scale (0 being the least happy that person has been and 20 being the happiest). Then interpret the resulting graph to determine whether the following statement is true or false: *On average, middle-aged people are less happy than young or older people are.*

Age	Happiness	Age (continued)	Happiness (continued)
12	16	33	10
13	15	44	8
20	18	55	10
15	12	80	10
40	5	15	13
17	17	40	8
18	18	17	15
19	15	18	17
42	7	19	20
70	17	22	16
45	10	27	15
60	12	36	9
63	15	33	10
22	14	44	6
27	15		

Bar Graphs

Bar graphs compare differences between categories or changes over a time. The data is grouped into categories or ranges and represented by rectangles. A bar graph's rectangles can be vertical or horizontal, depending on whether the dependent variable is placed on the x- or y-axis. Instead of the xy-plane, however, one axis is made up of categories (or ranges) instead of a numeric scale. Bar graphs are useful because the differences between categories are easy to see: the height or length of each bar shows the value for each category.

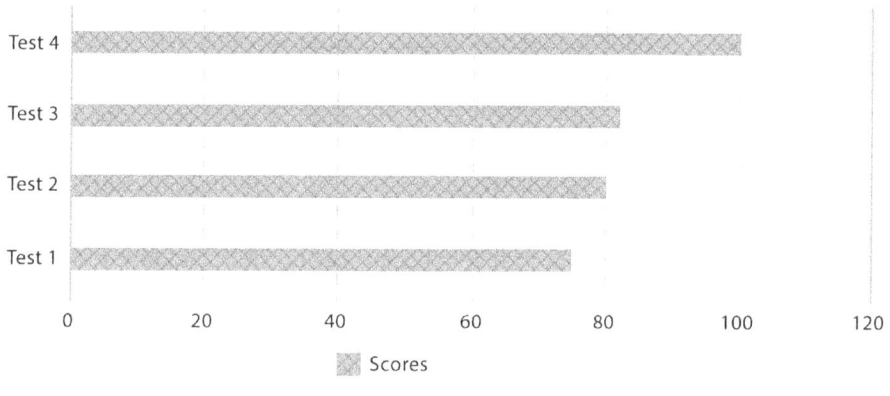

Figure 7.5. Bar Graph

Practice Question

8. A company X had a profit of $10,000 in 2010, $12,000 in 2011, $15,600 in 2012, and $20,280 in 2013. Create a bar graph displaying the profit from each of these four years.

Stem-and-Leaf Plots

Stem-and-leaf plots are ways of organizing large amounts of data by grouping it into classes. All data points are broken into two parts: a stem and a leaf. For instance, the number 512 might be broken into a stem of 5 and a leaf of 12. All data in the 500 range would appear in the same row (this group of data is a class). Usually a simple key is provided to explain how the data is being represented. For instance, $5|12 = 512$ would show that the stems are representing hundreds. The advantage of this display is that it shows general density and shape of the data in a compact display, yet all original data points are preserved and available. It is also easy to find medians and quartiles from this display.

Stem	Leaf
0	5
1	6, 7
2	8, 3, 6
3	4, 5, 9, 5, 5, 8, 5
4	7, 7, 7, 8
5	5, 4

Figure 7.6. Stem-and-Leaf Plot

Practice Question

9. The table gives the weights of wrestlers (in pounds) for a certain competition. What is the mean, median, and IQR of the data?

2	05, 22, 53, 40
3	07, 22, 29, 45, 89, 96, 98
4	10, 25, 34
6	21

Frequency Tables and Histograms

The frequency of a particular data point is the number of times that data point occurs. Constructing a frequency table requires that the data or data classes be arranged in ascending order in one column and the frequency in another column.

A histogram is a graphical representation of a frequency table used to compare frequencies. A histogram is constructed in quadrant I of the xy-plane, with data in each equal-width class presented as a bar and the height of each bar representing the frequency of that class. Unlike bar graphs, histograms cannot have gaps between bars. A histogram is used to determine the distribution of data among the classes.

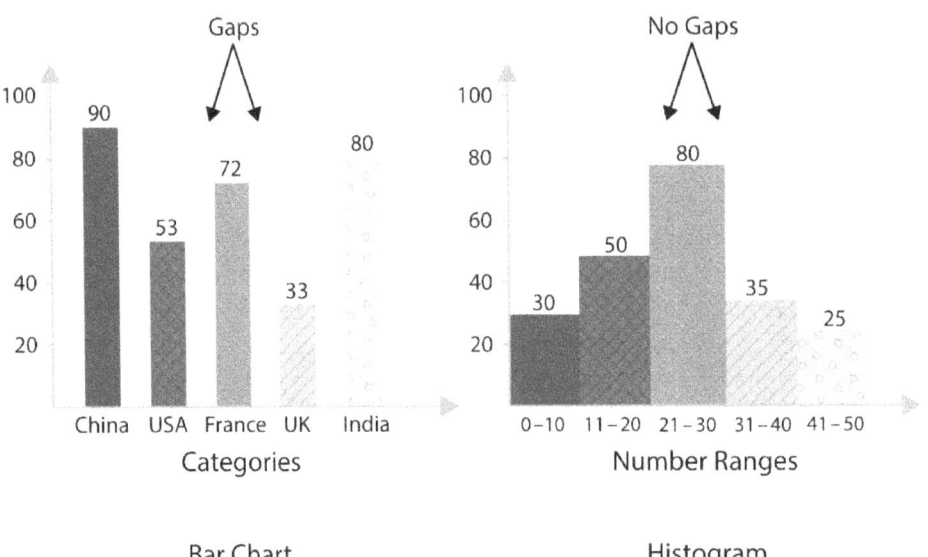

Figure 7.7. Bar Chart vs. Histogram

Histograms can be symmetrical, skewed left or right, or multimodal (data spread around). Note that **skewed left** means the peak of the data is on the *right*, with a tail to the left, while **skewed right** means the peak is on the *left*, with a tail to the right. This seems counterintuitive to many; the "left" or "right" always refers to the tail of the data. This is because a long tail to the right, for example, means there are high outlier values that are skewing the data to the right.

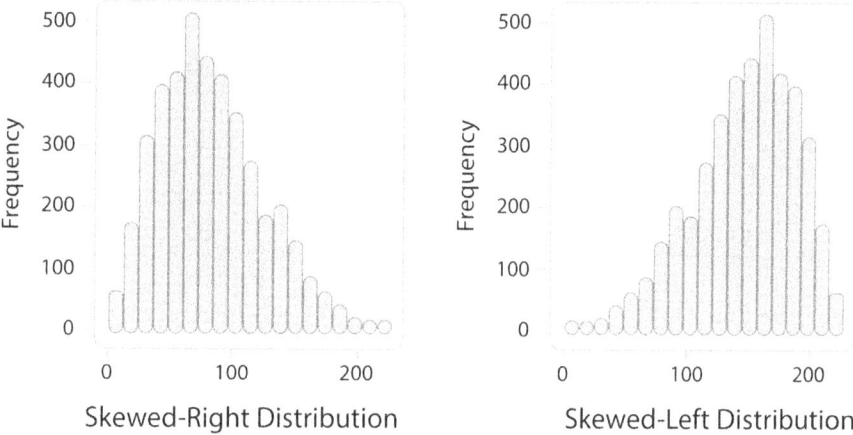

Figure 7.8. Histograms

A **two-way frequency table** compares **categorical data** (data in more than one category) of two related variables (bivariate data). Two-way frequency tables are also called **contingency tables** and are often used to analyze survey results. One category is displayed along the top of the table and the other category down along the side. Rows and columns are added and the sums appear at the end of the row or column. The sum of all the row data must equal the sum of all the column data.

From a two-way frequency table, the **joint relative frequency** of a particular category can be calculated by taking the number in the row and column of the categories in question and dividing by the total number surveyed. This gives the percent of the total in that particular category. Sometimes the **conditional relative frequency** is of interest. In this case, calculate the relative frequency confined to a single row or column.

Students by Grade and Gender					
	9th Grade	10th Grade	11th Grade	12th Grade	Total
Male	57	63	75	61	256
Female	54	42	71	60	227
Total	111	105	146	121	483

Figure 7.9. Two-Way Frequency Table

Practice Question

10. Cineflix movie theater polled its moviegoers on a weeknight to determine their favorite type of movie. The results are in the two-way frequency table below.

Moviegoers	Comedy	Action	Horror	Totals
Male	15	24	21	60
Female	8	18	17	43
Totals	23	42	38	103

Determine whether each of the following statements is true or false.

A) Action films are the most popular type of movie

B) About 1 in 5 moviegoers prefers comedy films

C) Men choose the horror genre more frequently than women do

11. A café owner tracked the number of customers he had over a twelve-hour period in the following frequency table. Display the data in a histogram and determine what kind of distribution there is in the data.

Time	Number of Customers
6 a.m. – 8 a.m.	5
8 a.m. – 9 a.m.	6
9 a.m. – 10 a.m.	5
10 a.m. – 12 p.m.	23
12 p.m. – 2 p.m.	24
2 p.m. – 4 p.m.	9
4 p.m. – 6 p.m.	4

Probability

Probability describes how likely something is to happen. In probability, an **event** is the single result of a trial, and an **outcome** is a possible event that results from a trial. The collection of all possible outcomes for a particular trial is called the **sample space**. For example, when rolling a die, the sample space is the numbers 1 – 6. Rolling a single number, such as 4, would be a single event.

Counting Principles

Counting principles are methods used to find the number of possible outcomes for a given situation. The **fundamental counting principle** states that, for a series of independent events, the number of outcomes can be found by multiplying the number of possible outcomes for each event. For example, if a die is rolled (6 possible outcomes) and a coin is tossed (2 possible outcomes), there are $6 \times 2 = 12$ total possible outcomes.

Combinations and permutations describe how many ways a number of objects taken from a group can be arranged. The number of objects in the group is written n, and the number of objects to be arranged is represented by r (or k). In a **combination**, the order of the selections does not matter because every available slot to be filled is the same. Examples of combinations include:

- Picking 3 people from a group of 12 to form a committee (220 possible committees)
- Picking 3 pizza toppings from 10 options (120 possible pizzas)

In a **permutation**, the order of the selection matters, meaning each available slot is different. Examples of permutations include:

- Handing out gold, silver, and bronze medals in a race with 100 participants (970,200 possible combinations)
- Selecting a president, vice-president, secretary, and treasurer from among a committee of 12 people (11,880 possible combinations)

The formulas for the both calculations are similar. The only difference—the $r!$ in the denominator of a combination—accounts for redundant outcomes. Note that both permutations and combinations can be written in several different shortened notations.

Permutation: $P(n, r) = nPr = \frac{n!}{(n-r)!}$

Combination: $C(n, r) = nCr = \binom{n}{r} = \frac{n!}{(n-r)!r!}$

Practice Question

12. A personal assistant is struggling to pick a shirt, tie, and cufflink set that go together. If his client has 70 shirts, 2 ties, and 5 cufflinks, how many possible combinations does he have to consider?

13. If there are 20 applicants for 3 open positions, in how many different ways can a team of 3 be hired?

14. Calculate the number of unique permutations that can be made with five of the letters in the word *pickle*.

15. Find the number of permutations that can be made out of all the letters in the word *cheese*.

Probability of a Single Event

The probability of a single event occurring is the number of outcomes in which that event occurs (called **favorable events**) divided by the number of items in the sample space (total possible outcomes):

$$P \text{ (an event)} = \frac{\text{number of favorable outcomes}}{\text{total number of possible outcomes}}$$

The probability of any event occurring will always be a fraction or decimal between 0 and 1. It may also be expressed as a percent. An event with 0 probability will never occur and an event with a probability of 1 is certain to occur. The probability of an event not occurring is referred to as that event's

complement. The sum of an event's probability and the probability of that event's complement will always be 1.

Practice Question

16. What is the probability that an even number results when a six-sided die is rolled? What is the probability the die lands on 5?

17. Only 20 tickets were issued in a raffle. If someone were to buy 6 tickets, what is the probability that person would not win the raffle?

18. A bag contains 26 tiles representing the 26 letters of the English alphabet. If 3 tiles are drawn from the bag without replacement, what is the probability that all 3 will be consonants?

Answer Key

1. Use the equation to find the mean of a sample:

$$\frac{1000 + 0.1 + 10 + 1}{4} = 252.78$$

2. Since there are an even number of data points in the set, the median will be the mean of the two middle numbers. Order the numbers from least to greatest: 0.1, 1, 10, and 1000. The two middle numbers are 1 and 10, and their mean is:

$$\frac{1 + 10}{2} = 5.5$$

3. Even though Josey does not know her test scores, she knows her average. Therefore, it can be assumed that each test score was 81, since four scores of 81 would average to 81. To find the score, x, that she needs use the equation for the mean of a sample:

$$\frac{4(81) + x}{5} = 83$$

$$324 + x = 415$$

$$x = 91$$

4. Use the equation for range.

$$R = largest\ point - smallest\ point = 169 - 3 = 166$$

Place the terms in numerical order and identify Q1, Q2, and Q3.

$$3$$
$$9$$
$$\rightarrow Q1 = \frac{49 + 9}{2} = 29$$
$$49$$
$$64$$
$$81$$
$$\rightarrow Q2$$
$$100$$
$$121$$
$$\rightarrow Q3 = \frac{121 + 144}{2} = 132.5$$
$$144$$
$$169$$

Find the IQR by subtracting Q1 from Q3.

$$IQR = Q3 - Q1 = 132.5 - 29 = \mathbf{103.5}$$

5. Create a frequency table to find the percentages and angle measurement for each category.

Category	Frequency	Percent	Angle Measurement
High School	30	24%	86.4
Associate	30	24%	86.4
Bachelor's	40	32%	115.2
Master's	20	16%	57.6

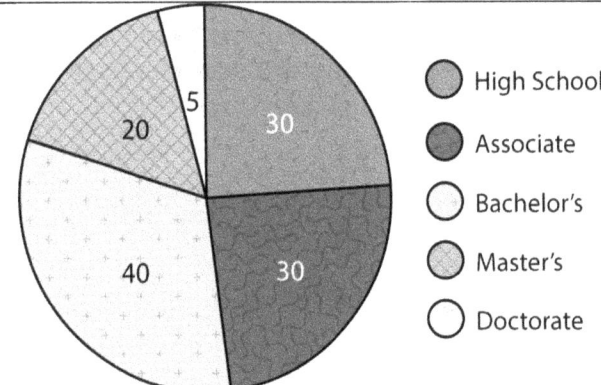

6. There is a somewhat weak positive correlation. As the number of hours spent studying increases, the average percent grade also generally increases.

7. To construct a line graph, the data must be ordered into consolidated categories by averaging the data of people who have the same age so that the data is one-to-one.

For example, there are 2 twenty- two-year-olds who are reporting. Their average happiness level is 15. When all the data has been consolidated and ordered from least to greatest, the table and graph below can be presented.

Age	Happiness
12	16
13	15
15	12.5
17	16
18	17.5
19	17.5
20	18
22	15

27	15
33	10
36	10.5
40	6.5
42	7
44	7
45	10
55	10
60	12
63	15
70	17
80	10

Average Happiness Rating Versus Age

The statement that, on average, middle-aged people are less happy than young or older people appears to be true.

According to the graph, people in their thirties, forties, and fifties are less happy than people in their teens, twenties, sixties, and seventies.

8. Place years on the independent axis, and profit on the dependent axis, and then draw a box showing the profit for each year.

9. Find the mean using the equation for the population mean.

$$\mu = \sum \frac{x}{N} = \frac{5281}{15} = 353.1 \text{ lbs}$$

Find the median and IQR by counting the leaves and identifying Q1, Q2, and Q3.

$$Q1 = 253$$
$$Q2 = 345$$
$$Q3 = 410$$
$$IQR = 410 - 253 = 157$$

The median is 345 lbs. The IQR is 157 lbs.

10. A) True. More people (42) chose action movies than comedy (23) or horror (38).

B) True. Find the ratio of total number of people who prefer comedy to total number of people. $\frac{23}{103} = 0.22$; 1 in 5 is 20%, so 22% is about the same.

C) False. The percentage of men who choose horror is less than the percentage of women who do.

$$part = \text{number of men who prefer horror} = 21$$
$$whole = \text{number of men surveyed} = 60$$
$$percent = \frac{part}{whole} = \frac{21}{60} = 0.35 = 35\%$$
$$part = \text{number of women who prefer horror} = 17$$
$$whole = \text{number of women surveyed} = 43$$
$$percent = \frac{part}{whole} = \frac{17}{43} = 0.40 = 40\%$$

11. Since time is the independent variable, it is on the x-axis and the number of customers is on the y-axis. For the histogram to correctly display data continuously, categories on the x-axis must be equal 2-hour segments. The 8 a.m.–9 a.m. and 9 a.m.–10 a.m. categories must be combined for a total of 11 customers in that time period.

Although not perfectly symmetrical, the amount of customers peaks in the middle and is therefore considered symmetrical.

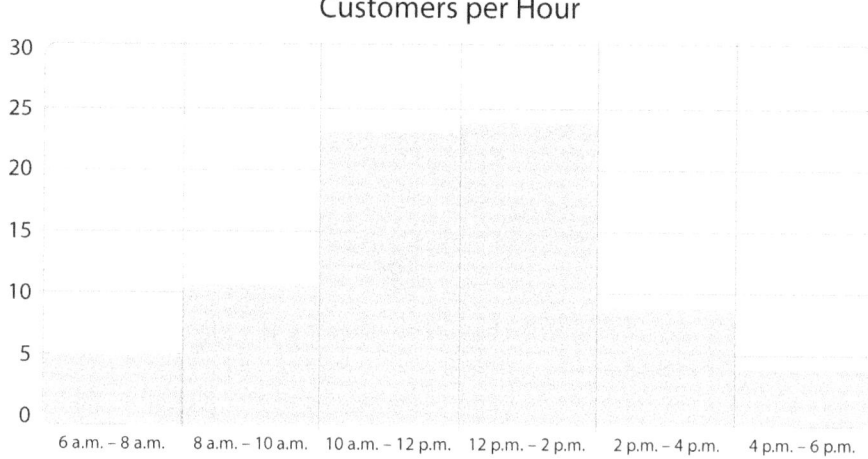

12. Multiply the number of outcomes for each individual event:

$$(70)(2)(5) = \textbf{700 outfits}$$

13. The order of the items doesn't matter, so use the formula for combinations:

$$C(n, r) = \frac{n!}{(n-r)!\,r!}$$

$$C(20, 3) = \frac{20!}{(20-3)!\,3!} = \frac{20!}{(17!\,3!)} = \frac{(20)(19)(18)}{3!} = \textbf{1140 possible teams}$$

14. To find the number of unique permutations of 5 letters in pickle, use the permutation formula:

$$P(n, r) = \frac{n!}{(n-r)!}$$

$$P(6, 5) = \frac{6!}{(6-5)!} = \frac{720}{1} = \textbf{720}$$

15. The letter e repeats 3 times in the word *cheese*, meaning some permutations of the 6 letters will be indistinguishable from others.

The number of permutations must be divided by the number of ways the three e's can be arranged to account for these redundant outcomes:

$$\text{total number of permutations} = \frac{\text{number of ways of arranging 6 letters}}{\text{number of ways of arranging 3 letters}}$$

$$\frac{6!}{3!} = 6 \times 5 \times 4 = \textbf{120}$$

7. Data Analysis, Probability, and Statistics

16. The probability of rolling an event happening can be found using the following fraction:

$$P(rolling\ even) = \frac{number\ of\ favorable\ outcomes}{total\ number\ of\ possible\ outcomes}$$

There are 3 even numbers on a die: 2, 4, and 6. Therefore, the number of favorable outcomes is 3, while the total number of possible outcomes is 6. This probability can be expressed as a fraction and simplified:

$$\frac{3}{6} = \frac{1}{2}$$

To find the probability of rolling a 5, consider how many sides of the die have a 5 on it. Because there is only 1 favorable outcome, the probability can be found using the following:

$$P(rolling\ 5) = \frac{number\ of\ favorable\ outcomes}{total\ number\ of\ possible\ outcomes} = \frac{1}{6}$$

17. To find the probability of not winning the raffle, the amount of tickets left must be found. This is done by subtracting the amount of tickets bought from the total number of tickets: $20 - 6 = 14$. Therefore, the remaining 14 tickets have a probability of winning, which can be shown through the following:

$$P(not\ winning) = \frac{number\ of\ favorable\ outcomes}{total\ number\ of\ possible\ outcomes} = \frac{14}{20} = \frac{7}{10}$$

18. Find the probability using the formula:

$$P = \frac{number\ of\ favorable\ outcomes}{total\ number\ of\ possible\ outcomes}$$

$$\frac{number\ of\ 3\ consonant\ combinations}{number\ of\ 3\ tile\ combinations} = \frac{\binom{21}{3}}{\binom{26}{3}}$$

First we solve the numerator $\binom{21}{3}$ with the combination formula:

$$C(n,r) = \frac{n!}{(n-r)!\,r!}$$

$$\frac{21!}{(21-3)!\,3!} = \frac{21!}{3!\,18!}$$

The factorial 18! Will cancel out from both the numerator and denominator leaving:

$$\frac{21 \times 20 \times 19}{3 \times 2 \times 1} = 1330$$

Next, we solve the denominator $\binom{26}{3}$ the same way.

$$\frac{26!}{(26-3)!\,3!} = \frac{26!}{3!\,23!}$$

The factorial 23! Cancels out, leaving:

$$\frac{26 \times 25 \times 24}{3 \times 2 \times 1} = 2600$$

Now, solve the problem to find probability.

$$\frac{1330}{2600} = 0.51 = \mathbf{51\%}$$

8. Scientific Practices

Scientific Inquiry

Science is defined simply as the study of the natural world. Although there are many disciplines within science, all scientific understanding is reached using a systematic gathering of observations and evidence. The investigations scientists use to gather this information can be descriptive, comparative, or experimental in nature. Once scientists conduct investigations using a range of methods and technology, they can begin to form explanations about natural phenomena. Over time, these explanations are collected in the general body of scientific knowledge and are used to form laws, or generalizations of the natural world, and theories, or explanations of laws.

Scientific inquiry is defined as the myriad ways in which scientists conduct their studies and form explanations. There is no one set path that all scientists must follow, but the **scientific method** provides a general framework for conducting scientific inquiry. The scientific method has five steps:

- Form a question.

  Observations about the natural world lead to questions about how or why the observed actions occur. The scientist should also do **research** on current knowledge of the topic in the scientific community. Together, observations and research can be used to create a question to be answered.

- Form a hypothesis.

  A proposed explanation of natural phenomena is also known as a **hypothesis**. A hypothesis consists of more than an educated guess; it is a testable proposition that scientists use as the basis for an investigation. If a proposition cannot be tested scientifically, it is not a hypothesis.

- Conduct an experiment.

  The next step is to design and conduct an experiment that tests the hypothesis. A scientific investigation contains an **experimental variable**, which scientists can manipulate during the course of the investigation, and **experimental controls**, which are variables that are kept constant.

- Collect and analyze data.

  Data should be collected during the experiment. This data can then be analyzed to look for statistically valid relationships and patterns.

- Draw a conclusion.

  Finally, experimental data is used to draw conclusions about the hypothesis. The hypothesis may be proven false, or the data may support the hypothesis.

Practice Question

1. Which of the following best defines a hypothesis?
    A) an educated guess
    B) a study of the natural world
    C) an explanation of natural phenomena
    D) a testable proposed scientific explanation

Designing Experiments

Scientists use a rigorous set of rules to design experiments. The protocols of **experimental design** are meant to ensure that scientists are actually testing what they set out to test. A well-designed experiment will measure the impact of a single factor on a system, thus allowing the experimenter to draw conclusions about that factor.

Every experiment includes variables—the factors or treatments that may affect the outcome of the experiment. **Independent variables** are controlled by the experimenter. They are usually the factors the experimenter has hypothesized will have an effect on the system. Often, a design will include a treatment group and a control group, which does not receive the treatment. The **dependent variables** are factors that are influenced by the independent variable.

For example, in an experiment investigating which type of fertilizer has the greatest effect on plant growth, the independent variable is the type of fertilizer used. The scientist is controlling, or manipulating, the type of fertilizer. The dependent variable is plant growth because the amount of plant growth depends on the type of fertilizer. The type of plant, the amount of water, and the amount of sunlight the plants receive are controls because those variables of the experiment are kept the same for each plant.

When designing an experiment, scientists must identify possible sources of **experimental error**. These can be **confounding variables**—factors that act much like the independent variable and thus can make it appear that the independent variable has a greater effect than it actually does. The design may also include unknown variables that are not controlled by the scientists. Finally, scientists must be aware of **human error**, particularly in collecting data and making observations, and of possible equipment errors.

> **Did You Know?**
>
> Reproducibility is an essential feature of a scientific finding. Under the same conditions and using the same experimental methods, multiple researchers should be able to produce identical results.

Practice Question

2. A chemistry student is conducting an experiment in which she tests the relationship between reactant concentration and heat produced by a reaction. In her experiment, she alters the reactant concentration and measures heat produced. The independent variable in the experiment is the
    A) reactant concentration.
    B) reaction rate.
    C) amount of heat produced by the reaction.
    D) product concentration.

Facts, Theories, and Laws

Scientific facts, *theories*, and *laws* are terms with specific, distinct definitions. **Scientific facts** are objective observations that have been repeatedly confirmed by data collected by multiple scientific **investigations**. Facts are generally accepted as truth, but they are never considered final proof. Facts are the observations themselves, rather than the explanations for a natural phenomenon.

Explanations of natural phenomena are the realm of hypotheses and theories. Hypotheses, as earlier defined, are proposed testable explanations of natural phenomena. In order to be testable, a hypothesis must contain specific observations researchers could expect to see if the hypothesis were confirmed. Hypotheses that are tested and confirmed time and time again could eventually accumulate enough data to be considered a **theory**. A theory is a well-founded explanation that is supported by large amounts of data and incorporates multiple sources of evidence. Unlike the everyday definition of *theory*, which suggests just an idea, a scientific theory is widely accepted as a valid explanation of phenomena.

Unlike theories, which are *explanations* of phenomena, scientific **laws** are a generalized *description* of natural phenomena based on multiple observations over time. Laws are distinguished from facts by their durability—or ability to stay constant over time—and their predictive nature. If multiple investigations are run under the exact same conditions over and over, the new observations will conform to the scientific law. If results are not as predicted, then the law can be modified and narrowed to incorporate the new information.

Practice Question

3. Why is the germ theory of disease considered to be a theory?
    A) There is insufficient evidence to support it.
    B) Valid alternative explanations exist.
    C) It is strongly supported by existing evidence.
    D) It has only limited clinical application.

Answer Key

1. D: A hypothesis must be testable and propose an explanation of observed natural phenomena.

2. A: The independent variable is deliberately changed in the course of the experiment. Here, the student is changing the reactant concentration. The heat produced is the dependent variable.

3. C: A scientific theory is typically strongly supported by evidence, despite public misunderstanding to the contrary.

9. Life Science

Biological Molecules

Molecules that contain carbon bound to hydrogen are **organic molecules**. Large organic molecules that contain many atoms and repeating units are **macromolecules**. Many macromolecules are **polymers** composed of repeating small units called **monomers**. There are four basic biological macromolecules that are common between all organisms: carbohydrates, lipids, proteins, and nucleic acids.

Carbohydrates, also called sugars, are polymers made of carbon, hydrogen, and oxygen atoms. The monomer for carbohydrates are **monosaccharides**, such as glucose and fructose, that combine to form more complex sugars called **polysaccharides**. Carbohydrates store energy and provide support to cellular structures.

Lipids, commonly known as fats, are composed mainly of hydrogen and carbon. They serve a number of functions depending on their particular structure: they make up the membrane of cells and can act as fuel, as steroids, and as hormones. Lipids are hydrophobic, meaning they repel water.

> **Did You Know?**
>
> An **enzyme** is a protein that accelerates a specific chemical reaction.

Proteins serve an incredibly wide variety of purposes within the body. As enzymes, they play key roles in important processes like DNA replication, cellular division, and cellular metabolism. Structural proteins provide rigidity to cartilage, hair, nails, and the cytoskeletons (the network of molecules that holds the parts of a cell in place). They are also involved in communication between cells and in the transportation of molecules.

Proteins are composed of individual **amino acids**, which are joined together by peptide bonds to form **polypeptides**. There are twenty amino acids, and the order of the amino acids in the polypeptide determines the shape and function of the molecule.

Nucleic acids store hereditary information and are composed of monomers called nucleotides. Each nucleotide includes a sugar, a phosphate group, and a nitrogenous base.

There are two types of nucleic acids. **Deoxyribonucleic acid (DNA)** contains the genetic instructions to produce proteins. It is composed of two strings of nucleotides wound into a double helix shape. The "backbone" of the helix is made from the nucleotide's sugar (deoxyribose) and phosphate groups. The "rungs" of the ladder are made from one of four nitrogenous bases: adenine, thymine, cytosine, and guanine. These bases bond together in specific pairs: adenine with thymine and cytosine with guanine.

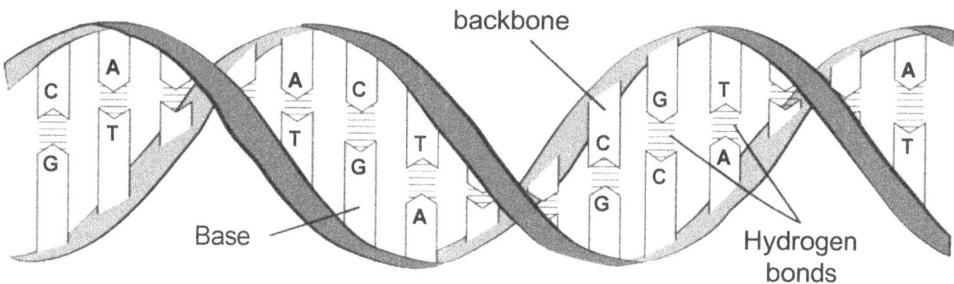

Figure 9.1. The Structure of DNA

Ribonucleic acid (RNA) transcribes information from DNA and plays several vital roles in the replication of DNA and the manufacturing of proteins. RNA nucleotides contain a sugar (ribose), a phosphate group, and one of four nitrogenous bases: adenine, uracil, cytosine, and guanine. It is usually found as a single-stranded molecule. There are three main differences between DNA and RNA:

1. DNA contains the nucleotide thymine; RNA contains the nucleotide uracil.
2. DNA is double-stranded; RNA is single-stranded.
3. DNA is made from the sugar deoxyribose; RNA is made from the sugar ribose.

Practice Question

1. Macromolecules are formed from small subunits called monomers. Which of the following are the monomers that make up a protein?
    A) monosaccharides
    B) nucleotides
    C) amino acids
    D) polypeptides

2. Which of the following is NOT true of RNA?
    A) Hydrogen bonds form between A–T and G–C bases.
    B) A sequence of RNA will not contain T bases but will contain U bases.
    C) RNA is single-stranded.
    D) RNA stores genetic information.

Nucleic Acids

DNA stores information by coding for proteins using blocks of three nucleotides called **codons**. Each codon codes for a specific amino acid; together, all the codons needed to make a specific protein are called a **gene**. In addition to codons for specific amino acids, there are also codons that signal "start" and "stop."

The production of a protein starts with **transcription**. During transcription, the two sides of the DNA helix unwind and a complementary strand of messenger RNA (mRNA) is manufactured using the DNA as a template.

This mRNA then travels outside the nucleus where it is "read" by a ribosome during **translation**. Each codon on the mRNA is matched to an anti-codon on a strand of tRNA, which carries a specific amino acid. The amino acids bond as they are lined up next to each other, forming a polypeptide.

When it is not being transcribed, DNA is tightly wound around proteins called **histones** to create **nucleosomes**, which are in turn packaged into **chromatin**. The structure of chromatin allows large amounts of DNA to be stored in a very small space and helps regulate transcription by controlling access to specific sections of DNA. Tightly folding the DNA also helps prevent damage to the genetic code. Chromatin is further bundled into packages of DNA called **chromosomes**. During cell division, DNA is replicated to create two identical copies of each chromosome called **chromatids**.

Somatic (body) cells are **diploid**, meaning they carry two copies of each chromosome—one inherited from each parent. Gametes, which are reproductive cells, are **haploid** and carry only one copy of each chromosome. Human somatic cells have forty-six chromosomes, while human egg and sperm each carry twenty-three chromosomes.

A **mutation** causes a change in the sequence of nucleotides within DNA. For example, the codon GAC codes for the amino acid aspartic acid. However, if the cytosine is swapped for adenine, the codon now reads GAA, which corresponds to the amino acid glutamic acid. Germ-line mutations, or mutations that occur in a cell that will become a gamete, can be passed on to the offspring of an organism. Somatic mutations cannot be passed on to the offspring of an organism.

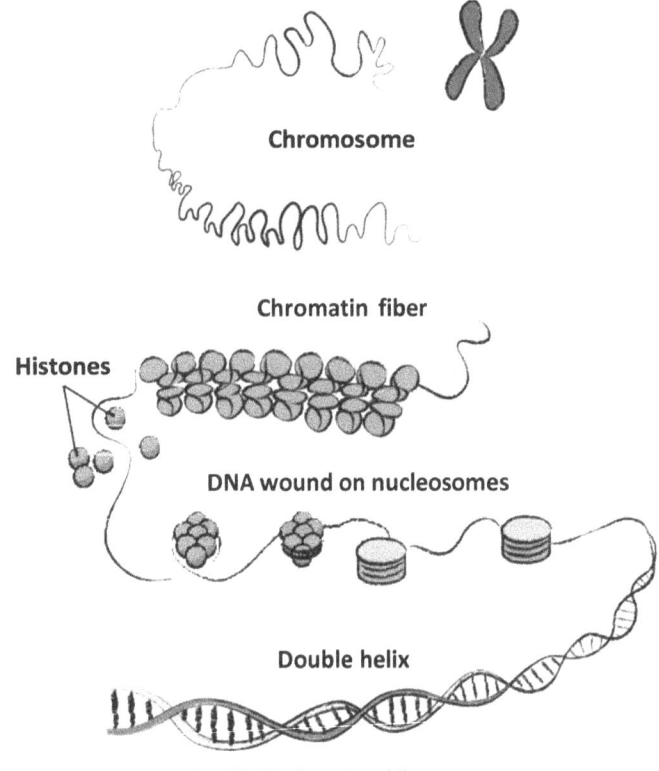

Figure 9.2. DNA, Chromatin, and Chromosomes

Practice Question

3. Which of the following processes uses the information stored in RNA to produce a protein?
   A) replication
   B) translation
   C) transcription
   D) mutation

Structure and Function of Cells

A cell is the smallest unit of life that can reproduce on its own. Unicellular organisms, such as amoebae, are made up of only one cell, while multicellular organisms are comprised of many cells. There are two basic types of cells: prokaryotic and eukaryotic. **Prokaryotic cells**, which include most bacteria, do not have a nucleus. The DNA in a prokaryotic cell is carried in the **cytoplasm**, which is the fluid that makes up the volume of the cell. **Eukaryotic cells** contain a nucleus where genetic material is stored.

Cells contain smaller structures called **organelles** that perform specific functions within the cell. These include **mitochondria**, which produce energy; **ribosomes**, which produce proteins; and **vacuoles**, which store water and other molecules.

Plant cells include a number of structures not found in animal cells. These include the **cell wall**, which provides the cell with a hard outer structure, and **chloroplasts**, where photosynthesis occurs.

The outer surface of human cells is made up of a **plasma membrane**, which gives the cell its shape. This membrane is primarily composed of a **phospholipid bilayer**, which itself is made up of two layers of lipids that face opposing directions. This functions to separate the inner cellular environment from the extracellular space, the space between cells. Molecules travel through the cell membrane using a number of different methods:

- **Diffusion** occurs when molecules pass through the membrane from areas of high to low concentration.

- **Facilitated diffusion** occurs with the assistance of proteins embedded in the membrane.

- **Osmosis** is the movement of water from areas of high to low concentration.

9. Life Science

During **active transport**, proteins in the membrane use energy (in the form of ATP) to move molecules across the membrane.

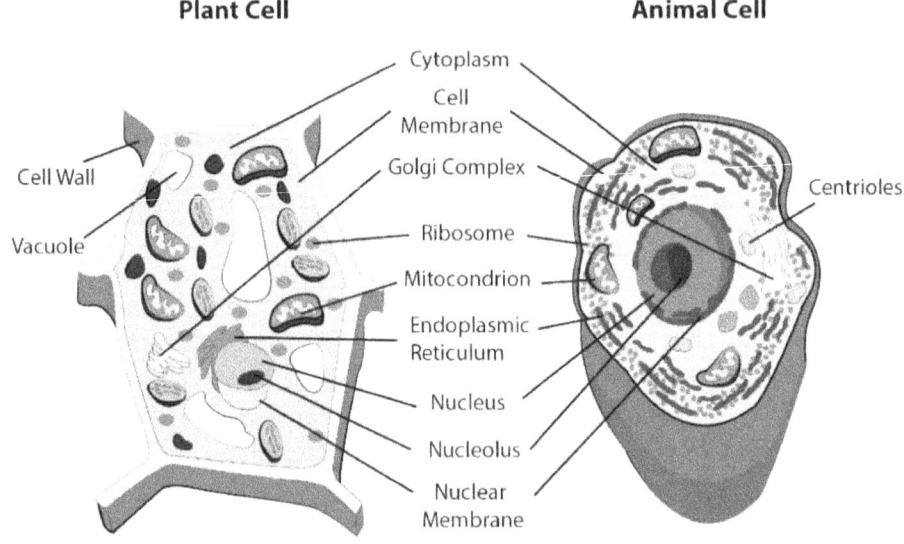

Figure 9.3. Cell Organelles

Practice Question

4. Which of the following structures produces proteins and is found in both prokaryotic and eukaryotic cells?
    A) nucleus
    B) chloroplast
    C) ribosome
    D) vacuole

5. The chromosomes of a eukaryotic organism would be found in the
    A) chloroplast.
    B) nucleus.
    C) mitochondria.
    D) cytoplasm.

Cellular Respiration

Organisms use chains of chemical reactions called **biochemical pathways** to acquire, store, and use energy. The molecule most commonly used to store energy is **adenosine triphosphate (ATP)**. When a phosphate group (Pi) is removed from ATP, creating **adenosine diphosphate (ADP)**, energy is released. The cell harnesses this energy to perform processes such as transport, growth, and replication.

Cells also transfer energy using the molecules **nicotinamide adenine dinucleotide phosphate (NADPH)** and **nicotinamide adenine dinucleotide (NADH)**. These molecules are generally used to carry energy-rich electrons during the process of creating ATP.

In **cellular respiration**, food molecules such as glucose are broken down, and the electrons harvested from these molecules are used to make ATP. The first stage of cellular respiration is an **anaerobic** (does not require oxygen) process called **glycolysis**. Glycolysis takes place in the cytoplasm of a cell and transforms glucose into two molecules of pyruvate. In the process, two molecules of ATP and two molecules of NADH are produced.

Under anaerobic conditions, pyruvate is reduced to acids and sometimes gases and/ or alcohols in a process called **fermentation**. However, this process is less efficient than aerobic cellular respiration and produces only two ATP.

Under aerobic conditions, pyruvate enters the second stage of cellular respiration— the **Krebs cycle**. The Krebs cycle takes place in the mitochondria, or tubular organelles, of a eukaryotic cell. Here, pyruvate is oxidized completely to form six molecules of carbon dioxide (CO_2). This set of reactions also produces two more molecules of ATP, ten molecules of NADH, and two molecules of $FADH_2$ (an electron carrier).

The electrons carried by NADH and $FADH_2$ are transferred to the **electron transport chain**, where they cascade through carrier molecules embedded in the inner mitochondrial membrane. Oxygen is the final electron receptor in the chain; it reacts with these electrons and hydrogen to form water. This sequential movement of electrons drives the formation of a proton (H^+) gradient, which is used by the enzyme ATP synthase to produce ATP. The electron transport chain produces thirty to thirty-two molecules of ATP.

The balanced chemical equation for cellular respiration is:

$$C_6H_{12}O_6 + 6O_2 \rightarrow 6CO_2 + 6H_2O$$

Figure 9.4. Cellular Respiration

Practice Question

6. Which of the following stages of cellular respiration produces the largest number of ATP molecules?
   A) glycolysis
   B) fermentation
   C) Krebs cycle
   D) electron transport chain

Photosynthesis

The sun powers nearly all biological systems on this planet. Plants, along with some bacteria and algae, harness the energy of sunlight and transform it into chemical energy through the process of **photosynthesis**.

Inside each chloroplast are stacks of flat, interconnected sacs called **thylakoids**. Within the membrane of each thylakoid sac are light-absorbing pigments called **chlorophyll**.

In the light-dependent reactions of photosynthesis, light penetrates the chloroplast and strikes the chlorophyll. The energy in the sunlight excites electrons, boosting them to a higher energy level. These excited electrons then cascade through the **electron transport chain**, creating energy in the form of ATP and NADPH. This reaction also splits water to release O_2.

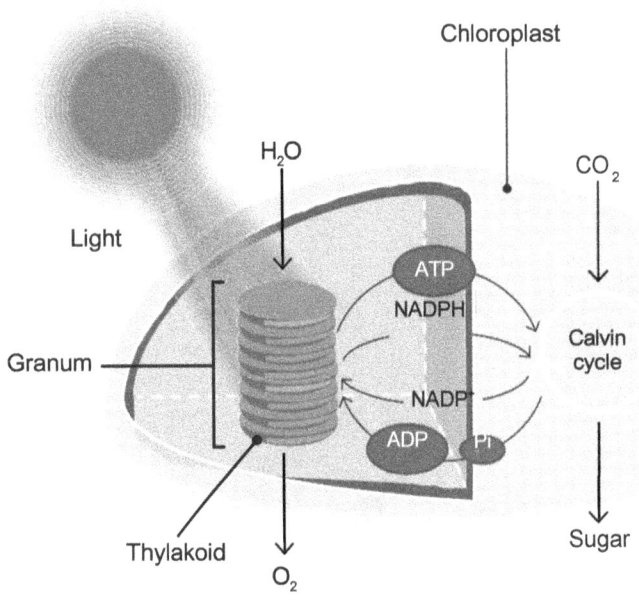

Figure 9.5. Photosynthesis

The ATP and NADPH created by the light-dependent stage of photosynthesis enters the **Calvin cycle**, which uses the energy to produce the carbohydrate glucose ($C_6H_{12}O_6$). The carbon needed for this reaction comes from atmospheric CO_2.

The balanced chemical equation for photosynthesis is:

$$6CO_2 + 6H_2O \rightarrow C_6H_{12}O_6 + 6O_2$$

TRIVIUM
— TEST PREP —

Practice Question

7. All of the following molecules are used in the Calvin cycle EXCEPT
   A) O_2.
   B) CO_2.
   C) ATP.
   D) NADPH.

Cell Division

The process of cell growth and reproduction is the **cell cycle**. Eukaryotic cells spend the majority of their lifespan in **interphase**, during which the cell performs necessary functions and grows. During interphase, the cell also copies its DNA. Then, during **mitosis** the two identical sets of DNA are pulled to opposite sides of the cell. The cell then splits during **cytokinesis**, resulting in two cells that have identical copies of the original cell's DNA.

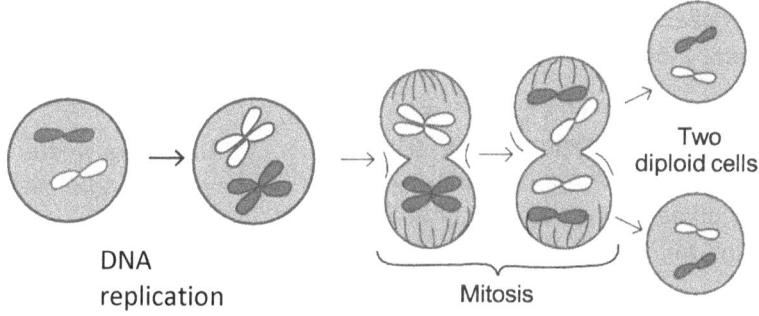

Figure 9.6. Mitosis

Meiosis is the process of sexual reproduction, or the formation of gametes (egg and sperm cells). During meiosis, the replicated DNA is separated to form two diploid cells. These cells in turn will separate again, with each cell retaining a single set of chromosomes. The result is four haploid cells.

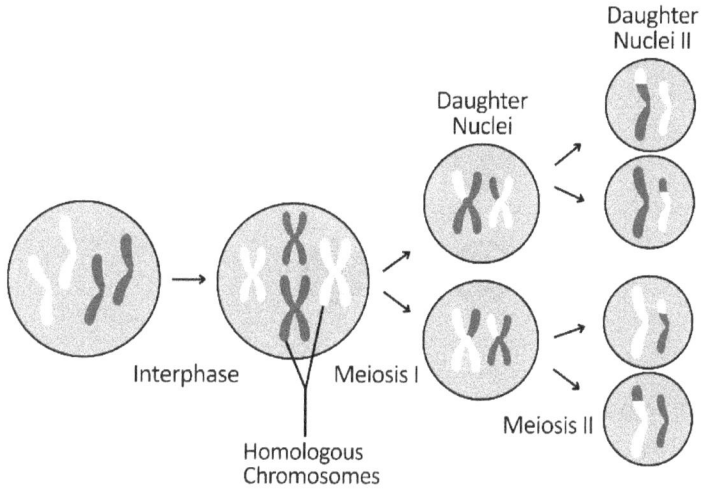

Figure 9.7. Meiosis

9. Life Science

Practice Question

8. The result of mitosis and cytokinesis is
    A) two haploid cells.
    B) four haploid cells.
    C) two diploid cells.
    D) four diploid cells.

Genetics

Genetics is the study of heredity—how characteristics are passed from parents to offspring. These characteristics, or traits, are determined by genes. Each individual has two versions of the same gene, called **alleles**, with one contributed by each parent. An individual is **homozygous** for a particular gene if both alleles are the same, and **heterozygous** if the two alleles are different.

For a particular gene, the **dominant** allele will always be expressed, and the **recessive** allele will only be expressed if the other allele is also recessive. In other words, a recessive trait is only expressed if the individual is homozygous for that allele.

The full set of genetic material in an organism is its **genotype**. The organism's **phenotype** is the set of observable traits in the organism. For example, brown hair is a phenotype. The genotype of this trait is a set of alleles that contain the genetic information for brown hair.

> **Did You Know?**
>
> Alleles are written as a single letter with the dominant allele capitalized (A) and the recessive allele lowercase (a).

The genotype, and resulting phenotype, of sexually reproducing organisms can be tracked using **Punnett squares**, which show the alleles of the parent generation on each of two axes. The possible genotype of the resulting offspring, called the F1 generation, are then shown in the body of the square.

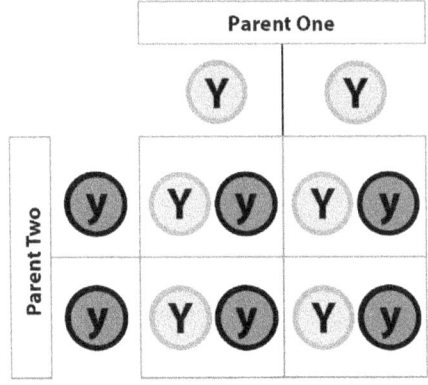

Figure 9.8. Punnett Square

In Figure 9.8., two heterozygous parents for trait Y are mated, resulting in the following genotypes and phenotypes for the offspring:

- One homozygous dominant (dominant phenotype)
- Two heterozygous (dominant phenotype)

- One homozygous recessive (recessive phenotype)

> **Did You Know?**
>
> Many of the rules of genetics were discovered by Gregor Mendel, a nineteenth century abbot who used pea plants to show how traits are passed down through generations.

Non-Mendelian inheritance describes patterns that do not follow the ratios described above. These patterns can occur for a number of reasons. Alleles might show **incomplete dominance**, where one allele is not fully expressed over the other, resulting in a third phenotype (for example, a red flower and white flower cross to create a pink flower). Alleles can also be **codominant**, meaning both are fully expressed (such as the AB blood type).

The expression of genes can also be regulated by mechanisms other than the dominant/recessive relationship. For example, some genes may inhibit the expression of other genes, a process called **epistasis**. The environment can also impact gene expression. For example, organisms with the same genotype may grow to different sizes depending on the nutrients available to them.

Practice Question

9. Which of the following is NOT a scenario in which the dominant allele will be expressed as a trait?
    A) a recessive allele from the father paired with a recessive allele from the mother
    B) a dominant allele from the father paired with a dominant allele from the mother
    C) a dominant allele from the father paired with a recessive allele from the mother
    D) a recessive allele from the father paired with a dominant allele from the mother

10. Alleles for brown eyes (B) are dominant over alleles for blue eyes (b). If two parents are both heterozygous for this gene, what is the percent chance that their offspring will have brown eyes?
    A) 25
    B) 50
    C) 75
    D) 100

Evolution

Evolution is the gradual genetic change in species over time. Natural selection alters the variation and frequency of certain alleles and phenotypes within a population. This increased variation and frequency leads to varying reproductive success, in which individuals with certain traits survive over others. Combined, these mechanisms lead to a gradual changes in the genotype of individual populations that, over time, can result in the creation of a new species.

> **Did You Know?**
>
> Why might a harmful mutation continue to exist in a population?

Natural selection is a process in which only the members of a population best adapted to their environment tend to survive and reproduce, which ensures that their favorable traits will be passed on to future generations of the species.

There are four basic conditions that must be met in order for natural selection to occur:

- Inherited variation

- Overproduction of offspring
- Fitness to environment
- Differential reproduction

The offspring with inherited variations best suited for their environment will be more likely to survive than others and are therefore more likely to pass on their successful genes to future populations through reproduction. This is referred to as **fitness**. An organism that is considered biologically "fit" will be more successful passing on its genes through reproduction compared to other members of the population. The frequency of certain alleles in a gene pool will change as a result.

Artificial selection occurs in a species when humans get involved in the reproductive process. Over time, humans have intentionally bred organisms with the same desirable traits in a process called selective breeding. This has led to the evolution of many common crops and farm animals that are bred specifically for human consumption, as well as among domesticated animals, such as horses or dogs.

Practice Question

11. Which of the following is NOT an example of natural selection?
    A) peahens selecting the most brightly colored peacocks as mates
    B) large bears chasing smaller rivals away from food sources
    C) sparrows with a certain beak shape reaching plentiful food sources
    D) farmers planting seeds only from the most productive corn plants

Ecology

Ecology is the study of organisms' interactions with each other and the environment. Ecologists break down the groups of organisms and abiotic features into hierarchal groups.

Groups of organisms of the same species living in the same geographic area are called **populations**. These organisms will compete with each other for resources and mates and will display characteristic patterns in growth related to their interactions with the environment. For example, many populations exhibit a carrying capacity, which is the highest number of individuals that the resources in a given environment can support. Populations that outgrow their carrying capacity are likely to experience increased death rates until the population reaches a stable level again.

Populations of different species living together in the same geographic region are called **communities**. Within a community there are many different interactions among individuals of different species. **Predators** consume **prey** for food, and some species are in **competition** for the same limited pool of resources. In a **symbiotic** relationship, two species have evolved to share a close relationship. Two species may also have a **parasitic** relationship in which one organism benefits to the detriment of the other, such as ticks feeding off a dog. Both species benefit in a **mutualistic** relationship, and in a **commensalistic** relationship, one species benefits and the other feels the effects.

Within a community, a species exists in a **food web**: every species either consumes or is consumed by another (or others). The lowest trophic level in the web is occupied by **producers**, which include plants and algae that produce energy directly from the sun. The next level are **primary consumers** (herbivores), which consume plant matter. The next trophic level includes **secondary consumers** (carnivores), which consume herbivores.

A food web may also contain another level of **tertiary consumers** (carnivores that consume other carnivores). In a real community, these webs can be extremely complex, with species existing on multiple trophic levels. Communities also include **decomposers**, which are organisms that break down dead matter.

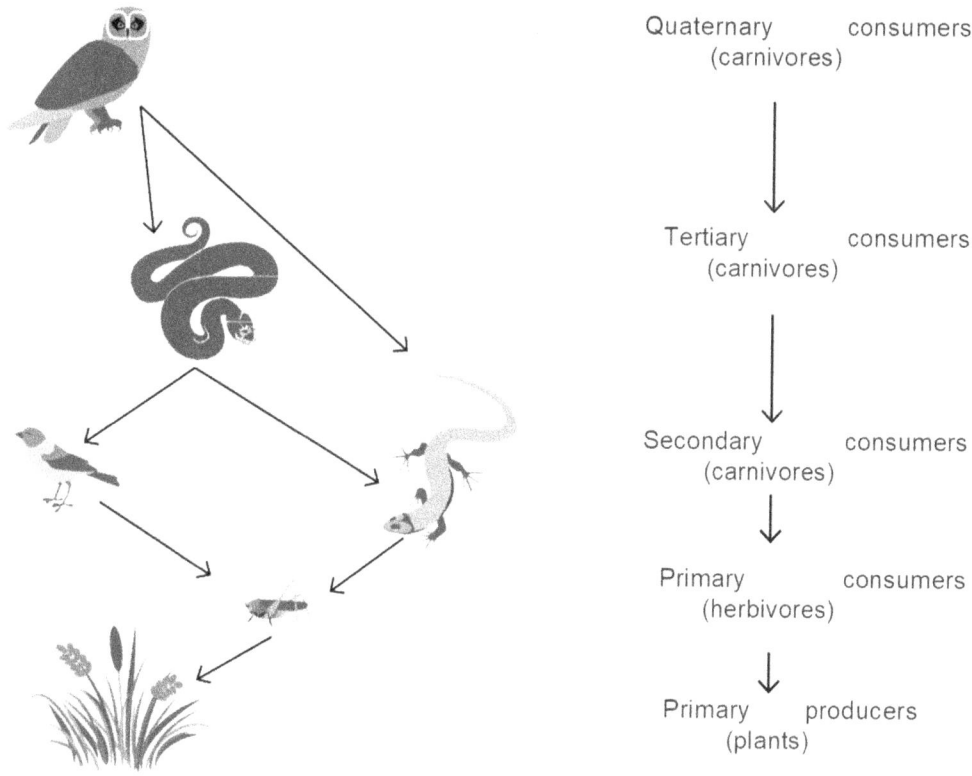

Figure 9.9. Food Web

The collection of biotic (living) and abiotic (nonliving) features in a geographic area is called an **ecosystem**. For example, in a forest, the ecosystem consists of all the organisms (animals, plants, fungi, bacteria, etc.), in addition to the soil, groundwater, rocks, and other abiotic features.

Biomes are collections of plant and animal communities that exist within specific climates. They are similar to ecosystems, but they do not include abiotic components and can exist within and across continents. For example, the Amazon rainforest is a specific ecosystem, while tropical rainforests in general are considered a biome that includes a set of similar communities across the world. Together, all the living and nonliving parts of the earth are known as the **biosphere**.

Terrestrial biomes are usually defined by distinctive patterns in temperature and rainfall, and aquatic biomes are defined by the type of water and organisms found there. Examples of biomes include:

- deserts: extreme temperatures and very low rainfall with specialized vegetation and small mammals

- tropical rainforests: hot and wet with an extremely high diversity of species

- temperate grasslands: moderate precipitation and distinct seasons with grasses and shrubs dominating

- temperate forests: moderate precipitation and temperatures with deciduous trees dominating

- tundra: extremely low temperatures and short growing seasons with little or no tree growth
- coral reefs: a marine (saltwater) system with high levels of diversity
- lake: an enclosed body of fresh water

If the delicate balance of an ecosystem is disrupted, the system may not function properly. For example, if all the secondary consumers disappear, the population of primary consumers would increase, causing the primary consumers to overeat the producers and eventually starve. **Keystone species** are especially important in a particular community, and removing them decreases the overall diversity of the ecosystem.

Practice Question

12. Which of the following is an example of an abiotic environmental factor that influences population size?
    A) food availability
    B) rate of precipitation
    C) interspecific competition
    D) competition

13. Which of the following terrestrial biomes is characterized by moderate rainfall and the dominance of deciduous trees?
    A) desert
    B) tropical rainforest
    C) temperate forest
    D) tundra

Human Anatomy and Physiology

In a multicellular organism, cells are grouped together into **tissues**, and these tissues are grouped into **organs**, which perform specific **functions**. The heart, for example, is the organ that pumps blood throughout the body. Organs are further grouped into **organ systems**, such as the digestive or respiratory systems.

> **Did You Know?**
>
> In science, a **system** is a collection of interconnected parts that make up a complex whole with defined boundaries. Systems may be closed, meaning nothing passes in or out of them, or open, meaning they have inputs and outputs.

Anatomy is the study of the structure of organisms, and **physiology** is the study of how these structures function. Both disciplines study the systems that allow organisms to perform a number of crucial functions, including the exchange of energy, nutrients, and waste products with the environment. This exchange allows organisms to maintain homeostasis, or the stabilization of internal conditions. The human body has a number of systems that perform vital functions, including the digestive, excretory, respiratory, circulatory, skeletal, muscular, immune, nervous, endocrine, and reproductive systems.

The **digestive system** breaks food down into nutrients for use by the body's cells. Food enters through the **mouth** and moves through the **esophagus** to the **stomach**, where it is physically and chemically broken down. The food particles then move into the **small intestine**, where the majority of nutrients are absorbed. Finally, the remaining particles enter the **large intestine**, which mostly absorbs water, and waste exits through the **rectum** and **anus**. This system also includes other organs, such as the **liver**, **gallbladder**, and **pancreas**, that manufacture substances needed for digestion.

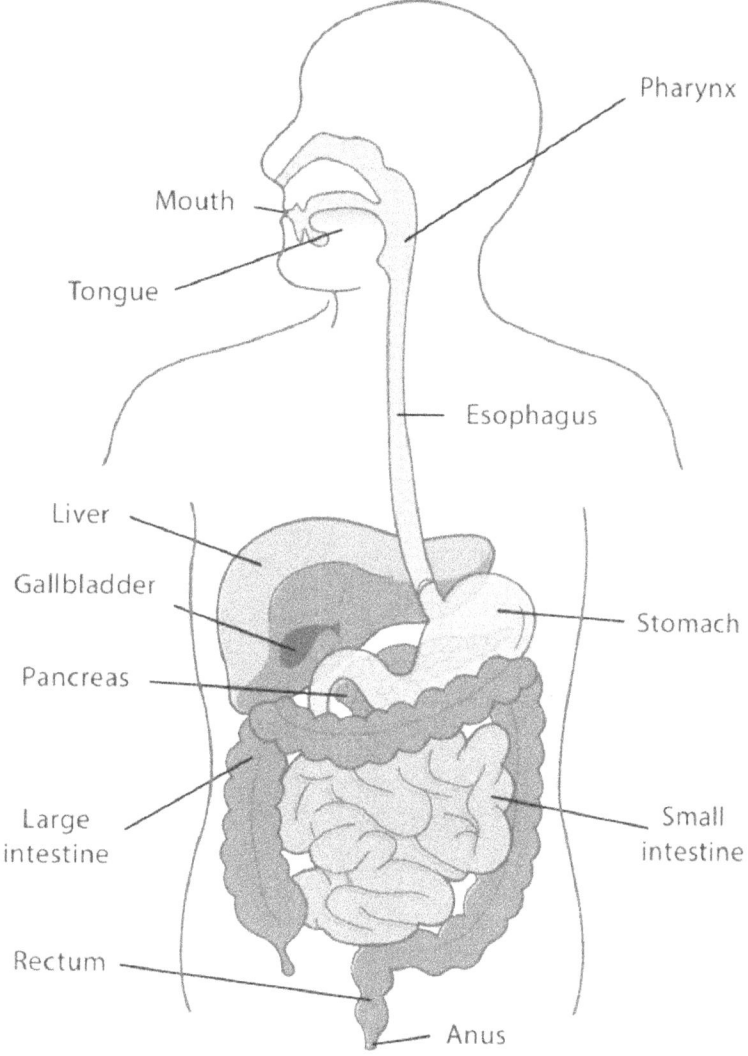

Figure 9.10. The Digestive System

The **genitourinary system** removes waste products from the body. Its organs include the liver, which breaks down harmful substances, and the **kidneys**, which filter waste from the bloodstream. The excretory system also includes the **bladder** and **urinary tract**, which expel the waste filtered by the kidneys; the lungs, which expel the carbon dioxide created by cellular metabolism; and the skin, which secretes salt in the form of perspiration.

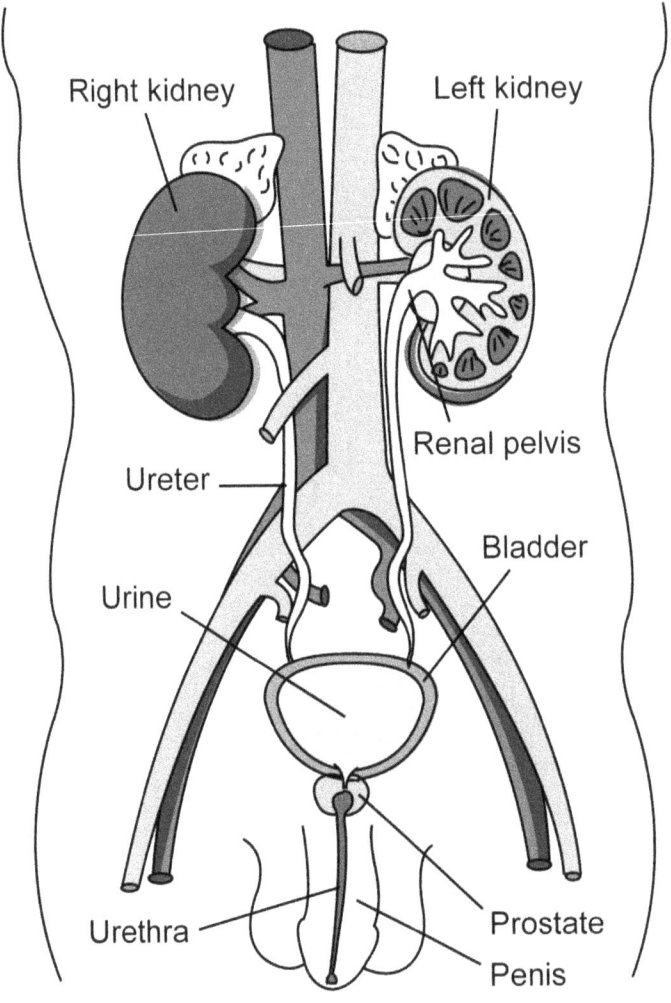

Figure 9.11. Genitourinary System

The **respiratory system** takes in oxygen (which is needed for cellular functioning) and expels carbon dioxide. Humans take in air primarily through the nose but also through the mouth. This air travels down the **trachea** and **bronchi** into the **lungs**, which are composed of millions of small structures called alveoli that allow for the exchange of gases between the blood and the air.

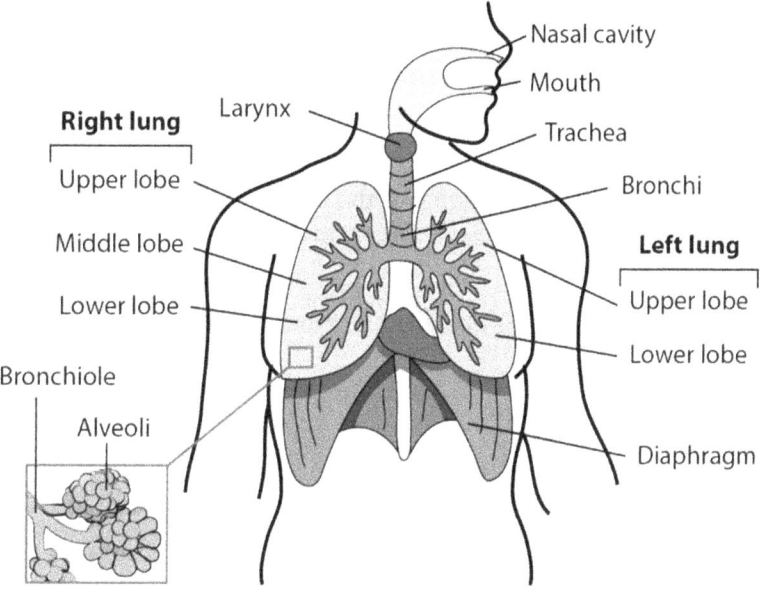

Figure 9.12. Respiratory System

The circulatory system carries oxygen, nutrients, and waste products in the blood to and from all the cells of the body. The **heart** is a four-chambered muscle that pumps blood throughout the body. The four chambers are the right atrium, right ventricle, left atrium, and left ventricle. Deoxygenated blood (blood from which all the oxygen has been extracted and used) enters the right atrium and then is sent from the right ventricle through the pulmonary artery to the lungs, where it collects oxygen. The oxygen-rich blood then returns to the left atrium of the heart and is pumped out the left ventricle to the rest of the body.

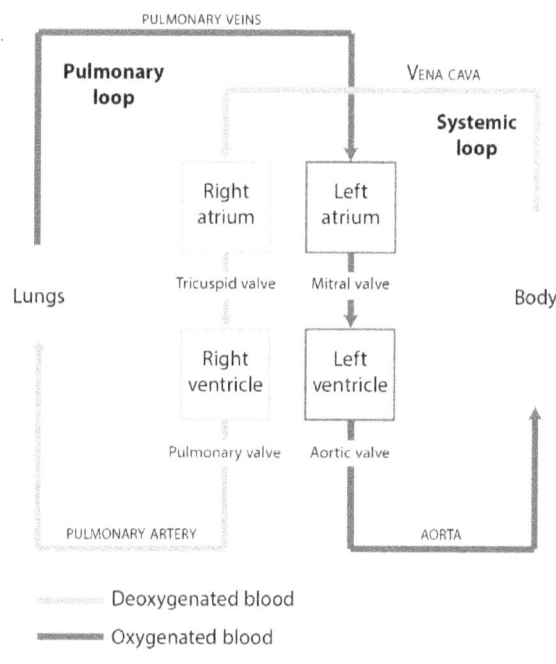

Figure 9.13. Circulatory System

9. Life Science

Blood travels through a system of vessels. **Arteries** branch directly off the heart and carry blood away from it. The largest artery is the aorta, which carries blood from the heart to the rest of the body. **Veins** carry blood back to the heart from other parts of the body. Most veins carry deoxygenated blood, but the pulmonary veins carry oxygenated blood from the lungs back to the heart to then be pumped to the rest of the body. Arteries and veins branch into smaller and smaller vessels until they become **capillaries**, which are the smallest vessels and the site where gas exchange occurs.

The **skeletal system**, which is composed of the body's **bones** and **joints**, provides support for the body and helps with movement. Bones also store some of the body's nutrients and produce specific types of cells. Humans are born with 237 bones. However, many of these bones fuse during childhood, and adults have only 206 bones.

Bones can have a rough or smooth texture and come in four basic shapes: long, flat, short, and irregular.

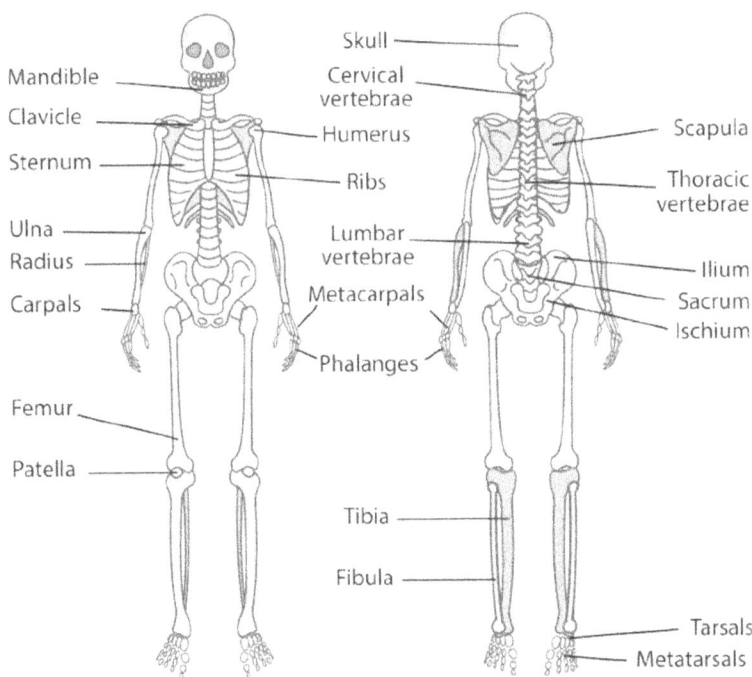

Figure 9.14. The Skeletal System

The **muscular system** allows the body to move and also moves blood and other substances through the body. The human body has three types of muscles. Skeletal muscles are voluntary muscles (meaning they can be controlled) that are attached to bones and move the body. Smooth muscles are involuntary muscles (meaning they cannot be controlled) that create movement in parts of the digestive tract, blood vessels, and the reproduction system. Finally, cardiac muscle is the involuntary muscle that contracts the heart, pumping blood throughout the body.

Did You Know?

Some skeletal muscles, such as the diaphragm and those that control blinking, can be voluntarily controlled but usually operate involuntarily.

The **immune system** protects the body from infection by foreign particles and organisms. It includes the **skin** and mucous membranes, which act as physical barriers, and a number of specialized cells that destroy foreign substances in the body. The human body has an adaptive immune system, meaning it can recognize and respond to foreign substances once it has been exposed to them. This is the underlying mechanism behind vaccines.

Did You Know?

Memory B cells are the underlying mechanisms behind vaccines, which introduce a harmless version of a pathogen into the body to activate the body's adaptive immune response.

The immune system is composed of **B cells**, or B lymphocytes, that produce special proteins called **antibodies** that bind to foreign substances, called antigens, and neutralize them. **T cells**, or T lymphocytes, remove body cells that have been infected by foreign invaders like bacteria or viruses. **Helper T cells** coordinate production of antibodies by B cells and removal of infected cells by T cells. **Killer T cells** destroy body cells that have been infected by invaders after they are identified and removed by T cells. Finally, **memory cells** remember antigens that have been removed so the immune system can respond more quickly if they enter the body again.

The **nervous system** processes external stimuli and sends signals throughout the body. It is made up of two parts. The central nervous system (CNS) includes the brain and spinal cord and is where information is processed and stored. The brain has three parts: the cerebrum, cerebellum, and medulla. The **cerebrum** is the biggest part of the brain, the wrinkly gray part at the front and top, and controls different functions like thinking, vision, hearing, touch, and smell. The **cerebellum** is located at the back and bottom of the brain and controls motor movements. The **medulla**, or brain stem, is where the brain connects to the spinal cord and controls automatic body functions like breathing and heartbeat.

The peripheral nervous system (PNS) includes small cells called **neurons** that transmit information throughout the body using electrical signals. Neurons are made up of three basic parts: the cell body, dendrites, and axons. The cell body is the main part of the cell where the organelles are located. Dendrites are long arms that extend from the main cell body and communicate with other cells' dendrites through chemical messages passed across a space called a synapse. Axons are extensions from the cell body and transmit messages to the muscles.

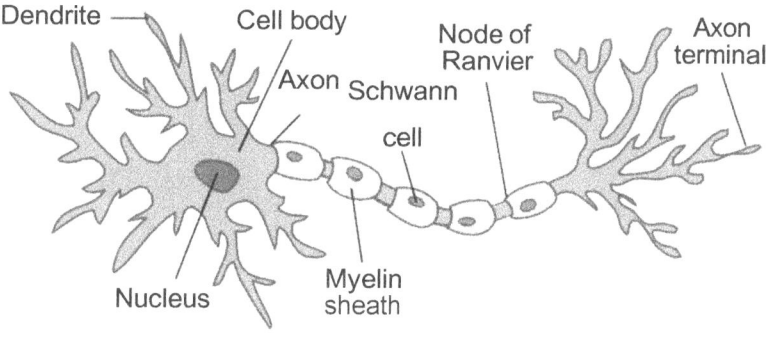

Figure 9.15. Neuron

The **endocrine system** is a collection of organs that produce **hormones**, which are chemicals that regulate bodily processes. These organs include the pituitary gland, hypothalamus, pineal gland, thyroid gland, parathyroid glands, adrenal glands, testes (in males), ovaries (in females), and the placenta (in pregnant females). Together, the hormones these organs produce regulate a wide variety of bodily functions, including hunger, sleep, mood, reproduction, and temperature. Some organs that are part of other systems can also act as endocrine organs, including the pancreas and liver.

The reproductive system includes the organs necessary for sexual reproduction. In males, sperm is produced in the testes (also known as **testicles**) and carried through a thin tube called the **vas deferens** to the **urethra**, which carries sperm through the **penis** and out of the body. The **prostate** is a muscular gland approximately the size of a walnut that is located between the male bladder and penis and produces a fluid that nourishes and protects sperm.

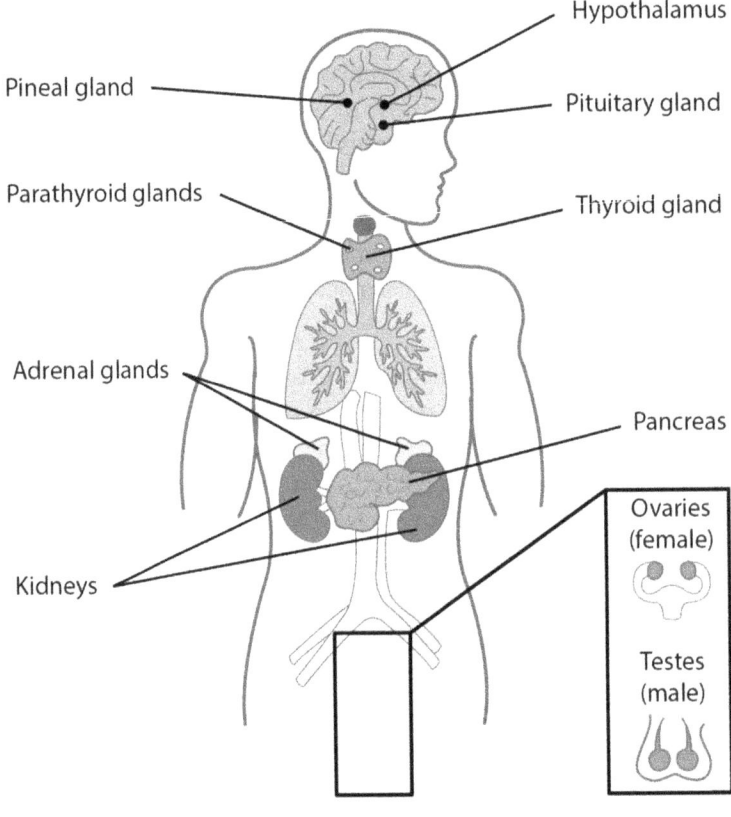

Figure 9.16. Endocrine System

In the female reproductive system, eggs are produced in the **ovaries** and released roughly once a month to move through the **fallopian tubes** to the **uterus**. If an egg is fertilized, the new embryo implants in the lining of the uterus and develops over the course of about nine months.

At the end of **gestation**, the baby leaves the uterus through the cervix, and exits the body through the **vagina**. If the egg is not fertilized, the uterus will shed its lining.

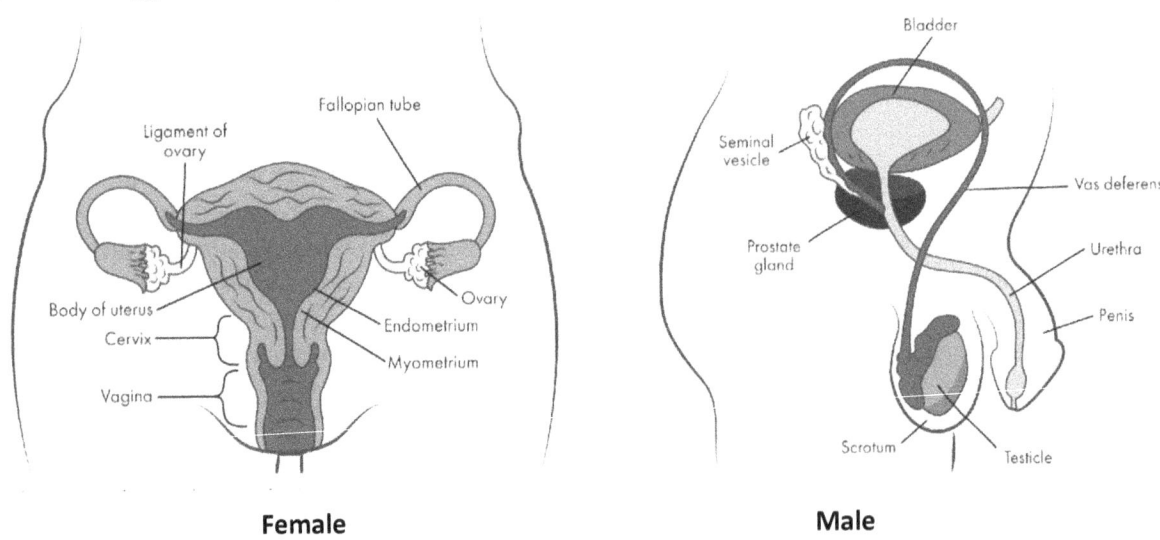

Female **Male**

Figure 9.17. Reproductive System

Practice Question

14. Which of the following structures are small air sacs that function as the site of gas exchange in the lungs?
    A) capillaries
    B) bronchi
    C) alveoli
    D) cilia

15. Where in the digestive tract are most of the nutrients absorbed?
    A) small intestine
    B) rectum
    C) stomach
    D) large intestine

Answer Key

1. C: Amino acid monomers are the building blocks of proteins.

2. A: These are the complementary base pairs that form in DNA.

3. B: Translation is the process of matching codons in RNA to the correct anti-codon to manufacture a protein.

4. C: Ribosomes consist of two subunits built from ribosomal RNA and protein. They are not bound by a membrane.

5. B: The nucleus is the organelle that carries the DNA of eukaryotic organisms.

6. D: The electron transport chain produces thirty to thirty-two molecules of ATP made during cellular respiration. The other choices each produce only two molecules of ATP.

7. A: O_2 is released during the light-dependent stage of photosynthesis and is not used during the Calvin cycle. The other choices are all used during the Calvin cycle to produce glucose.

8. C: The daughter cells produced during mitosis are genetically identical to their diploid (2n) parent.

9. A: This genotype is homozygous, and the recessive trait is the only trait that can be expressed.

10. C: The Punnett square shows that there is a 75 percent chance the child will have the dominant B gene, and thus have brown eyes.

	B	b
B	BB	Bb
b	Bb	bb

11. D: Farmers choosing specific traits in plants is an example of artificial selection.

12. B: Precipitation is a nonliving (abiotic) factor that influences population size.

13. C: Temperate forests have moderate rainfall and are dominated by deciduous trees.

14. C: The alveoli are sacs found at the terminal end of each bronchiole in the lungs and are the site of gas exchange with the blood.

15. A: Most nutrients are absorbed by the small intestine.

10. Physical Science

The Structure of the Atom

All matter is composed of very small particles called **atoms**. Atom can be further broken down into subatomic particles. **Protons**, which are positive, and **neutrons**, which are neutral, form the nucleus of the atom. Negative particles called **electrons** orbit the nucleus.

While electrons are often depicted as orbiting the nucleus like a planet orbits the sun, they're actually arranged in cloud-like areas called **shells**. The shells closest to the nucleus have the lowest energy and are filled first. The high-energy shells farther from the nucleus only fill with electrons once lower-energy shells are full.

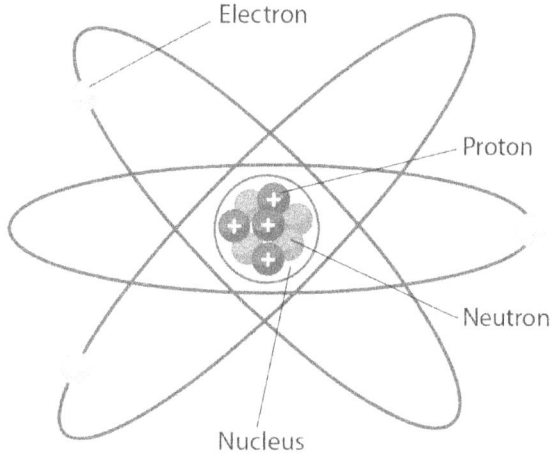

Figure 10.1. Structure of the Atom

The outermost electron shell of an atom is its **valence shell**. The electrons in this shell are involved in chemical reactions. Atoms are most stable when their valence shell is full (usually with eight electrons), so the atom will lose, gain, or share electrons to fill its valence shell.

A neutral atom will have an equal number of protons and electrons. When a neutral atom loses or gains electrons, it gains or loses charge accordingly, forming an **ion**. An ion with more protons than electrons has a positive charge and is called a **cation**. An ion with more electrons than protons has a negative charge and is considered an **anion**.

For example, the element oxygen (O) has eight protons and eight electrons. A neutral oxygen atom is represented simply as O. However, if it gains two electrons, it becomes an anion with a charge of −2 and is written as O^{2-}.

All atoms with the same number of protons are the same **element** and cannot be further reduced to a simpler substance by chemical processes. Each element has a symbol, which is a one- or two-letter abbreviation for the element's name. The number of protons in an atom is that atom's **atomic number**.

Along with atomic charge, atoms have measurable mass. Protons and neutrons are significantly more massive than electrons (about 1,800 times), so the mass of electrons is not considered when calculating the mass of an atom. Thus, an element's **mass number** is the number of protons and neutrons present in its atoms.

Practice Question

1. What is the charge of an atom with five protons and seven electrons?
    A) 12
    B) −12
    C) 2
    D) −2

2. Which ion has the greatest number of electrons?
    A) K^+
    B) Cl^-
    C) Ca^+
    D) P^{3-}

The Periodic Table of the Elements

Elements are arranged on the **Periodic Table of the Elements** by their atomic number, which increases from top to bottom and left to right on the table. Hydrogen, the first element on the periodic table, has one proton while helium, the second element, has two, and so on.

The rows of the periodic table are called **Periods**, and the vertical columns are called **groups**. Each group contains elements with the same number of valence electrons, meaning the elements have similar chemical properties.

The majority of the elements in the periodic table are metals. Metals have the following properties:

- They are hard, opaque, and shiny.
- They are ductile and malleable.
- They conduct electricity and heat.
- With the exception of mercury, they are solids.

Metals begin on the left side of the periodic table and span across the middle of the table, almost all the way to the right side. Examples of metals include gold (Au), tin (Sn), and lead (Pb).

Nonmetals are elements that do not conduct electricity and tend to be more reactive than metals. They can be solids, liquids, or gases. The nonmetals are located on the right side of the periodic table. Examples of nonmetals include sulfur (S), hydrogen (H), and oxygen (O).

Metalloids, or semimetals, are elements that possess both metal and nonmetal characteristics. For example, some metalloids are shiny but do not conduct electricity well. Metalloids are located between the metals and nonmetals on the periodic table. Some examples of metalloids are boron (B), silicon (Si), and arsenic (As).

The Periodic Table

Figure 10.2. Periodic Table

Practice Question

3. Bismuth is a
    A) metal.
    B) nonmetal.
    C) metalloid.
    D) transition element.

4. The lithium ion Li^+ combines with the fluorine ion F^- to form the ionic compound LiF. Which of the following elements is fluorine most likely to also form an ionic compound with?
    A) nickel (Ni)
    B) beryllium (Be)
    C) sodium (Na)
    D) argon (Ar)

Chemical Bonds

Chemical bonds are attractions between atoms that create molecules, which are substances consisting of more than one atom. There are three types of bonds: ionic, covalent, and metallic.

In an **ionic bond**, one atom "gives" its electrons to the other, resulting in one positively and one negatively charged atom. The bond is a result of the attraction between the two ions. Ionic bonds form between atoms on the left side of the periodic table (which will lose electrons) and those on the right side (which will gain electrons). Table salt (NaCl) is an example of a molecule held together by an ionic bond.

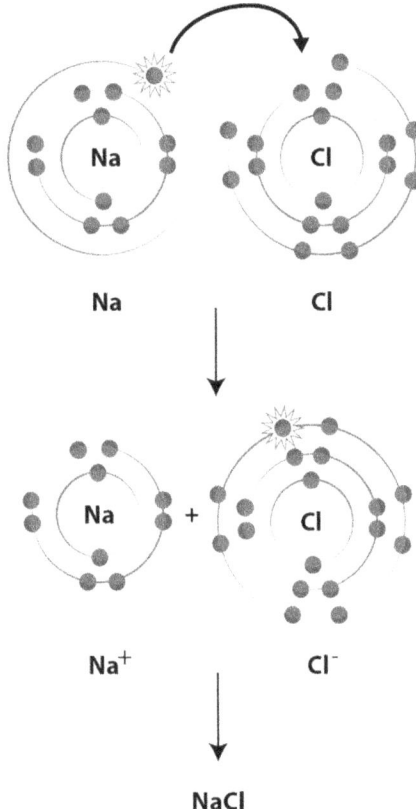

Figure 10.3. The Ionic Bond in Table Salt

A **covalent bond** is created by a pair of atoms sharing electrons to fill their valence shells. In a **nonpolar** covalent bond, the electrons are shared evenly. In a **polar** covalent bond, the electrons are shared unevenly. One atom will exert a stronger pull on the shared electrons, giving that atom a slight negative charge. The other atom in the bond will have a slight positive charge.

Water (H_2O) is an example of a polar molecule.

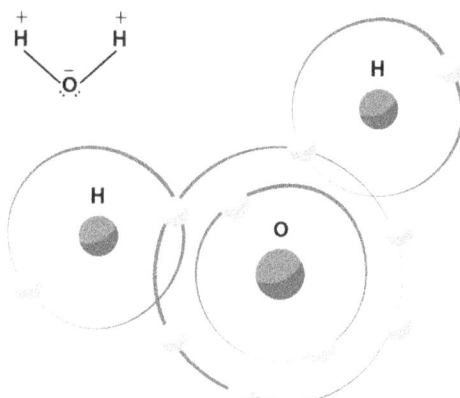

Figure 10.4. Polar Covalent Bond

Metals can form tightly packed arrays in which each atom is in close contact with many neighbors. The valence electrons are free to move between atoms and create a "sea" of delocalized charge. Any excitation, such as an electrical current, can cause the electrons to move throughout the array. The high electrical and thermal conductivity of metals is due to this ability of electrons to move throughout the lattice. This type of delocalized bonding is called **metallic bonding**.

> **Did You Know?**
>
> The polar nature of water is responsible for many of its unique properties. The small charges within a water molecule cause attraction between the molecules. The molecules then "stick" to each other (cohesion) and to other surfaces (adhesion).

Practice Question

5. Which of the following compounds is held together by a polar covalent bond?
    A) LiF
    B) CO_2
    C) H_2
    D) NaOH

Properties of Matter

Matter is any substance that takes up space. The amount of matter in an object is that object's **mass**, which is measured in grams or kilograms. Mass is different from **weight**, which is a measure of the gravitational force exerted on an object.

An object's mass never changes, but its weight will change if the gravitational force changes. The **density** of an object is the ratio of an object's mass to its volume.

> **Did You Know?**
>
> Objects weigh less on the moon than on the earth because the pull of gravity on the moon is lower than that on earth. However, the mass of the object is the same no matter where in the universe it is.

10. Physical Science

Properties of substances are divided into two categories: physical and chemical. **Physical properties** are those that are measurable and can be seen without changing the chemical makeup of a substance. In contrast, **chemical properties** are those that determine how a substance will behave in a chemical reaction. Chemical properties cannot be identified simply by observing a material. Instead, the material must be engaged in a chemical reaction in order to identify its chemical properties. A **physical change** is a change in a substance's physical properties, and a **chemical change** is a change in its chemical properties.

Table 10.1. Properties of Matter	
Physical Properties	**Chemical Properties**
mass	heat of combustion
temperature	flammability
density	toxicity
color	chemical stability
viscosity	enthalpy of formation

Temperature is the name given to the kinetic energy of all the atoms or molecules in a substance. While it might look like matter is not in motion, in fact, its atoms have kinetic energy and are constantly spinning and vibrating. The more energy the atoms have (meaning the more they spin and vibrate) the higher the substance's temperature.

Did You Know?

In both physical and chemical changes, matter is always conserved, meaning it can never be created or destroyed.

Heat is the movement of energy from one substance to another. Energy will spontaneously move from high-energy (high-temperature) substances to low-energy (low- temperature) substances.

Practice Question

6. Which of the following describes a physical change?
    A) Water becomes ice.
    B) Batter is baked into a cake.
    C) A firecracker explodes.
    D) An acid is neutralized with a base.

States of Matter

All matter exists in different **states** (or phases) that depend on the energy of the molecules in the matter. **Solid** matter has densely packed molecules and does not change volume or shape. **Liquids** have more loosely packed molecules and can change shape but not volume. **Gas** molecules are widely dispersed, and gases can change both shape and volume.

Changes in temperature and pressure can cause matter to change states. Generally, adding energy (in the form of heat) changes a substance to a higher energy state (e.g., solid to liquid). Transitions from a high to lower energy state (e.g., liquid to solid) release energy. Each of these changes has a specific name, summarized in the table below.

Table 10.2. Changes in State of Matter				
Name	From	To	Occurs At	Energy Change
evaporation	liquid	gas	boiling point	uses energy
condensation	gas	liquid	boiling point	releases energy
melting	solid	liquid	freezing point	uses energy
freezing	liquid	solid	freezing point	releases energy
sublimation	solid	gas	---	uses energy
deposition	gas	solid	---	releases energy

Practice Question

7. The process that takes place when water reaches its boiling point is called
   A) condensation.
   B) evaporation.
   C) melting.
   D) sublimation.

Chemical Reactions

A **chemical reaction** occurs when one or more substances react to form new substances. **Reactants** are the substances that are consumed or altered in the chemical reaction, and the new substances are **products**. Equations are written with the reactants on the left, the products on the right, and an arrow between them. The state of the chemical compounds are sometimes noted using the labels *s* (solid), *l* (liquid), *g* (gas), or *aq* (aqueous, meaning a solution).

The equation below shows the reaction of hydrogen gas (H_2) and chlorine gas (Cl_2) to form hydrogen chloride (HCl), an acid.

$$H_2 \, (g) + Cl_2 \, (g) \rightarrow 2HCl \, (aq)$$

Chemical reactions follow the **law of conservation of matter**, which states that matter cannot be created or destroyed. In a reaction, the same types and numbers of atoms that appear on the left side must also appear on the right. To **balance** a chemical equation, coefficients (the numbers before the reactant or product) are added. In the equation above, a coefficient of two is needed on HCl so that two hydrogen and two chlorine atoms appear on each side of the arrow.

There are five main types of chemical reactions; these are summarized in the table below.

Table 10.3. Types of Reactions

Type of Reaction	General Formula	Example Reaction
Synthesis	$A + B \rightarrow C$	$2H_2 + O_2 \rightarrow 2H_2O$
Decomposition	$A \rightarrow B + C$	$2H_2O_2 \rightarrow 2H_2O + O_2$
Single displacement	$AB + C \rightarrow A + BC$	$CH_4 + Cl_2 \rightarrow CH_3Cl + HCl$
Double displacement	$AB + CD \rightarrow AC + BD$	$CuCl_2 + 2AgNo_3 \rightarrow Cu(NO_3)_2 + 2AgCl$
Combustion	$C_xH_yO_z + O_2 \rightarrow CO_2 + H_2O$	$2C_8H_{18} + 25O_2 \rightarrow 10CO_2 + 18H_2O$

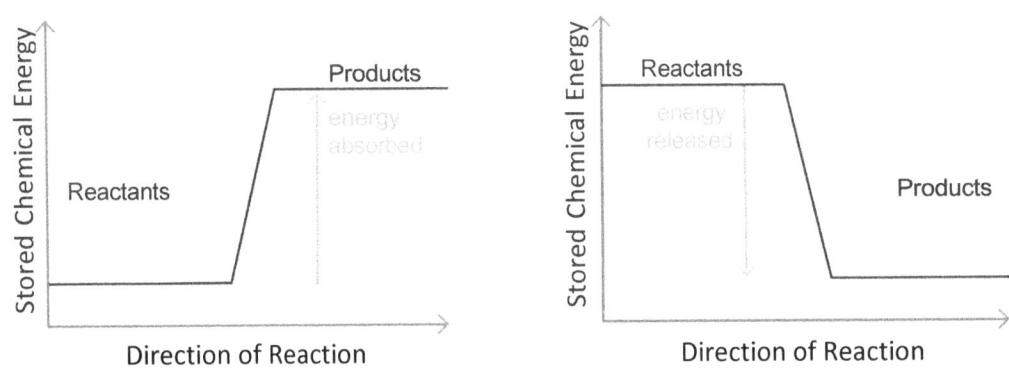

Figure 10.5. Stored Energy in Endothermic and Exothermic Reactions

Energy is required to break chemical bonds, and it is released when bonds form. The total energy absorbed or released during a chemical reaction will depend on the individual bonds being broken and formed. A reaction that releases energy is **exothermic**, and a reaction that absorbs energy is **endothermic**.

Practice Question

8. Which of the following types of reactions is shown below?

$$Pb(NO_3)_2 + K_2CrO_4 \rightarrow PbCrO_4 + 2KNO_3$$

A) combustion
B) decomposition
C) double displacement
D) single replacement

9. Which of the following equations is a balanced equation?
A) $2KClO_3 \rightarrow KCl + 3O_2$
B) $KClO_3 \rightarrow KCl + 3O_2$
C) $2KClO_3 \rightarrow 2KCl + 3O_2$
D) $6KClO_3 \rightarrow 6KCl + 3O_2$

Mixtures

When substances are combined without a chemical reaction to bond them, the resulting substance is called a **mixture**. Physical changes can be used to separate mixtures. For example, heating salt water until the water evaporates, leaving the salt behind, will separate a salt water solution.

In a mixture, the components can be unevenly distributed, such as in trail mix or soil. These mixtures are described at **heterogeneous**. Alternatively, the components can be **homogeneously**, or uniformly, distributed, as in salt water.

Did You Know?

Solutions can exist as solids, liquids, or gases. For example, carbonated water has a gaseous solute (CO_2) and a liquid solvent (water). A solution formed by combining two solid metals, such as stainless steel, is an **alloy**.

A **solution** is a special type of stable homogeneous mixture. The components of a solution will not separate on their own and cannot be separated using a filter. The substance being dissolved is the **solute**, and the substance acting on the solute, or doing the dissolving, is the **solvent**.

The **solubility** of a solution is the maximum amount of solute that will dissolve in a specific quantity of solvent at a specified temperature. Solutions can be saturated, unsaturated, or supersaturated based on the amount of solute dissolved in the solution.

A **saturated** solution has the maximum amount of solute that can be dissolved in the solvent.

An **unsaturated** solution contains less solute than a saturated solution would hold.

A **supersaturated** solution contains more solvent than a saturated solution. A supersaturated solution can be made by heating the solution to dissolve additional solute and then slowly cooling it down to a specified temperature.

Practice Question

10. Which of the following is a heterogeneous mixture?
    A) a mixture in which the atoms or molecules are distributed unevenly
    B) a mixture in which two substances are in different states
    C) a mixture of covalent and ionic compounds
    D) a mixture of polar and nonpolar molecules

11. Which of the following terms describes a solution in which more solvent can be dissolved?
    A) unsaturated
    B) saturated
    C) supersaturated
    D) homogeneous

Acids and Bases

Acids and bases are substances that share a distinct set of physical properties. **Acids** are corrosive, sour, and change the color of vegetable dyes like litmus from blue to red. **Bases**, or alkaline solutions, are slippery, bitter, and change the color of litmus from red to blue.

There are a number of different ways to define acids and bases, but generally acids release hydrogen ions (H^+) in solution, while bases release hydroxide (OH^-) ions. For example, hydrochloric acid (HCl) ionizes, or breaks apart, in solution to release H+ ions:

Did You Know?

A **buffer**, or buffer solution, is a solution that resists changes in pH when small quantities of acids or bases are added. A buffer can do this because it contains a weak acid to react with any added base and a weak base to react with any added acid.

$$HCl \rightarrow H^+ + Cl$$

The base sodium hydroxide (NaOH) ionizes to release OH^- ions:

$$NaOH \rightarrow Na^+ + OH^-$$

Acids and bases combine in a **neutralization reaction**. During the reaction, the H^+ and OH^- ions join to form water, and the remaining ions combine to form a salt:

$$HCl + NaOH \rightarrow H_2O + NaCl$$

The strength of an acid or base is measured on the **pH scale**, which ranges from 1 to 14, with 1 being the strongest acid, 14 being the strongest base, and 7 being neutral.

A substance's pH value is a measure of how many hydrogen ions are in the solution. The scale is logarithmic, meaning an acid with a pH of 3 has ten times as many hydrogen ions as an acid with a pH of 4. Water, which separates into equal numbers of H^+ and OH^- ions, has a neutral pH of 7.

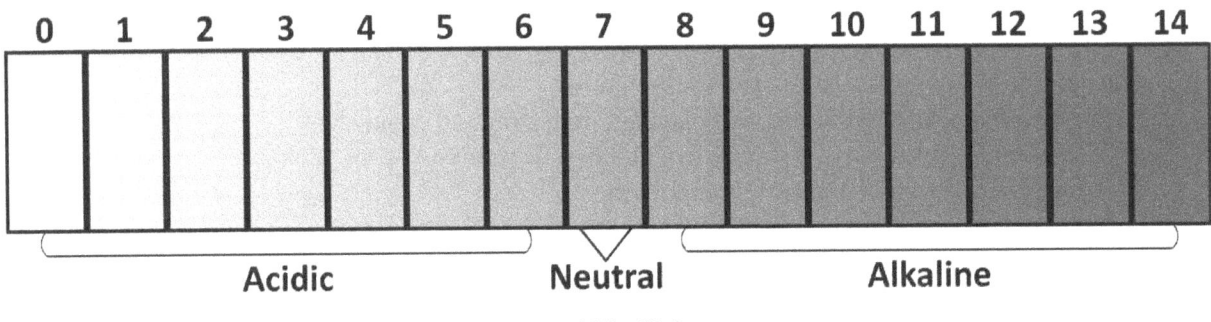

Figure 10.6. The pH Scale

Practice Question

12. Which of the following is the product of a neutralization reaction?
    A) a base
    B) a buffer
    C) hydrogen ions
    D) a salt

13. What will happen to the pH of a nitric acid solution that is diluted by a factor of ten?
    A) The pH will go up ten units.
    B) The pH will go down ten units.
    C) The pH will go up one unit.
    D) The pH will go down one unit.

Motion

To study motion, it is necessary to understand the concept of scalars and vectors.

Scalars are measurements that have a quantity but no direction. **Vectors**, in contrast, have both a quantity and a direction. **Distance** is a scalar: it describes how far an object has traveled along a path. Distance can have values such as 54 m or 16 miles. **Displacement** is a vector: it describes how far an object has traveled from its starting position. A displacement value will indicate direction, such as 54 m east or –16 miles.

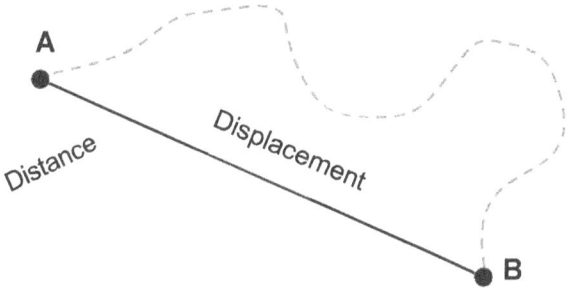

Figure 10.7. Distance versus Displacement

Speed describes how quickly something is moving. It is found by dividing distance by time, and so is a scalar value. **Velocity** is the rate at which an object changes position. Velocity is found by dividing displacement by time, meaning it is a vector value. An object that travels a certain distance and then returns to its starting point has a velocity of zero because its final position did not change. Its speed, however, can be found by dividing the total distance it traveled by the time it took to make the trip.

Acceleration describes how quickly an object changes velocity. It is also a vector: when acceleration is in the same direction as velocity, the object will move faster. When the acceleration is in the opposite direction of velocity, the object will slow down.

Practice Question

14. A person starts from rest and increases his velocity to 5 m/s over a time period of 1 second. What is his acceleration?
    A) -5 m/s^2
    B) 0 m/s^2
    C) 5 m/s^2
    D) 10 m/s^2

Forces

A push or pull that causes an object to move or change direction is called a force. Forces can arise from a number of different sources.

Gravity is the attraction of one mass to another mass. For example, the earth's gravitational field pulls objects toward it, and the sun's gravitational field keeps planets in motion around it.

Electrical force is the creation of a field by charged particles that will cause other charged objects in that field to move.

Tension is found in ropes pulling or holding up an object.

Friction is created by two objects moving against each other.

Normal force occurs when an object is resting on another object.

Buoyant force is the upward force experienced by floating objects.

In 1687, Isaac Newton published **three laws of motion** that describe the behavior of force and mass. Newton's first law is also called the **law of inertia**. It states that an object will maintain its current state of motion unless acted on by an outside force.

Newton's **second law** is an equation, $F = ma$. The equation states that increasing the force on an object will increase its acceleration. In addition, the mass of the object will determine its acceleration: under the same force, a small object will accelerate more quickly than a larger object.

An object in equilibrium is either at rest or is moving at constant velocity; in other words, the object has no acceleration, or $a = 0$. Using Newton's second law, an object is in equilibrium if the net force on the object is 0, or $F = 0$ (this is called the equilibrium condition).

Newton's **third law** states that for every action (force), there will be an equal and opposite reaction (force). For instance, if a person is standing on the floor, there is a force of gravity pulling him toward the earth. However, he is not accelerating toward the earth; he is simply standing at rest on the floor (in equilibrium). So, the floor must provide a force that is equal in magnitude and in the opposite direction to the force of gravity.

Practice Question

15. When a car moving forward stops abruptly, which of the following describes what happens to the driver if she is wearing a seat belt?
    A) The driver's body will continue to move forward due to inertia, and the seat belt will apply the required force to keep her in her seat.
    B) The driver is inside the car, so she will stop with the car whether or not she is wearing a seat belt.
    C) Due to inertia, the driver's body wants to be at rest, so she will stop automatically once the car stops moving.
    D) The driver's body will slow down because inertia is passed from the seat belt in the car to the driver.

16. Which example describes an object in equilibrium?
    A) a parachutist after he jumps from an airplane
    B) an airplane taking off
    C) a person sitting still in a chair
    D) a soccer ball when it is kicked

Work

Work is a scalar value that is defined as the application of a force over a distance. It is measured in Joules (J).

A person lifting a book off the ground is an example of someone doing work. The book has a weight because it is being pulled toward the earth. As the person lifts the book, her hand and arm are producing a force that is larger than that weight, causing the book to rise. The higher the person lifts the book, the more work is done.

The sign of the work done is important. In the example of lifting a book, the person's hand is doing positive (+) work on the book. However, gravity is always pulling the book down, which means that during a lift, gravity is doing negative (−) work on the book. If the force and the displacement are in the same direction, then the work is positive (+). If the force and the displacement are in opposite directions, then the work is negative (−). In the case of lifting a book, the net work done on the book is positive.

Practice Question

17. Which situation requires the most work done on a car?
    A) pushing on the car, but it does not move
    B) towing the car up a steep hill for 100 meters
    C) pushing the car 5 meters across a parking lot
    D) painting the car

Energy

Energy is an abstract concept, but everything in nature has an energy associated with it. Energy is measured in Joules (J). There are many types of energy:

- mechanical: the energy of motion
- chemical: the energy in chemical bonds
- thermal: the energy of an object due to its temperature
- nuclear: the energy in the nucleus of an atom
- electric: the energy arising from charged particles
- magnetic: the energy arising from a magnetic field

10. Physical Science

There is an energy related to movement called the **kinetic energy (KE)**. Any object that has mass and is moving will have a kinetic energy.

Potential energy (PE) is the energy stored in a system; it can be understood as the potential for an object to gain kinetic energy. There are several types of potential energy.

Electric potential energy is derived from the interaction between positive and negative charges.

Compressing a spring stores **elastic potential energy**.

Energy is also stored in chemical bonds as **chemical potential energy**.

The energy stored by objects due to their height is **gravitational potential energy**.

Energy can be converted into other forms of energy, but it cannot be created or destroyed. This principle is called the **conservation of energy**. A swing provides a simple example of this principle. Throughout the swing's path, the total energy of the system remains the same. At the highest point of a swing's path, it has potential energy but no kinetic energy (because it has stopped moving momentarily as it changes direction). As the swing drops, that potential energy is converted to kinetic energy, and the swing's velocity increases. At the bottom of its path, all its potential energy has been converted into kinetic energy (meaning its potential energy is zero). This process repeats as the swing moves up and down. At any point in the swing's path, the kinetic and potential energies will sum to the same value.

Figure 10.8. Conservation of Energy in a Swing

Practice Question

18. Imagine a roller coaster that does not have its own power and starts on a hill at a height of 100 meters. There is no air resistance or friction. It falls down to a height of 50 meters in the first dip and begins to move up the next hill, which is 200 meters high. What will happen to the coaster on this hill?
    A) It will slow down but will make it over the 200 meter hill.
    B) It will make it 150 meters up the hill and move back down to the first dip.
    C) It will make it 100 meters up the hill and move back down to the first dip.
    D) It will make it 75 meters up the hill and move back down to the first dip.

19. A pendulum with mass m is swinging back and forth. Which of the following statements about the pendulum's speed is true?
   A) The maximum speed of the mass will occur when it's closest to the ground.
   B) The maximum speed of the mass will occur when it's farthest from the ground.
   C) The mass will always travel at the same speed.
   D) The maximum speed of the mass will occur when it is halfway between its lowest and highest point.

Waves

Energy can also be transferred through **waves**, which are repeating pulses of energy. Waves that travel through a medium, like ripples on a pond or compressions in a Slinky, are called **mechanical waves**. Waves that vibrate up and down (like the ripples on a pond) are **transverse waves**, and those that travel through compression (like the Slinky) are **longitudinal waves**. Mechanical waves will travel faster through denser mediums; for example, sound waves will move faster through water than through air.

Longitudinal Wave

Transverse Wave

Figure 10.9. Types of Waves

Waves can be described using a number of different properties. A wave's highest point is called its **crest**, and its lowest point is the **trough**. A wave's **midline** is halfway between the crest and trough; the **amplitude** describes the distance between the midline and the crest (or trough). The distance between crests (or troughs) is the wavelength. A wave's **period** is the time it takes for a wave to go through one complete cycle, and the number of cycles a wave goes through in a specific period of time is its **frequency**.

Sound is a special type of longitudinal wave created by vibrations. Our ears are able to interpret these waves as particular sounds. The frequency, or rate, of the vibration determines the sound's **pitch**. **Loudness** depends on the amplitude, or height, of a sound wave.

The **doppler effect** is the difference in perceived pitch caused by the motion of the object creating the wave. For example, as an ambulance approaches an observer, the siren's pitch will appear to increase, and then as the ambulance moves away, the siren's pitch will appear to decrease. This occurs because sound waves are compressed as the ambulance approaches the observer and are spread out as the ambulance moves away from the observer.

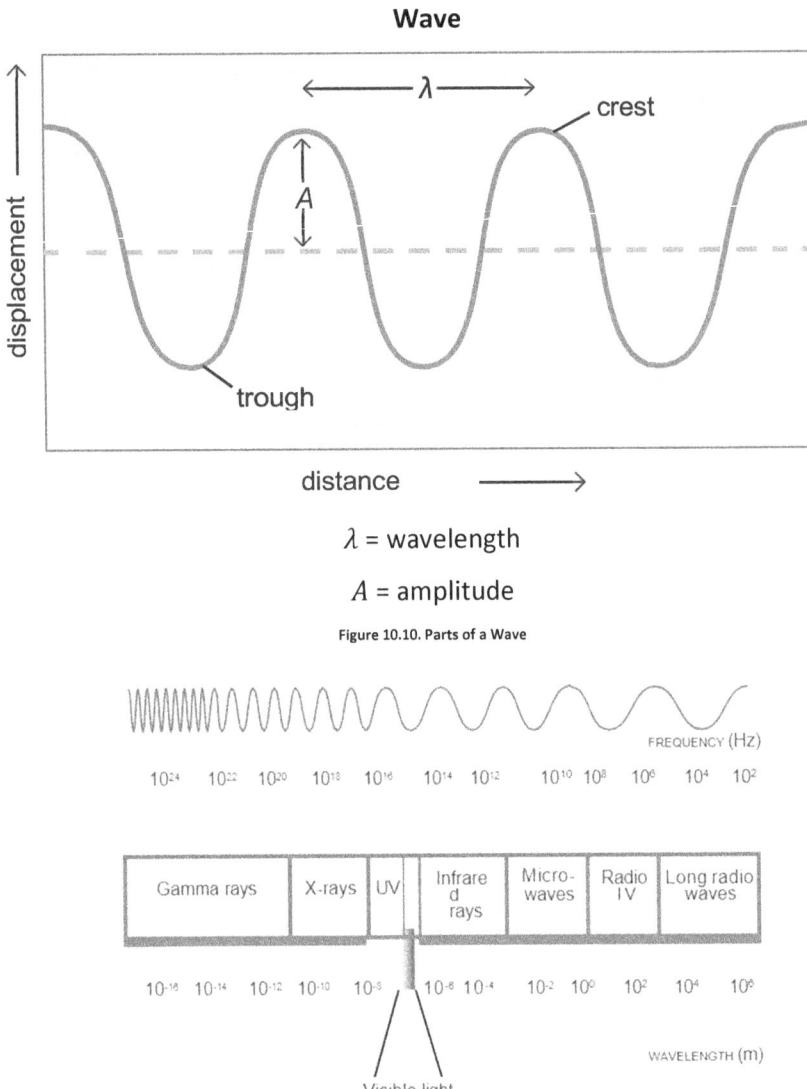

Figure 10.10. Parts of a Wave

Figure 10.11. The Electromagnetic Spectrum

Electromagnetic waves are composed of oscillating electric and magnetic fields and thus do not require a medium through which to travel. The electromagnetic spectrum classifies the types of electromagnetic waves based on their frequency. These include radio waves, microwaves, X-rays, and visible light.

The study of light is called **optics**. Because visible light is a wave, it will display properties that are similar to other waves. It will **reflect**, or bounce off, surfaces, which can be observed by shining a flashlight on a mirror. Light will also **refract**, or bend, when it travels between substances. This effect can be seen by placing a pencil in water and observing the apparent bend in the pencil.

Curved pieces of glass called **lenses** can be used to bend light in a way that affects how an image is perceived. Some microscopes, for example, make objects appear larger through the use of specific types of lenses. Eyeglasses also use lenses to correct poor vision.

The frequency of a light wave is responsible for its color, with red/orange colors having a lower frequency than blue/violet colors. White light is a blend of all the frequencies of visible light. Passing white light through a prism will bend each frequency at a slightly different angle, separating the colors and creating a rainbow. Sunlight passing through raindrops can undergo this effect, creating large rainbows in the sky.

Practice Question

20. Which type of wave is a longitudinal wave?
    A) ocean wave
    B) light wave
    C) sound wave
    D) X-ray wave

21. Which of the following events is caused by refraction?
    A) a rainbow during a rainstorm
    B) an echo in a cave
    C) a candle appearing in a mirror
    D) the Doppler effect

Electricity and Magnetism

Electric charge is created by a difference in the balance of protons and electrons, which creates a positively or negatively charged object. Charged objects create an **electric field** that spreads outward from the object. Other charged objects in that field will experience a force: objects that have opposite charges will be attracted to each other, and objects with the same charge will be repelled, or pushed away, from each other.

Because protons cannot leave the nucleus, charge is created by the movement of electrons. **Static electricity**, or electrostatic charge, occurs when a surface has a buildup of charges. For example, if a student rubs a balloon on her head, the friction will cause electrons to move from her hair to the balloon. This creates a negative charge on the balloon and a positive charge on her hair; the resulting attraction will cause her hair to move toward the balloon.

Electricity is the movement of electrons through a conductor, and an electric circuit is a closed loop through which electricity moves. Circuits include a **voltage** source, which powers the movement of electrons known as **current**. Sources of voltage include batteries, generators, and wall outlets (which are in turn powered by electric power stations). Other elements, such as lights, computers, and microwaves, can then be connected to the circuit and then powered by its electricity.

Magnets are created by the alignment of spinning electrons within a substance. This alignment will occur naturally in some substances, including iron, nickel, and cobalt, all of which can be used to produce permanent magnets. The alignment of electrons creates a magnetic field, which, like an electric or gravitational field, can act on other objects. Magnetic fields have a north and a south pole that act similarly to electric charges: opposite poles will attract, and same poles will repel each other. However, unlike electric charge, which can be either positive or negative, a magnetic field ALWAYS has two poles. If a magnet is cut in half, the result is two magnets, each with a north and a south pole.

10. Physical Science

Electricity and magnetism are closely related. A moving magnet creates an electric field, and a moving charged particle creates a magnetic field. A specific kind of temporary magnet known as an **electromagnet** can be made by coiling a wire around a metal object and running electricity through it. A magnetic field will be created when the wire contains a current but will disappear when the flow of electricity is stopped.

Practice Question

22. What part of the atom flows through a circuit to power a light bulb?
    A) protons
    B) neutrons
    C) electrons
    D) nucleus

23. Which metal attracts magnets?
    A) iron
    B) copper
    C) silver
    D) gold

Answer Key

1. D: The total charge of an atom is the difference between the number of protons and electrons. Subtract the number of electrons from the number of protons: $5 - 7 = -2$.

2. C: Calcium has an atomic number of 20 (found on the Periodic table), meaning it has 20 protons. For a Ca ion to have a charge of 1+, it must have nineteen electrons. All the other ions have eighteen electrons.

3. A: Bismuth is a metal.

4. C: Lithium and sodium are both in Group 1 of the periodic table, so they have similar chemical properties. Sodium will form the ion Na^+ and join with F^- to form NaF.

5. B: Carbon and oxygen are both nonmetals that combine through a covalent bond. Oxygen has a strong pull on their shared electrons, so CO_2 is polar. In hydrogen gas (H_2), the identical hydrogen atoms share electrons equally, so the compound is nonpolar. Choices A and D are ionic compounds.

6. A: When water changes form, it does not change the chemical composition of the substance. Once water becomes ice, the ice can easily turn back into water by increasing its temperature.

7. B: Evaporation is the process of conversion from liquid to gas that occurs at the boiling point.

8. C: In the reaction, the Pb and K exchange their anions in a double-displacement reaction.

9. C: In this equation, there are equal numbers of each type of atom on both sides (2 K atoms, 2 Cl atoms, and 6 O atoms).

10. A: A heterogeneous mixture is any non-uniform mixture, which means that the atoms or molecules are unevenly distributed.

11. A: An unsaturated solution has less solute than can be dissolved in the given amount of solvent.

12. D: A neutralization reaction occurs when an acid and a base combine to form a salt and water.

13. C: The pH will go up: diluting an acid will decrease the concentration of H^+ ions, and higher pH values represent lower concentrations of H^+ ions. Diluting the acid by a factor of ten will change the pH one unit because the pH scale is logarithmic.

14. C: Acceleration is the change in velocity over the change in time:

$$a = \frac{v}{t} = \frac{5\ m/s - 0\ m/s}{1\ s} = 5\ m/s^2$$

15. A: The driver's body will continue moving forward due to inertia. A force is required to slow the driver down (Newton's first law).

16. C: A person sitting in a chair is not accelerating. All the other choices describe objects that are accelerating, or changing velocity.

17. B: A steep hill requires a large force to counter the gravitational force. The large distance will also lead to a large amount of work done. Less work is done in choice C), and no work is done in choice A). Choice D) is incorrect because painting the car is "work," but not the technical definition of work. The car is not moving while being painted, so no work is done on the car.

18. C: Its maximum energy is from its starting point, the potential energy at 100 meters, so it can never move higher than 100 meters.

19. A: The mass always has the same total energy. When the height is the lowest, the potential energy is at its minimum, and so the kinetic energy is at its maximum. When kinetic energy is high, the mass's velocity will be at its height.

20. C: Sound waves are longitudinal waves because the vibrations travel in the same direction as the energy.

21. A: The light of the sun hits rain droplets and bends into a band of colors. The bending of waves is refraction.

22. C: Electrons are negatively charged subatomic particles that exist outside the nucleus of an atom. A power source forces moving electrons through a circuit.

23. A: Magnets readily attract iron. The other metals are not attracted to magnets.

11. Earth and Space Science

Astronomy

Astronomy is the study of space. Our planet, **Earth**, is just one out of a group of planets that orbit the sun, which is the star at the center of our solar system. Other planets in our solar system include Mercury, Venus, Mars, Jupiter, Saturn, Uranus, and Neptune.

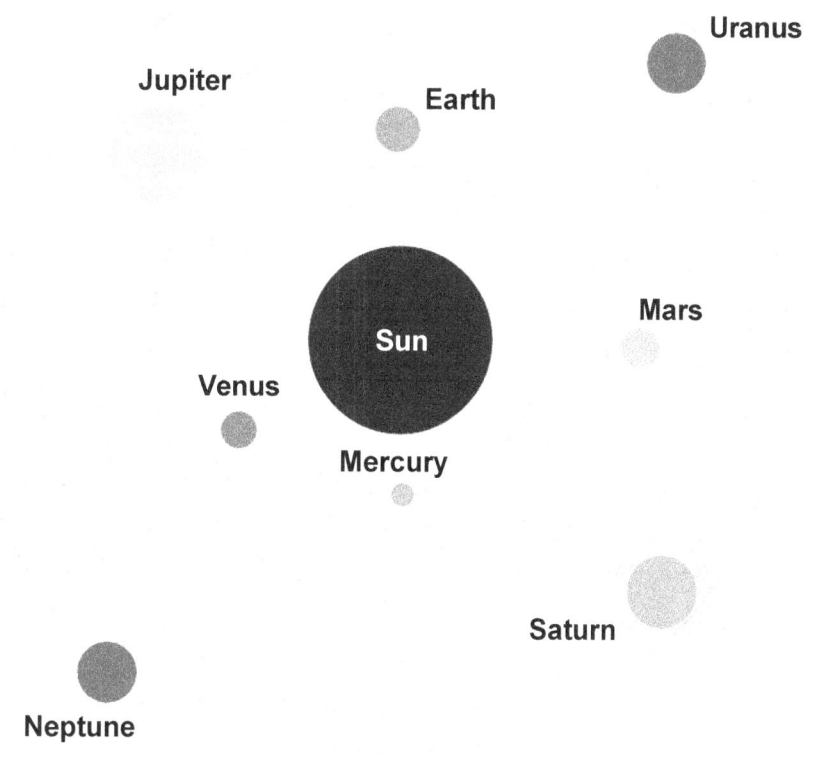

Figure 11.1. Solar System

Every planet, except Mercury and Venus, has **moons**, or naturally occurring satellites that orbit a planet. Our solar system also includes **asteroids** and **comets**, small rocky or icy objects that orbit the Sun. Many of these are clustered in the **asteroid belt**, which is located between the orbits of Mars and Jupiter.

Our solar system is a small part of a bigger star system called a **galaxy**. (Our galaxy is called the Milky Way.) Galaxies consist of stars, gas, and dust held together by gravity and contain millions of **stars**, which are hot balls of plasma and gases. The universe includes many types of stars, including supergiant stars, white dwarfs, giant stars, and neutron stars. Stars form in **nebulas**, which are large clouds of dust and gas. When very large stars collapse, they create **black holes**, which have a gravitational force so strong that light cannot escape.

Earth, the moon, and the sun interact in a number of ways that impact life on our planet. When the positions of the three align, eclipses occur. A **lunar eclipse** occurs when Earth lines up between the moon and the sun; the moon moves into the shadow of Earth and appears dark in color. A **solar eclipse** occurs when the moon lines up between Earth and the sun; the moon covers the sun, blocking sunlight.

The cycle of day and night and the seasonal cycle are determined by the earth's motion. It takes approximately 365 days, or one **year**, for Earth to revolve around the sun. While Earth is revolving around the sun, it is also rotating on its axis, which takes approximately twenty-four hours, or one **day**. As the planet rotates, different areas alternately face toward the sun and away from the sun, creating night and day.

The earth's axis is not directly perpendicular to its orbit, meaning the planet tilts on its axis. The **seasons** are caused by this tilt. When the Northern Hemisphere is tilted toward the sun, it receives more sunlight and experiences summer. At the same time that the Northern Hemisphere experiences summer, the Southern Hemisphere, which receives less direct sunlight, experiences winter. As the earth revolves, the Northern Hemisphere will tilt away from the sun and move into winter, while the Southern Hemisphere tilts toward the sun and moves into summer.

Practice Question

1. What term describes what occurs when the moon moves between the earth and the sun?
    A) aurora
    B) lunar eclipse
    C) black hole
    D) solar eclipse

Geology

Geology is the study of the minerals and rocks that make up the earth. A **mineral** is a naturally occurring, solid, inorganic substance with a crystalline structure. There are several properties that help identify a mineral, including color, luster, hardness, and density. Examples of minerals include talc, diamonds, and topaz.

> **Did You Know?**
>
> Luster describes how light reflects off the surface of a mineral. Terms to describe luster include dull, metallic, pearly, and waxy.

Although a **rock** is also a naturally occurring solid, it can be either organic or inorganic and is composed of one or more minerals. Rocks are classified based on their method of formation. The three types of rocks are igneous, sedimentary, and metamorphic. **Igneous rocks** are the result of tectonic processes that bring magma, or melted rock, to the earth's surface; they can form either above or below the surface. **Sedimentary rocks** are formed from the compaction of rock fragments that results from weathering and erosion. Lastly, **metamorphic rocks** form when extreme temperature and pressure cause the structure of pre-existing rocks to change.

The **rock cycle** describes how rocks form and break down. Typically, the cooling and solidification of magma as it rises to the surface creates igneous rocks. These rocks are then subject to **weathering**, the mechanical and/or chemical processes by which rocks break down. During **erosion** the resulting sediment is deposited in a new location.

As sediment is deposited, the resulting compaction creates new sedimentary rocks. As new layers are added, rocks and minerals are forced closer to the earth's core where they are subjected to heat and pressure, resulting in meta- morphic rock. Eventually, they will reach their melting point and return to magma, starting the cycle over again. This process takes place over hundreds of thousands or even millions of years.

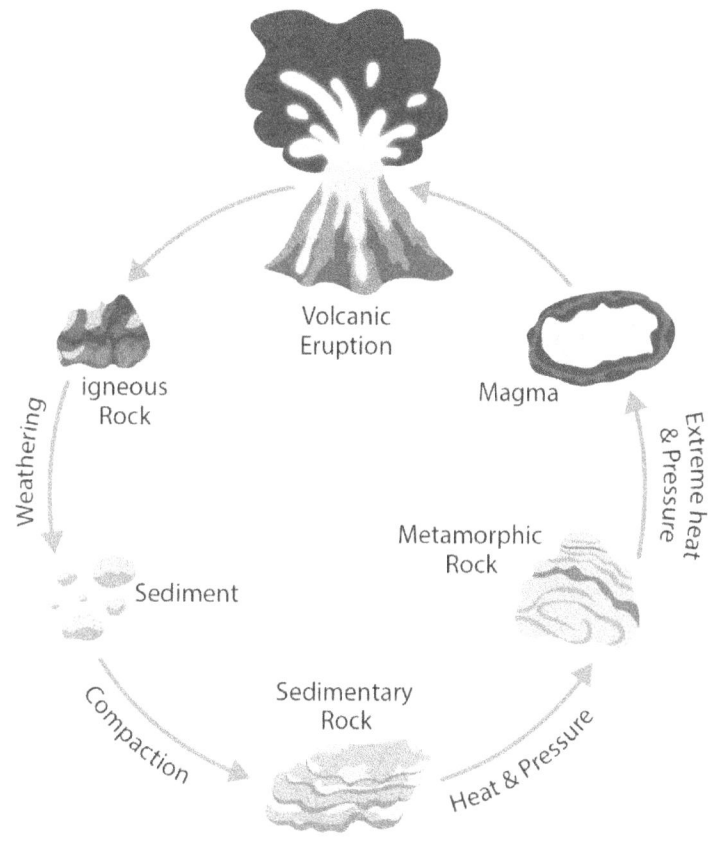

Figure 11.2. The Rock Cycle

Paleontology, the study of the history of life on Earth, is sometimes also considered part of geology. Paleontologists study the rock record, which retains biological history through **fossils**, the preserved remains and traces of ancient life. Fossils can be used to learn about the evolution of life on the planet, particularly bacteria, plants, and animals that have gone extinct. Throughout Earth's history, there have been five documented catastrophic events that caused major extinctions. For each mass extinction, there are several theories about the cause but no definitive answers. Theories about what triggered mass extinctions include climate change, ice ages, asteroid and comet impacts, and volcanic activity.

The surface of the earth is made of large plates that float on the less dense layer beneath them. These **tectonic plates** make up the lithosphere, the planet's surface layer. Over 200 million years ago, the continents were joined together in one giant landmass called **Pangea**. Due to **continental drift**, or the slow movement of tectonic plates, the continents gradually shifted to their current positions.

The boundaries where plates meet are the locations for many geologic features and events. **Mountains** are formed when plates collide and push land upward, and **trenches** form when one plate is pushed beneath another. In addition, the friction created by plates sliding past each other is responsible for most **earthquakes**.

Volcanoes, which are vents in the earth's crust that allow molten rock to reach the surface, frequently occur along the edges of tectonic plates. However, they can also occur at hotspots located far from plate boundaries.

> **Did You Know?**
>
> The magnitude of an earthquake refers to the amount of energy it releases, measured as the maximum motion during the earthquake. This can indirectly describe how destructive the earthquake was.

The outermost layer of the earth, which includes tectonic plates, is called the **lithosphere**. Beneath the lithosphere are, in order, the **asthenosphere**, **mesosphere**, and **core**. The core includes two parts: the **outer core** is a liquid layer, and the **inner core** is composed of solid iron. It is believed the inner core spins at a rate slightly different from the rest of the planet, which creates the earth's magnetic field.

Practice Question

2. Which type of rock forms when lava cools and solidifies?
    A) igneous
    B) sedimentary
    C) metamorphic
    D) sandstone

Hydrology

The earth's surface includes many bodies of water that together form the **hydrosphere**. The largest of these are the bodies of salt water called **oceans**. There are five oceans: the Arctic, Atlantic, Indian, Pacific, and Southern. Together, the oceans account for 71 percent of the earth's surface and 97 percent of the earth's water.

Oceans are subject to cyclic rising and falling water levels at shorelines called **tides**, which are the result of the gravitational pull of the moon and sun. The oceans also experience **waves**, which are caused by the movement of energy through the water.

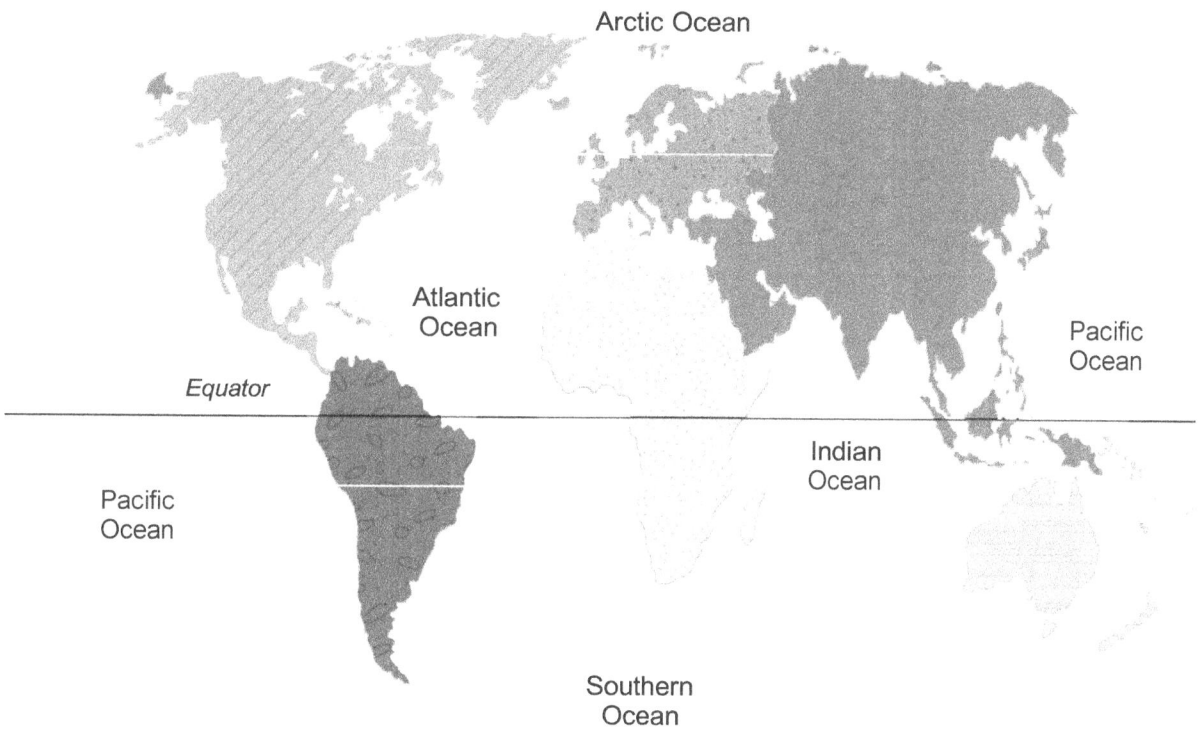

Figure 11.3. The Earth's Oceans

Other bodies of water include **lakes**, which are usually freshwater, and **seas**, which are usually saltwater. **Rivers** and streams are moving bodies of water that flow into lakes, seas, and oceans. The earth also contains groundwater, or water that is stored underground in rock formations called **aquifers**.

> **Did You Know?**
>
> 97 percent of the water on earth is saltwater. 68 percent of the remaining freshwater is locked up in ice caps and glaciers.

Much of the earth's water is stored as **ice**. The North and South Poles are usually covered in large sheets of ice called polar ice. **Glaciers** are large masses of ice and snow that move. Over long periods of time, they scour Earth's surface, creating features such as lakes and valleys. Large chunks of ice that break off from glaciers are called **icebergs**.

The **water cycle** is the circulation of water throughout the earth's surface, atmosphere, and hydrosphere. Water on the earth's surface evaporates, or changes from a liquid to a gas, and becomes water vapor. Plants also release water vapor through transpiration. Water vapor in the air then comes together to form clouds. When it cools, this water vapor condenses into a liquid and falls from the sky as precipitation, which includes rain, sleet, snow, and hail.

Precipitation replenishes groundwater and the water found in features such as lakes and rivers, thus starting the cycle over again.

Figure 11.4. The Water Cycle

Practice Question

3. During the water cycle, groundwater is replenished by
   A) transpiration.
   B) glaciers.
   C) lakes.
   D) precipitation.

Meteorology

Above the surface of Earth is the mass of gases called the **atmosphere**. The atmosphere includes the **troposphere**, which is closest to the earth, followed by the **stratosphere**, **mesosphere**, and **thermosphere**. The outermost layer of the atmosphere is the **exosphere**, which is located 6,200 miles above the surface. Generally, temperature in the atmosphere decreases with altitude. The **ozone layer**, which captures harmful radiation from the sun, is located in the stratosphere.

The **humidity**, or amount of water vapor in the air, and the **temperature** are two major atmospheric conditions that determine weather, the day-to-day changes in atmospheric conditions. A **warm front** occurs when warm air moves over a cold air mass, causing the air to feel warmer and more humid. A **cold front** occurs when cold air moves under a warm air mass, causing a drop in temperature.

> **Did You Know?**
>
> Between each layer, a boundary exists where conditions change. This boundary takes the first part of the name of the previous layer followed by "pause." For example, the boundary between the troposphere and stratosphere is called the tropopause.

Sometimes, weather turns violent. Tropical cyclones, or hurricanes, originate over warm ocean water. Hurricanes have destructive winds of more than 74 miles per hour and create large storm surges that can cause extensive damage along coast- lines. Hurricanes, typhoons, and cyclones are all the same type of storm; they just have different names based on where the storm is located. **Hurricanes** originate in the Atlantic or Eastern Pacific Ocean, **typhoons** in the Western Pacific Ocean, and **cyclones** in the Indian Ocean. **Tornadoes** occur when unstable warm and cold air masses collide and a rotation is created by fast-moving winds.

The long-term weather conditions in a geographic location are called **climate**. A climate zone is a large area that experiences similar average temperature and precipitation. The three major climate zones, based on temperature, are the polar, temperate, and tropical zones. Each climate zone is subdivided into subclimates that have unique characteristics. The **tropical climate zone** (warm temperatures) can be subdivided into tropical wet, tropical wet and dry, semiarid, and arid. The **temperate climate zones** (moderate temperatures) include Mediterranean, humid subtropical, marine West Coast, humid continental, and subarctic. The **polar climate zones** (cold temperatures) include tundra, highlands, nonpermanent ice, and ice cap. Polar climates are cold and experience prolonged, dark winters due to the tilt of the earth's axis.

Practice Question

4. Which layer of the atmosphere absorbs harmful ultraviolet radiation from the sun?
    A) mesosphere
    B) stratosphere
    C) troposphere
    D) thermosphere

Answer Key

1. D: When the moon moves between the earth and the sun, a solar eclipse occurs, blocking sunlight from the planet.

2. A: Igneous rocks form when liquid rock cools and solidifies.

3. D: Precipitation such as rain and snow seep into the ground to add to the groundwater supply.

4. B: The stratosphere contains a sublayer called the ozone layer, which absorbs harmful ultraviolet radiation from the sun.

12. United States History

North America Before European Contact

Prior to European colonization, diverse Native American societies controlled the continent; they would later come into economic and diplomatic contact, and military conflict, with European colonizers and United States forces and settlers.

Major civilizations that would play an important and ongoing role in North American history included the **Iroquois** and **Algonquin** in the Northeast. Both of those tribes would also be important allies of the English and French, respectively, in future conflicts, in that part of the continent.

Later, the young United States would come into conflict with the **Shawnee, Lenape, Kickapoo, MIAMI**, and other tribes in the Midwest during early western expansion. These tribes formed the Northwest Confederacy to fight the United States.

In the South, major tribes included the **Chickasaw, Choctaw,** and **Creek** (Muscogee), who were the descendants of the **Mississippi Mound Builders** or Mississippian cultures, societies that built mounds from around 2,100 to 1,800 years ago as burial tombs or the bases for temples. It is thought that the **Cherokee** migrated south to present-day Georgia sometime long before European contact, where they remained until they were forcibly removed in 1832.

Farther west, tribes of the Great Plains like the **Sioux, Cheyenne, Apache, Comanche,** and **Arapaho** would later come into conflict with American settlers as westward expansion continued. Traditionally nomadic or semi-nomadic, these tribes depended on the **Buffalo** for survival.

The **Navajo** controlled territory in the Southwest. The Navajo were descendants of the **Ancestral Pueblo** or **Anasazi**, who had settled in the Four Corners area.

In the Pacific Northwest, fishing was a major source of sustenance, and Native American peoples like the **Coast Salish** and **Chinook** created and used canoes to engage in the practice.

Ultimately, through both violent conflict and political means, Native American civilizations lost control of most of their territories and were forced onto reservations by the United States. Negotiations continue today over rights to land and opportunities and reparations for past injustices.

Colonial North America

The Americas were quickly colonized by Europeans after Christopher Columbus first laid claim to them for the Spanish, and the British, French, and Spanish all held territories in North America throughout the sixteenth, seventeenth, eighteenth, and nineteenth centuries.

Spanish *conquistadors* explored what is today the Southwestern United States, claiming land inhabited by local tribes for Spain. Spanish colonization not only included the control and settlement of land but also the mission to spread Christianity. The Spanish Crown granted *encomiendas*, land grants to individuals to establish settlements, allowing the holder to ranch or mine the land and demand tribute and forced labor from local Native peoples.

Forced labor and diseases like **smallpox** had decimated Native American populations in Mexico and the Southwest. Consequently, to exploit these resource-rich lands, Spanish colonizers took part in the European-driven **transatlantic slave trade**, kidnapping African people or purchasing them on the West African coast, bringing them to the Americas, and forcing them into slavery in mines and plantations in the Western Hemisphere.

> **Did You Know?**
>
> Eventually France would control much of the Great Lakes and the Mississippi region through Louisiana and New Orleans, valuable trade routes. French explorers included **Jacques Cartier** and **Samuel de Champlain**, who founded New France.

Unlike Spain, which sought not only profit but also to settle the land and convert Native Americans to Christianity, France was mainly focused on trade. French explorers reached the Northeast and the eastern Great Lakes region as early as the seventeenth century in search of fur and beaver pelts.

While the Spanish and French arrived generally as single men for trade, who would intermarry with local inhabitants, the English brought their families and settled in North America, with the goal of establishing agricultural settlements. In the sixteenth century, Sir Walter Raleigh established the Roanoke colony in present-day Virginia; while this settlement disappeared by 1590, interest in colonization reemerged as **joint stock companies** sought royal charters to privately develop colonies on the North American Atlantic coast.

The first established colony, **Jamestown**, was also located in Virginia, which became so profitable that the English Crown took it over as a colony in 1624. Tobacco and rice grew in Virginia, the Carolinas, and Georgia. Appropriate for plantation farming, these crops required unskilled labor, and the southern colonies became socially stratified, with a society composed mainly of large numbers of enslaved Africans, indentured servants, and landowners.

In New England, **Separatists**, members of the Church of England who believed it had strayed too far from its theological roots, had come to North America seeking more religious freedom. The first group of Separatists, the Pilgrims, arrived on the Mayflower in 1620 and had drawn up the **Mayflower compact**, guaranteeing government by the consent of the governed. They were later joined by the **Puritans**, who had been persecuted in England. These philosophies would later inform the American Revolution.

Despite differences from the South, social stratification existed in New England as well: according to Puritan belief, wealth and success showed that one was a member of the elect, or privileged by God. Poorer farmers were generally tenant farmers; they did not own land and rarely made a profit.

> **Did You Know?**
>
> The mid-Atlantic colonies were also founded on the basis of religious tolerance in the Quaker spirit inspired by the Quaker William Penn.

The North American colonial economy was part of the **Atlantic World**, taking part in the **triangular trade** between the Americas, Africa and Europe, where people from Africa who were enslaved were exchanged in the Americas for raw materials shipped to Europe to be processed into goods for the benefit of the colonial powers. Sometimes those goods were also exchanged for slaves in Africa. In this way, North America was part of the **Columbian Exchange**, the intersection of goods and people throughout the Atlantic World.

British policy toward the Colonies had been one of **salutary neglect**, allowing them great autonomy. However, an emerging culture of independence in the Thirteen Colonies caught the attention of the British Crown; it passed the **Navigation Acts** in 1651 to prevent colonial trade with any other countries. An early sign of colonial dis- content, **Bacon's Rebellion** in 1676 against Governor Berkeley of Virginia embodied the growing resentment of landowners, who wanted to increase their own profit rather than redirect revenue to Britain.

American colonists were also increasingly influenced by Enlightenment thought. John Locke's *Second Treatise* was published in 1689; critical of absolute monarchy, it became popular in the Colonies. Locke argued for **republicanism**: that the people must come together to create a government for the protection of themselves and their property, thereby giving up some of their natural rights. However, should the government overstep its bounds, the people have the right to overthrow it and replace it.

In the mid-eighteenth century, a sense of religious fervor called the **Great Awakening** spread throughout the Colonies; people became devoted to God beyond the confines of traditional Christianity. The Great Awakening helped develop a more singularly North American religious culture. It also created a divide between traditional European Christianity and emerging North American faiths.

Meanwhile, North America served also as a battleground for France and England, already in conflict in Europe and elsewhere. In the mid-seventeenth century, the two colonial powers fought the proxy Beaver and Chickasaw wars in alliances with Native American tribes in the Northeast and Southeast.

The Seven Years' War broke out in Europe in 1756; this conflict between the British and French in North America was known as the **French and Indian War**. Following defeats by strong colonial military leaders like **George Washington** and despite its strong alliances and long-term presence on the continent, France eventually sur- rendered. Britain gained control of French territories in North America—as well as Spanish Florida—in the 1763 **Treaty of Paris** which ended the Seven Years' War. In the Proclamation of 1763, Britain also promised Native American tribes that it would not expand its colonies farther west.

Revolution and the Early United States

As a result of the French and Indian War and subsequent unrest, Britain once again discarded its colonial policy of salutary neglect. Furthermore, Britain was in desperate need of cash, as the war had nearly bankrupted the country. The Crown sought ways to increase its revenue from the Colonies.

King George III enforced heavy taxes and restrictive acts in the colonies to generate income for the Crown and punish disobedience. These included the **Sugar Act** in 1764 and the **Quartering Act**, requiring colonists to provide shelter to British troops stationed in the region.

The 1765 **Stamp Act**, the first direct tax on the colonists, triggered more tensions. Any document required a costly stamp, the revenue reverting to the British government.

As a result, colonists began boycotting British goods and engaging in violent protest. In response, officials enforced the punitive **Townshend Acts** which imposed more taxes and restrictions on the colonies. Samuel Adams continued to stir up rebellion with his **Committees of Correspondence**, which distributed anti-British propaganda.

Protests against the Quartering Act in Boston led to the **Boston Massacre** in 1770, when British troops fired on a crowd of protesters. By 1773, colonists protested the latest taxes on tea levied by the **Tea Act** in the famous **Boston Tea Party** by dressing as Native Americans and tossing tea off a ship in Boston Harbor. In response, the government passed the **Intolerable Acts**, closing Boston Harbor and bringing Massachusetts back under direct royal control.

In response to the Intolerable Acts, colonial leaders met in Philadelphia at the **First Continental Congress** in 1774 and issued the *Declaration of Rights and Grievances*, presenting colonial concerns to the King, who ignored it. However, violent conflict began in 1775 at **Lexington and Concord**, when American militiamen (**minutemen**) had gathered to resist British efforts to seize weapons and arrest rebels in Concord. On June 17, 1775, the Americans fought the British at the **Battle of Bunker Hill**; despite American losses, the number of casualties the rebels inflicted caused the king to declare that the colonies were in rebellion. Troops were deployed to the colonies; the Siege of Boston began.

In May 1775, the **Second Continental Congress** met at Philadelphia to debate the way forward. Debate between the wisdom of continued efforts at compromise and negotiations and declaring independence continued. **Thomas Paine** published his pamphlet *Common Sense*; taking Locke's concepts of natural rights and the obligation of a people to rebel against an oppressive government, it popularized the notion of rebellion against Britain.

By summer of 1776, the Continental Congress agreed on the need to break from Britain; on July 4, 1776, it declared the independence of the United States of America and issued the **Declaration of Independence**, drafted mainly by **Thomas Jefferson** and heavily influenced by Locke. Pro-revolution Americans were known as **Patriots**; those against were **Tories**. The American Revolution had begun.

George Washington was appointed head of the Continental Army and led a largely unpaid and unprofessional army; despite early losses and the military and financial superiority of the British, Washington and the colonists gained ground due to strong leadership, superior knowledge of the land, and international support. In the 1783 **Treaty of Paris**, the United States was recognized as a country. The American Revolution would go on to inspire revolution around the world.

Did You Know?

The new country was heavily in debt. Currency was weak, and high taxes led to instability in the form of minor rebellions like **Shays' Rebellion**, a revolt of indebted farmers, and the **Whiskey Rebellion**. Furthermore, debt and disorganization made the country appear weak and vulnerable to Great Britain and Spain.

If the United States was to remain one country, it needed a stronger federal government.

Joy in the victory over Great Britain was short-lived. Fearful of tyranny, the Second Continental Congress had provided for only a weak central government, adopting the **Articles of Confederation** to organize the Thirteen Colonies—now states—as a loosely united country. However, it soon became clear that the Articles of Confederation were not strong enough to keep the nation united.

Alexander Hamilton and **James Madison** called for a **Constitutional Convention** to write a Constitution as the foundation of a stronger federal government. Madison and other **federalists** like **John Adams** believed in **separation of powers**, republicanism, and a strong federal government.

Despite the separation of powers provided for in the Constitution, **anti-federalists** like **Thomas Jefferson** called for even more limitations on the power of the federal government. The first ten amendments to the Constitution, or the **Bill of Rights**, a list of guarantees of American freedoms, was a concession to the anti-Federalists, who would later become the **Democratic-Republican Party** (eventually, the Democratic Party).

In order to convince the states to ratify the Constitution, Hamilton, Madison, and John Jay wrote the *Federalist Papers*, articulating the benefits of federalism. Likewise, the Bill of Rights helped convince the hesitant. In 1791, the Constitution was ratified. **George Washington** was elected president, with John Adams serving as vice president; Washington appointed Hamilton as Secretary of the Treasury and Jefferson as Secretary of State.

Federalists favored taxation and centralized financial management, which Anti- Federalists—who became known as **Democratic-Republicans**—vehemently opposed. The US tried to remain neutral in international affairs but was accosted by Britain and France at sea and in conflict in the Northwest Indian Wars.

In President Washington's **Farewell Address**, he recommended the United States follow a policy of neutrality in international affairs, setting a precedent for early American history. Vice President John Adams, a Federalist, became the second president.

During the Adams administration, the Federalists passed the harsh **Alien and Sedition Acts** that increased executive power. Divisions between the Federalists and the Democratic-Republicans were deeper than ever and the presidential elections of 1800 were tense and controversial; nevertheless, Thomas Jefferson was elected to the presidency in 1801 in a historical non-violent transfer of power.

Jefferson shrank the federal government. The Alien and Sedition Acts were repealed. Economic policies favored small farmers and landowners, in contrast to Federalist policies, which supported big business and cities. However, Jefferson also oversaw the **Louisiana purchase**, which nearly doubled the size of the United States. This troubled some Democratic-Republicans, who saw this as federal overreach, but the Louisiana Purchase would be a major step forward in westward expansion.

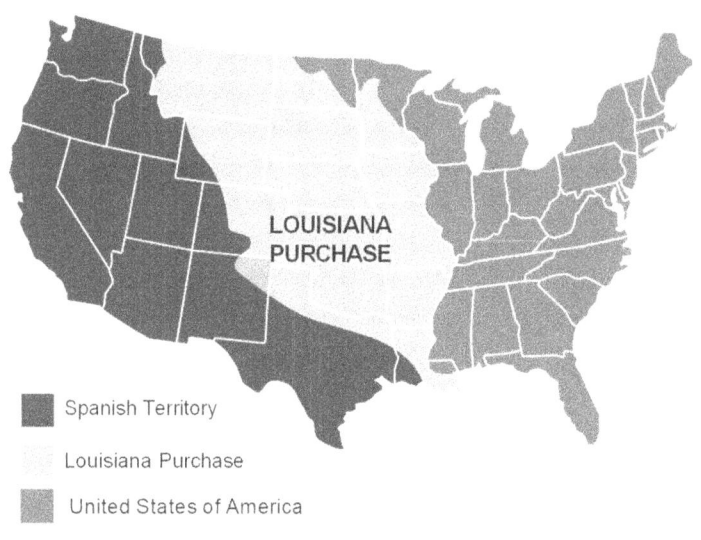

Figure 12.1. Louisiana Purchase

Continuing British provocation at sea and in the northwest led to the **War of 1812**. Growing nationalism in the United States pressured Madison into pushing for war after the **Battle of Tippecanoe** in Indiana, when **General William Henry Harrison** fought the **northwest confederacy**, a group of tribes led by the Shawnee leader **Tecumseh**. Despite the Confederacy's alliance with Britain, the United States prevailed. Congress declared war under Madison with the intent to defend the United States, end chaotic trade practices and treatment of Americans on the high seas, and penetrate British Canada.

The war resulted in no real gains or losses for either the Americans or the British. Yet at the war's end, the United States had successfully defended itself as a country and reaffirmed its independence. Patriotism ran high.

With the Louisiana Purchase, the country had almost doubled in size. In the nineteenth century, the idea of **Manifest destiny**, or the sense that it was the fate of the United States to expand westward and settle the continent, prevailed. The **Monroe Doctrine**, James Monroe's policy that the Western Hemisphere was "closed" to any further European colonization or exploration, asserted US hegemony in the region.

Westward expansion triggered questions about the expansion of slavery, a divisive issue. Slavery was profitable for the southern states which depended on the plantation economy, but increasingly condemned in the North with the growing **Abolitionist** movement. The **Missouri Compromise**, also known as the **Compromise of 1820**, allowed Missouri to join the union as a slave state, but provided that any other states north of the **thirty-sixth parallel (36°30')** would be free. However, more tension and compromises over the nature of slavery in the West were to come.

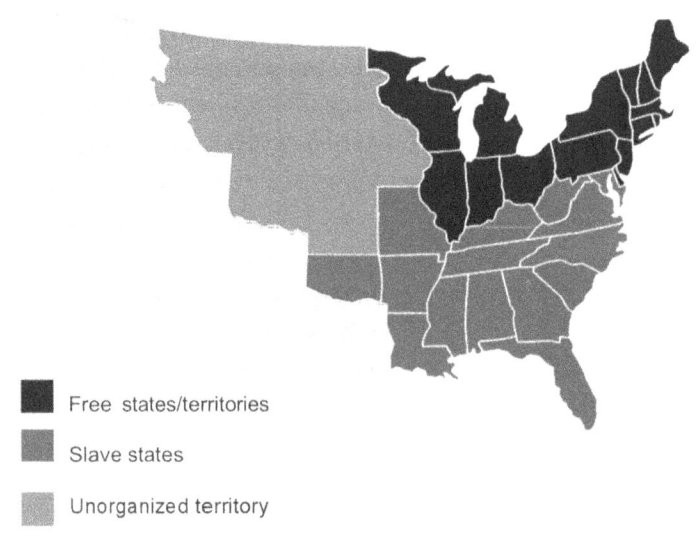

Figure 12.2. Missouri Compromise

Demographics were changing throughout the early nineteenth century. Techno-logical advances such as the **cotton gin** had allowed exponential increases in cotton; therefore, more persons were enslaved than ever before, bringing more urgency to the issue of slavery. In addition, **immigration** from Europe to the United States was increasing—mainly Irish Catholics and Germans. Reactionary **nativist** movements like the **know-nothing party** feared the influx of non-Anglo Europeans, particularly Catholics, and discrimination was widespread, especially against the Irish. Other technological advances like the **railroads** and **steamships** were speeding up westward expansion and improving trade throughout the continent; a large-scale **market economy** was emerging. With early industrialization and changing concepts following the Second Great Awakening, women were playing a larger role in society, even though they could not vote.

Most states had extended voting rights to white men who did not own land or substantial property: **universal manhood suffrage**. Elected officials would increasingly come to better reflect the electorate, and the brash war hero Andrew Jackson was popular among the "common man." During this period, the **two-party system** also emerged.

Jackson's popularity with the "common man," white, male farmers and workers who felt he identified with them, and the fact that owning property was no longer a requirement to vote, gave him the advantage and a two-term presidency. Jackson rewarded his supporters, appointing them to important positions as part of the **spoils system**.

Jackson's administration faced economic crises that exacerbated divisions between northern, industrial interests that supported tariffs, and southern, agrarian interests that opposed them. Jackson also supported further continental expansion, which brought conflict with Native Americans. The 1830 **Indian Removal Act** forced thousands of people to travel mainly on foot, with all of their belongings, to Indian Territory (today, Oklahoma) on the infamous **Trail of Tears**, to make way for white settlers.

Practice Question

1. What advantage did the colonists have in the American Revolution?
    A) vast financial wealth and resources
    B) superior weaponry and equipment
    C) strong leadership and knowledge of the terrain
    D) a professional military and access to mercenaries

Civil War and Westward Expansion

In 1845, Texas, which had declared independence from Mexico in 1836, joined the Union; this event, in the context of US westward expansion, triggered the **Mexican-American War**. As a result, the United States obtained territory in the Southwest, including gold-rich California. The population of California would grow rapidly with the **gold rush** as prospectors in search of gold headed west to try their fortunes. However, Californians of Hispanic descent who had lived in the region under Mexico lost their land and also suffered from racial and ethnic discrimination.

Meanwhile, social change in the Northeast and growing Midwest continued. As the market economy and early industry developed, so did an early **Middle Class**. Activists like **Susan B. Anthony** and **Elizabeth Cady Stanton** worked for women's rights. Women were also active in the temperance movement.

Reform movements continued to include abolitionism, which ranged from moderate to radical. An activist leader and writer, slave **Frederick Douglass** publicized the movement along with the American Anti-Slavery Society and publications like Harriet Beecher Stowe's *Uncle Tom's Cabin*. The radical abolitionist **John Brown** led violent protests against slavery.

Competing factions in Congress had continued to battle over the expansion of slavery, resulting in the unsuccessful 1846 **Wilmot Proviso**; the **Compromise of 1850**, which admitted the populous California as a free state; and the **Fugitive Slave Act**, which allowed slave owners to pursue escaped slaves to free states and recapture them. Congress passed the **Kansas-Nebraska Act of 1854** effectively repealing the Missouri Compromise. Violence broke out in Kansas between pro- and anti-slavery factions in what became known as **Bleeding Kansas**.

In 1856, an escaped slave, **Dred Scott**, took his case to the Supreme Court to sue for freedom. The Court upheld the Fugitive Slave Act, nullified the Missouri Com- promise, and essentially decreed that African Americans were not entitled to rights under US citizenship.

In 1858, a series of debates between Illinois senate candidates, Republican **Abraham Lincoln** and Democrat **Stephen Douglas**, showed the deep divides in the nation over slavery and states' rights. During the **Lincoln-Douglas Debates**, Lincoln spoke out against slavery, while Douglas supported the right of states to decide its legality on their own. In 1860, Lincoln was elected to the presidency. Given Lincoln's outspoken stance against slavery, South Carolina seceded immediately thereafter, followed by Mississippi, Alabama, Florida, Louisiana, Georgia, and Texas. They formed the Confederate States of America, or the **Confederacy**, on February 1, 1861.

Shortly after secession, Confederate forces attacked Union troops in Charleston Harbor, South Carolina; the **Battle of Fort Sumter** sparked the Civil War. As a result, Virginia, Tennessee, North Carolina, and Arkansas seceded and joined the Confederacy.

Did You Know?

Gettysburg, Pennsylvania, was the site of the bloodiest battle in US history up to that point. President Lincoln later delivered the Gettysburg Address there, in which he framed the Civil War as a battle for human rights and equality.

The Confederacy had experienced military leadership and vast territory. The Union had a larger population (strengthened by immigration) and stronger industrial capacity (including weapons-making capacity). Both sides believed the conflict would be short-lived; however it became clear that the war would not end quickly.

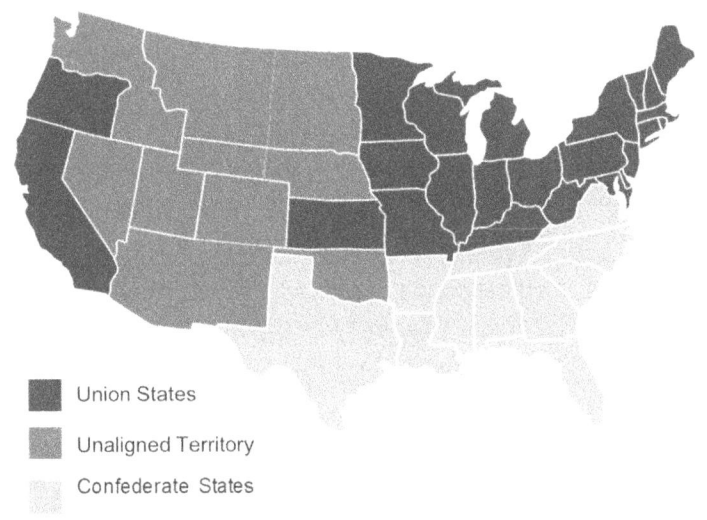

Figure 12.3. Union and Confederacy

The Union developed a blockade to prevent the Confederacy from trading inter- nationally, since the South depended on international cotton trade for much of its income. Several years of bloody battles and economic stagnation resulted in Confederate surrender at Appomattox, Virginia, on April 9, 1865, where General Lee surrendered to General Grant. The war ended shortly after and **reconstruction** began.

On January 1, 1863, President Lincoln had already decreed the end of slavery in the rebel states with the **Emancipation Proclamation**. Before his assassination just a few days after Confederate surrender, Lincoln had crafted the **ten percent plan** permitting a Southern state's readmission to the Union if ten percent of the population swore allegiance to the Union. However Lincoln's vice president, Andrew Johnson, enforced Reconstruction weakly and the white supremacist **Ku Klux Klan** emerged; likewise, states developed the oppressive **black codes** to limit the rights of African Americans.

Congress passed the **Civil Rights Act** in 1866, granting citizenship to African Americans and guaranteeing African American men the same rights as white men (later reaffirmed by the **Fourteenth Amendment**). Eventually former Confederate states also had to ratify the 1865 **Thirteenth Amendment**, which abolished slavery; the **Fourteenth Amendment**, which upheld the provisions of the Civil Rights Act; and the **Fifteenth Amendment**, which in 1870 granted African American men the right to vote.

In 1867, a Republican-led Congress passed the **Reconstruction Acts**, placing former Confederate states under the control of the US Army, effectively declaring martial law, but modernizing Southern education systems, tax collection, and infrastructure. The **Freedmen's Bureau** was tasked with assisting freed slaves in the South.

While enslaved African Americans had been freed, many were not aware of this; others still remained voluntarily or involuntarily on plantations. All slaves were eventually freed; however, few had education or skills. Furthermore, oppressive social structures remained: the **Jim Crow Laws** enforced **segregation** in the South. In 1896, the Supreme Court upheld segregation in **Plessy v. Ferguson** when a mixed-race man, Homer Plessy, was forced off a whites-only train car. When Plessy challenged the law, the Court held that segregation was, indeed, constitutional; according to the Court, *separate but equal* did still ensure equality under the law. This would remain the law until **Brown v. Board of Education** in 1954.

Resentment over the Reconstruction Acts never truly subsided, and military control of the South finally ended with the **Compromise of 1877**, which resolved the disputed presidential election of 1876, granting Rutherford B. Hayes the presidency and removing Union troops from the South.

Did You Know?

Americans of Asian descent moved beyond California and settled in western cities like Denver. They were an important part of the labor force that built the transcontinental railroads.

While the Civil War raged, and during the chaotic post-war Reconstruction period, settlement of the West continued. California had already grown in population due to the gold rush. In the mid-nineteenth century, **Chinese Immigrants** came in large numbers to California. While Chinese Americans faced racism, Americans of European descent were encouraged to settle the Frontier by the **Homestead Act of 1862**. Meanwhile, ranching and herding cattle became popular and profitable. White settlers also hunted the buffalo; mass buffalo killings threatened Native American survival.

Meanwhile, the Great Plains and Rockies were already populated with the Sioux, Cheyenne, Apache, Comanche, Arapaho, Pawnee, and others. Conflict between Native American tribes and white settlers was ongoing. The **Ghost Dance Movement** united Plains tribes in a spiritual movement and in the belief that whites would eventually be driven from the land. In 1890, the military forced the Sioux to cease this ritual; the outcome was a massacre at **Wounded Knee** and the death of the Sioux chief, **Sitting Bull**.

In 1887, the **Dawes Act** ended federal recognition of tribes, withdrew tribal land rights, and forced the sale of reservations—tribal land. It also dissolved Native American families: children were sent to boarding schools, where they were forced to assimilate to the dominant American culture.

Back in the Northeast, the market economy and industry were flourishing. The **Gilded Age** saw an era of rapidly growing income inequality, justified by theories like **Social Darwinism** and the **Gospel of Wealth**, which argued that the wealthy had been made rich by God and were socially more deserving of it.

12. United States History

Practice Question

2. Following the Civil War, the United States ratified the Thirteenth, Fourteenth and Fifteenth Amendments to the Constitution. What did these amendments guarantee?
- A) an end to slavery, equal rights for all Americans, and voting rights for all Americans, respectively
- B) an end to slavery, equal rights for all Americans, and voting rights for all African Americans, respectively
- C) an end to slavery, equal rights for all American men, and voting rights for all African American men, respectively
- D) an end to slavery, equal rights for Americans, and voting rights for African American men, respectively

Industrialization and the Progressive Era

Following the war, the **Industrial Revolution** accelerated in the United States. The Industrial Revolution had begun on the global level with textile production in Great Britain, had been fueled in great part by supplies of Southern cotton, and was evolving in the United States with the development of heavy industry—what would come to be called the **Second Industrial Revolution**. Westward expansion required railroads; railroads required steel, and industrial production required oil: all these commodities spurred the rise of powerful companies like John D. Rockefeller's Standard Oil and Andrew Carnegie's US Steel.

The creation of **monopolies** and **trusts** helped industrial leaders consolidate their control over the entire economy. **Monopolies** let the same business leaders control the market for their own products. Business leaders in varying industries (monopolies) organized into **trusts**, ensuring their control over each other's industries.

With limited governmental controls or interference in the economy, American **Capitalism**—the free market system—was dominated by the elite. Government corruption led only to weak restrictive legislation like the **Interstate Commerce Act** of 1887, which was to regulate the railroad industry, and the **Sherman Antitrust Act** (1890), which was intended to break up monopolies and trusts, in order to allow for a fairer marketplace. However, these measures would remain largely toothless until President Theodore Roosevelt's "trust-busting" administration in 1901.

To continue fueling economic growth, the United States needed more markets abroad. *New Imperialism* described the US approach to nineteenth and early twentieth century imperialism as practiced by the European powers. Rather than controlling territory as the European powers did, the US sought economic connections with countries around the world.

While the free markets and trade of the **capitalist** economy spurred national economic and industrial growth, the **working class**, many of whom were immigrants, suffered from dangerous working conditions and other abuses. As the railroads expanded westward, white farmers, Native Americans, and Mexican Americans suffered: they lost their land to corporate interests. African Americans in the South, though freed from slavery, were also struggling under **sharecropping**, in which many worked the same land owned by former slaveholders, leasing land and equipment at unreasonable rates and unable to profit.

The **People's (Populist) Party** formed in response to corruption and industrialization injurious to farmers (later, it would also support reform in favor of the working class and women and children). Farmers were also concerned about fiscal policy and debt.

At the same time, the **Labor Movement** emerged to support mistreated industrial workers in urban areas using **strikes** and **collective bargaining** to gain protections and fair pay for the unskilled workers who had come to cities seeking industrial jobs. With the continual rise of the **Middle Class**, women took a more active role in advocating for the poor and for themselves. Women activists also aligned with labor and the emerging **progressive movement** to ensure better treatment for workers and immigrants.

With the Progressive **Theodore Roosevelt's** ascension to the presidency in 1901, the Progressive Era reached its apex. The *Trust-Buster* Roosevelt broke up monopolies and obtained fairer treatment for workers. The Progressive Era also saw a series of acts to protect workers, health, farmers, and children.

> **Did You Know?**
>
> Jacob Riis' groundbreaking book and photo essay How the Other Half Lives revealed the squalor and poverty the poor urban classes endured, leading to more public calls for reform.
>
> Check it out to get a better understanding of life in the early twentieth century and prepare for images you might see on HiSET questions. It's available online for free!

Roosevelt also continued overseas expansion following McKinley's **Spanish-American War** (1898 – 1901), in which the US gained control over Spanish territory in the Caribbean, Asia, and the South Pacific. The **Roosevelt Corollary** to the Monroe Doctrine promised US intervention in Latin America in case of European aggression, asserting US dominance in the region.

Practice Question

3. Workers organized labor unions for all of the following reasons EXCEPT
   A) not being paid fairly for their work
   B) shifts that were frequently twelve to fourteen hours a day
   C) to overthrow capitalists like Carnegie and Rockefeller
   D) dangerous working conditions

The United States Becomes a Global Power

Debate had arisen within the US between **interventionism** and **isolationism**—whether the US should intervene in international matters or not. Interventionists believed in spreading US-style democracy, while isolationists believed in focusing on development at home. This debate became more pronounced with the outbreak of World War I in Europe.

Several inflammatory events triggered US intervention in WWI. With victory in 1918, the US had proven itself a superior global military and industrial power. Interventionist **President Woodrow Wilson** played an important role in negotiating the peace. However, divisions between interventionists and isolationists continued.

On the home front, fear of homegrown radicals—particularly of communists and anarchists—and xenophobia against immigrants led to the **Red Scare** in 1919 and a series of anti-immigration laws. In response to widespread xenophobia and a sentiment of isolationism following the First World War,

Congress limited immigration specifically from Asia, Africa, Eastern Europe, and Southern Europe with the racist **Emergency Quota Act** of 1921 and **National Origins Act** of 1924.

The **great migration** of African Americans to the North that had begun after the Civil War continued, but tensions increased with urban race riots in 1919. In the South, the Ku Klux Klan was growing in power, and blacks faced intimidation, violence, and death. **Lynchings**, in which African Americans were kidnapped and murdered, sometimes publicly, occurred frequently. At the same time, African American culture flourished with the **Harlem Renaissance** and become an integral part of a growing American popular culture.

Did You Know?

Japanese-Americans faced oppression and discrimination at home simply due to their race. Forced into internment camps, Japanese Americans challenged this violation of their rights in Korematsu v. US; however, the Supreme Court ruled that this forced displacement was constitutional. In 1988, the US government apologized for its actions.

Following WWI, the United States had experienced an era of consumerism and corruption. The government sponsored **Laissez-Faire** policies and supported **manufacturing**, flooding markets with cheap consumer goods. Union membership suffered; so did farmers, due to falling crop prices. While mass-production helped the emerging middle class afford more consumer goods and improve their living standards, many families resorted to **credit** to fuel consumer spending. These risky consumer loans, **overspeculation** on crops and the value of farmland, and weak banking protections helped bring about the **great depression**. On October 29, 1929, or **Black Tuesday**, the stock market collapsed. During the same time period, a major drought occurred in the Great Plains, affecting farmers throughout the region. Millions of Americans faced unemployment and poverty.

Following weak responses by the Hoover administration, **Franklin Delano Roosevelt** was elected to the presidency in 1932. FDR offered Americans a *New Deal*: a plan to bring the country out of the Depression. During the *first hundred days* of FDR's administration, a series of emergency acts (known as an *Alphabet Soup* of acts due to their many acronyms) was passed for the immediate repair of the banking system. A number of acts also provided relief to the poor and unemployed.

Figure 12.4. Soup Kitchen During the Great Depression

The entire world suffered from the Great Depression, and Europe became increasingly unstable. With the rise of the radical Nazi Party in Germany, the Nazi leader Adolf Hitler led German takeovers of several European countries and became a threat to US allies, bombing Britain. However, the United States, weakened by the Great Depression and reluctant to engage in international affairs due to continuing public and political support for isolationism, remained militarily uncommitted in the war.

After the Japanese attack on **Pearl Harbor** on December 7, 1941, the US entered World War II on the side of the Allies in Europe and the Pacific. The war ended with Japanese surrender in 1945 after the US bombed the Japanese cities **Hiroshima** and **Nagasaki**, the only times that **atomic weapons** have been used in conflict. With most of Europe destroyed, the victorious United States and the Soviet Union emerged as the two global **superpowers**.

The US-led **Marshall Plan** was a program to rebuild Europe, but the USSR consolidated its presence and power in eastern European countries, forcing them to reject aid from the Marshall Plan. This division would destroy the alliance between the Soviets and the West, leading to the **Cold War** between the two superpowers and the emergence of a **Bipolar World**.

With the collapse of the relationship between the USSR and the US, distrust and fear of **communism** grew. Accusations of communist sympathies against public figures ran rampant during the **McCarthy Era** in the 1950s, reflecting domestic anxieties.

President Harry S. Truman's **Truman Doctrine** stated that the US would support any country threatened by authoritarianism (communism), leading to the **Korean War** (1950 – 1953), a conflict between the US and Soviet-backed North Korean forces, which ended in a stalemate. The policy of **containment**, to contain Soviet (communist) expansion, defined US foreign policy. According to **domino theory**, once one country fell to communism, others would quickly follow.

Meanwhile, in Southeast Asia, communist forces in North Vietnam were gaining power. Congress never formally declared war in Vietnam but gave the president authority to intervene militarily there through the **Gulf of Tonkin Resolution** (1964). However, the resulting protracted conflict—the **Vietnam War**—also led to widespread domestic social unrest.

Practice Question

4. How did the United States change in the 1920s?
   A) The Great Migration ceased.
   B) African American culture became increasingly influential.
   C) The Great Depression caused high unemployment.
   D) Thanks to the New Deal, millions of Americans found jobs.

Postwar and Contemporary United States

During the 1960s, the US experienced social and political change, starting with the election of the young and charismatic **John F. Kennedy** in 1960. Kennedy and his successor after his assassination, **Lyndon B. Johnson**, embraced **Liberalism**, believing that government should fight poverty at home, and play an interventionist role abroad (in this era, by fighting communism). **Johnson**'s administration envisioned a **Great Society**, passing legislation in support of the poor and of civil rights in the tradition of the Progressives. Johnson launched a **War on Poverty**, passing reform legislation to support the poor, providing housing, health care, and education.

The **Civil Rights Movement**, led by activists like the **Rev. Dr. Martin Luther King, Jr.** and **Malcolm X**, fought for African American rights in the South, including the abolition of segregation, and also for better living standards for blacks in northern cities. Civil rights came to the forefront with the 1954 Supreme Court case ***Brown v. Board of Education***, when the Court found segregation unconstitutional.

Civil rights became a major domestic political issue with widespread public support. Civil rights workers organized the **March on Washington** in 1963, when Dr. King delivered his famous, *I have a dream* speech. In 1964, Congress passed the **Civil Rights Act**, which outlawed segregation. However, African Americans' voting rights were still not sufficiently protected. In 1965, led by President Lyndon B. Johnson, Congress passed the **Voting Rights Act**, which forbade restrictions impeding the ability of African Americans to vote.

Figure 12.5. March on Washington

The Civil Rights Movement extended beyond the Deep South. **Cesar Chavez** founded the **United Farm Workers (UFW)**, which organized Hispanic and migrant farm workers in California and the Southwest to advocate for unionizing and collective bargaining. The Civil Rights Movement also included **feminist** activists who fought for fairer treatment of women in the workplace and for women's reproductive rights. The **American Indian Movement (AIM)** addressed injustices and discrimination suffered by Native Americans, achieving more tribal autonomy. The 1969 **Stonewall Riots** occurred in New York City in response to police repression of the gay community. These riots and subsequent organized activism are seen as the beginning of the LGBT rights movement.

Conservatism strengthened in response to the heavy role of government in public life throughout the 1960s, high rates of government spending, and social challenges to traditional values. During the administration of the conservative President **Richard Nixon**, the conflict in Vietnam ended and a diplomatic relationship with China began. Nixon also oversaw economic reforms. However, the **Watergate Scandal**, when the president was involved in a break-in at the headquarters of the **Democratic National Committee**, forced Nixon to resign. Nixon's resignation further destroyed many Americans' faith in their government.

> **Did You Know?**
>
> At the same time, LBJ's overseas agenda in Vietnam was increasingly unpopular due to high casualties, the draft (which forced young American males to fight overseas) and what seemed to many to be the purposelessness of the war. Protests swept the nation against the war, and popular counterculture usurped government authority and challenged traditional values.

After political and economic instability in the 1970s, the conservative president **Ronald Reagan** championed domestic tax cuts and an aggressive foreign policy against the Soviet Union. However, tax cuts forced Congress to cut or eliminate social programs that benefitted millions. Enormous military investment—the **Arms Race** with the Soviet Union—helped bring about the end of the Cold War with the 1991 fall of the USSR and later, a new era of globalization. It also increased government debt. Finally, the Reagan Revolution ushered in an era of conservative values in the public sphere.

With the collapse of the Soviet Union, the balance of international power changed. The bipolar world became a unipolar world, and the United States was the sole super- power. US intervention in the Middle East during the **Gulf War**, or **Operation Desert Storm** (1991)—cemented its status as the world's sole superpower.

With the election of President **Bill Clinton** in 1992, the US took an active role in international diplomacy. Society became increasingly liberal. Technology like the **internet** facilitated national and global communication, media, and business; minority groups like the LGBT community engaged in more advocacy; and environmental issues became more visible.

As part of **globalization**, the facilitation of global commerce and communication, the Clinton administration prioritized free trade. The United States signed the **North American Free Trade Agreement (NAFTA)** with Mexico and Canada, removing trade restrictions throughout North America. Many American jobs went overseas, especially manufacturing jobs, where labor was cheaper, benefitting companies but causing unemployment. Furthermore, globalization began facilitating the movement of people as methods of communication and transportation transformed. **Immigration Reform** would be a major issue into the twenty-first century.

By the end of the twentieth century, the United States had established itself as the dominant global economic, military, and political power. Due to its role in global conflict from the Spanish-American War onward, the US had established a military presence worldwide. The US dominated global trade. American popular culture was widely popular.

However, globalization also facilitated global conflict. On **September 11, 2001 (9/11)**, the terrorist group **Al Qaeda** attacked the US, triggering an aggressive military and foreign policy under the administration of President **George W. Bush**, who declared a *war on terror*, an open-ended global conflict against terrorist organizations and their supporters. The US attacked al Qaeda bases in Afghanistan. President

Bush believed in the doctrine of **preemption**, that if the US was aware of a threat, it should preemptively attack the source of that threat. Preemption would drive the invasion of Iraq in 2003.

At home, Congress passed the **Usa Patriot Act** to respond to fears of more terrorist attacks on US soil. This legislation gave the federal government unprecedented—and, some argued, unconstitutional—powers of surveillance over the American public.

Despite the tense climate, social liberalization continued in the US. Following the Bush administration, during which tax cuts and heavy reliance on credit helped push the country into the **Great Recession**, the first African American president, **Barack Obama**, was elected in 2008. Under his presidency, the US emerged from the recession, ended its occupations of Iraq and Afghanistan, passed the Affordable Care Act, which reformed the healthcare system, and legalized same-sex marriage. The Obama administration also oversaw the passage of consumer protection acts, increased support for students, and safety nets for homeowners.

Yet change persists in the United States. In 2016, the country was deeply divided as the television personality and real estate developer **Donald Trump** was elected president on a platform of conservatism and isolationism. However, his opponent, former senator and Secretary of State **Hillary Rodham Clinton**, won the popular vote. Many Americans viewed Trump as racist and sexist, and grassroots opposition movements developed. Still, his supporters remained committed. Some argued he understood the harms of rising income inequality better than Clinton, despite her work to support the poor and working class. Some researchers believe the election showed deeper divisions among Americans than had previously been understood.

Practice Question

5. Which of the following BEST describes the approach taken by the Reagan administration to counter the Soviet Union?
    A) bilateral diplomacy
    B) direct military confrontation
    C) engagement in multilateral pact such as the United Nations
    D) escalation of arms production and proxy warfare

Answer Key

1. C: The colonial military had strong leaders and an intimate knowledge of the terrain; many of its military leaders were born and raised in North America.

2. D: The Thirteenth Amendment abolished slavery; the Fourteenth Amendment promised equal protection under the law to all U.S. citizens; the Fifteenth Amendment ensured that (male) African Americans and former slaves could vote.

3. C: Labor unions sought improved working conditions, not the overthrow of capitalism.

4. B: The Harlem Renaissance is one example of the emergence of African American culture in the public imagination; as US popular culture developed, African American contributions had a strong influence.

5. D: The Reagan administration focused on arms buildup, weapons spending, and supporting anti-Soviet movements around the world.

13. Civics and Government

The Constitution

Any study of the United States government must begin with its founding document: the **Constitution**. It was written as both an expression of ideals and as a practical framework for the functioning of the country. Designed to be a "living document," the Constitution and how it is interpreted has changed in the almost 230 years since it was written. However, its core principles have not. They continue to serve as the foundation and guiding light of American government and politics. In order to understand the government that emerged from the US Constitution, it is necessary to understand its historical context.

Historical Background

In 1781 the Second Continental Congress had convened to organize a government for the emerging nation. The colonies had broken away from Britain because of what they viewed as the oppressive rule of an overbearing central government. As a result, the first government they created, whose framework was called the **Articles of Confederation**, was intentionally weak. Called a "firm league of friendship," it was designed to create a loose confederation between the colonies (now states) while allowing them to retain much of their individual sovereignty.

> **Did You Know?**
>
> While influenced by philosophy, the Constitution is actually a very practical document. It lays out the overarching structure of the government. However, each decision made about the structure of the government was an attempt to either prevent the re-emergence of tyranny or fix the mistakes of the first, failed government.

As a result, the Articles established a political system which consisted of a **Unicameral Legislature** (only one house) with extremely limited authority. The Congress of the Confederation, as it was called, did not have the power to levy taxes or raise an army. Any laws had to be passed by a two-thirds vote, and any changes to the Articles had to be passed unanimously—essentially an impossible feat. The legislature was intentionally subordinate to the states. Representatives were selected and paid by state legislatures.

It quickly became clear that this government was too weak to be effective, and by 1787 the new government of the United States was already in crisis. Without the power to levy taxes, the federal government had no way to alleviate its debt burden from the war. In addition, without an organizing authority, states began issuing their own currencies and crafting individual trade agreements with foreign nations, halting trade and sending inflation through the roof. Without a national judicial system, there was no mechanism to solve the inevitable economic disputes.

Discontent was particularly strong among farmers, who were losing their property at devastating rates. Violence exploded in 1786 when Daniel Shays led a rebellion against Massachusetts tax collectors and banks. Unable to raise an army, the Congress of the Confederation was powerless to intervene. The rebellion was finally suppressed when citizens of Boston contributed funds to raise a state militia. **Shays' Rebellion** made it clear that the new government was unable to maintain order.

A convention of the states was called to address problems in the young United States. At the **Constitutional Convention** in 1787, a decision was made to completely throw out the old Articles and write a new governing document from scratch. There were five main goals for the new Constitution:

- The protection of property
- Granting increased, but limited, power to the federal government
- The protection of and limitations on majority rule
- The protection of individual rights
- The creation of a flexible framework for government

Each of these reflects the desire to balance authority and liberty, the core of the framework of the American government.

The federal government was reorganized under the Constitution, shifting from a one-body political system to a three-branch system as conceived by the Enlightenment philosopher **Montesquieu**. In addition to a now bicameral (two house) legislature, a legitimate executive branch was added as well as a judicial. Following Montesquieu's model of **separation of powers**, the now-increased powers of the federal government were divided among these branches. In addition, each branch was given powers that would limit the power of the other branches in a system called **Checks and Balances**.

> **Did You Know?**
>
> It was clear that a stronger central government was needed. However, the states did not want a central government that was so strong that it would oppress the states or the people. The solution? Increase the power of the government, but prevent the concentration of power by dividing it.

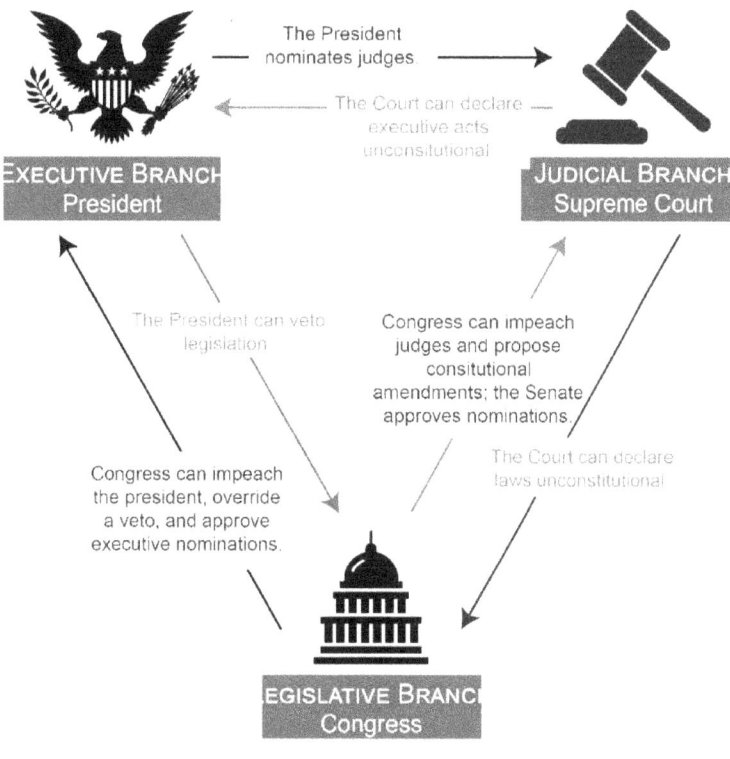

Figure 13.1. Checks and Balances

13. Civics and Government

For example:

- The executive branch—via the role of president—has the power to veto (reject) laws passed by the legislature.
- The legislative branch can override the president's veto (with a two-thirds vote) and pass the law anyway.
- The judicial branch can determine the constitutionality of laws (the principle of judicial review).

Enlightenment Philosophy

The founders of the United States were all educated in the philosophy of the **enlightenment**. Several key elements of this philosophy are reflected in the Constitution.

Rule of Law: The very desire for a written constitution—a law above all others— reflected Enlightenment thinking, as it ensures a rule of law, rather than a rule of man. In a nation ruled by man, governance is at the whim of an individual or small group of individuals. Decisions are arbitrary based on the interests and needs of those in authority. In a nation ruled by law, governance is based on a body of written, or otherwise codified, law (such as the Constitution). No individual can make a governing decision in conflict with those laws.

Reason: The Constitution is a document based on reason, and is therefore relatively simple and straightforward. It lays out the structure of government without detailing every single function of that government. Rather than simply empowering authority, the Constitution aims to limit government while still allowing it to fulfill its function. It also insists that governing decisions are made outside the scope of religion, by actively separating the two.

Social Contract: The document begins "We the People..." because the founders believed that government was a social contract, legitimized only by the consent of the people. This is also known as **popular sovereignty**. The Constitution protects individual liberty, life, and property, the fundamental natural laws laid out by the Enlightenment philosopher **John Locke**.

Social Progress: Enlightenment thinkers believed strongly that social progress was possible. As a result, the writers of the Constitution built in a means for *amending* the Constitution, allowing it to progress with the nation it governed.

Governmental Powers

Governmental powers in the Constitution can be divided into six types:

Expressed Powers or **Enumerated Powers** are powers that are specifically granted to the federal government only. An example of an expressed power is the power to make treaties with foreign nations.

Implied Powers are powers the federal government has that are not in the Constitution. They derive from the elastic clause of the Constitution, Article I, Section 8. The **elastic clause** gives Congress the right to "make all laws necessary and proper" for carrying out other powers. For example, over time as new technologies have emerged, such as radio and television, the commerce clause has been expanded to allow the federal government to regulate them.

The idea of implied powers was supported by the Supreme Court in *McCulloch v. Maryland* (1819). The state of Maryland tried to tax the Maryland branch of the Bank of the United States. When the bank refused to pay the tax, the case landed in the Maryland Court of Appeals; the court ruled that the Bank of the United States was unconstitutional, as the Constitution did not expressly give the federal government the power to operate a bank. Later, the Supreme Court overturned the ruling, citing the elastic clause.

Reserved Powers are powers that are held by the states through the Tenth Amendment, which states that all powers not expressly given to the federal government belong to the states. For example, the management of public education is a reserved power.

Inherent Powers are powers that derive specifically from US sovereignty and are inherent to its existence as a nation. For example, the powers to make treaties and to wage war are both inherent powers.

Concurrent Powers are powers that are shared equally by both the national and state government. The power to tax and the power to establish courts are both concurrent powers.

Prohibited Powers are powers that are denied to both the national government and the state governments. Passing bills of attainder (laws that declare someone guilty without a trial) is a prohibited power.

The separation of powers limited the powers within the federal government, but did not address the power relationship between the federal government and the states. Under the Articles, the federal government was completely beholden to the states for its very existence. However, it was clear that complete state sovereignty did not work. Instead, the Constitution created a **federal** relationship between the two levels of government. **Federalism** is a system in which both the state government and federal government retain sovereignty by dividing up the areas for which they are responsible.

Under the Constitution, the federal government is charged with matters that concern the population at large: for example, handling federal lands, coining money, and maintaining an army and navy. It also handles conflicts between the states via the federal judiciary and by regulating interstate trade. Matters of regional or local concern are handled by state or local governments. This relationship is best codified in the Tenth Amendment, which states that any powers not explicitly given to the federal government are reserved for the states. However, according to the **supremacy clause** (Article VI, Clause 2) the Constitution is the "supreme law of the land." Therefore, in cases of conflict between the states and the federal government, the federal government's authority generally supersedes that of the states.

The division of power has shifted over time with more power going to the federal government as its scope has expanded. The federal government also can exert influence over state governments through **grant-in-aid**, money that is provided for a particular purpose. The federal government can attach stipulations to this funding. For example, grant-in-aid was given to the states in the late 1970s for highway improvement. However, states who accepted the money were required to set the drinking age at twenty-one years old in their state. This was a way for the government to influence law that was technically beyond their purview.

Practice Question

1. In the American federal system of government, the power of state governments derives from
    A) the Constitution
    B) the people of the nation
    C) the state legislatures
    D) the people of that state

Organization of the Federal Government

The Legislative Branch

At the writing of the Constitution, the branch of the federal government endowed with the most power was the legislative branch. Called **Congress**, this branch is composed of a bicameral legislature (two houses). Based on the British model, most colonies—and then states—had bicameral legislatures with an upper and lower house. While this structure was not originally adopted under the Articles of Confederation, the framers chose it when reorganizing the government. This was in large part due to a dispute at the convention over the structure of the legislative body—specifically the voting power of each state.

> **Did You Know?**
>
> The bicameral system had other advantages. The House of Representatives would be directly elected by the people, and the Senate by the state legislatures. This supported the federal structure of the government: one house would serve the needs of the people directly, and the other would serve the needs of the states. Also, it curbed federal power by fragmenting it and slowing down the legislative process.

Small states advocated equal representation, with each state having the same number of representatives, each with one vote. Called the **New Jersey Plan,** this plan distributed decision- making power equally among the states, regardless of land mass or population. The more populous states found this system to be unfair. Instead, they argued for a plan called the **Virginia Plan**, based on **proportional representation**. Each state would be assigned a number of representatives based on its population (enslaved people deprived of their rights would even be counted among the population, benefiting those states with large slave populations). In the end, the **Great Compromise** was reached. There would be two houses: the **House of Representatives** (the lower house) would have proportional representation, and the **Senate** (the upper house) would have equal representation.

The structure and powers of Congress are outlined in Article I of the Constitution. As the most representative branch of government, the legislative branch was also designed to be the most powerful. Hence, it has the most expressed powers in the Constitution. The table below contains eighteen clauses listing specific powers which can be divided into peacetime powers and war powers:

Table 13.1. Powers of Congress			
Clause	Peacetime Powers	Clause	War Powers
1	To establish and collect taxes, duties, and excises	10	To define and punish crimes at sea; define violations of international law
2	To borrow money	11	To declare war; to make laws regarding people captured on land and water

Table 13.1. Powers of Congress

Clause	Peacetime Powers	Clause	War Powers
3	To regulate foreign and interstate commerce	12	To raise and support armies
4	To create naturalization laws; to create bankruptcy laws	13	To provide and maintain a navy
5	To coin money and regulate its value; regulate weights and measures	14	To make laws governing land and naval forces
6	To punish counterfeiters of federal money	15	To provide for summoning the militia to execute federal laws, suppress uprisings, and repel invasions
7	To establish post offices and roads	16	To provide for organizing, arming, and disciplining the militia and governing it when in the service of the Union
8	To grant patents and copyrights	17	To exercise exclusive jurisdiction over Washington, D.C. and other federal properties
9	To create federal courts below the Supreme Court	18	To make all laws necessary and proper to the execution of the other expressed powers (elastic clause)

The **House of Representatives** is the house which was designed to directly represent the people, and it was originally the only part of the federal government that was directly elected by the citizens. It is the larger of the houses with the number of representatives from each state based on the states' population (**proportional representation**). Every state is guaranteed at least one representative. Apportionment of representatives is based on the census, so seats are reapportioned every ten years with the new census.

At the convention, Southern states argued that their (non-voting) slave population should count towards their overall population, therefore entitling them to more representatives. Northern states with few slaves disagreed. This issue was settled with the **Three-Fifths Compromise** which declared that each slave would be counted as three-fifths of a person for the purpose of the census. (Women, who could not vote until the ratification of the Nineteenth Amendment, were also counted in the census.)

The size of the House grew every ten years along with the population of the United States until 1929, when Congress set the number at 435 voting representatives where it has remained since. Today, each member of Congress represents approximately 700,000 people. Residents of Washington D.C. and territories held by the United States (Guam, American Samoa, and the US Virgin Islands) are represented by non-voting observers; Puerto Rico is represented by a resident commissioner.

Each state legislature divides its state into essentially equally populated congressional districts. This process can become political, with political parties attempting to draw the lines to ensure the maximum number of seats for their party. This is called **gerrymandering**. The Supreme Court has made several rulings to limit gerrymandering, including requiring each district to have equal population and contiguous or connected lines. It is also unconstitutional to draw lines based solely on race.

Members of the House of Representatives are elected for two-year terms in an effort to keep them beholden to the people. The Constitution lays out basic requirements for membership in the House. In order to qualify, candidates must be at least twenty-five years old, have been a US citizen for at least seven years, and live in the state they are representing at the time of the election. The leader of the House is called the **Speaker of the House**. He or she is the leader of the majority party in the House.

- Although it is technically considered the lower house, there are still powers that belong only to the House of Representatives:
- All revenue bills must start in the house. While the Senate may amend the bills, the framers wanted to keep fiscal power in the hands of the house most beholden to the people.
- The House may bring charges of impeachment against the president or a Supreme Court justice. Impeachment is the process by which a federal official can be officially charged with a crime. If found guilty, he or she is removed from office. In order to impeach a president or justice, a simple majority is required. Only two presidents have ever been tried for impeachment: Andrew Johnson and Bill Clinton.

The House must choose the president if there is no majority in the Electoral College. The House has only selected the president once: in 1824, Andrew Jackson, John Quincy Adams, and Henry Clay split the electoral vote. Jackson had the plurality (the greatest percentage), but did not win a majority. The vote went to the House, and, after some backroom politics, they voted for John Quincy Adams.

The **Senate** was designed to be the house of the states. To signify that no one state is more important than any other, representation in the Senate is apportioned equally, with two senators per state, making a total of 100 senators. The framers designed the Senate so that representatives were chosen by the state legislatures; there was no direct connection between the Senate and the people. However, as the power of the federal government grew, the people increasingly came to think of it as representing themselves rather than their states. Corrupt state legislatures sold Senate seats to the highest bidder rather than electing the most qualified individual. As a result, the Senate seemed dis- connected from the democratic process, a corrupt millionaire's club.

The tension between the people's perception of their relationship to the federal government and the mechanism of Senate elections came to a head during the Progressive Era. Political machinations led to deadlocks in state legislatures over appointments, leaving Senate seats vacant for months at time. In 1913, the **Seventeenth Amendment** to the Constitution was ratified; it required the direct election of senators by the people of a state.

As the upper house, the Senate was designed to have greater autonomy with stricter qualifications. Senators are elected for six year terms to allow them time to make decisions that might not be popular but that are best for the nation. They are staggered in three groups; one group is up for election every two years. This ensures that all senators do not face re-election at the same time, allowing for more consistent governance.

To be a senator, candidates must be at least thirty years old, have been a citizen of the United States for nine years, and—at the time of the election—live in the state they will represent. The president of the Senate is the US vice president. However, he or she only has the power to vote in case of a tie. The vice president is often absent from the Senate, in which case the **president pro tempore** presides. He or she is generally the longest- serving member of the Senate.

Much like the House, the Senate has certain unique powers:

- Whereas the House has the power to impeach, the Senate acts as the jury in the impeachment of a president and determines his or her guilt. In order to remove, or oust, a president from office, the Senate must vote two-thirds in favor. Removal has never happened in American history.

- The Senate approves executive appointments and appointments to federal positions in the judicial system. These include, among others, members of the Supreme Court and other federal courts, the attorney general, cabinet members, and ambassadors.

- The Senate ratifies (approves) all treaties signed by the president. The president is in charge of foreign relations and is responsible for negotiating all treaties; however, as part of the system of checks and balances, the president requires the Senate's approval before any treaty becomes a permanent agreement.

The primary function of the legislature is to write and pass laws. Approximately 5,000 bills are introduced in Congress each year, only 2.5 percent of which become laws. There are no restrictions on who can write a bill. In fact, most are not written by Congress, but begin either in the executive branch or are written by special interest groups. A member of Congress is required, however, to introduce the bill. With the exception of revenue bills, bills can start in either house. Since the two houses have parallel processes, the same bill often starts in both houses at the same time.

Once it is placed in the "hopper," the bill is assigned a number and sent to the appropriate committee. Committees and their subcommittees are where most of the hard work of lawmaking is actually done. Here bills are read, debated, and revised. It is also where most bills die, by either being **tabled** (put aside) in subcommittee or committee, or by being voted down. If a bill does get voted out of committee, it goes to the floor for debate. In the House of Representatives, the powerful **rules Committee** not only determines which bills make it to the floor for debate, but also sets time limits for debate on each bill.

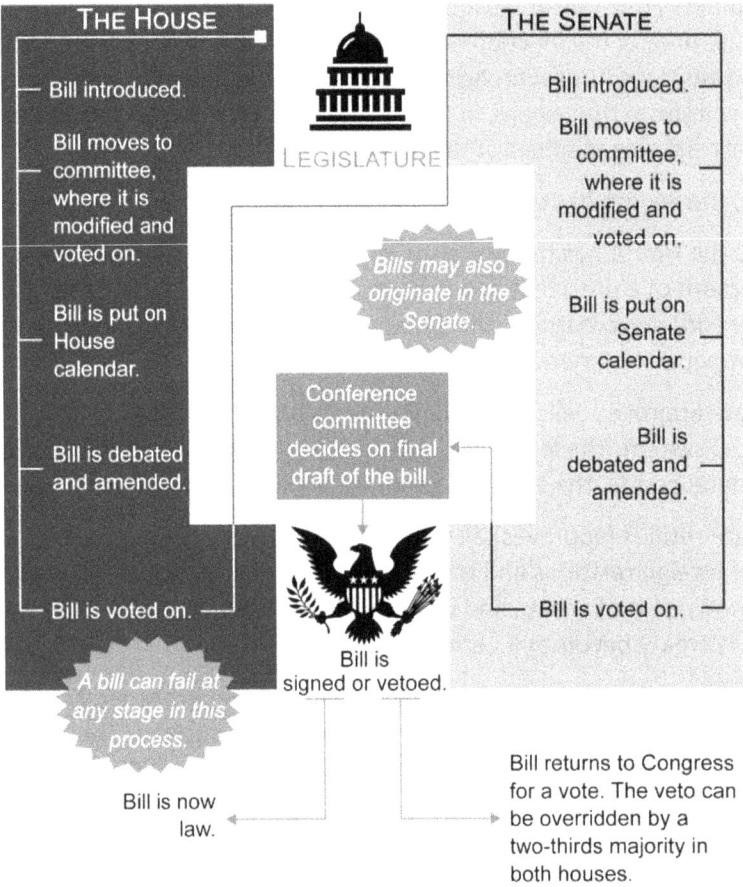

Figure 13.2. Bill to Law

In the Senate, debate is unlimited. This allows for a unique tactic called the **filibuster**, in which a senator or group of senators continues debate indefinitely to delay the passage of a bill. Sixty votes are needed to end a filibuster, so senators often attempt to gather sixty or more votes for a bill before it comes to the floor to ensure it is not filibustered.

After debate has ended, the members of each house vote on the bill. If it passes out of both houses, it moves to the **Conference Committee** which must transform the two very different draft bills (as different revisions and amendments were made as the bill made its way through each house) into one. Once that is done, the unified bill returns to both houses for a final vote. If it passes, it then proceeds to the president for signature or veto. If the president does veto the bill, it returns to Congress where both houses can vote again. If two-thirds of each house vote in favor of the bill, Congress will override the veto and the bill will become law anyway. However, this rarely happens.

Congress is responsible for another significant legislative process: amending the Constitution. The framers understood that they could not possibly foresee every threat to state sovereignty and personal liberty nor every need that would require government management. So they added Article V to the Constitution, which lays out a procedure for amending it. This is one of the most significant aspects of the Constitution as it makes it a "living document."

Amendments to the Constitution can either come from Congress or from the state legislatures. For Congress to propose an amendment to the Constitution, two-thirds of each house must vote in favor of the amendment. Alternatively, an amendment can be proposed if two-thirds of the states call for a national constitutional convention. All amendments to date, however, have been proposed by Congress. Either way, once the amendment has been officially proposed, it is not ratified until three-quarters of state legislatures (or special conventions convened by each state) approve it. There are twenty-seven amendments to the Constitution, the first ten of which were passed immediately in 1791.

> **Did You Know?**
>
> The process by which laws are written and passed is intentionally cumbersome and complicated. The framers of the Constitution believed that the longer the process took, the more deliberation there would be, decreasing the risk of abuse of power.

These first ten amendments, called **The Bill of Rights**, were a condition for ratification imposed by those who thought the new government wielded too much power. These **Anti-Federalists** argued that individual liberty had to be explicitly protected from federal intervention.

According to the amendments, the government may not:

- Amendment I: prohibit freedom of religion, speech, press, petition, and assembly
- Amendment II: prohibit the right to bear arms
- Amendment III: quarter troops in citizens' homes
- Amendment IV: conduct unlawful search and seizures
- Amendment V: force anyone to testify against themselves or be tried for the same crime twice
- Amendment VI: prohibit the right to a fair and speedy trial
- Amendment VII: prohibit the right to a jury trial in civil cases (remember the original Constitution only guaranteed a jury in criminal cases)
- Amendment VIII: force citizens to undergo cruel and unusual punishment
- Amendment IX: violate rights that exist but are not explicitly mentioned in the Constitution
- Amendment X: usurp any powers from the states not given to them in the Constitution (so all other powers not listed in the Constitution belong to the states)

While the only official way to change the Constitution is through the amendment process, other loopholes for change exist within its framework. These include:

Clarifying Legislation: Using the **elastic clause**, much legislation has been passed whose purpose is to clarify or expand the powers of the federal government. For example, the Constitution only provides directly for the Supreme Court, but empowers Congress to create other courts. The Judiciary Act of 1789 created the federal judiciary.

Executive Actions: Although Congress holds most lawmaking power, the president is able to issue executive actions which have the force of law without having to involve Congress. The most famous of these is Abraham Lincoln's Emancipation Proclamation.

Judicial Decisions: In *Marbury v. Madison* (1803) the Supreme Court established the precedent of **judicial review**, the power of the Supreme Court to determine the constitutionality of laws. *Marbury v. Madison* not only illustrated how judicial decisions can expand federal power in general, but it also broadened the power of the Supreme Court in particular, laying the groundwork for future decisions that would have a similar impact.

Political Parties: The rise of political parties changed the political landscape as well. Some aspects of American politics—like how the Speaker of the House is chosen and nomination conventions for presidential candidates— have come from political parties rather than through a formal legislative process.

Although Congress was made much more powerful by the Constitution, a real fear of tyranny existed among the framers. While Section VIII of the Constitution lists the powers of Congress, Section IX lists what Congress cannot do.

The most notable are:

- No suspension of habeas corpus: A writ of habeas corpus is a legal demand a prisoner can make to appear in court in order to profess their innocence. Essentially a means of preventing unreasonable imprisonment, habeas corpus was viewed as an essential element of a just government. The Constitution forbids its suspension except in cases of rebellion or invasion. (Abraham Lincoln, during the Civil War, was the first president to suspend habeas corpus.)

- No bills of attainder: A bill of attainder is a law that declares an individual or a group guilty of a crime without holding a trial. Much like with the writ of habeas corpus, this was seen as an essential protection in a fair society.

- No ex post facto laws: An ex post facto law is a law which punishes an individual or group for breaking a law that was not a law when the act was committed. For example, slavery was abolished in 1865. If an ex post facto law was passed at that time, it would have punished anyone who had owned slaves before 1865.

- No titles of nobility: It was important to the framers to provide safeguards against a return to monarchy. Therefore, they prohibited an American nobility of any kind.

Practice Question

2. Why did the framers give the House of Representatives the power to start revenue bills?
    A) Based on their qualifications, members of the House would have more economic knowledge.
    B) Members of the House would be less influenced by outside forces and political parties than members of the Senate.
    C) The House was more truly a national legislature; therefore, it should be in charge of the national budget.
    D) The frequency of elections for House of Representatives would make them more responsive to the will of the people in terms of spending.

The Executive Branch

Defined by Article II of the Constitution, the executive branch enforces all federal law. Article II only provides for a president, vice president, and an unspecified number of executive departments. However, the federal government has expanded considerably over the past 225 years, in large part due to the expansion of the executive branch. Today, the executive branch is also responsible for administering a federal bureaucracy that spends $3 trillion a year and employs 2.7 million people.

Of the three mentioned, the president is the only executive role that is specifically defined in the Constitution. The president serves a term of four years and may be re-elected up to two times. While the term length was set in the original Constitution, the term limit was added in the Twenty-Second Amendment in 1951, in response to Franklin Delano Roosevelt's four elections to the presidency. Many felt that allowing unlimited terms opened the door for a de facto dictator and threatened liberty.

In order to qualify for the presidency, candidates must be natural-born American citizens, at least thirty-five years old, and have resided in the United States for at least fourteen years. While the Constitution does not specifically list requirements for the vice presidency, it does state that the vice president becomes the president in case of death, resignation, or impeachment. As a result, the vice president must meet the same qualifications as the president.

The **Cabinet** consists of the heads of the executive departments and may advise the president on a variety of matters. It is not directly referred to at all in the Constitution. Instead, it was derived from one line in Section 2: "[the president] may require the opinion, in writing, of the principal officer in each of the executive departments, upon any subject relating to the duties of their respective offices." However, the cabinet as we know it today was established immediately under George Washington. He established four executive departments, so the first cabinet consisted of four positions: the Secretary of State, the Secretary of the Treasury, the Secretary of War (now, the Secretary of Defense) and the Attorney General, or head of the Justice Department. Over time, eleven new executive departments were added, for a total of fifteen cabinet positions.

- Department of State
- Department of the Treasury
- Department of Defense
- Department of Justice
- Department of Interior
- Department of Agriculture
- Department of Commerce
- Department of Labor
- Department of Energy
- Department of Education
- Department of Housing and Urban Development
- Department of Transportation
- Department of Veterans Affairs

Did You Know?

While you do not need to memorize every department for the HiSET, you should understand they have a wide-ranging effect on American society. How has your life been affected by these departments? For instance, if you pay taxes, your life is affected by the Treasury Department, which controls the Internal Revenue Service (IRS).

- Department of Health and Human Services
- Department of Homeland Security

These fifteen departments employ more than two-thirds of all federal employees.

In addition to managing their departments, the members of the cabinet are also all in the line of presidential succession as established by the Presidential Succession Act (first passed in 1792 but most recently amended in 1947). The line of succession is as follows: following the vice president is the Speaker of the House, then the president pro tempore of the Senate, followed by each cabinet member in the order of the department's creation, beginning with the Secretary of State and ending with the Secretary of Homeland Security.

Article II is considerably shorter than Article I because the framers intended the role and powers of the president to be more limited than those of Congress. However, the president does have a number of expressed powers.

One of the most significant presidential powers is the power to appoint federal officials. The president's **appointment power** is far-ranging and includes cabinet members, heads of independent agencies, ambassadors, and federal judges. Through this power, the president not only controls the entirety of the executive branch as well as foreign policy, but also wields significant and long-term influence over the judicial branch. This power, however, is not unlimited. Based on the advise and consent clause of the Constitution, the Senate must approve all presidential appointments. The president does have the power to remove any of his or her appointees from office—with the exception of judges—without Senate approval.

The first line of section 2 of Article II declares the president **Commander-in-chief** of the army and navy. In this role, the president is the supreme leader of US military forces. He or she can deploy troops and dictate military policy. However, this power is checked as well. While the president controls the military, Congress retains the power to declare war. Presidents have circumvented this check in the past, however, by deploying troops without requesting a formal declaration of war. In the twentieth century, this happened most notably in the Vietnam War, which was never officially declared. In 1964, Congress passed the Gulf of Tonkin Resolution in response to the perceived attack on an American ship in the Gulf of Tonkin. The resolution essentially gave the president a blank check for military action in Vietnam, which led to a rapid and massive escalation of US military spending and troops. Because of this, in 1974 Congress passed the **war powers resolution**; this resolution requires the president to inform Congress within forty-eight hours of a troop deployment and restricts deployment unsupported by congressional authorization to sixty days.

The president is also considered the **Chief diplomat** of the United States. In this capacity, the president has the power to recognize other nations, receive ambassadors, and negotiate treaties. However, any treaties negotiated by the president must be approved by the Senate before taking effect.

Many of the president's diplomatic powers are informal. In the twentieth century, the US became a superpower, transforming the role of the president into that of a world leader as well as the leader of the nation. As a result, the president is now expected to manage international crises, negotiate executive agreements with other countries, and monitor and maintain confidential information related to the security of the nation and to the rest of the world.

While the executive and judicial branches are quite separate, the president has powers intended to check the power of the judicial branch. Primarily, this is the power to appoint federal judges. The president may also grant pardons and reprieves for individuals convicted of federal crimes. The purpose of this is to provide a final option for those who have been unfairly convicted. This is one of the president's more controversial powers, as pardons are often seen to be politically motivated or a tool for those with political or personal connections.

Like the judicial branch, the president is constitutionally accorded some **legislative powers** in order to limit the powers of the legislative branch. All laws that are passed end up on the president's desk. He or she has the choice to either sign the bill—in which case it becomes a law—or to **veto** the bill. The president's veto prevents the bill from becoming law (unless Congress overrides the veto). The president is required to either fully accept or fully reject a bill; he or she may not veto only sections of it.

This is called a **line-item veto**, and the Supreme Court declared it unconstitutional in 1996. If the president does not wish to take such a clear stand on a bill, he or she can also simply ignore it. If the president does nothing for ten days, the bill automatically becomes law, even without a signature. If, however, there are less than ten days left in Congress's session, and the president does not sign the bill, it automatically dies. This is called a **pocket veto**.

The president also has the power to convene both houses of Congress to force them to consider matters requiring urgent attention. While this is technically the extent of the president's legislative powers, in reality the position has a much greater legislative impact. The president sets the policy agenda both as the leader of his or her party and through the **State of the Union** address. Section 3 of Article II states, "He [or she] shall from time to time give to the Congress information of the state of the union, and recommend to their consideration such measures as he [or she] shall judge necessary and expedient." This has evolved into an annual formalized address to Congress in which the president lays out executive legislative priorities.

Many bills originate in the executive branch, either from the president's office or from one of the executive departments. The president also often uses the power of the veto to influence legislation. By threatening to veto, the president can force changes to bills that align more with her or his political agenda.

Almost half of Article II is dedicated to describing the process of electing the president. The framers wanted to ensure the president represented all of the states and was immune from the mob rule of democracy. As a result, they created the **Electoral College.** Over the years, the political parties have expanded the process into a nine- month series of elections by various groups of people.

The first step in choosing a president is selecting the candidates. Originally, this was done in smoke-filled back rooms; it then became the provenance of party caucuses and then conventions, eventually evolving into the current system of primaries and caucuses. In a **primary** election, members of a political party in a state vote at a polling place for whom they believe is the best candidate for their party. In ten states, a **Caucus** system is used, in which members of a party in a state gather together at party meetings and vote for the candidate using raised hands or by gathering in groups.

Then, in July of the election year, the party holds a **national nominating convention**. Historically, this is where the candidate was chosen after days of heated debate and dealings. However, because of the primary and caucus systems, delegates at the convention arrive already knowing whom their state supports. The delegates vote for the candidate who won their primary or caucus. The candidate with the most votes becomes the party's nominee.

Presidential elections are held nationwide every four years on the Tuesday following the first Monday in November. Today, all American citizens over the age of eighteen are allowed to vote, but this was not always the case. The framers viewed the electorate as a small, select segment of the population.

However, no voter qualifications are written into the Constitution; those were left to the states. In 1789, in every state, only propertied white men—one in fifteen white men—were allowed to vote. Starting with the removal of property qualifications during the Jacksonian era (1830s), views of democracy began to change, and the electorate expanded. Aside from property requirements, each expansion resulted from a new amendment to the Constitution.

Table 13.2. Constitutional Amendments Expanding Voting Rights		
Amendment	Year	Provision
Fifteenth	1870	All male citizens, regardless of race, are allowed to vote.
Nineteenth	1920	Women are allowed to vote.
Twenty-Third	1961	Residents of the District of Columbia are allowed to vote in presidential elections.
Twenty-Fourth	1964	Poll taxes, an indirect restriction of black voting rights, are prohibited.
Twenty-Sixth	1971	All citizens over the age of eighteen are allowed to vote (in most states the voting age had previously been twenty-one years).

While the popular vote is tallied on Election Day, it does not determine the outcome of the presidential election. That is the job of the Electoral College. The **Electoral College** is composed of electors from each state who vote for the president. Electors are apportioned based on population; the number of a state's electors is the same as its number of representatives plus its number of senators (so each state has at least three electors).

In the January following the election, electors gather in their states to cast their votes for president. Technically, electors are not bound to vote in line with their state's popular vote. However, rarely has an elector taken advantage of this, and it has never affected the outcome of an election. Today, most states are winner-take-all, meaning the electors are expected to all vote in line with the outcome of the state's popular vote. The president must win a majority—not a plurality—of the Electoral College in order to win. This is 270 votes.

The Electoral College was designed to elect a president for a nation that was scattered and had greater regional than national loyalty. It favors small states and minority groups, giving them greater influence on the election than they would have in a direct election system. Today many people feel that the Electoral College is outdated and ill-fitting. They argue it is undemocratic, and that it gives undue importance to certain states based on their number of electoral votes. Instead, they support a direct election system.

Did You Know?

A state's number of electors is equal to its number of representatives plus its number of senators (which is two for every state). So, every state (and Washington, DC) has at least three electoral votes. There are a total of 538 votes available.

Practice Question

3. The Electoral College represents which of the beliefs of the framers of the Constitution?
    A) Government derives its authority from the consent of the people.
    B) Concentration of power can lead to tyranny.
    C) The federal government derives its authority from the states.
    D) The federal government needs greater power to provide stability to the nation.

The Judicial Branch

The Constitution's framework for the judicial branch is the least detailed of the three branches. It is also a passive branch. Where the legislative branch creates laws, and the executive branch takes actions to enforce those laws, the judicial branch can only weigh in when an actual case is presented to it. It may not rule or make decisions based on hypotheticals. Yet this branch has grown to be at least as influential as the other two branches both in setting policy and molding the size and shape of the federal government.

The United States has a complex **dual court system**; each state has its own multi- part judicial system in addition to the federal one. Even though federal district courts handle over 300,000 cases a year, ninety-seven percent of criminal cases are heard in state and local courts. While the federal courts hear more civil cases than criminal, the majority of these are still handled within the states. Because of the federal system, state courts have **jurisdiction**—or the authority to hear a case—over most cases. Only cases that meet certain criteria (e.g. a dispute between two states, a case involving federal employees or agencies, or a violation of federal law) are heard in federal courts. Most cases also can only be **appealed**—or reviewed by a higher court—up to the state supreme court. For the federal Supreme Court to review a state supreme court's decision, there must be an issue involving the interpretation of the federal Constitution.

The federal court system is composed of three levels of courts. First are the district courts. There are ninety-four district courts in the country, served by 700 judges. They handle 80 percent of all federal cases. The next level of courts are the twelve circuit courts of appeal. These courts review district court decisions and the decisions of federal regulatory agencies.

Did You Know?

Article III, the article of the Constitution which discusses the judicial branch, only details the Supreme Court. It then empowers Congress to create the rest of the judiciary, which it did beginning with the Judiciary Act of 1789.

At the top is the **Supreme Court**. Sometimes called the "court of last resort," the Supreme Court reviews cases from the circuit court and from state supreme courts, and is the final arbiter of constitutionality. Decisions made by the Supreme Court establish **precedents**, rulings that guide future court decisions at all levels of the judicial system.

While the Constitution delineates which kinds of cases the Supreme Court may hear, its real power was established by the precedent of an early case, *Marbury v. Madison* (1803). In this case, William Marbury—citing the Judiciary Act of 1789— sought relief from the court when James Madison, Secretary of State to the newly inaugurated Thomas Jefferson, did not deliver the federal appointment Marbury was given under the previous president, John Adams. The court, under Chief Justice John Marshall, ruled that while Madison was in the wrong, the section of the Judiciary Act allowing Marbury to petition the Supreme Court was unconstitutional because it extended the jurisdiction of the court beyond the scope established in

Article III. This established **judicial review**, the Supreme Court's power to determine the constitutionality of laws. This has become the most significant function of the court, and has allowed it to shape public policy.

There are nine justices who serve on the Supreme Court.

Appointed by the president and approved by the Senate, Supreme Court justices serve for life. The Constitution does not provide any criteria for serving on the court. However, unofficial requirements do exist: justices must demonstrate competence through high level credentials or through prior experience. Today, all of the justices on the Supreme Court hold law degrees from major universities and first served in federal district or appellate courts. They also generally share policy preferences with the president who appointed them, although judicial inclinations do not always neatly align with political ones.

Did You Know?

You do not need to memorize all the important Supreme Court cases to do well on the HiSET. Instead, focus on understanding why they were important and how they affected US government and society.

There are several significant Supreme Court cases to know, some of which are listed in Table 13.3.

Table 13.3. Supreme Court Cases

Case Name	Ruling
Marbury v. Madison (1803)	This case established judicial review.
McCulloch v. Maryland (1819)	The court ruled that states could not tax the Bank of the United States; this ruling supported the implied powers of Congress.
Dred Scott v. Sandford (1857)	The Supreme Court ruled that enslaved persons were not citizens; it also found the Missouri Compromise unconstitutional, meaning Congress could not forbid expanding slavery to US territories.
Plessy v. Ferguson (1896)	This case established the precedent of separate but equal (segregation).
Korematsu v. US (1945)	This case determined that the internment of Japanese Americans during WWII was lawful.
Brown v. Board of Education (1954)	The Supreme Court overturned *Plessy v. Ferguson*; it ruled that separate but equal, or segregation, was unconstitutional.
Gideon v. Wainwright (1963)	The Supreme Court ruled that the court must provide legal counsel to poor defendants in felony cases.
Miranda v. Arizona (1966)	This ruling established that defendants must be read their due process rights before questioning.

Table 13.3. Supreme Court Cases

Case Name	Ruling
Tinker v. Des Moines (1969)	This case established "symbolic speech" as a form of speech protected by the First Amendment.
Roe v. Wade (1973)	This case legalized abortion in the first trimester throughout the United States.
Bakke v. Regents of University of California (1978)	This case ruled that while affirmative action was constitutional, the university's quota system was not.
Citizens United v. Federal Elections Commission (2010)	The court ruled that restricting corporate donations to political campaigns was tantamount to restricting free speech; this ruling allowed the formation of influential super PACs, which can provide unlimited funding to candidates running for office.
Obergefell v. Hodges (2015)	The court ruled that same-sex marriage was legal throughout the United States.

Civil Liberties and Rights

Influenced by the ideas of the Enlightenment and fresh from revolution, the framers of the Constitution valued **civil liberties**. Civil liberties are rights—provided for either directly by the Constitution or through its historical interpretations—which protect individuals from arbitrary acts of the government. The framers protected some liberties explicitly in the Constitution via the prohibited powers, and expanded on them in the **Bill of Rights**. Each of these amendments restricts the actions of the federal government rather than actually granting a freedom to the people.

The liberties most central to the American identity are articulated in the **First Amendment**: speech, press, petition, assembly, and religion. The first four are all closely related. No liberty is truly unlimited, however, and the court has imposed restrictions on **freedom of speech** over time. It has upheld laws banning libel, slander, obscenity, and symbolic speech that intends to incite illegal actions.

The **freedom of religion** comes from two clauses in the First Amendment: the **establishment clause** and the **free exercise clause**. The first prohibits the government from establishing a state religion or favoring one religion over another. The second prohibits the government from restricting religious belief or practice. Again, this is not unlimited. The court has found that religious practice can be banned if it requires engagement in otherwise illegal activity. There are also continuing debates on allowing prayer in schools and granting vouchers to students to attend parochial schools.

Most of the civil liberties written into the body of the Constitution addressed the rights of the accused, including prohibitions on bills of attainder, ex post facto laws, and denials of writs of habeas corpus. Three of the amendments in the Bill of Rights address this as well.

The **Fourth Amendment** restricts unlawful searches and seizures. In *Mapp v. Ohio* (1961), the Supreme Court ruled that evidence obtained illegally—so in violation of the Fourth Amendment—could not be used in court. This **exclusionary rule** is very controversial, and the courts have struggled since to determine when and how to apply it.

The **Fifth Amendment** protects the accused from self-incrimination. Drawing on this amendment, the Supreme Court ruled in *Miranda v. Arizona* (1966) that arrestees must be informed of their due process rights before interrogation in order to protect them from self-incrimination. These rights, along with those in the Sixth Amendment, are now colloquially known as **Miranda rights**.

> **Did You Know?**
>
> What rights do Americans enjoy under these constitutional amendments and court rulings? To do well on the exam, it is more important to have an understanding of citizens' rights than to memorize each court case and amendment.

The **Sixth Amendment** guarantees the accused the right to a fair, speedy, and public trial, as well as the right to counsel in criminal cases. While originally this only applied at the federal level, in *Gideon v. Wainwright* (1963) the Supreme Court ruled that states must provide counsel to those who cannot afford it.

The Court's ruling in *Gideon v. Wainwright* was based on the Fourteenth Amendment's **equal protection clause**. Ratified in 1868, the amendment's original purpose was to ensure the equal treatment of African Americans under the law after the abolition of slavery. However, its use has been expanded far beyond that original purpose. The equal protection clause has been used to protect the **civil rights**—protections against discriminatory treatment by the government—of individuals of a variety of groups.

The courts have regularly protected political and legal equality, as well as equality of opportunity (like the *Brown v. Board of Education* decision in 1954). However, the courts do not recognize a right to economic equality. The Supreme Court also recognizes the need for reasonable classifications of people, and allows discrimination along those lines. For example, age restrictions on alcohol consumption, driving, and voting are all considered constitutional.

The Supreme Court has also used the **Fourteenth Amendment** over time to extend federal civil liberties to the state level. Today, all states are held to the same standard as the federal government in terms of civil liberties.

The second part of the Fourteenth Amendment extends the Fifth Amendment's **due process** guarantees to the state level. "No person shall be deprived of life, liberty or property without the due process of law..." While this typically refers to the processes of the accused, as discussed above, it has also come to represent certain unnamed, or implied, rights. At the heart of most of these **implied rights** is the right to privacy, which is not specifically protected in the Constitution. However, the court has ruled that it is implied by the Fourth, Fifth, and Fourteenth Amendments. This was the basis for its decision to legalize abortion in *Roe v. Wade* (1973).

Practice Question

4. Which of the following is NOT considered protected speech?
    A) burning the American flag
    B) writing an article criticizing the government
    C) publishing a false list of supposed KKK members
    D) protesting outside of an abortion clinic

Political Parties

Although the framers envisioned a political system without political parties, by the election of 1800, two official parties existed. A **political party** is a group of citizens who work together in order to win elections, hold public office, operate the government, and determine public policy. Some countries have one-party systems; others have multiple parties.

Although party names and platforms have shifted over the years, the United States has maintained a two-party system. Since 1854, our two major parties have been the **democratic party** and the **republican party**. Democrats generally follow a liberal political ideology, while Republicans have a conservative ideology. The parties operate at every level of government in every state. Although many members of a party serve in elected office, political parties have their own internal organization. Parties are hierarchical: they are comprised of national leaders, followed by state chairpersons, county chairpersons, and local activists.

The parties serve an important role in the American political system, fulfilling functions that aid government operations. These include:

- recruiting and nominating candidates for office
- running political campaigns
- articulating positions on various issues
- connecting individuals and the government

In Congress, parties have become integral to the organization of both houses. The leadership of each house is based on the leadership of whichever party has the majority.

The majority party also holds all of the committee chairs, assigns bills to committees, holds a majority in each committee, controls the important Rules Committee, and sets the legislative agenda.

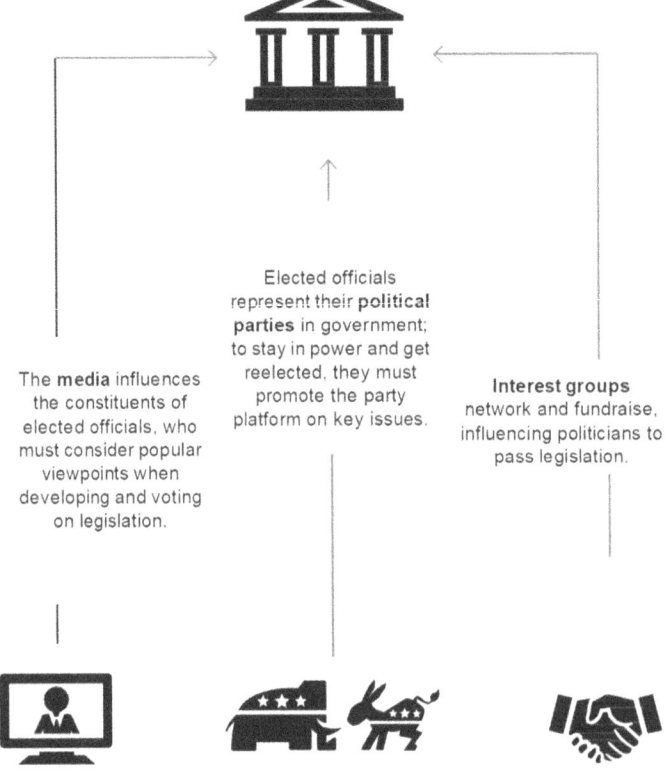

Figure 13.3. Political Influence

While still very important, the power of political parties has declined dramatically since the beginning of the twentieth century. In response to the dominance and corruption of political machines, many states implemented **direct primaries** to circumvent the parties. Individual politicians can now build power without the party machinery.

Although the United States has a two-party system, third parties still emerge from time to time. These parties are always relatively small and come in three types:

- Charismatic leadership parties are dominated by an engaging and forceful leader. Examples include the Bull Moose Party (Teddy Roosevelt, 1912), the American Independent Party (George Wallace, 1972), and the Reform Party (Ross Perot, 1992 and 1996).

- Single-issue parties are organized around one defining issue. Examples include the Free Soil Party and the Know Nothing Party in the 1840s, and the Right to Life Party in the 1970s and 1980s.

- Ideological parties are organized around a particular non-mainstream ideology. Examples include the Green Party and the Libertarian Party.

Although they rarely succeed in gaining major political office, these third parties play an important role in American politics. The two main parties tend toward the middle in an attempt to garner the majority of votes. Third parties, on the other hand, target select populations and are thus able to express strong views on controversial issues. Because their views are usually shared by the most extreme elements of one of the major parties, their stances often push the major parties into more radical positions. They also can affect the outcome of an election, even without winning it. By siphoning off a segment of the vote from one of the dominant parties, they can "spoil" the election for that party. For example, in the 2000 presidential election, Ralph Nader, the Green Party candidate, did not win any electoral votes. However, he drew away votes that most likely otherwise would have gone to Al Gore, contributing to George W. Bush's election.

Practice Question

5. Third parties primarily impact presidential elections by
    A) increasing voter turnout.
    B) preventing either party from winning a majority in the Electoral College.
    C) encouraging more voters to officially join a political party.
    D) bringing forward issues to be adopted by the major parties later.

Other Groups

Organizations and individuals who are not politicians or employed by the government still have a role to play in politics. Washington, DC and state capitals are home to many interest groups, and the media is key in governance.

Interest Groups

An **interest group** is a private organization made up of individuals who share policy views on one or more issues. Organized together, the group then tries to influence public opinion to its own benefit. Interest groups play an important role in American politics. Much like political parties (and often even more directly than political parties), they connect citizens to the government. They act as a two-way street, both bringing their members' concerns and perspective to government officials and sharing information with their members about government policy. They wield more influence than the average citizen: they speak for many, and they raise money to influence policymakers, thereby influencing policy.

> **Did You Know?**
>
> Interest groups play an increasingly dominant role in American political life. The number of groups increased from 6,000 in 1959 to 22,000 in 2010.

Most interest groups focus on one core issue or on a set of issues and draw their membership from people interested in those issues. For example, the National Rifle Association (NRA) focuses on protecting the right to gun ownership. Other organizations focus on a specific group of people, and then determine their interests based on the interests of that group. The AARP (American Association of Retired Persons) is an example of this type of interest group. It determines which issues are most relevant to senior citizens (who make up their membership), and pursues those issues. In addition, large corporations, industry organizations, agricultural groups, professional associations, and unions act as interest groups.

Interest groups **lobby** lawmakers to try to effect the change they wish to see. To lobby means to attempt to persuade policymakers to make a certain decision. There are about 30,000 lobbyists in Washington D.C., making $2 billion a year. It is their full-time job to advance the agenda of their interest groups. They do this by testifying before congressional committees, meeting with aides, connecting influential constituents to lawmakers, drafting legislation, and providing relevant technical information to members of Congress.

When all else fails, interest groups will turn to the courts to help them achieve their goals. They write amicus briefs (supporting documents arguing for a side) in Supreme Court cases or initiate court cases to challenge existing laws. They also can play a significant role in determining who is nominated to the federal courts, including the Supreme Court.

Another tool interest groups use to influence policymakers is the **political action committee**, also known as a PAC. These are committees that interest groups form with the purpose of raising money to support the campaigns of specific candidates who can further their interests. PACs are limited to contributions of $5000 per candidate per election. In 2010, however, the Supreme Court ruled in *Citizens United v. Federal Elections Commission* that limiting corporate donations to candidates was tantamount to limiting free speech. This controversial decision resulted in the creation of super PACs which have no limits on spending.

The role of lobbying, and most specifically PACs and super PACs, in American politics is a hotly debated one. Some political analysts are concerned that politics and money have become too closely tied together. Others argue that the sheer number of special interest groups is a benefit because they each balance each other out. In order to accomplish anything, politicians must bargain and compromise, creating solutions that are ultimately better for more people. Others still argue that rather than creating solutions, the number of competing interests leaves politicians scared to take any action for fear that they will anger one interest group or another.

Mass Media

Any means of communication—newspapers, magazines, radio, television, or blogs— that reaches a broad and far-reaching audience is considered part of the **mass media**. Although certainly not a formal part of the political process, the mass media has a significant impact on American politics. It connects people to the government by providing them with inside information on its people and processes, through reports, interviews, and exposés. The media also can help set the political agenda by drawing attention to issues through its coverage. For example, the medical treatment of veterans became a significant political issue after two lengthy exposés in the *Washington Post* on the conditions at Walter Reed Medical Center in 2007.

Mass media has also reshaped American campaigns. Campaigns have become more candidate-centered rather than issue-centered, as candidates now must consider their image on television and other video sources. They also have to be media savvy, making appearances on popular nightly shows and radio programs. The need for a strong media presence is largely responsible for the increase in campaign spending, as candidates work to maintain an up-to-date web presence and spend millions of dollars on television advertising space. Candidates' lives and pasts are also more visible to the public as journalists research their backgrounds to a further extent than ever before. In the 1960 presidential campaign, John F. Kennedy and Richard Nixon engaged in the first televised presidential debate in American history. Those who listened to it on the radio declared Nixon—who was confident in speech, but sweaty and uncomfortable on camera—the winner, while those who watched it on television saw the suave and image-savvy Kennedy as the victor. Many credit this debate for Kennedy's eventual win, demonstrating the new importance of crafting a public image for politicians.

Practice Question

6. Throughout the twentieth and twenty-first centuries, changes in politics have coincided with the emergence of new media or a change in the organization of media. This shows that:
    A) Politics is responsive to changes in how people communicate.
    B) Media has a greater impact on the functioning of government than other political systems.
    C) There is no connection between the functioning of media and politics.
    D) New media develops in response to political changes.

Answer Key

1. D: Each state government is a democratic republic in which authority is derived from the consent of the governed.

2. D: The framers thought it was important that those who spent the money be held most accountable to the people to avoid corruption and misuse.

3. C: The Electoral College is designed to balance the power of the states and to best represent their interests without allowing a single state to dominate.

4. C: Incorrectly alleging that someone is a member of a white supremacist group is considered libel (if written) or slander (if spoken). This is not protected by the Constitution.

5. D: This is by far the most significant role third parties play. They are able to discuss more controversial issues and espouse more radical positions. This often pushes the major parties to discuss the issues as well and take a stand.

6. A: Politicians are always trying to find the best way to connect to their constituencies; therefore they must be adaptable to new media as it emerges. Also, new media changes the way in which politics is reported, which then changes the way it functions.

14. Economics

Economists study how goods and services are produced and distributed. Economic activity is generally assumed to occur on the market (although there are different economic systems).

The **market** refers to how goods and services are bought and sold. Historically, a market was an actual location where merchants would buy and sell goods; this remains true today. However, the term *market* also refers more abstractly to commercial networks of buying, selling, and production on the local, regional, national, and international scale. There are different types of markets: investors buy and sell stocks and bonds in the financial markets, individuals can find food and clothing in the retail market, and the housing market varies from city to city and region to region as home prices rise and fall.

Production is the creation of goods and services that are sold on the market for profit. Producers, or **firms**, **profit** when they sell a product for a higher price than it cost to create the product. Goods and services are **distributed** through the market: that is, they are made available for **consumption**, or purchase.

Labor refers to the work done by humans in an economy to produce goods and services. **Capital** is something that produces income. Capital might be a farmer's tractors, a restaurant's kitchen equipment, or a contractor's tools. Labor turns capital into goods and services that are then sold on the market. The people that do the labor are compensated for it with **wages**.

Types of Economic Systems

There are four kinds of economic systems. A **traditional economy** is a pre-industrialized economy, guided by tradition, and often using **bartering** rather than currency. For instance, farmers in medieval societies might have traded crops for handmade goods like tools.

A **pure command economy** is usually found in **communist** societies. In a pure command economy, the government—rather than the market—determines all aspects of production. Today, they are very rare; North Korea is an example.

A **pure market economy**, also known as **capitalism**, is governed by the laws of supply and demand with no outside interference. The economist **Adam Smith** theorized that the **"invisible hand"** of the market would direct activity to maximize economic efficiency. Government should let the economy behave freely—a concept called *laissez-faire*, or "let do" in French. Pure market economies are usually found where there is weak or no government, for instance in parts of Somalia.

A **mixed economy** is governed by both the market and the government. The people may decide what is produced by what they are willing to buy, but the government regulates different aspects of the economy with regards to the safety of the population. Most modern economies are mixed economies. The United States economy is based on capitalism, but it is a mixed economy because the government intervenes in some aspects.

Practice Question

1. In the 1870s in the United States, Americans favored laissez-faire economics, minimizing government regulations and controls on business. This most closely resembles which type of economy?
    A) traditional
    B) market
    C) command
    D) mixed

Functions of the Market

There are several defining principles of a market economy. **Private property**: The market favors private ownership of most economic resources. Private ownership leads to innovation and investment, which in turn lead to growth. It also allows for trade (of services and goods). Economists often point to the inefficiency of the United States Postal Service (USPS) as compared to private carriers like FedEx or UPS to illustrate this point. FedEx and UPS have an incentive to provide better service, in order to stay in business and grow. The better their services, the more likely consumers are to choose them, keeping their businesses alive and thriving. USPS, as a publicly owned entity, is guaranteed survival by the government. So even if the USPS provides bad service, it will not lose government support (though customers may choose to send packages by FedEx or UPS instead).

Freedom of choice: In a market economy, all individuals are free to acquire, use, and sell resources without restriction or regulation. This allows market forces to function properly. Two important elements in the market are supply and demand. If there was a restriction on buying large cars, for example, this would artificially alter demand, and throw off the functioning of the automobile market.

Private property and freedom of choice create the two primary driving forces of the market: self-interest and competition.

Economists assume that people are motivated by **self-interest** as they use their own resources. The seller in the market wants to maximize resources (or profit). The buyer wants to maximize utility (or happiness). As a result, the seller offers goods that will maximize the happiness of buyers in order to attract sales. Self-interest, then, leads to innovation and quality, as it creates a market where the best products are available to buyers. For example, Apple has noted that technological integration brings buyers a great deal of happiness, so the company works to continually innovate new ways of integrating technology (like the Apple watch) in its quest for profit.

Because all individuals are motivated by self-interest, new sellers will enter the market when they determine that there is a possibility for profit. And, because all individuals have freedom of choice, buyers will buy from the sellers whose products maximize their happiness (either through prices or quality). Therefore, sellers compete with each other to attract buyers by appealing to their maximum happiness. **competition** leads to lower prices and higher quality.

Consequently, the primary communication tool of the market is **price**. Because of competition, prices are set by the market rather than by individuals. As a result, price signals buyers and sellers who, in turn, use it to make decisions about how to use their resources. Prices communicate the relative value of products in the market and deliver to both sellers and buyers what they seek through their own self-interest: profit and happiness, respectively.

Economic Behavior

Economists assume that all people have unlimited wants; however, there are limited resources to satisfy those wants. This concept is called **scarcity**. Scarcity forces individuals to make a **choice**, to select one want over another. In making choices, people seek to maximize their **utility**, the point of greatest happiness.

For example, a student wants to go to the movies with her friends, but also wants to do well on her exams the next day. Her resource—in this case, time—is limited, so she must choose between the options. She will weigh the cost, or value lost, of not studying for her exam, against the benefit, or value attained, of seeing the movie, and vice versa. The value of the option *not* selected is called the **opportunity cost**. So, the opportunity cost of staying home to study is the lost fun of seeing the movie and strengthening the bonds with friends.

Resources, also called **factors of production**, fall into four basic categories:

- Labor
- Land/natural resources
- Physical capacity
- Entrepreneurial ability, or know-how

Each of the four factors of production is necessary for producing anything in the marketplace. They are considered some of the most basic parts of the business equation.

Practice Question

2. Which of the following is NOT an example of the principle of scarcity?
   A) a pharmaceutical company lowers the price of a commonly used drug
   B) overfishing in key coastal waters
   C) drought reduces the number of pumpkins sold in fall farmer's markets
   D) flu season ramps up and flu vaccines are hard to find

Demand And Supply

The **Law of demand** is simple. As the price for a good or service increases, the demand for it will decrease. In other words, if the price goes up, purchases usually go down. For example, a coffee shop sells coffee for $1 a cup and sales skyrocket. The coffee shop then quadruples the price to $4 a cup, and sales plummet.

Whereas demand addresses the behavior of buyers, supply deals with the behavior of sellers. The **Law of supply** states that as the price of a good increases, suppliers will increase the quantity of the good they supply. This is because of **increasing marginal costs**: as suppliers increase the amount they are supplying, the marginal costs of pro- duction (the costs of capital, labor, etc.) increase as well. Therefore, they will only increase supply if price is high enough to offset that cost.

For example, at the holidays, a toy company decides to double its supply of its most popular toy. In order to do this, the company must hire more workers, keep the factory open longer, run the machines longer, pay more in electricity, and pay more in packing materials and shipping costs to get the toys to the stores. If they decided to triple the supply, these costs would only increase. So, the price of the toy would need to be high enough to generate enough revenue to offset these additional costs.

The interplay of supply, demand, and price is used to describe the state of the market. When the quantity demanded equals the quantity supplied at a given price, the market is in a state of **equilibrium**. Essentially, this means that both suppliers and buyers are satisfied with the price.

When the quantity demanded exceeds the quantity supplied, a **shortage**, or **excess demand**, exists. Shortages occur when prices are low because low prices lead to high demand but low supply. For example, if the market price of a television is $20, demand for these inexpensive TVs will be high, but increasing supply would be too expensive for producers because they are not making enough money to offset production costs. Therefore, producers would not make more TVs to meet demand, keeping the supply low.

> **Did You Know?**
>
> When have you been affected by price changes due to demand and supply? For instance, stores heavily discount leftover Valentine's Day candy on February 15 because demand for it drops after the holiday.

When the quantity supplied exceeds the quantity demanded, a **surplus**, or **excess supply**, exists. Again, this is caused by the supply and demand's opposing relationships to price. If the TVs are now $2,000 each, fewer buyers will be willing to purchase one. However, the high price allows the supplier to clearly outstrip the costs of production.

The market always tends toward equilibrium. So, in the case of a shortage, buyers will offer to pay more for the television, and suppliers will begin to increase supply. This trend will continue until they reach equilibrium. On the flip side, when a surplus exists, suppliers will lower prices in order to attract buyers, thereby increasing demand until equilibrium is reached.

The Basic Categories of Financial Assets

Stocks and bonds are securities, monetary units that can be exchanged. Public and private interests and individuals may invest in stocks as stockholders, or in bonds as lenders. Stocks and bonds are traded on the **stock market**, a venue where private individuals, businesses, government agencies, and even foreign investors and foreign countries can invest.

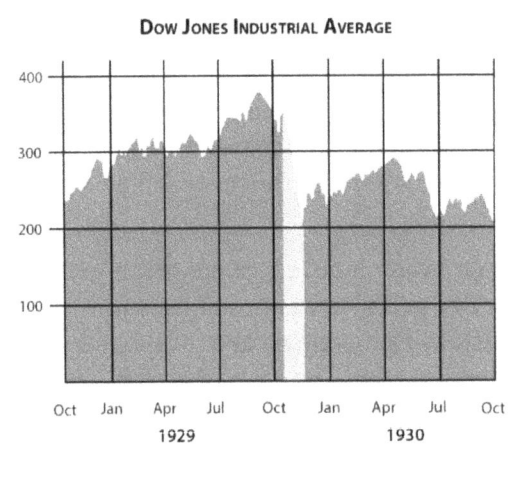

Figure 14.1. Stock Market Crash and Consequences

Stocks are essentially shares of any given company or corporation that has "gone public" or offered its stock for sale to the highest bidder, whomever that may be. In the last century, the value of the stock market has come to reflect the state of the American economy as never before.

In 1929, the stock market was the precursor to an economic downturn that history has called the **great depression**. It was not just an American economic downturn. Most of the world was affected by the stock market crash in 1929 and the decade of depression that followed. The graph below shows the pitfalls of more than a decade of questionable buying practices by investors of all economic demographics.

The American economy is still more or less a mirror reflection of the American stock market. Its movement, both up and down, is the fodder of presidential campaigns and Congressional debate. For smaller investors, the risks and rewards can be high. There are fortunes to be made and lost for anyone who wants to take the risk. This graph explores the three different stock measures over a period of several years.

Figure 14.2. Stock Measures

Money market funds invest in short-term investments like treasury bonds. These are considered safe and solid investments much like bank deposits, but encompass a broader scope for large scale investors.

The Allocation of Resources

Allocation of resources, or how resources are distributed across an economy, can fall to either the government or the market, depending on the type of economy. Within a specific firm, the allocation of resources is determined by profit maximization: how can the resources be used most efficiently?

One of the best ways to explain government control of the allocation of resources is to look at rationing during the Second World War in the United States. Rather than allow the public to hoard goods and create shortages, the federal government decided to control the flow of goods to civilians by allocating only a small amount of goods to the public on a weekly and monthly basis. Most resources are limited. In this case, economists determine the best way to allocate resources that does the least harm to all parties.

Public goods are products that an individual can consume without reducing their availability to other individuals. Public goods are also equally available to all. Basic television, plumbing infrastructure, and sewage systems are all examples of public goods. Some people now argue that internet access should be a public good. In a pure market economy, the market would provide for all public goods. However, in reality, often private markets fail to provide the allocatively efficient level of public goods, and providing them falls to the government.

Practice Question

3. Which of the following is NOT an example of a public good?
   A) public parks
   B) streetlights
   C) air travel
   D) radio broadcasts

Government Intervention

In the United States, one of the government's most important roles in the economy is to foster **competition** to guarantee a fair market and help ensure that consumers have choices. **antitrust Laws** promote a competitive market environment. Antitrust laws exist to protect consumers from illegal mergers and other unfair business practices. Antitrust laws emerged out of the Progressive movement of the nineteenth century in response to the monopolies and trusts dominated by banking and heavy industry in the Second Industrial Revolution.

The richest businessmen of the nineteenth century were called **robber barons** because they controlled vast amounts of money and property. For the robber barons, controlling all aspects of one given industry was simply good business practice. For example, a steel magnate might control the steel industry of a given region of the United States. That means he or she controls the mines where raw ingredients are mined from the earth as well as the miners, even providing company houses and a company store. Furthermore, the magnate controls the railroad that hauls raw ingredients to the steel foundries and the railroads that carry the finished product to its destination.

> **Did You Know?**
>
> Understanding the US government's basic role in the economy will be an asset on the exam.

Competition is key to a market economy and a capitalist system. Establishing a **trust**—control over the entire industrial process—defeats that purpose. It was for that reason that the US government set out to break the trusts of the late nineteenth and early twentieth centuries.

The government also intervenes in the form of taxation. In theory, progressive taxes tax the income of the wealthy more than other groups in society. These taxes increase gradually as income rises for an individual, but in a free market economy, taxes are adjusted to account for income losses in business, charitable contributions, and other circumstances. Therefore, in reality, tax rates may vary considerably across income levels.

Other forms of taxation include **proportional** and **regressive taxes. Proportional taxes** are similar to flat rate taxes in that all taxpayers are taxed at the same rate or at the same proportion of their incomes.

regressive taxes affect everyone at the same rate without a sliding proportional scale, making life more expensive for the lower classes.

Practice Question

4. Which of the following statements is true of antitrust laws?
    A) They are designed to modify perfect competition markets.
    B) They are designed to protect controlling firms in trusts.
    C) They are designed to shift markets towards monopolies.
    D) They are designed to decrease the power of monopolists.

The Federal Reserve

The federal reserve behaves as a central bank of the United States and ensures the safety of the American monetary system. In the century since its inception, the role of the Fed has expanded tremendously, but the Fed's primary role at the end of the day is to maximize employment and stabilize prices in the United States.

> **Did You Know?**
>
> You do not need to memorize every responsibility of the Fed for the GED, but you should know its purpose.

The Federal Reserve was created in 1913 to help thwart the rising numbers of financial panics that seized the nation every few years. The Fed was created to stabilize the US money supply and to moderate interest rates. As mentioned earlier, the Fed's duties have also expanded to include monitoring and maintaining reserves for US banks. With its own seal and flag, the Federal Reserve is among the most important components of the US federal government.

The Federal Reserve is the arbiter of interest rates for mortgages, the stock market, and any other monetary policy involving interest (such as money markets). **Equilibrium interest rates**, regulated by the Fed, occur only when interest rates and the money supply are roughly equivalent

Figure 14.3. The Federal Reserve

The interest rate set by the Federal Reserve is established by a number of factors, including the federal funds rate, the interest that the Federal Reserve charges banks. Figure 3.4 shows the fluctuating interest rates that banks have paid in recent decades and how they ultimately trickled down to consumers.

The Federal Reserve also monitors **monetary stabilization**: efforts to keep prices, unemployment, and the money supply, among other fiscal indicators, relatively stable. Monetary stabilization helps to prevent the economy from oscillating between inflation and recession.

Figure 14.4. Federal Funds Rate

Practice Question

5. Which of the following is NOT a responsibility of the Federal Reserve?
    A) to set interest rates
    B) to determine government spending
    C) to maximize employment
    D) to stabilize prices

Fiscal Policy

Fiscal policy is an approach to economic management in which the government is deeply involved in managing the economy. When an individual or firm spends or saves money, those choices impact that individual's or firm's own finances. When the government makes similar choices, the government's decisions impact the economy as a whole. These economic decisions are called **multipliers.**

Countries experience business cycles. In a **business cycle**, businesses tend to expand and grow. Consumer spending and employment increase. Then, the economy experiences a period of contraction and slowdown. The contraction period is known as **recession** and is marked by unemployment, low wages, and low consumer spending. A particularly harsh recession is a **depression**. After a period of time, recession is followed by **recovery**, which may be stimulated by government intervention, and growth begins anew.

In **inflation**, the price of goods and services in an economy outpaces the ability of the local currency to purchase them. Inflation is not necessarily related to the business cycle.

In **expansionary fiscal policy**, the government either increases spending or decreases taxes to counteract a recession. When the economy experiences inflation, government uses **contractionary fiscal policy**: reducing government spending or increasing taxes.

A **tariff** is a tax or duty paid on anything imported or exported into or from a given country. Low tariffs encourage foreign goods to enter the market. Countries may do this to stimulate trade or in exchange for other trade agreements. For example, the North American Free Trade Agreement (NAFTA) essentially eliminated tariffs among Canada, the United States, and Mexico. This is also known as **free trade**.

High tariffs protect domestic industry by making foreign goods more expensive. This is known as **Protectionism**. However, they also risk slowing trade. For example, between World War I and World War II, the United States passed a very high protectionist tariff. In response, other countries instituted retaliatory tariffs to block American trade as Americans had blocked foreign trade. Consequently, world trade ground to a halt.

When governments make changes to spending and taxes, it affects the government's budget. When revenue (primarily money from taxes) exceeds spending, the government has a **surplus**. When spending exceeds revenues, the government has a **deficit**. A deficit is not the same thing as a debt. A deficit is simply the gap between what the government has spent and what it has earned. In order to cover that deficit, it must borrow money, generating government debt. National debt develops over years of deficits.

Changes in **currency** are caused by and impact the strength of a nation's economy. **Currency appreciation** occurs when a country's money gains value in national and international markets. This increases foreign investment, as other countries are able to gain more value for their money. However, a strong currency makes that nation's exports more expensive, which can affect trade.

Currency depreciation occurs when a country's money loses value in national and international markets. Currency depreciation may point to instabilities in the nation's economy (such as high rates of inflation). However, when carried out in an intentional and orderly manner, it can increase a nation's global competiveness by lowering the cost of its exports. For example, China has used intentional currency depreciation to build a strong export-based economy and foster economic growth.

Practice Question

6. Which of the following would NOT be an example of contradictory fiscal policy?
    A) freezing annual increases on government employees' salaries
    B) reducing the operating hours of national parks
    C) increasing property taxes
    D) financing a new dam

Answer Key

1. B: Laissez-faire economics essentially means to leave the market alone to function. The United States came close to having a pure market economy in the 1870s.

2. A: The lowered price by itself does not create scarcity, as the supply of the drug is not impacted.

3. C: Air travel is not available to everyone; it is restricted by price. Also, once one person "consumes" air travel by taking up a seat on a plane, the passenger prevents someone else from "consuming" that good.

4. D: With the rise of the robber barons and the consolidation of market power in several industries (including steel, railroads, and oil), the government took action to reduce that power and restore balance in the market.

5. B: Although the Federal Reserve plays an important role in fiscal policy, it has no control over government spending.

6. D: If the government builds a new dam, it injects new spending into the economy, thereby expanding the economy.

15. Geography and World History

Geography

Human-Environment Interaction

Humans have always modified the environment to suit their needs. For example, with the advent of agriculture, humans began loosening the topsoil to make planting easier. A looser topsoil is more susceptible to erosion from wind and rain, allowing greater changes to the physical landscape. Cities are also a prime example. Cities significantly reduce the amount of exposed ground in an area and lead to a concentration of fuel and resource consumption.

The environment has also shaped human activity. For example, the main economic activities of a place—farming, fishing, trade—have historically been determined, in large part, by the physical characteristics of the place. People living in deserts have traditionally been nomadic because restricted access to food and water requires them to continually move around in search of it. Climate impacts clothing, housing, and work and leisure patterns. For example, a period of rest in the middle of the day is common in cultures in hot climates.

> **Did You Know?**
>
> Trees can be considered both renewable and nonrenewable. If managed properly, they can be replanted and grown again. However, the rapid consumption of old growth forests uses up a resource that essentially cannot be replaced. Also, the land trees are on is often repurposed for farm land, urbanization, or mining, resulting in a permanent loss of the resource.

One of the most significant ways humans have impacted their environment is through the use of natural resources. Some resources are **renewable resources**, meaning they are virtually unlimited or can be grown and regrown. Wind, sun, and plants are all examples of renewable resources. Other resources are **non-renewable resources** because they cannot be replaced once they are consumed. Iron ore, coal, and petroleum are three of the most important nonrenewable resources.

Consuming nonrenewable resources—and consuming renewable resources too quickly—is a growing concern as industrialization has greatly increased overall consumption. Many countries are searching for ways to promote **sustainable development**, the use of natural resources and the growth of new ones at a rate that can be maintained from one generation to the next. The **United Nations commission on sustainable development** defines several criteria for global sustainable development: caring for the soil, avoiding overfishing, preserving the forest, protecting species from extinction, and reducing air pollution.

Other sustainability efforts focus on indirect factors impacting the earth's natural resources. For example, efforts to reduce fuel consumption are motivated by both the finite quantity of oil and also by the **greenhouse effect** caused by industrialization. Industrial production unleashes carbon dioxide, methane, and other gases. These create a vapor that transforms radiation into heat, which leads to **global warming**, an overall rise in the earth's temperature. As a result, the ice caps are melting prematurely, leading to rising sea levels and changes in oceanic patterns.

Practice Question

1. Which of the following statements is true about sustainable development?

    A) Sustainable development requires a prohibition on the use of nonrenewable resources.
    B) Sustainable development only applies to energy resources like wind, sun, oil, and coal.
    C) Sustainable development requires the proper management of renewable resources like trees and fish.
    D) Sustainable development contributes to the greenhouse effect and increases global warming.

Human Characteristics of Place

The human characteristics of a place make up its **culture**. These characteristics include the shared values, language, and religion of the people living in a location or region. Culture also includes the ways people feed, clothe, and shelter themselves. Cultures can be very specific or regional, like **folk cultures**, or they can be diffuse and widespread, like **popular culture**.

There are eight locations where formal culture—meaning the development of agriculture, government, and urbanization—began. These locations are known as **culture hearths**.

In the Americas, culture began in Andean America and Mesoamerica. In Africa, the culture hearths were in West Africa and the Nile River Valley. In the Middle East, culture began in Mesopotamia, and in Asia, hearths existed in the Indus River Valley, the Ganges River delta, and along the Wei and Huang Rivers in China. In each of these hearths, similar innovations—the seeds of culture—developed completely independently of one another.

Settlements are the cradles of culture. They allow for the development of political structures, the management of resources, and the transfer of information to future generations. While settlements differed greatly, they did all share some commonalities. Settlements all began near natural resources that can support life, namely water and a reliable food source. The success and growth of a settlement was based on its proximity to these natural resources and its ability to collect and move raw materials. As each of these characteristics reached a new level of sophistication, population in that area began to concentrate near the point of resource allocation and production.

The spatial layout of these settlements, then, was determined by the environment and the primary function of the settlement. For example, European villages were clustered on hillsides to more easily protect against invaders and to leave the flat areas for farming. Settlements that rose up around trade, like those on the outskirts of the Saharan desert, concentrated around access to the trade routes and were generally more dispersed.

Later in history, successful settlements also needed an ample work force, and the ability to produce and deliver finished products elsewhere. Once transportation methods were developed, the populations of these settlements became mobile, allowing for a faster diffusion of culture, and—eventually—the development of industrial centers. These industrial centers became cities. A **city** is a major hub of human settlement with a high population density and a concentration of resource creation or allocation. Today, more than half of the world's population lives in cities. In more developed regions the percentages are even higher. With the development of cities, three types of areas emerged: **urban** (in the city itself), **suburban** (near the city), and **rural (away from the city)**. In some cases, urban and suburban areas or multiple urban areas merge into a **megalopolis**, or super-city. The Northeast Corridor from Washington, DC, to Boston is one such example.

Practice Question

2. The majority of people in the world today live in
    A) urban areas.
    B) suburban areas.
    C) rural areas.
    D) megalopolises.

Development and Globalization

As areas develop and economies grow, manufacturing becomes increasingly important to the functioning of the economy. This phenomenon is called **industrialization**. Because industrialization requires a shift in the labor force, it pairs with a decline in subsistence farming: the rural labor force moves to cities.

Industrialization is a relatively recent phenomenon. The **industrial revolution** began in Great Britain in the 1760s, then diffused to Western Europe and North America by 1825. The discovery of new energy sources like coal (which was later replaced by oil) and technological advancements that allowed machines to replace human labor led to the emergence of manufacturing centers and a shift in the functioning of the economy. As people left rural areas in search of manufacturing jobs, urban areas grew: this phenomenon is called **urbanization**.

Economic growth is strongly connected to **development**, the use of technology and knowledge to improve the living conditions of people in a country. While economic in its foundation, development focuses on a range of quality of life issues like access to basic goods and services, education, and healthcare. Countries on the wealthier side of the spectrum are called **more developed countries (MDCs)**, while those on the poorer side are called **less developed countries (IDCs)**. MDCs are concentrated primarily in the Northern Hemisphere. Their primary economic concern is maintaining growth. LDCs, found mostly in the Southern Hemisphere, face the challenge of improving their economic conditions by stimulating significant and sustainable economic growth.

Globalization is the trend of increasing interdependence and spatial interaction between disparate areas of the world economically, politically, and culturally. At its core, globalization is an economic trend; however it has significant cultural and political impacts as well. For example, the exportation of American fast food restaurants, like McDonald's, to other parts of the world reflects the capitalist drive to find new markets. Furthermore, the introduction of this type of food has a significant impact on one of the major distinguishing cultural traits of other countries—their cuisine.

The primary driving force of globalization is **multinational corporations (MNCs)** or **transnational corporations (TNCs)**. These are companies whose headquarters are located in one country and whose production is located in one or more different countries. The process of moving production to a different country is called **outsourcing**. Outsourcing benefits the MNC because of reduced labor costs, lower tax rates, cheaper land prices, and usually fewer regulations on safety and environmental standards.

Demography is the study of human population. More than half of the world's population today lives in cities. While this is a relatively recent change, the population has always been unevenly distributed based on resources. So, as cities have become better at obtaining and allocating resources, they have attracted more people. Seventy-five percent of all people live on only 5 percent of the earth's land.

Over the last 300 years, the population of Earth has exploded; population has been growing at an exponential rate, meaning the more people are added to the population, the faster it grows. In 1765, the global population was 300 million people. Today it is six billion. This increase has raised concerns for many demographers, particularly in the areas with a higher population concentration. To determine if an area is at risk, demographers determine its **carrying capacity**, the number of people the area can support.

The carrying capacity of various areas can differ greatly depending on technology, wealth, climate, available habitable space, access, and **infrastructure**, or institutions that support the needs of the people. When a country exceeds its carrying capacity, it suffers from **overpopulation**. Countries in danger of overpopulation may attempt to

> **Did You Know?**
>
> While much of the world's wealth is concentrated in North America and Western Europe, 80 percent of people live in poor, developing countries in South America, Asia, and Africa. The most populated area in the world is East Asia, which is home to 25 percent of the world's population. In terms of population, East Asia is followed by Southeast Asia, and then Europe, from the Atlantic Ocean to the Ural Mountains.

restrict their growth, like China did through its one-child policy.

In spite of the population boom, some countries actually suffer from **underpopulation**. They have a much greater carrying capacity—due to their high levels of production, amount of land, or abundance of natural resources—than their population uses.

Migration is the permanent relocation of an individual or group from one home region to another region. As globalization has increased, so has global mobility, both in frequency and length of migrations. Some migration is internal—people moving from one place to another within the same region, like urbanization. Other migration involves people moving from one region of the world to another. Many immigrants have migrated to the United States from other countries around the world.

Push factors are the negative aspects of the home region that make someone want to leave it; **pull factors** are the positive aspects of the new region that make someone want to move there. Push factors include high taxes, high crime rates, resource depletion, and corrupt governments. Migrants who cross inter- national borders fleeing persecution, governmental abuse, war, or natural disaster are called **refugees**. People who migrate intra-nationally by moving from one part of a country to another are called **internally displaced persons**.

> **Did You Know?**
>
> According to the UN, at least 40 percent of Syria's population was internally displaced in 2014, fleeing violence in that country's civil war. In 2015, millions of refugees from Syria and elsewhere in the Middle East, Asia, and North Africa began migrating to Europe, seeking safety from violent conflict.

Not all migration is voluntary. History has many examples of **forced migration**, when a group of people is forcibly removed from their home and brought to a new region. The African slave trade and the removal of Native American tribes from the Southeastern United States are both examples of forced migration.

Practice Question

3. Canada produces more resources than its population can consume. This is an example of
   A) overpopulation.
   B) carrying capacity.
   C) underpopulation.
   D) graying population.

World History

Early Civilizations and the Great Empires

Around 2500 BCE (or possibly earlier) the **Sumerians** emerged in the Near East (eventually expanding into parts of Mesopotamia). Developing irrigation and advanced agriculture, they were able to support settled areas that developed into cities. They also developed **cuneiform**, the earliest known example of writing to use characters to form words.

Did You Know?

To do well on the HiSET, focus on understanding historical trends and why they occurred. Don't worry about memorizing dates.

Around the eighteenth-century BCE, **Babylonia** dominated Southern Mesopotamia and **Assyria** to the north. King Hammurabi in Babylonia had developed courts and an early codified rule of law—**the code of Hammurabi**—which meted out justice on an equal basis: "an eye for an eye, a tooth for a tooth."

Meanwhile, development had been under way in the **Nile Valley** in ancient **Egypt.** Despite the surrounding Sahara Desert, the fertile land on the banks of the Nile River lent itself to agriculture, and the early Egyptians were able to develop settled communities thanks to agriculture and irrigation. Known for their pyramids, art, and pictorial writing (**hiero-glyphs**), the ancient Egyptians emerged as early as 5000 BCE; evidence of Egyptian unity under one monarch, or **pharaoh**, dates to around 3000 BCE.

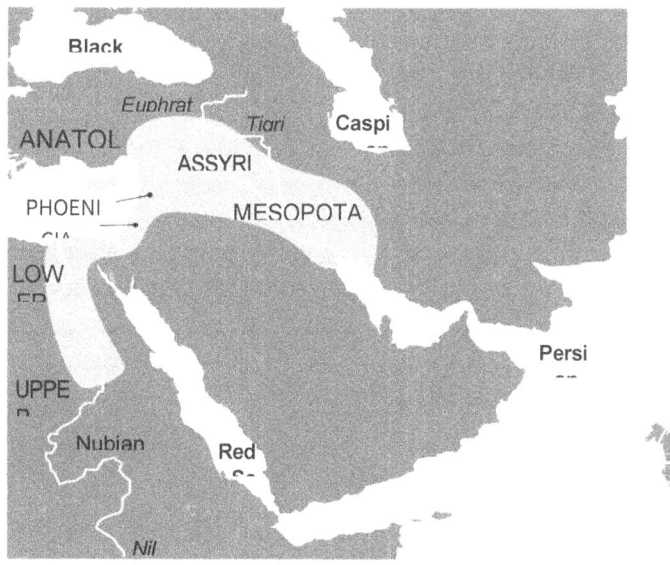

Figure 15.1. Fertile Crescent

15. Geography and World History
267

Early civilizations also developed farther east. The **Indus Valley civilizations** flourished in the Indian Subcontinent and the Indus and Ganges river basins. The **Harapan** civilization was based in Punjab from around 3000 BCE. Concurrent with the Roman Empire, the **Gupta Empire** emerged in India. During this period, known as the Golden Age of India, the region was economically strong; there was active trade by sea with China, East Africa, and the Middle East in spices, ivory, silk, cotton, and iron, which was highly profitable as an export.

In China, the **Shang Dynasty**, the first known dynasty, ruled the **Huang He** or **Yellow River** area around the second millennium BCE and developed the earliest known Chinese writing, which helped unite Chinese-speaking people throughout the region. The concept of the **Mandate of Heaven**, in which the emperor had a divine mandate to rule, emerged from the understanding that land was divinely inherited. **Confucius** taught harmony and respect for hierarchy.

Under the Qin and Han Dynasties, China developed centralized administration, expanded infrastructure, standardization in weights and measures, standardized writing, a standardized currency, and strict imperial control. The administrative **bureaucracy** established by the emperor was the foundation of Chinese administration until the twentieth century. In addition, the Emperor constructed the **Great Wall of China**.

Throughout Mesoamerica, civilizations like the **Olmec** had developed irrigation as early as 1200 BCE to expand and enrich agriculture, similar to developments in the Fertile Crescent. In South America, artistic evidence remains of the **Chavin**, **Moche**, and **Nazca** peoples, who preceded the later Inca civilization and empire.

The **Maya** came to dominate the Yucatan peninsula around 300. They developed a complex spiritual belief system accompanied by relief art, and built pyramidal temples that still stand today. In addition, they developed a detailed calendar and a written language using pictographs similar to Egyptian hieroglyphs; they studied astronomy and mathematics. Maya political administration was organized under monarchical city-states until around 900, when the civilization began to decline.

Persia conquered the Babylonians in the sixth century BCE.

Persian rule extended from the Indus Valley to Egypt, and north to **Anatolia** by about 400 BCE, where the Persians encountered the ancient **Greeks**.

Greece was comprised of **city-states** like **Athens**, the first known **democracy**, and the military state **Sparta**. Historically these city-states had been rivals; however, they temporarily united to defeat Persia. Much of Greece became unified under Athens following the war. During this **Golden Age** of Greek, or Hellenic Age, civilization, art, architecture, and philosophy emerged that would influence European civilization. **Socrates** began teaching, influencing later philosophers like **Plato** and **Aristotle**, who established the basis for modern western philosophical and political thought.

> **Did You Know?**
>
> The term democracy comes from the Greek word demokratia— "people power." It was participatory rather than representative; officials were chosen by groups rather than elected.
>
> Athens was the strongest of the many small political bodies.

In Italy, the city of **Rome** was founded as early as the eighth century BCE; it became strong thanks to its importance as a trade route for the Greeks and other Mediterranean peoples.

Originally a kingdom, Rome became a **republic** and elected lawmakers (senators) to the **Senate**. The Romans developed highly advanced infrastructure, including aqueducts and roads, some still in use today. Economically powerful Rome began conquering areas around the Mediterranean with its increasingly powerful military, holding territory thanks to its infrastructure.

However, the Senate became corrupt, and divisions grew throughout the Republic between the wealthy ruling class and the working, poor, and military. The popular military leader **Julius Caesar** forced the corrupt Senate to give him control and began to transition Rome from a republic to an empire. His nephew **Octavian** became the first emperor.

At this time, Rome reached the height of its power, and the Mediterranean region enjoyed a period of stability known as the ***Pax Romana.*** Rome controlled the entire Mediterranean region and lands stretching as far north as Germany and Britain, territory into the Balkans, far into the Middle East, Egypt, North Africa, and Iberia. In this time of relative peace and prosperity, Latin literature flourished, as did art, architecture, philosophy, mathematics, science, and international trade throughout Rome and beyond into Asia and Africa. A series of emperors would follow and Rome remained a major world power, but it would never again reach the height of prosperity and stability that it did under Augustus.

Figure 15.2. Pax Romana

Practice Question

4. Rome was able to maintain imperial control over a vast amount of territory thanks in part to
    A) the idea that the Roman emperor had a divine mandate to rule: the Mandate of Heaven.
    B) a powerful military and strong infrastructure (like roads) throughout the empire.
    C) the concept of one God, and shared religion throughout the empire.
    D) how easy it was to obtain Roman citizenship and all the benefits that came with it.

Feudalism Through the Era of Expansion

After the fall of Rome, the Byzantine Empire—formerly the eastern part of the Roman Empire, based in Constantinople—remained a strong civilization and a place of learning. Constantinople was a strategically located commercial center that connected Asian trade routes with Europe. Later, missionaries traveled north to Slav-controlled Russia, spreading Christianity and literacy. Russian Christianity was influenced by the Byzantine doctrine, what would become Greek Orthodox Christianity.

Despite the chaos in Western Europe, the Christian Church in Rome remained strong, becoming a stabilizing influence. However, differences in doctrine between Rome and Constantinople became too wide to overcome. Beginning in 1054, a series of **schisms** developed in the now-widespread Christian religion between the **Roman Catholic Church** and the **Greek Orthodox Church** over matters of doctrine and some theological concepts. Eventually the two would become entirely separate churches.

In Europe, the early Middle Ages (or **Dark Ages**) from the fall of Rome to about the tenth century, were a chaotic, unstable, and unsafe time. What protection and stability existed were represented and maintained by the Catholic Church and the feudal system.

Society and economics were characterized by decentralized, local governance, or **feudalism**, a hierarchy where land and protection were offered in exchange for loyalty. Feudalism was the dominant social, economic, and political hierarchy of the European Middle Ages.

In exchange for protection, **vassals** would pledge **fealty**, or **pay homage to lords**, landowners who would reward their vassals' loyalty with land, or **fiefs.** Economic and social organization consisted of **manors**, self-sustaining areas possessed by lords but worked by peasants. The peasants were **serfs**, not slaves but not entirely free. Tied to the land, they worked for the lord in exchange for protection; however they were not obligated to fight. Usually they were also granted some land for their own use, but they could not leave the manor. While not true slaves, their lives were effectively controlled by the lord.

Warriors who fought for lords, called **knights**, were rewarded with land and could become minor lords in their own right. Lords themselves could be vassals of other lords; that hierarchy extended upward to kings or the Catholic Church. The Catholic Church itself was a major landowner and political power. In a Europe not yet dominated by sovereign states, the **pope** was not only a religious leader, but also a military and political one.

Did You Know?

Charlemagne brought stability to Western and Central Europe during a period when two powerful, organized, non- Christian civilizations—the Vikings in the north and the Islamic powers in the south—threatened what was left of western Christendom, and when insecurity was growing to the east with the decline of the Byzantines.

In what is considered the reemergence of centralized power in Europe, parts of Western and Central Europe were organized under Charlemagne, who was crowned emperor of the Roman Empire by Pope Leo III in **800 CE**. While in retrospect this seems long after the end of Rome, at the time many Europeans still perceived them- selves as somehow still part of a Roman Empire.

It was also under Charlemagne that the feudal system became truly organized, bringing more stability to Western Europe. The Catholic Church would dominate Europe from Ireland towards Eastern Europe—an area of locally controlled duchies, kingdoms, and alliances. In **962**, the pope crowned the first emperor of the Holy Roman Empire in Central Europe, a confederation of small states which remained an important European power until its dissolution in **1806**.

Meanwhile, in the wake of the decline of the Byzantine Empire, **Arab-Islamic empires** characterized by brisk commerce, advancements in technology and learning, and urban development arose in the Middle East.

In Arabia itself, Judaism, Christianity, and animist religions were practiced by the Arab majority. The Prophet **Muhammad** was born in Mecca around 570; he began preaching Islam around 613. Muhammad and his followers established Islam and Arab rule in the region, and the Arabs went on to conquer the Byzantine Empire and Persia in a series of *caliphates*, or empires: first the Umayyad caliphate based in Damascus, and then the Abbasid Caliphate based in Baghdad. By 750, they would control territory from Iberia (Spain) to parts of Central Asia and what is today Pakistan.

Stability permitted open trade routes, economic development, and cultural inter- action throughout Asia, the Middle East, North Africa, and parts of Europe. Thanks to the universality of the Arabic language, scientific and medical texts from varying civilizations—Greek, Persian, Indian—could be translated into Arabic and shared throughout the Islamic world. Arab thinkers studied Greek and Persian astronomy and engaged in further research. The Arabs studied mathematics and developed algebra, and fostered literary culture.

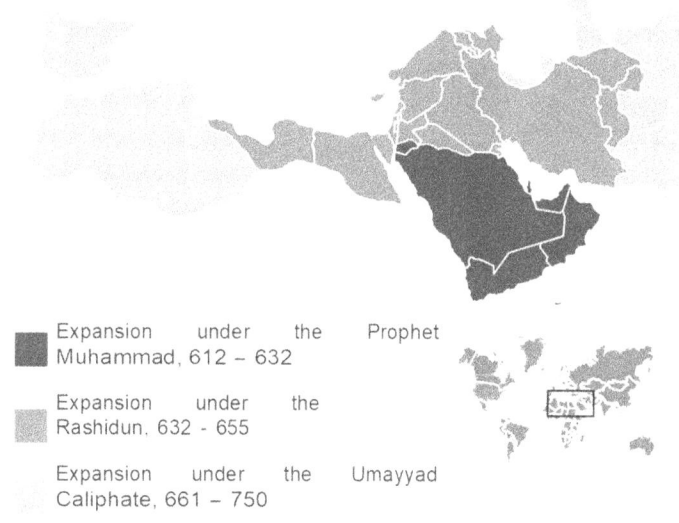

Figure 15.3. Islamic Expansion

Around this time, the **Song Dynasty (960 – 1276)** controlled most of China. Under the Song, China experienced tremendous development and economic growth. Characterized by increasing urbanization, the Song featured complex administrative rule, including the difficult competitive written examinations required to obtain prestigious bureaucratic positions in government.

Most traditions recognized as Chinese emerged under the Song, including the consumption of tea and rice and common Chinese architecture. The Song engaged not only in overland trade along the Silk Road, exporting silk, tea, ceramics, jade, and other goods, but also sea trade with Korea, Japan, Southeast Asia, India, Arabia, and even East Africa.

International commerce was vigorous along the **silk road,** trading routes which stretched from the Arab-controlled Eastern Mediterranean to Song Dynasty China. The Silk Road reflected the transnational nature of Central Asia: the nomadic culture of Central Asia lent itself to trade between the major civilizations of China, Persia, the Near East, and Europe. Buddhism and Islam spread into China. Chinese,

Islamic, and European art, pottery, and goods were interchanged between the three civilizations— early globalization. The Islamic tradition of the **hajj**, or the pilgrimage to Mecca, also spurred cultural interaction. Islam had spread from Spain throughout North Africa, the Sahel, the Middle East, Persia, Central Asia, India, and China; peoples from all these regions traveled and met in Arabia as part of their religious pilgrimage.

Islam also spread along trans-Saharan trade routes into West Africa and the Sahel. Brisk trade between the gold-rich **Kingdom of Ghana** and Muslim traders based in Morocco brought Islam to the region around the eleventh century. The Islamic **Mali Empire** (1235 – 1500), based farther south in **Timbuktu**, eventually extended beyond the original Ghanaian boundaries all the way to the West African coast, and controlled the valuable gold and salt trades. It became a center of learning and commerce. At the empire's peak, the ruler **Mansa Musa** made a pilgrimage to Mecca in 1324. However, by 1500, the **Songhai Empire** had overcome Mali and eventually dominated the Niger River area.

Figure 15.4. The Silk Road

Loss of Byzantine territory to the Islamic empires meant loss of Christian lands in the Levant—including Jerusalem and Bethlehem—to Muslims. In **1095 CE**, the Byzantine emperor asked **the pope** for help to defend Jerusalem and protect Christians. With a history of Muslim incursions into Spain and France, anti-Muslim sentiment was strong in Europe and Christians there were easily inspired to fight them in the Levant, or **holy land**; the Pope offered lords and knights the chance to keep lands and bounty they won from conquered Muslims (and Jews) in this *crusade*. He also offered Crusaders **indulgences**— forgiveness for sins committed in war and guarantees they would enter heaven. The **crusades** continued over several centuries.

Meanwhile, the Abbasid Caliphate went into decline in the tenth century and control in the region splintered. The collapse of the Abbasid Caliphate led to instability and decentralization of power, and production and economic development declined. China closed its borders and trade on the Silk Road declined.

Despite conflict in Europe, Christians found they had more in common with each other than with Muslims, and united to fight in the Middle East. While the ongoing Crusades never resulted in permanent European control over the Holy Land, they did open up trade routes and information exchange between Europe and the Middle East, stretching all the way along the Silk Road to China. This increasing interdependence led to the European Renaissance.

Ongoing interactions between Europeans and Muslims exposed Europeans, who could now afford them thanks to international trade, to improved education and goods. However, the **Bubonic (Black) Plague** also spread to Europe as a result of global exchange, killing off a third of its population from 1347–1351. The plague had a worldwide impact: empires fell in its wake.

Back in Europe, instability reached its height throughout the thirteenth and fourteenth centuries known as the **hundred years' war** (1337 – 1453), a chaotic time of conflict between France and England. In Islamic Spain, Christian raids and conflict were ongoing during the lengthy period of the **Reconquista**, which did not end until 1492 when Christian powers led by Ferdinand and Isabella united Spain as one Christian kingdom.

In Southwest Asia, the **Mongol invasions** destroyed agriculture, city life and planning, economic patterns and trade routes, and social stability for some time. The **Mongol empire** was based in Central Asia; led by **Genghis Khan**, the Mongols expanded thanks to their abilities in horsemanship and archery. The continent was vulnerable: Central Asia lacked one dominant culture or imperial power; Southwest Asia was fragmented following the decline of the Abbasids. These weaknesses allowed the Mongols to take over most of Eurasia. In China, they did maintain infrastructure, but they established their own dynasty, the Yuan Dynasty, in 1271, with Mongols at the top of the social and political hierarchy.

> **Did You Know?**
>
> The HiSET will not test you on dates or names directly. Instead, you will be asked to analyze reading passages and images. However, you will need to be familiar with historical events and major figures to do well on the test.

Eventually in China, the Ming Dynasty reasserted Chinese control and continued traditional methods of administration; the construction of the **forbidden city**, the home of the Emperor in Beijing, helped consolidate imperial rule. The Ming also emphasized international trade; demand for ceramics in particular, in addition to silk and tea, was high abroad, and contact with seafaring traders like the Portuguese and Dutch in the sixteenth century was strong. The Ming also encouraged trade and exploration by sea.

In Russia, **Ivan the Great** brought Moscow from Mongol to Slavic Russian control. In the late fifteenth century, Ivan had consolidated Russian power over neighboring Slavic regions. Through both military force and diplomacy, Ivan achieved Moscow's independence in 1480. Turning Russian attention toward Europe, he set out to bring other neighboring lands under Russian rule. Ivan achieved a centralized, consolidated Russia that was the foundation for an empire and a sovereign nation that sought diplomatic status with Europe.

A century later, **Ivan the Terrible** set out to expand Russia further, to integrate it into Europe, and to strengthen Russian Orthodox Christianity. Named the first **tsar**, or emperor, Ivan reformed government, strengthening centralization and administrative bureaucracy and disempowering the nobility. He led the affirmation of orthodox Christianity and reorganized the military. However, overextension of resources and oppression depopulated the state and gave him the reputation as a despotic ruler.

Despite the instability inland, Indian Ocean trade routes had continued to function since at least the seventh century. These oceanic routes connected the Horn of Africa, the East African Coast, the Arabian Peninsula, Southern Persia, India, Southeast Asia, and China. The ocean acted as a unifying force throughout the region, and the **monsoon winds** permitted Arab, Persian, Indian, and Chinese merchants to travel to East Africa in search of goods such as ivory and gold—and slaves.

Many civilizational advances were achieved on the backs of enslaved persons. The **East African slave trade** remained vigorous until the nineteenth century. Arabs, Asians, and other Africans kidnapped African people and sent them to lives of slavery throughout the Arab world and South Asia. Later, Europeans would take part in the trade, forcing Africans into slavery in colonies throughout South and Southeast Asia, and on plantations in Indian Ocean islands such as Madagascar.

The major East African port was **Zanzibar**, from which gold, coconut oil, ivory, other African exports, and enslaved people made their way to Asia and the Middle East. However, enslaved persons from Sub-Saharan Africa were also forced north overland to markets in **Cairo**, where they were sold and dispersed throughout the Arab-Islamic empires and later, the Ottoman Empire.

Islam also spread throughout the African coast and inland; given the cosmopolitan nature of the coastline, the **Swahili** language adopted aspects of Arabic and other Asian languages.

Further north, the Ottoman Turks represented a threat to Central Europe. Con- trolling most of Anatolia from the late thirteenth century, the Ottomans spread west into the Balkans. In 1453 they captured Istanbul, from which the **Ottoman Empire** would come to rule much of the Mediterranean world and eventually the Middle East and North Africa until the nineteenth century. Christians left Constantinople and Greece for Italy, bringing Greek, Middle Eastern, and Asian learning with them and enriching the emerging European Renaissance.

Renaissance and Exploration

The **European Renaissance**, or *rebirth,* included the revival of ancient Greek and Roman learning, art, and architecture. However, the roots of the Renaissance stretched farther back to earlier interactions between Christendom, the Islamic World, and China during the Crusades and through Silk Road trade. Not only did the Renaissance inspire new learning and prosperity in Europe, enabling exploration, colonization, profit, and later imperialism, but it also led to scientific and religious questioning and rebellion against the Catholic Church and, later, monarchical governments.

The fall of Constantinople precipitated the development of **humanism** in Europe, a mode of thought emphasizing human nature, creativity, and an overarching concept of truth in philosophy. Humanism represented a threat to religious, especially Catholic, orthodoxy, as it allowed for the questioning of religious teaching. Ultimately humanism would be at the root of the **reformation** of the sixteenth century.

Art, considered not just a form of expression but also a science in itself, flourished in fifteenth century Italy, particularly in **Florence**. Major figures who explored anatomy in sculpture, design and perspective, and innovation in architecture included Leonardo da Vinci, Bramante, Michelangelo, Rafael, and Donatello. Leonardo is particularly known for his scientific pursuits in addition to his artistic achievement. Interest in classical (ancient Greek and Roman) artistic work enjoyed a resurgence.

Meanwhile, scholars like Galileo, Isaac Newton, and Copernicus made discoveries in what became known as the **scientific revolution**, rooted in the scientific knowledge of the Islamic empires, which had been imported through economic and social contact initiated centuries prior in the Crusades. Scientific study and discovery threatened the power of the Church.

> **Did You Know?**
>
> How might an illiterate European peasant whose only education was from the local church react to news of scientific discoveries?

Also in the mid-fifteenth century, **Johann Gutenberg** invented the **printing press**; the first book to be published would be the Bible. With the advent of printing, texts could be more widely and rapidly distributed, and people had more access to information. Here lay the roots of the **Enlightenment**, the basis for reinvigorated European culture and political thought that would drive its development for the next several centuries—and inspire revolution.

Transnational cultural exchange had also resulted in the transmission of technology to Europe. During the sixteenth century, European seafaring knowledge, navigation, and technology benefitted from Islamic and Asian expertise; European explorers and traders could now venture beyond the Mediterranean. Portuguese and Dutch sailors eventually reached India and China, where they established ties with the Ming Dynasty. Trade was no longer dependent on the Silk Road. Improved technology also empowered Europeans to explore overseas, eventually landing in the Western Hemisphere.

Interest in exploration grew in Europe during the Renaissance period. Technological advancements made complex navigation and long-term sea voyages possible, and economic growth resulting from international trade drove interest in market expansion. Global interdependence got a big push from Spain when King Ferdinand and Queen Isabella agreed to sponsor **Christopher Columbus'** exploratory voyage in 1492 to find a sea route to Asia, in order to speed up commercial trade there. Instead, he stumbled upon the Western Hemisphere, which was unknown to Europeans, Asians, and Africans to this point.

Columbus landed in the Caribbean; he and later explorers would claim the Caribbean islands and eventually Central and South America for Spain and Portugal. However, those areas were already populated by the major American civilizations.

By around 1400, two major empires dominated Central and South America: the Incas and the Aztecs. These two empires would be the last indigenous civilizations to dominate the Americas before European colonization of the Western Hemisphere.

Their military power and militaristic culture allowed the **Aztecs** to dominate Mexico and Mesoamerica and regional trade in precious objects. The main city of the Aztec empire, **Tenochtitlan**, was founded in 1325 and, at its height, home to several million people. Aztec civilization was militaristic in nature and divided on a class basis: it included slaves, indentured servants, serfs, an independent priestly class, military, and ruling classes. The Aztecs shared many beliefs with the preceding Mayan civilization.

Meanwhile, in the Andes, the **Incas** had emerged. Based in **Cuzco**, the Incas had consolidated their power around 1300. Domesticated llamas and alpacas allowed the military to transport supplies through the mountains. Inca engineers built the citadel of **Machu Picchu** and imperial infrastructure, including roads throughout the Andes. They grew crops at high altitudes. To subdue local peoples, they moved conquered groups elsewhere in the empire and repopulated conquered areas with Incas.

With its weapons and technological superiority, Spain took over the silver- and gold-rich Mesoamerican and Andean territories. The Spanish *conquistador* Hernán Cortés conquered the Aztecs, and Francisco Pizarro the Incas. In the Caribbean islands, sugar became an important cash crop.

The economic system of **mercantilism** developed, in which the colonizing or ***mother country*** took raw materials from the territories they controlled for the colonizers' own benefit. Governments amassed

15. Geography and World History

wealth through protectionism and increasing exports at the expense of other rising colonial powers. This eventually involved developing goods and then selling them back to those colonized lands at an inflated price. The *encomienda* system granted European landowners the "right" to hold lands in the Americas and demand labor from the local inhabitants. Spreading Christianity was another important reason for European expansion. Local civilizations and resources were exploited and destroyed.

The **Columbian exchange** enabled mercantilism to flourish. Conflict and illness brought by the Europeans—especially **smallpox**—decimated the Native Americans, and the Europeans were left without labor to mine the silver and gold or to work the land. **African slavery** was their solution.

Slavery was an ancient institution in many societies worldwide; however, with the Columbian Exchange slavery came to be practiced on a mass scale the likes of which the world had never seen. Throughout Africa and especially on the West African coast, Europeans traded for slaves with some African kingdoms and also raided the land, kidnapping people. Europeans took captured Africans in horrific conditions to the Americas; those who survived were enslaved and forced to work in mining or agriculture for the benefit of expanding European imperial powers.

The Columbian Exchange described the **triangular trade** across the Atlantic: Europeans took kidnapped African people from Africa to the Americas along the "Middle Passage," sold them at auction and exchanged them for sugar and raw materials; these materials were traded in Europe for consumer goods, which were then exchanged in Africa, and so on.

Figure 15.5. Triangular Trade

Throughout this period, Africans did resist both on ships and later, in the Americas; **maroon communities** of escaped slaves formed throughout the Western Hemisphere, the **Underground Railroad** in the nineteenth-century United States helped enslaved persons escape the South, and **Toussaint L'Ouverture** led a successful slave rebellion in Haiti, winning independence from the French for that country in 1803. However, the slave trade continued for centuries.

> **Did You Know?**
>
> The Haitian Revolution nearly bankrupted France, and was one reason for the sale of its territory in Louisiana to the early United States. Haiti was the first independent state in Latin America.

During the eighteenth century, Spain and Portugal were preeminent powers in global trade thanks to colonization and **imperialism**, the possession and exploitation of land overseas. However, Great Britain became an important presence on the seas; it would later dominate the oceans throughout the nineteenth century.

Practice Question

5. Major influences on the European Renaissance included
    A) cultural discoveries in North America.
    B) African music and culture.
    C) Greek Orthodox Christianity and learning brought by Byzantine missionaries.
    D) scientific knowledge from the Islamic empires and Greco-Roman philosophy and art.

Reformation and Revolution

While Spain and Portugal consolidated their hold over territories in the Americas, conflict ensued in Europe. The power of the Catholic Church was threatened; new scientific discoveries and secular Renaissance thought were at odds with many teachings of the Church. The Catholic monk **Martin Luther** wrote a letter of protest to the Pope in 1517 known as the **ninety-five theses**, outlining ways he believed the Church should reform. His ideas gained support, especially among rulers who wanted more power from the Church. Triggering the **reformation**, or movement for reform of the Church, Luther's ideas led to offshoots of new versions of Christianity in Western Europe. Protestant thinkers like Luther and **John Calvin** addressed particular grievances, condemning the **infallibility** of the Pope (its teaching that the Pope was without fault) and the selling of **indulgences**, or guarantees of entry into heaven.

Conflict between Protestants and Catholics was fierce on the Continent as well. The **thirty years' war** (1618 – 1648) began in Central Europe between Protestant nobles in the Holy Roman Empire who disagreed with the strict Catholic **Ferdinand II**, who ruled parts of Central Europe. Elected Holy Roman Emperor in 1619, Ferdinand II was a leader of the **counter-reformation**, attempts at reinforcing Catholic dominance throughout Europe during and after the Reformation in the wake of the Renaissance and related social change. Ferdinand was also closely allied with the Catholic **Habsburg** Dynasty, which ruled Austria and Spain.

At the same time, France came into conflict with its Catholic neighbors—Habsburg-ruled Spain and Austria—despite their shared faith. Threatened by a strengthened Spain and Holy Roman Empire, France declared war. European politics began emphasizing state sovereignty over religious solidarity.

> **Did You Know?**
>
> International relations today are based on the principles of the Treaty of Westphalia.

The tangled alliances between European powers resulted in widespread conflict. In the 1648 **Treaty of Westphalia**, European powers agreed to recognize **state sovereignty** and practice **non-interference** in each other's matters—at the expense of family and religious allegiance. 1648 marked a transition into modern international relations when politics and religion would no longer be inexorably intertwined.

The end of the Thirty Years' War represented the end of the notion of the domination of the Catholic Church over Europe and the concept of religious regional dominance, rather than ethnic state divisions. Over the next several centuries, the Church and religious empires would eventually lose control over ethnic groups and their lands, later giving way to smaller **nation-states**.

Peace did not last, and in 1756, the **Seven Years' War** began between Prussia and Austria, drawing in other allied countries. In Europe, this war further cemented concepts of state sovereignty and delineated rivalries between European powers engaged in colonial adventure and overseas imperialism—especially Britain and France. It would kick-start British dominance in Asia. In North America, it was known as the French and Indian War; France lost its territory there to Britain.

This time of change in Europe would affect Asia. European concepts of social and political organization became constructed around national sovereignty and nation- states. European economies had become dependent upon colonies and were starting to industrialize, enriching Europe at the expense of the Americas, Africa, and increasingly Asia.

Industrialization and political organization allowed improved militaries, which put Asian governments at a disadvantage. The major Asian powers—India, China, the Ottoman Empire, and Persia—would eventually succumb to European influence or come under direct European control.

Monarchies in Europe had been weakened by the conflicts between Catholicism and Protestant faiths; despite European presence and increasing power overseas, as well as its dominance in the Americas, instability on the continent and in the British Isles made the old order vulnerable. Enlightenment ideals like democracy and republicanism, coupled with political instability, would trigger revolution against **absolute monarchy**. Revolutionary actors drew on the philosophies of Enlightenment thinkers like **John Locke, Jean-Jacques Rousseau,** and **Montesquieu**, whose beliefs, such as **republicanism**, the **social contract**, the **separation of powers**, and the **rights of man** would drive a series of revolutions.

In the seventeenth century, conflict following the **English Civil War** between the **royalists**, who supported the monarchy, and the **parliamentarians**, who wanted a republic, eventually resulted in a constitutional monarchy.

The **American Revolution**, heavily influenced by Locke, broke out a century later. Chapter One, *US History*, contains details.

The **French Revolution** was the precursor to the end of the feudal order in most of Europe. **King Louis XIV**, the *Sun King* (1643 – 1715), had consolidated the monarchy in France, taking true political and military power from the nobility. Meanwhile, French Enlightenment thinkers like **Jean-Jacques Rousseau, Montesquieu,** and **Voltaire** criticized absolute monarchy and the repression of freedom of speech and thought. In 1789, the French Revolution broke out.

The power of the Catholic Church had weakened and the Scientific Revolution and the Enlightenment had fostered social and intellectual change. Colonialism and mercantilism were fueling the growth of an early middle class: people who were not traditionally nobility or landowners under the feudal system were becoming wealthier and more powerful thanks to early capitalism. This class, the **bourgeoisie**, chafed under the rule of the nobility, which had generally inherited land and wealth (while the bourgeoisie earned their wealth in business).

In France, the problem was most acute as France had the largest population in Europe at the time. At the same time, France had one of the most centralized monarchies in Europe and entrenched nobilities. With a growing bourgeoisie and peasant class paying increasingly higher taxes to the nobility, resentment was brewing.

Louis XIV had strengthened the monarchy by weakening the nobility's control over the land and centralizing power under the king. However, his successors had failed to govern effectively or win the loyalty of the people; both the nobility and the monarch were widely resented. Furthermore, the bourgeoisie resented their lack of standing in government and society. Moreover, advances in medicine had permitted unprecedented population growth, further empowering the peasantry and bourgeoisie.

The French government was struggling financially, having supported the American Revolution, and needed to increase taxes. The burden of taxation traditionally fell on the Third Estate, the middle class and the poor peasants, not the wealthier nobility, who were unwilling to contribute. In fact, peasants had to **tithe**, paying ten percent of their earnings to the nobles.

After a poor harvest in 1788, unrest spread throughout the country. On July 14 the people stormed the **Bastille** prison. The peasantry then revolted in the countryside. The National Constituent Assembly was formed and took control. While unrest continued in France, the French Revolution is noteworthy for having inspired revolutionary movements throughout Europe and beyond.

In 1804 **Napoleon Bonaparte** emerged as emperor of France and proceeded to conquer much of Europe. French occupation of Spain weakened that country enough that revolutionary movements in its colonies strengthened. Latin American countries led by **Simón Bolivar** joined Haiti and the United States in revolution against colonial European powers. By 1815, other European powers had managed to halt France; at the **Congress of Vienna** in 1815, European powers agreed on a **balance of power** in Europe.

Did You Know?

The Congress of Vienna was the first real international peace conference and set the precedent for European political organization.

Practice Question

6. Which of the following best describes the motivation for Protestant reformers?
    A) Protestants, including Martin Luther, originally sought to develop a new form of Christianity separate from the Catholic Church.
    B) Protestants like Martin Luther were unhappy with the teachings of the Church, including papal indulgences and corruption in the Church, and originally sought reform.
    C) Protestants were initially influenced by European political leaders, who used them to limit the power of the Church.
    D) Protestants such as Martin Luther wanted to topple the Catholic Church, believing it to have become too corrupt.

Nationalism, Industry, and Imperialism

The nineteenth century was a period of change and conflict, and the roots of the major twentieth century conflicts—world war and decolonization—are found in it. Modern European social and political structures and norms, including **nationalism** and the **nation-state**, would begin to emerge. Economic theories based in the Industrial Revolution like **socialism** and eventually **communism** gained traction with the stark class divisions brought on by **urbanization** and industry.

> **Did You Know?**
>
> World War I was rooted in complex alliances among countries going back to the mid-nineteenth century.

Following the Napoleonic Wars, Prussia had come to dominate the German-speaking states that had composed the Holy Roman Empire. **Otto Von Bismarck** unified the linguistically and culturally German states of Central Europe. Prussian power had been growing, fueled by **nationalism** and the **nation-state,** or the idea that individuals with shared experience (including ethnicity, language, religion, and cultural practices) should be unified under one government. In 1871, the **German Empire** became a unified state. Bismarck encouraged economic cooperation, instituted army reforms, and cultivated an image of Prussia as a defender of German culture and nationhood.

In the Balkans, Southwest Asia and North Africa, the Ottoman Empire was in decline. The Ottoman Empire had long been a major force in Europe, controlling the bulk of the Balkans. However, the empire had lost land in Europe to the Austrians and in Africa to British and French imperialists. In the Balkans, rebellion among small nations supported by larger European powers would put an end to Ottoman power in Europe for good.

Eventually tension between Russia and Austria-Hungary—which was supported by Germany—led to the breakdown of Russian relationships with those countries. At the same time, Russian relations with Great Britain and France improved. In 1894, Russia and France became allies. This alliance would culminate in the 1907 **Triple Entente**, setting the stage for the system of alliances at the heart of the First World War.

Continued European involvement in the Balkans accelerated the ongoing loss of Ottoman influence there due to phenomena like nationalism, **pan-Slavism** (by which Balkan nations like Serbia and Bulgaria were empowered to rebel against the Ottoman Empire by identifying with Russia), military and political power, and religious influence. The Balkan nations continued rebellion against Ottoman rule, and European powers proceeded into the area.

Eventually, instability in the region would lead to the First World War which was triggered by the assassination of the Austro-Hungarian **Archduke Franz Ferdinand** by the Serbian nationalist **Gavrilo Princip** in Bosnia-Herzegovina in 1914.

Meanwhile, European powers were expanding their reach overseas. As colonialism in the fifteenth and sixteenth centuries had been driven by mercantilism, conquest, and Christian conversion, so was seventeenth, eighteenth and nineteenth century imperial-ism driven by capitalism, European competition, and conceptions of racial superiority.

In 1837, **Queen Victoria** ascended to the English throne. During her reign (1837 – 1901) the British Empire would expand enormously, controlling much of Sub-Saharan Africa, South Asia, and the Pacific. The concept of the *white man's burden*, wherein white Europeans were "obligated" to bring their "superior" culture to other civilizations around the globe, also drove imperialism, popularizing it at home in Britain and elsewhere in Europe.

The European powers were immersed in what became known as the *scramble for Africa*; the industrial economies of Europe would profit from the natural resources abundant in that continent, and the "white man's burden" continued to fuel colonization. At the **1884 Berlin conference**, control over Africa was divided among European powers without regard for or consultation with existing civilizations on the continent.

To gain access to closed **Chinese** markets, Britain forced China to buy Indian opium; the **Opium Wars** ended with the **Treaty of Nanking (1842)**. As a consequence, China lost great power to Britain and later, other European countries, which gained **spheres of influence**, or areas of China they effectively controlled, and **extraterritoriality**, or privileges in which their citizens were not subject to Chinese law.

However, not all non-European countries fell to European imperialism. **Ethiopia** was never colonized, having repelled Italian forces. In Asia, the Emperor Meiji promoted modernization of technology, especially the military, during the **Meiji restoration** of 1868. Japan proved itself a world power when it defeated Russia in the **Russo-Japanese war** in 1905, and would play a central role in twentieth century conflict.

Figure 15.6. Imperial Africa

Raw goods from colonies fueled European economic growth and development, leading to the **Industrial Revolution** in the nineteenth century. Industrialization began in Manchester, where factories produced textiles using cotton from the colonies. Poor people moved from rural areas to cities for higher-paying jobs in factories, beginning **urbanization**.

Early industrial technology sped up the harvesting and transport of crops and their conversion to textiles. This accelerated manufacturing was based on **capitalism**, the *laissez-faire* (or **free market**) theory developed by **Adam Smith**, who believed that an *invisible hand* should guide the marketplace—that government should stay out of the economy regardless of abuses, as the economy would eventually automatically correct for inequalities, price problems, and any other problematic issues.

To access the raw materials needed to produce manufactured goods, Britain and other industrializing countries in Western Europe needed resources—hence the drive for imperialism. Cotton was harvested in India and Egypt for textile mills; minerals were mined in South Africa and the Congo for industry. Furthermore, as industrialization and urbanization led to the development of early middle classes in Europe and North America, imports of luxury goods from Asia increased to meet consumer demand. Colonial powers also profited by selling manufactured goods back to the colonies.

Largely unbridled capitalism had led to the dangerous conditions of the early Indus- trial Revolution; workers suffered from poor treatment and unsafe working environments. The German philosophers **Karl Marx** and **Friedrich Engels** were appalled by these injustices. They developed **socialism**, the philosophy that workers, or the **proletariat**, should own the means of production and reap the benefits, rather than the **bourgeoisie**, who were only concerned with profit. Later, Marx and Engels wrote the *communist manifesto*, a pamphlet laying out their ideas and calling for revolution.

Communism inspired the Russian intellectuals **Vladimir Lenin** and **Leon Trotsky**, paving the way for the political and economic organization of the Soviet Union. In Russia, Tsar Nicholas faced dissent at home due to a humiliating defeat by Japan in the 1905 Russo-Japanese War; discontent was fueled by longer-term economic hardship compared to industrial Europe and limited freedoms. Workers began striking, and peasants rebelled against oppressive taxation. Following a period of revolution and instability, Lenin's party, the **Bolsheviks**, would gain power and eventually take over the country. Installing a communist government, they established the Soviet Union in 1921.

Practice Question

7. The Meiji Restoration was
    A) an attempt to restore traditional Japan as it had been before Western incursions into the country.
    B) a period of modernization and westernization in Japan.
    C) the early stage of Japanese imperialism in Asia, when it invaded Korea.
    D) a cultural movement in Japan to reinvigorate Shintoism and traditional poetry.

Twentieth Century

Global Conflicts

The assassination of the Austro-Hungarian Archduke **Franz Ferdinand** in Sarajevo on June 28, 1914, kicked off the **system of alliances** that had been in place among European powers, setting off the First World War.

Austria-Hungary declared war on Serbia, and Russia came to Serbia's aid. An ally of Austria-Hungary as part of the **Triple Alliance**, Germany declared war on Russia.

Russia's ally France prepared for war; as Germany traversed Belgium to invade France, Belgium pleaded for aid from other European countries and so the United Kingdom declared war on Germany. After several provocations, in 1917 the United States would join the war on the side of the **Triple Entente** (France, Russia, and the United Kingdom), helping defeat Germany.

Figure 15.7. WWI Alliances

Germany had been emphasizing military growth since the consolidation of the empire under Bismarck. Now, under **Kaiser Wilhelm II**, who sought expanded territories in Europe and overseas for Germany, it was a militarized state and an important European power.

According to the **Schlieffen Plan**, Germany had planned to fight a war on two fronts against both Russia and France. However, Russia's unexpectedly rapid mobilization stretched the German army too thin on the Eastern Front, while it became bogged down in **trench warfare** on the Western Front against the British, French, and later the Americans. Germany lost the war and was punished with the harsh **Treaty of Versailles**. The treaty brought economic hardship on the country by forcing it to pay **reparations** for the war. German military failure and consequent economic collapse set the stage for the rise of fascism and Adolf Hitler.

> **Did You Know?**
>
> The treaty also created the League of Nations, an international organization designed to prevent conflict; however, it was largely powerless, especially because the United States did not join.

The end of WWI also marked the end of the Ottoman Empire, which was officially dissolved in 1923. From the end of the nineteenth century, the British had been increasing their influence throughout Ottoman territory in Egypt and the Persian Gulf, seeking control over the Suez Canal and petroleum resources in the Gulf. The Ottomans had already lost their North African provinces to France in the mid-nineteenth century.

In 1916, France and Britain concluded the **Sykes-Picot agreement**, which secretly planned for the Middle East following the defeat of the Ottoman Empire. The agreement divided up the region into spheres of influence to be controlled by each power; Palestine would be governed internationally. In 1917, the secret **Balfour Declaration** promised the Jewish people an independent state in Palestine, but Western powers did not honor this agreement. The state of Israel was not established until 1948.

At the end of the war the area was indeed divided into **mandates** controlled by Britain and France. Most of those borders remain today dividing the modern Middle East. After the First World War, the nationalist Turkish leader **Mustafa Ataturk** kept European powers out of Anatolia and abolished the Caliphate in 1924, establishing modern Turkey.

> **Did You Know?**
>
> The first international war to use industrialized weaponry, WWI was called "the Great War" because battle on such a scale had never before been seen.

After the dissolution of the Ottoman Empire, the future of the Middle East was uncertain. Despite its weaknesses, the Ottoman Empire had been the symbolic center of Islam, controlling Mecca and Medina. The Ottoman sultan held the title of Caliph, or the one entrusted with the leadership of those two cities holy in Islam. With the region broken up into European-controlled protectorates and an independent, nationalist, secular Turkey turned toward Europe, the social and political fabric of the region was becoming undone.

The roots of two competing ideologies, **pan-Arabism** and **Islamism**, developed in this context. According to **pan-Arabism**, Arabs and Arabic speakers should be aligned regardless of international borders. Similar to Pan-Slavism, Pan-Arabism eventually became an international movement espousing Arab unity in response to European and US influence and presence later in the twentieth century. **Islamism** or political Islam began as a social and political movement, where Islam, rather than Arabic and Arab culture, was a unifying factor. It influenced political thinkers and groups, including violent extremists, into the twenty-first century.

In the Soviet Union, following Lenin's death in 1924, the Secretary of the Communist Party, **Josef Stalin**, took power. The USSR became socially and politically repressive; the Communist Party and the military underwent **purges** where any persons who were a potential threat to Stalin's power were imprisoned or executed.

The general population suffered under the **great terror** throughout the 1920s. Any hint of dissent was to be reported to the secret police and usually resulted in imprisonment in *gulags*, forced labor camps. Stalin also enforced **russification** policies, persecuting ethnic and religious minorities.

> **Did You Know?**
>
> In the 1920s, around twenty million Russians were sent to the gulags, usually hundreds or thousands of miles from their homes. Millions died.

In 1931, Stalin enforced the **collectivization** of land and agriculture in an attempt to consolidate control over the countryside and improve food security. The government confiscated land and imprisoned land-owners; by 1939, most farming and land was controlled by the government, and most peasants lived on collective land. Collectivizing the farms encouraged more peasants to become industrial workers. However, systemic disorganization in the 1920s and early 1930s resulted in famine and food shortages.

As part of modernizing Russia, Stalin focused on accelerating industrial development. Targeting heavy industry, these **Five-Year Plans** increased production of industrial materials and developed major infrastructure. The USSR quickly became an industrial power, but at the expense of millions who lost their lives in purges, forced labor camps, and famine.

Similar rapid modernization occurred in East Asia. Japan had undergone rapid modernization as part of the Meiji Restoration in the nineteenth century. After the Russo- Japanese War, Japan turned towards imperialism throughout Asia, gaining control of parts of China, Korea, and the Pacific Islands in the early twentieth century, which Japan considered its *sphere of influence*.

While Japan was building its global reputation and military and economic strength in Asia, China was undergoing political change. Dynastic Chinese rule ended in 1911 with a revolution. After a short-lived republic, China came under the control of two rival factions: the **Kuomintang (KMT)**, or Nationalist Party led by **Jiang Jieshi (Chiang Kai-Shek)**, and the **Chinese Communist Party (CCP)** led by **Mao Zedong**. In the 1920s and 1930s, parts of coastal and northern China were controlled by Japan; the KMT controlled much of the south, although peasants there supported the communists, and the CCP had been driven north by the KMT in the arduous **Long March**.

Figure 15.8. The Long March

Meanwhile, Germany suffered under the provisions of the Treaty of Versailles. In 1919, a democratic government was established—the **Weimar Republic**. But debt from **reparations** owed for WWI set off **hyperinflation**, impoverishing the country and its people. Economic crisis was amplified by the stock market crash in 1929 and the Great Depression. In this climate, the National Socialist Party, or **Nazi Party**, led by **Adolf Hitler**, became powerful as an alternative to the ineffective Weimar government.

Hitler's charisma and popular platform—to cancel the Treaty of Versailles—allowed him to become chancellor and then *Führer*, or *leader*, by 1934. Nazi ideals and effective propaganda appealed strongly to both industrial interests and workers in the face of global economic depression. Hitler and the Nazis consolidated total control by banning political parties and trade unions and establishing the violent **Gestapo**, or secret police. They also set into motion their agenda of racism and genocide against Jewish people, Roma, Slavic people, homosexuals, disabled people, people of color, communists, and others. So-called "undesirables," particularly the Jews in Germany and eventually other European countries, were discriminated against, forced into ghettoes, and later imprisoned and murdered in **concentration camps**. At least six million European Jews were murdered by the Nazis in the **Holocaust**.

Hitler sought to restore Germany's power and expand its reach by annexing **Austria** and part of what is today the Czech Republic. He invaded the rest of **Czechoslovakia** and formed an alliance with **Italy**. In 1939, Germany invaded **Poland** in what is commonly considered the beginning of the **Second World War (WWII)**. Europe descended into conflict again. Despite staying out of combat, in 1941 the **United States** enforced the **Lend-Lease Act** which provided support and military aid to Britain. The two also released the **Atlantic Charter**, outlining common goals.

Japan joined the **Axis Powers** of Germany and Italy, bringing conflict in Asia into the Second World War. Japan had invaded and occupied parts of China and other parts of East and Southeast Asia controlled by Europe, threatening European imperial and economic interests. In December of 1941, Japan attacked the United States at Pearl Harbor. Consequently, the US joined the war in Europe and in the Pacific, deploying thousands of troops in both theaters. In 1944, the Allies invaded France on **D-Day**; as the US led forces from the west and the USSR pushed from the east, Germany surrendered in the spring of 1945.

Did You Know?

The Atlantic Charter described values shared by the US and Britain, including restoring self-governance in occupied Europe and liberalizing international trade.

The war in the Pacific would continue until the summer of 1945, when the US used atomic bombs against the Japanese cities of **Hiroshima** and **Nagasaki**. The tremendous civilian casualties forced the Emperor to surrender; the Second World War came to an end.

The **Chinese Civil War** between Mao Zedong's CCP and Jiang Jieshi's KMT had halted as Chinese forces united against Japanese invasion. By the end of the war, the CCP was stronger than ever, with widespread support from many sectors of Chinese society. By 1949 the communists had emerged victorious and China became a communist country.

Allied forces took the lead in rebuilding efforts: the US occupied areas in East Asia and Germany, while the Soviet Union remained in Eastern Europe. The Allies had planned to rebuild Europe according to the **Marshall Plan**; however, Stalin broke his promise made at the 1945 **Yalta Conference** held by the Allies to allow Eastern European countries to hold free elections after the war. Instead, the USSR occupied these countries and they came under communist control. The **Cold War** had begun.

Stalin ensured that communists came to power in Eastern Europe, setting up satellite states at the Soviet perimeter. The Soviet rationale was to establish a buffer zone following its extraordinarily heavy casualties in WWII. Germany was divided into east and west, and eventually a wall built dividing the city of Berlin. An *Iron Curtain* had come down across Europe, dividing east from west.

Consequently, western states organized the North Atlantic Treaty Organization or **NATO**, a **collective security** agreement in the face of the Soviet expansionist threat.

Figure 15.9. Cold War Europe

The United States adopted a policy of **containment**, the idea that communism should be *contained*, as part of the **Truman Doctrine** of foreign policy.

In response, the Soviet Union created the **Warsaw Pact**, a similar organization consisting of Eastern European communist countries. **atomic weapons**, especially the development of the extremely powerful **hydrogen bomb**, raised the stakes of the conflict. During the **Cuban Missile Crisis** in 1962, the world came closer than ever to nuclear war when the US found out the Soviet Union was building missile bases in communist Cuba. Diplomacy averted disaster.

> **Quick Review**
>
> What factors caused the Cold War to erupt between the Allies and the Soviet Union?

According to the Truman Doctrine, communism needed to be contained. Furthermore, according to **Domino Theory**, if one country became communist, then more would, too, like a row of dominoes falling. Therefore, the United States, by way of the United Nations, became involved in the **Korean War** (1950 – 1953) which divided the country into North and South Korea.

United States pursued conflict in **Vietnam** for almost a decade beginning in the early 1960s. Supporting anti-communist fighters, the US battled North Vietnamese forces, including the guerrilla fighters called **Viet Cong**, in a war for Vietnamese sovereignty throughout the 1960s. Despite being outnumbered, the Viet Cong's familiarity with the difficult terrain, support from Russia and China, and determination eventually resulted in victory. Extreme objection to the war within the United States, high casualties, and demoralization resulted in US withdrawal in 1973.

Toward the end of the 1960s and into the 1970s, the Cold War reached a period of **détente**, or a warming of relations. The US and USSR signed the **nuclear non-proliferation treaty**, in which they and other nuclear powers agreed not to further spread nuclear weapons technology. Later, the USSR and the US signed the **SALT I** (Strategic Arms Limitation Treaty), limiting strategic weaponry. Some cultural exchanges and partnerships in outer space took place also.

At the same time, the United States began making diplomatic overtures toward communist China. Despite its status as a communist country, China and the USSR had difficult relations due to their differing views on the nature of communism. Nikita Khrushchev, Soviet leader from Stalin's death until the 1970s, took a moderate approach to world communism, while Mao supported active revolution. Following the **Sino-Soviet split** of the 1960s, China had lost much Soviet support for its modernization programs. Despite advances in agriculture and some industrialization, Mao's programs like the **Great Leap Forward** and the **Cultural Revolution** had taken a toll on the people. In 1972, President Nixon visited China, establishing relations between the communist government and the United States.

The climate would change again, however, in the 1970s and 1980s. The US and USSR found themselves supporting opposing sides in regional conflicts throughout the world. **President Ronald Reagan** pursued a militaristic policy, prioritizing weapons development with the goal of outspending the USSR on weapons technology. The **arms race** was underway.

Meanwhile, the former colonies of the fallen European colonial powers had won or were in the process of gaining their independence through **decolonization**. These newly formed countries constituted the *third world*, an alternative to the countries directly dominated by the democratic-capitalist and communist spheres of the US and USSR. However, the global superpowers fought for dominance worldwide by arming different sides in smaller regional conflicts (fighting *proxy wars*) and influencing regional and global politics.

Already, the leader **Mohandas Gandhi** had led a peaceful independence movement in **India** against the British, winning Indian independence in 1949. His assassination by Hindu radicals led to conflict between **Hindus** and **Muslims** in the **subcontinent**, resulting in **partition,** the violent division of India into India, Pakistan and later, Bangladesh.

African countries became independent through both revolution and thanks to strong leadership by African nationalist leaders and thinkers. The **apartheid** regime in South Africa, where segregation between races was enforced and people of color lived in oppressive conditions, was not lifted until the 1990s; **Nelson Mandela** led the country in a peaceful transition process.

In the Middle East, post-Ottoman *protectorates* became independent states with arbitrary borders drawn and rulers installed by the Europeans. The creation of the state of **Israel** was especially contentious: in the 1917 **Balfour declaration**, the British had promised the **Zionist** movement that the Jews would be given a homeland in the British-controlled protectorate of Palestine. However, the US assured the Arabs in 1945 that a Jewish state would not be founded there. Israel emerged from diplomatic confusion, chaos, and tragedy after the murder of millions of Jewish people in Europe, and violence on the ground in Palestine carried out by both Jews and Arabs. This legacy of conflict persists in the Middle East.

In Egypt, **Gamal Abdul Nasser** led the Pan-Arabist movement in the region, which included creating an Arab alliance against Israel. Arab allies fought Israel in the 1967 Six-Day War and again in the 1973 Yom Kippur War, but Israel held on to and even gained territory. In 1978, the US brokered a peace agreement between Egypt and Israel—the **Camp David Accords**. By the 1970s, Pan-Arabism was no longer the popular, unifying movement it had once been.

Proxy wars between the US and the USSR were fought around the world. In 1979, the USSR invaded **Afghanistan**, an event which would contribute to the Soviet collapse; in response, the US began supporting anti-Soviet *Mujahideen* forces there. Other examples include the Nicaraguan Revolution, the **Angolan civil war**, the **Mozambican civil war**, and conflict in the Horn of Africa.

> **Quick Review**
>
> What is a proxy war? Why were proxy wars important in the context of the Cold War?

While never officially colonized, **Iran** had been under the oppressive regime of the western-supported **shah** for decades. By the 1970s, the Shah's corrupt, oppressive regime was extremely unpopular in Iran, but it was propped up by the West. Following the 1979 **Iranian Revolution**, Islamist revolutionaries took over the country. The new theocracy was led by the **Ayatollah Khomeini**, who instituted political and social reforms, including stricter interpretations of Islamic laws and traditions. Later that year, radical students stormed the US embassy and held a number of staff hostage for over a year; the **Iran Hostage Crisis** would humiliate the United States.

Following the Iranian Revolution, the Iraqi leader **Saddam Hussein** declared war against Iran. Saddam feared Iran would trigger a similar revolution there. Iraq also sought control over strategic territories. The Iran-Iraq war raged from 1980 – 1990.

Practice Question

8. The Warsaw Pact was a supranational organization created in response to
    A) NATO.
    B) the United Nations.
    C) the European Union.
    D) the League of Nations.

Post-Cold War World

In 1991, the Soviet Union fell when Soviet Premier **Mikhail Gorbachev**, who had implemented reforms like *glasnost* and *perestroika* (or *openness* and *transparency*), was nearly overthrown in a coup. A movement led by **Boris Yeltsin**, who had been elected president of Russia, stopped the coup. The USSR was dissolved later that year and Yeltsin became president of the Russian Federation. The war in Afghanistan and military overspending in an effort to keep up with American military spending had weakened the USSR to the point of collapse, and the Cold War ended.

In 1990, Saddam Hussein, the leader of Iraq, invaded Kuwait and took over its oil reserves and production facilities. In response, an international coalition led by the United States expelled Iraq from Kuwait and protected Saudi Arabia, regaining control of the world's petroleum reserves in the **Gulf War**. This event cemented the US status as the sole world superpower.

Despite stability throughout most of Europe, the changes following the fall of the Iron Curtain led to instability in the Balkans. The **Bosnian War** raged from 1992 to 1995, resulting in the deaths of thousands of civilians and another European genocide— this time, of Bosnian Muslims. Also following the Cold War, instability in the devel- oping world continued as a result of colonialism and proxy wars. In 1994, conflict in Central Africa resulted in the **Rwandan Genocide**. In the 1980s, drought in the Horn of Africa led to widespread famine; humanitarian affairs and issues came into the public eye and the general public became more concerned about providing foreign aid.

The balance of economic and political power began to change. The **g-20**, the world's twenty most important economic and political powers, includes many former colonies and non-European countries. The **BRICS**—Brazil, Russia, India, China, and South Africa—are recognized as world economic and political leaders.

Steps toward European unification had begun as early as the 1950s; the **European Union**, as it is known today, was formed after the **Maastricht Treaty** was signed in 1992. As the former Soviet satellite states moved from communism to more democratic societies and capitalistic economies, more countries partnered with the EU and eventually joined it; as of 2015, twenty-eight countries are members, with more on the path to membership.

Continental integration exists beyond Europe. In Africa, the **African Union**, originally the Organization of African Unity, has become a stronger political force in its own right, organizing peacekeeping missions throughout the continent. An organization similar to the EU, the AU is a forum for African countries to organize and align political, military, economic, and other policies.

In this era of **globalization**, international markets became increasingly open through free-trade agreements like **NAFTA** (the North American Free Trade Agreement) and **MEROSUR** (the South American free-trade zone). The **World Trade Organization** oversees international trade. Technological advances like improvements in transportation infrastructure and the **internet** made international communication faster, easier, and cheaper.

However, more reliable international transportation and faster, easier worldwide communication brought risks, too. In the early twenty-first century, the United States was attacked by terrorists on **September 11, 2001**, resulting in thousands of civilian casualties. Consequently, the US launched a major land war in Afghanistan and another later in Iraq.

Following the attacks on 9/11, the United States attacked Afghanistan as part of the **war on terror**. Afghanistan's radical Islamist **Taliban** government was providing shelter to the group that took responsibility for the attacks, **al Qaeda**. Led by **Osama Bin Laden**, al Qaeda was inspired by radical Islamism. Bin Laden had fought the Soviets with the US-supported Afghan *mujahideen* during the 1980s; despite that alliance, bin Laden and his followers were angered by US involvement in the Middle East throughout the 1990s and its support of Israel. While bin Laden was killed by the United States in 2011, and while control of Afghan security was turned over from the US to the US-backed government in 2014, the US still maintains a strong military presence in the country.

> **Did You Know?**
>
> While benefits of international trade include lower prices and more consumer choice, unemployment often increases in more developed countries and labor and environmental violations are more likely in developing countries. How do you feel about international trade?

The **Iraq War** began in 2003 when the US invaded that country under the faulty premises that Saddam Hussein's regime was involved with al Qaeda, supported inter- national terrorism, and illegally possessed weapons of mass destruction. Iraq descended into chaos, with thousands of civilian and military casualties, Iraqi and American alike. While the country technically and legally remains intact under a US-supported government, the ethnically and religiously diverse country is de facto divided as a result of the disintegration of central power.

Elsewhere in the Middle East, reform movements began via the 2011 **Arab Spring** in Tunisia, Egypt, Bahrain, and Syria. Some dictatorial regimes have been replaced with democratic governments; other countries still enjoy limited freedoms or even civil unrest. In Syria, unrest erupted into civil war. One consequence has been enormous movements of **refugees** into Europe. Uprisings in Israeli-occupied West Bank and Gaza have continued sporadically. Long-term peace efforts have failed and conflict continues.

Practice Question

9. In the twenty-first century, which phenomenon has so far characterized global governance?
    A) international terrorism
    B) globalized political and economic organization
    C) worldwide war and conflict
    D) the European Union and the African Union

Answer Key

1. C: The goal of sustainable development is to ensure resources are available to the next generation. Therefore, renewable resources must be managed to make sure consumption does not outpace the rate of replacement.

2. A: More than half of the world's population lives in cities.

3. C: When a country does not have enough people to utilize its resources, it is underpopulated.

4. B: Strong infrastructure facilitated trade, communication, and military movement throughout the empire, ensuring unity and security.

5. D: Science and technology imported from the Middle East during the Crusades, coupled with a resurgence of Classical philosophy, art, and scholarship imported by Byzantine refugees, inspired the Renaissance.

6. B: Martin Luther and his followers opposed corruption in the Church and wanted changes.

7. B: The Meiji Restoration was a period of industrialization and westernization in Japan.

8. A: Following the creation of NATO, a military alliance formed to counter the Soviet Union, the USSR and the countries of the Eastern Bloc came to an agreement on collective defense—the Warsaw Pact.

9. B: While the United States remains a leading world power, the emergence of international organizations like the BRICS, the EU, the G-20, and the AU has empowered other countries; furthermore, international trade agreements are helping mold the balance of power. However, the AU, EU, and other organizations do not dominate the world in their own right, so they do not characterize global governance. Nor has the world descended into total chaos, so conflict and terrorism do not characterize global governance, either.

Practice Test #1

Language Arts: Reading Comprehension

Directions: Read the question, passage, or figure carefully, and choose the best answer.

Questions 1–5 refer to the following passage.

Taking a person's temperature is one of the most basic and common health care tasks. Everyone from nurses to emergency medical technicians to concerned parents should be able to grab a thermometer to take a patient or loved one's temperature. But what's the best way to get an accurate reading? The answer depends on the situation.

The most common way people measure body temperature is orally. A simple digital or disposable thermometer is placed under the tongue for a few minutes, and the task is done. There are many situations, however, when measuring temperature orally isn't an option. For example, when a person can't breathe through his nose, he won't be able to keep his mouth closed long enough to get an accurate reading. In these situations, it's often preferable to place the thermometer in the rectum or armpit. Using the rectum also has the added benefit of providing a much more accurate reading than other locations can provide.

It's also often the case that certain people, like **agitated** patients or fussy babies, won't be able to sit still long enough for an accurate reading. In these situations, it's best to use a thermometer that works much more quickly, such as one that measures temperature in the ear or at the temporal artery. No matter which method is chosen, however, it's important to check the average temperature for each region, as it can vary by several degrees.

1. Which statement is NOT a detail from the passage?
   A) Taking a temperature in the ear or at the temporal artery is more accurate than taking it orally.
   B) If an individual cannot breathe through the nose, taking his or her temperature orally will likely give an inaccurate reading.
   C) The standard human body temperature varies depending on whether it's measured in the mouth, rectum, armpit, ear, or temporal artery.
   D) The most common way to measure temperature is by placing a thermometer in the mouth.

2. What is the author's primary purpose in writing this essay?
   A) to advocate for the use of thermometers that measure temperature in the ear or at the temporal artery
   B) to explain the methods available to measure a person's temperature and the situation where each method is appropriate
   C) to warn readers that the average temperature of the human body varies by region
   D) to discuss how nurses use different types of thermometers depending on the type of patient they are examining

3. What is the best summary of this passage?
   A) It's important that everyone know the best way to take a person's temperature in any given situation.
   B) The most common method of taking a person's temperature—orally— isn't appropriate in some situations.
   C) The most accurate way to take a temperature is placing a digital thermometer in the rectum.
   D) There are many different ways to take a person's temperature, and which is appropriate will depend on the situation.

4. According to the passage, why is it sometimes preferable to take a person's temperature rectally?
   A) Rectal readings are more accurate than oral readings.
   B) Many people cannot sit still long enough to have their temperatures taken orally.
   C) Temperature readings can vary widely between regions of the body.
   D) Many people do not have access to quick-acting thermometers.

5. What is the meaning of the word *agitated* in the last paragraph?
   A) obviously upset
   B) quickly moving
   C) violently ill
   D) slightly dirty

Questions 6–10 refer to the following passage.

In recent decades, jazz has been associated with New Orleans and festivals like Mardi Gras, but in the 1920s, jazz was a booming trend whose influence reached into many aspects of American culture. In fact, the years between World War I and the Great Depression were known as the Jazz Age, a term coined by F. Scott Fitzgerald in his famous novel *The Great Gatsby*. Sometimes also called the Roaring Twenties, this time period saw major urban centers experiencing new economic, cultural, and artistic vitality. In the United States, musicians flocked to cities like New York and Chicago, which would become famous hubs for jazz musicians. Ella Fitzgerald, for example, moved from Virginia to New York City to begin her much-lauded singing career, and jazz pioneer Louis Armstrong got his big break in Chicago.

Jazz music was played by and for a more expressive and freed populace than the United States had previously seen. Women gained the right to vote and were openly seen drinking and dancing to jazz music. This period marked the emergence of the flapper, a woman determined to make a statement about her new role in society. Jazz music also provided the soundtrack for the explosion of African American art and culture now known as the Harlem Renaissance. In addition to Fitzgerald and Armstrong, numerous musicians, including Duke Ellington, Fats Waller, and Bessie Smith, promoted their distinctive and complex music as an integral part of the emerging African American culture.

6. What is the main idea of the passage?
   A) People should associate jazz music with the 1920s, not modern New Orleans.
   B) Jazz music played an important role in many cultural movements of the 1920s.
   C) Many famous jazz musicians began their careers in New York City and Chicago.
   D) African Americans were instrumental in launching jazz into mainstream culture.

7. What is a reasonable inference that can be drawn from this passage?
   A) Jazz music was important to minority groups struggling for social equality in the 1920s.
   B) Duke Ellington, Fats Waller, and Bessie Smith were the most important jazz musicians of the Harlem Renaissance.
   C) Women gained the right to vote with the help of jazz musicians.
   D) Duke Ellington, Fats Waller, and Bessie Smith all supported women's right to vote.

8. What is the author's primary purpose in writing this essay?
   A) to explain the role jazz musicians played in the Harlem Renaissance
   B) to inform the reader about the many important musicians playing jazz in the 1920s
   C) to discuss how jazz influenced important cultural movements in the 1920s
   D) to provide a history of jazz music in the 20th century

9. Which of the following is NOT a fact stated in the passage?
   A) The years between World War I and the Great Depression were known as the Jazz Age.
   B) Ella Fitzgerald and Louis Armstrong both moved to New York City to start their music careers.
   C) Women danced to jazz music during the 1920s to make a statement about their role in society.
   D) Jazz music was an integral part of the emerging African American culture of the 1920s.

10. What can the reader conclude from the passage above?
    A) F. Scott Fitzgerald supported jazz musicians in New York and Chicago.
    B) Jazz music is no longer as popular as it once was.
    C) Both women and African Americans used jazz music as a way of expressing their newfound freedom.
    D) Flappers and African American musicians worked together to produce jazz music.

Questions 11–16 refer to the following passage.

The most important part of brewing coffee is getting the right water. Choose a water that you think has a nice, neutral flavor. Anything with too many minerals or contaminants will change the flavor of the coffee, and water with too few minerals won't do a good job of extracting the flavor from the coffee beans. Water should be heated to between 195 and 205 degrees Fahrenheit. Boiling water (212 degrees Fahrenheit) will burn the beans and give your coffee a scorched flavor.

While the water is heating, grind your beans. Remember, the fresher the grind, the fresher the flavor of the coffee. The number of beans is entirely dependent on your personal taste. Obviously, more beans will result in a more robust flavor, while fewer beans will give your coffee a more subtle taste. The texture of the grind should be not too fine (which can lead to bitter coffee) or too large (which can lead to weak coffee).

Once the beans are ground and the water has reached the perfect temperature, you're ready to brew. A French press (which we recommend), allows you to control brewing time and provide a thorough brew. Pour the grounds into the press, then pour the hot water over the grounds and let it steep. The brew shouldn't require more than five minutes, although those of you who like your coffee a bit harsher can leave it longer. Finally, use the plunger to remove the grounds and pour.

11. Which of the following best describes the structure of the text?
    A) chronological
    B) cause and effect
    C) problem and solution
    D) contrast

12. According to the passage, which of the following lists the steps for brewing coffee in the correct sequence?
    A) Choose a water that doesn't have too many or two few minerals. Then, heat water to boiling and pour over coffee grounds.
    B) Grind the beans to the appropriate texture and pour into the French press. Then, heat water to boiling and pour over the ground beans. Finally, use the plunger to remove the grounds and pour.
    C) Grind beans to the appropriate texture, and then heat water to 195 degrees Fahrenheit. Next, pour water over the grounds and steep for no more than five minutes. Finally, remove the grounds using the plunger.
    D) Choose the right type of water and heat it to the correct temperature. Next, grind the beans and put them in the French press. Then, pour the hot water over the grounds and let the coffee steep.

13. Which of the following statements based on the passage should be considered an opinion?
    A) While the water is heating, grind your beans.
    B) A French press (which we recommend), allows you to control brewing time and provide a thorough brew.
    C) Anything with too many minerals or contaminants will change the flavor of the coffee, and water with too few minerals won't do a good job of extracting the flavor from the coffee beans.
    D) Finally, use the plunger to remove the grounds and pour.

14. What is the author's intent in writing this passage?
    A) to describe how to make hot beverages
    B) to argue that grinding beans makes a better cup of coffee
    C) to claim that coffee is better than tea
    D) to explain how to brew a cup of coffee

15. Which of the following conclusions is best supported by the passage?
    A) Coffee should never be brewed for longer than five minutes.
    B) It's better to use too many coffee beans when making coffee than too few.
    C) Brewing quality coffee at home is too complicated for most people to do well.
    D) The best way to brew coffee is often determined by personal preferences.

16. Which of the following would be an appropriate title for this passage?
    A) How to Brew the Perfect Cup of Coffee
    B) Why Drinking Coffee Is the Best Way to Start the Day
    C) How to Use a French Press to Make Coffee
    D) The Importance of Grinding Coffee Beans

Questions 17–22 refer to the following passage.

Influenza (also called the flu) has historically been one of the most common, and deadliest, human infections. While many people who contract the virus will recover, many others will not. Over the past 150 years, tens of millions of people have died from the flu, and millions more have been left with lingering complications such as secondary infections.

Although it's a common disease, the flu is not actually highly infectious, meaning it's relatively difficult to contract. The flu can only be transmitted when individuals come into direct contact with bodily fluids of people infected with the flu or when they are exposed to expelled aerosol particles (which result from coughing and sneezing). Because the viruses can only travel short distances as aerosol particles and will die within a few hours on hard surfaces, the virus can be contained with fairly simple health measures like hand washing and face masks.

However, the spread of the flu can only be contained when people are aware such **measures** need to be taken. One of the reasons the flu has historically been so deadly is the amount of time between when people become infectious and when they develop symptoms. Viral shedding—the process by which the body releases viruses that have been successfully reproducing during the infection—takes place two days after infection, while symptoms do not usually develop until the third day of infection. Thus, infected individuals have at least twenty-four hours in which they may unknowingly infect others.

17. Which of the following correctly describes the flu?
    A) The flu is easy to contract and always fatal.
    B) The flu is difficult to contract and always fatal.
    C) The flu is easy to contract and sometimes fatal.
    D) The flu is difficult to contract and sometimes fatal.

18. What is the main idea of the passage?
    A) The flu is a deadly disease that's difficult to control because people become infectious before they show symptoms.
    B) For the flu to be transmitted, individuals must come in contact with bodily fluids from infected individuals.
    C) The spread of the flu is easy to contain because the viruses do not live long either as aerosol particles or on hard surfaces.
    D) The flu has killed tens of millions of people and can often cause deadly secondary infections.

19. Why is the flu considered to not be highly infectious?
    A) Many people who get the flu will recover and have no lasting complications, so only a small number of people who become infected will die.
    B) The process of viral shedding takes two days, so infected individuals have enough time to implement simple health measures that stop the spread of the disease.
    C) The flu virus cannot travel far or live for long periods of time outside the human body, so its spread can easily be contained.
    D) Twenty-four hours is a relatively short period of time for the virus to spread among a population.

20. What is the meaning of the word measures in the last paragraph?
    A) a plan of action
    B) a standard unit
    C) an adequate amount
    D) a rhythmic movement

21. Which statement is NOT a detail from the passage?
    A) Tens of millions of people have been killed by the flu virus.
    B) There is typically a twenty-four hour window during which individuals are infectious but not showing flu symptoms.
    C) Viral shedding is the process by which people recover from the flu.
    D) The flu can be transmitted by direct contact with bodily fluids from infected individuals or by exposure to aerosol particles.

22. What can the reader conclude from the passage?
    A) Preemptively implementing health measures like hand washing and face masks could help stop the spread of the flu virus.
    B) Doctors are not sure how the flu virus is transmitted, so they are unsure how to stop it from spreading.
    C) The flu is dangerous because it is both deadly and highly infectious.
    D) Individuals stop being infectious three days after they are infected.

Questions 23–27 refer to the following passage.

It had been a long morning for Julia. She'd been woken up early by the sound of lawn mowers outside her window and despite her best efforts, had been unable to get back to sleep. So, she'd reluctantly got out of bed, showered, and prepared her morning cup of coffee. At least, she tried to anyway. In the kitchen she'd discovered she was out of regular coffee and had to settle for a decaffeinated cup instead.

Once on the road, her caffeine-free mug of coffee didn't help make traffic less annoying. In fact, it seemed to Julia like the other drivers were sluggish and surly as well—it took her an extra fifteen minutes to get to work. And when she arrived, all the parking spots were full.

By the time she'd finally found a spot in the overflow lot, she was thirty minutes late for work. She'd hoped her boss would be too busy to notice, but he'd already put a pile of paperwork on her desk with a note that simply said "Rewrite." She wondered if she should point out to her boss that she hadn't been the one to write the reports in the first place, but decided against it.

When the fire alarm went off an hour later, Julia decided she'd had enough. She grabbed her purse and headed outside with her coworkers. While everyone else stood around waiting for the alarm to quiet, Julia determinedly walked to her car, fired up the engine, and set a course for home.

23. Which of the following lists Julia's actions in the correct sequence?
    A) Julia woke up early and found she didn't have any regular coffee. When she got to work, her boss had a lot for her to do. When the fire alarm went off, she decided to go home.
    B) Julia got to work and decided she was too tired to do the work her boss asked for, so she went home to get a cup of coffee.
    C) Julia woke up when the fire alarm went off and couldn't get back to sleep. She then got stuck in traffic and arrived at work thirty minutes late.
    D) Julia was woken up early by a lawnmower and then got stuck in traffic on the way to her office. Once there, she found that the office was out of coffee and she had a lot of work to do. When the fire alarm went off, she decided to go home.

24. Which of the following is the most likely reason Julia did not return to work after the alarm?
    A) She was embarrassed that should could not finish the work her boss asked for.
    B) She was tired and wanted to go home.
    C) She got stuck in traffic and could not get back to her office.
    D) Her boss gave her the afternoon off.

25. Which of the following statements based on the passage should be considered an opinion?
    A) Julia's boss asked her to do work to help one of her coworkers.
    B) Julia was late to work because of traffic.
    C) It was irresponsible for Julia to leave work early.
    D) Julia was tired because she'd been woken up early.

26. The passage states that Julia set a course for home. Which of the following is the most accurate interpretation of this sentence?
    A) Julia is looking up directions to her house.
    B) Julia is planning to drive home.
    C) Julia wants to go home but will go back to work.
    D) Julia is worried the fire at her office will spread to her home.

27. Which of the following conclusions is best supported by the passage?
    A) Julia will find a job closer to her home.
    B) Julia will be fired.
    C) Julia will feel guilty and return to work.
    D) Julia will drive home and go to sleep.

Questions 28–33 refer to the following passage.

The bacteria, fungi, insects, plants, and animals that live together in a habitat have evolved to share a pool of limited resources. They've competed for water, minerals, nutrients, sunlight, and space—sometimes for thousands or even millions of years. As these communities have evolved, the species in them have developed complex, long- term interspecies interactions known as symbiotic relationships.

Ecologists characterize these interactions based on whether each party benefits. In mutualism, both individuals benefit, while in synnecrosis, both organisms are harmed. A relationship where one individual benefits and the other is harmed is known as parasitism. Examples of these relationships can easily be seen in any ecosystem. Pollination, for example, is mutualistic—pollinators get nutrients from the flower, and the plant is able to reproduce—while tapeworms, which steal nutrients from their host, are parasitic.

Practice Test #1

There's yet another class of symbiosis that is controversial among scientists. As it's long been defined, commensalism is a relationship where one species benefits and the other is unaffected. But is it possible for two species to interact and for one to remain completely unaffected? Often, relationships described as commensal include one species that feeds on another species' leftovers; remoras, for instance, will attach themselves to sharks and eat the food particles they leave behind. It might seem like the shark gets nothing from the relationship, but a closer look will show that sharks in fact benefit from remoras, which clean the sharks' skin and remove parasites. In fact, many scientists claim that relationships currently described as commensal are just mutualistic or parasitic in ways that haven't been discovered yet.

28. What is the meaning of the word *controversial* in the last paragraph?
    A) debatable
    B) objectionable
    C) confusing
    D) upsetting

29. What is the author's primary purpose in writing this essay?
    A) to argue that commensalism isn't actually found in nature
    B) to describe the many types of symbiotic relationships
    C) to explain how competition for resources results in long-term interspecies relationships
    D) to provide examples of the many different ways individual organisms interact

30. Which of the following is NOT a fact stated in the passage?
    A) Mutualism is an interspecies relationship where both species benefit.
    B) Synnecrosis is an interspecies relationship where both species are harmed.
    C) The relationship between plants and pollinators is mutualistic.
    D) The relationship between remoras and sharks is parasitic.

31. Epiphytes are plants that attach themselves to trees and derive nutrients from the air and surrounding debris. Sometimes, the weight of epiphytes can damage the trees on which they're growing. The relationship between epiphytes and their hosts would be described as ____.
    A) mutualism
    B) commensalism
    C) parasitism
    D) synnecrosis

32. Why is commensalism controversial among scientists?
    A) Many scientists believe that an interspecies interaction where one species is unaffected does not exist.
    B) Some scientists believe that relationships where one species feeds on the leftovers of another should be classified as parasitism.
    C) Because remoras and sharks have a mutualistic relationship, no interactions should be classified as commensalism.
    D) Only relationships among animal species should be classified as commensalism.

33. What can the reader conclude from this passage about symbiotic relationships?
    A) Scientists cannot decide how to classify symbiotic relationships among species.
    B) The majority of interspecies interactions are parasitic because most species do not get along.
    C) If two species are involved in a parasitic relationship, one of the species will eventually become extinct.
    D) Symbiotic relationships evolve as the species that live in a community adapt to their environments and each other.

Questions 34–39 refer to the following passage.

Popcorn is often associated with fun and festivities, both in and out of the home. It's eaten in theaters, usually after being salted and smothered in butter, and in homes, fresh from the microwave. But popcorn isn't just for fun—it's also a multimillion-dol- lar-a-year industry with a long and fascinating history.

While popcorn might seem like a modern invention, its history actually dates back thousands of years, making it one of the oldest snack foods enjoyed around the world. Popcorn is believed by food historians to be one of the earliest uses of cultivated corn. In 1948, Herbert Dick and Earle Smith discovered old popcorn dating back 4,000 years in the New Mexico Bat Cave. For the Aztec people who called the caves home, popcorn (or momochitl) played an important role in society, both as a food staple and in ceremonies. The Aztecs cooked popcorn by heating sand in a fire; when it was heated, kernels were added and would pop when exposed to the heat of the sand.

The American love affair with popcorn began in 1912, when popcorn was first sold in theaters. The popcorn industry flourished during the Great Depression when it was advertised as a wholesome and economical food. Selling for five to ten cents a bag, it was a luxury that the downtrodden could afford. With the introduction of mobile popcorn machines at the World's Columbian Exposition, popcorn moved from the theater into fairs and parks. Popcorn continued to rule the snack food kingdom until the rise in popularity of home televisions during the 1950s.

The popcorn industry reacted to the decline in sales quickly by introducing pre- popped and unpopped popcorn for home consumption. However, it wasn't until microwave popcorn became commercially available in 1981 that at-home popcorn consumption began to grow exponentially. With the wide availability of microwaves in the United States, popcorn also began popping up in offices and hotel rooms. However, the home still remains the most popular popcorn eating spot: today, 70 percent of the 16 billion quarts of popcorn consumed annually in the United States are eaten at home.

34. What can the reader conclude from the passage above?
    A) People ate less popcorn in the 1950s than in previous decades because they went to the movies less.
    B) Without mobile popcorn machines, people would not have been able to eat popcorn during the Great Depression.
    C) People enjoyed popcorn during the Great Depression because it was a luxury food.
    D) During the 1800s, people began abandoning theaters to go to fairs and festivals.

35. What is the meaning of the word *staple* in the second paragraph?
    A) something produced only for special occasions
    B) something produced regularly in large quantities
    C) something produced by cooking
    D) something fastened together securely

36. What is the author's primary purpose in writing this essay?
    A) to explain how microwaves affected the popcorn industry
    B) to show that popcorn is older than many people realize
    C) to illustrate the history of popcorn from ancient cultures to modern times
    D) to demonstrate the importance of popcorn in various cultures

37. Which factor does the author of the passage credit for the growth of the popcorn industry in the United States?
    A) the use of popcorn in ancient Aztec ceremonies
    B) the growth of the home television industry
    C) the marketing of popcorn during the Great Depression
    D) the nutritional value of popcorn

38. What is the best summary of this passage?
    A) Popcorn is a popular snack food that dates back thousands of years. Its popularity in the United States has been tied to the growth of theaters and the availability of microwaves.
    B) Popcorn has been a popular snack food for thousands of years. Archaeologists have found evidence that many ancient cultures used popcorn as a food staple and in ceremonies.
    C) Popcorn was first introduced to America in 1912, and its popularity has grown exponentially since then. Today, over 16 billion quarts of popcorn are consumed in the United States annually.
    D) Popcorn is a versatile snack food that can be eaten with butter or other toppings. It can also be cooked in a number of different ways, including in microwaves.

39. Which of the following is NOT a fact stated in the passage?
    A) Archaeologists have found popcorn dating back 4000 years.
    B) Popcorn was first sold in theaters in 1912.
    C) Consumption of popcorn dropped in 1981 with the growing popularity of home televisions.
    D) Seventy percent of the popcorn consumed in the United States is eaten in homes.

Questions 40–50 refer to the following passage (and graph), which is adapted from an article entitled "NASA Contributes to First Global Review of Arctic Marine Mammals," published online by the National Aeronautics and Space Administration in April 2015. This was initially published to NASA's Cryosphere Science Research Portal, alongside an article entitled "Current State of the Sea Ice Cover."

[1] Many human communities want answers about the current status and future of Arctic marine mammals, including scientists who dedicate their lives to studying them and indigenous people whose traditional ways of subsistence are intertwined with the fate of species such as ice seals, narwhals, walruses, and polar bears.

[2] But there are many unknowns about the current status of eleven species of marine mammals who depend on Arctic sea ice to live, feed and breed, and about how their fragile habitat will evolve in a warming world.

[3] A recently published multinational study attempted to gauge the population trends of Arctic marine mammals and changes in their habitat, identify missing scientific information, and provide recommendations for the conservation of Arctic marine mammals over the next decades.

The Arctic sea ice cover, made of frozen seawater floating on top of the Arctic Ocean and its neighboring seas, naturally grows in the fall and winter and melts during the spring and summer every year. But over the past decades, the melt season has grown longer and the average extent of Arctic sea ice has diminished, changing the game for many Arctic marine mammals—namely beluga, narwhal and bowhead whales; ringed, bearded, spotted, ribbon, harp and hooded seals; walruses; and polar bears.

"This research would not have been possible without support from NASA," said Kristin Laidre, lead author of the new study and a polar scientist with University of Washington in Seattle. "NASA backed us on research related to the biodiversity and ecology of Arctic marine mammals, as well as the development of metrics for the loss of sea ice, their habitat."

Laidre's team used the Arctic sea ice record derived from microwave measurements taken by NASA and Department of Defense satellites. This record began in late 1978, is uninterrupted, and relies on NASA-developed methods for processing the microwave data.

"It's really our best global view of the Arctic sea ice," said Harry Stern, author of the paper with Laidre and a mathematician specializing in sea ice and climate at University of Washington.

[4] Stern divided the Arctic Ocean into twelve regions. Using daily sea ice concentration data from the satellite record, he calculated changes in the dates of the beginning of the melt season in spring and the start of the fall freeze-up from 1979 to 2013. He found that, in all regions but one, the melt season had grown longer (mostly by five to ten weeks, and by twenty weeks in one region).

"Sea ice is critical for Arctic marine mammals because events such as feeding, giving birth, molting, and resting are closely timed with the availability of their ice platform," Laidre said. "It is especially critical for the ice-dependent species—seals and polar bears. Ice seals use the sea ice platform to give birth and nurse pups during very specific weeks of the spring, and polar bears use sea ice for feeding, starting in late winter and continuing until the ice breaks up."

[5] Pacific walrus use the floating pack ice both as a platform on which to rest between feeding bouts and as a passive transport around their habitat.

"Loss of sea ice has resulted in walrus hauling out on land in Alaska and Russia in massive numbers—these land haul outs result in trampling of their young," Laidre said. "Also, now walrus must travel a longer way to reach their feeding areas, which is energetically costly."

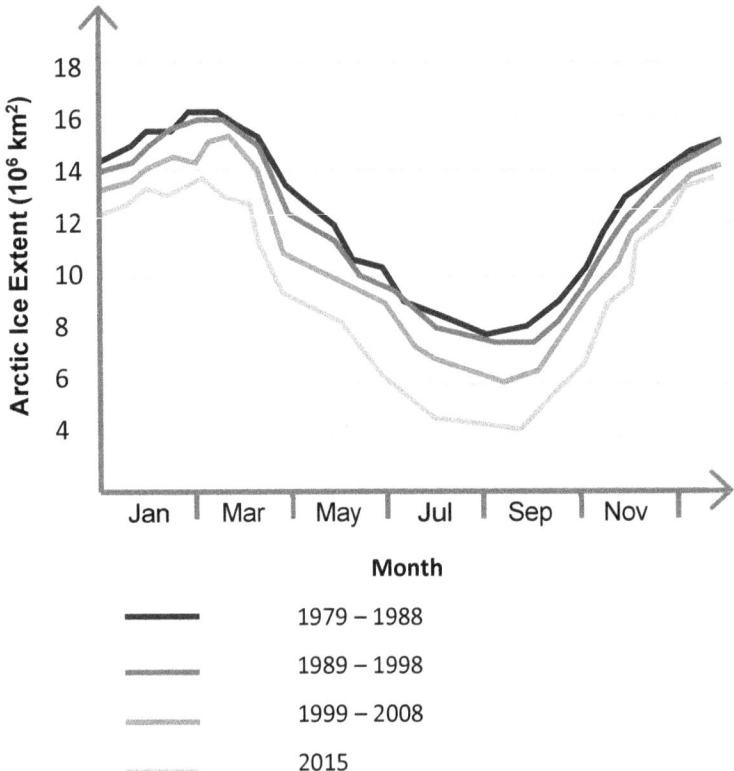

[6] In the case of Arctic whales, the changes in sea ice might benefit their populations, at least in the short term: the loss and earlier retreat of sea ice opens up new habitats and, in some areas of the Arctic, has also led to an increase in food production and the length of their feeding season.

[7] In the future, Stern said higher-resolution satellite microwave data might come in handy when studying the interactions of Arctic marine mammals with their icy habitat.

"For example, we know that narwhals congregate in specific areas of the Arctic in the wintertime, so maybe a higher spatial resolution in these areas might help us better understand their relationship with the ice," Stern said. "But mainly, just continuing daily coverage is what's important for the long-term monitoring of habitat changes."

40. In paragraph 1, the author includes a detail about indigenous people of the Arctic in order to
    A) provide readers with a relatable story to consider as they read the article.
    B) emphasize the importance of protecting the habitats of Arctic marine mammals.
    C) challenge readers to make Arctic preservation efforts their top priority.
    D) illustrate a contrast between the indigenous people and the scientists mentioned in the first part of the sentence.

41. In paragraph 4, the author indicates that while fluctuation in sea ice extent is expected throughout the year,
    A) variability from year to year is a recent phenomenon.
    B) the fluctuation is usually minute.
    C) daily changes in sea ice extent are becoming more typical.
    D) changes in the populations of Arctic mammals are not.

42. Why does the author include the list of Arctic marine mammals in paragraph 4?
    A) to illustrate a discrepancy between the number of Arctic species and the number of species that depend on sea ice for survival
    B) to challenge the assertion that the recession of sea ice is significant
    C) to articulate a general truth about life in the Arctic
    D) to highlight the number of species that depend on sea ice for their survival

43. When it comes to research about sea ice and the animals who rely on it, according to the passage
    A) scientists know everything they need to know.
    B) data collection is rarely a simple process.
    C) very few answers currently exist.
    D) vigilant observation is an essential tool in gaining insight.

44. What is the meaning of the word fragile in paragraph 2?
    A) brittle
    B) flimsy
    C) breakable
    D) unstable

45. Which excerpt from the text provides the best evidence for the answer to the previous question?
    A) "Using daily sea ice concentration data from the satellite record, he calculated changes in the dates of the beginning of the melt season in spring and the start of the fall freeze-up from 1979 to 2013."
    B) "Sea ice is critical for Arctic marine mammals because events such as feeding, giving birth, molting, and resting are closely timed with the availability of their ice platform."
    C) "The Arctic sea ice cover, made of frozen seawater floating on top of the Arctic Ocean and its neighboring seas, naturally grows in the fall and winter and melts during the spring and summer every year."
    D) "But over the past decades, the melt season has grown longer and the average extent of Arctic sea ice has diminished, changing the game for many Arctic marine mammals."

46. According to the passage, in a little over three decades, the length of the melt seasons in most regions of the Arctic
    A) decreased by more than two months.
    B) increased by more than two months.
    C) decreased by more than a month.
    D) increased by more than a month.

Practice Test #1   305

47. In paragraphs 9 through 12, the author indicates that
    A) most, but not all, animals struggle when the availability of sea ice decreases.
    B) many animals will continue to thrive despite the change in climate.
    C) all Arctic mammals use sea ice for the same reason.
    D) all Arctic mammals struggle when the availability of sea ice decreases.

48. What is the meaning of the word retreat in paragraph 12?
    A) surrender
    B) refuge
    C) recession
    D) departure

49. Which excerpt from the text provides the best evidence for the answer to the previous question?
    A) "But there are many unknowns about the current status of eleven species of marine mammals who depend on Arctic sea ice to live, feed, and breed, and about how their fragile habitat will evolve in a warming world."
    B) "Using daily sea ice concentration data from the satellite record, he calculated changes in the dates of the beginning of the melt season in spring and the start of the fall freeze-up from 1979 to 2013."
    C) "In the future, Stern said higher-resolution satellite microwave data might come in handy when studying the interactions of Arctic marine mammals with their icy habitat."
    D) "But mainly, just continuing daily coverage is what's important for the long-term monitoring of habitat changes."

50. Which claim about Arctic ice extent is supported by the graph?
    A) Arctic ice extent has remained steady over the last three decades.
    B) Patterns of formation and recession are largely unpredictable.
    C) Arctic ice extent during late summer is significantly lower today than it was in 1979.
    D) Sea ice extent during winter was significantly lower in 1979 than it is today.

Language Arts: Writing

Grammar

Directions: Read the passage and choose the best answer. The underlined sentences in the passage correspond to a question number. For each question, choose the revision that makes the most grammatical sense while keeping the idea of the original text.

Becoming a Police Officer

Some (1) careers, especially those in the public eye, lend themselves to controversy and caricatures. In the twenty-first century, police work lands squarely in this category: (2) crooked cops and detectives with donuts are commonplace in the worlds of media and entertainment. Still, officers of the law and public investigators play an essential role in our criminal justice system, a role that comes with a great deal of responsibility. (3) They must first be strong communicators, as they must be able to gather information and effectively communicate that information in written reports. In order to evaluate and respond to situations quickly and appropriately, they must also be highly perceptive and must possess good judgment. In addition, physical strength and stamina are a necessity for officers of the law, as the job can be strenuous and demanding. Finally, they must be empathetic, as they must be able to relate to and treat the people of their community (4) with sincere care and unwavering equity.

To become a police officer, one must complete a rigorous series of hiring requirements, (5) which begin with providing proof of citizenship, age, education, and criminal history. After meeting these basic requirements, each candidate must pass a series of (6) evaluations, which are intended to determine (7) their suitability for police work. First, the candidate must pass a series of challenging physical tests and written exams, which are intended to evaluate the candidate based on his or her physical and mental fitness. Then, each candidate must pass a series of challenging inter- views, during which he or she may be asked to complete lie detector and drug tests. Finally, an applicant who meets all of these requirements must gain acceptance into (8) his or her agency's academy to begin training.

Academy training is extensive for officers of the law. In addition to physical training in (9) self-defense firearms, emergency response and first aid, candidates must also complete a series of classes in constitutional law, state and local law, civil rights, and ethics. Federal agents or officers with specialized responsibilities must complete even more training.

An officer who is successful in his or her initial role as patrolman or first responder may find him- or herself in the position of receiving a promotion. Often, this first promotion elevates the person to the role of detective or special investigator. Detectives and special investigators are responsible for (10) investigating reported crimes, to gather and protecting evidence, conducting interviews, and for solving crimes in specialized areas such as homicide, vice, or special victims.

1.
   A) NO CHANGE
   B) careers—especially those in the public eye
   C) careers, especially those in the public eye—
   D) careers, especially those in the public eye

2. Which of the following best supports the claim made earlier in the paragraph?
   A) NO CHANGE
   B) however, it is an extremely challenging profession, and its significance should not be underestimated.
   C) the work itself is challenging, but the perks that come along with it are substantial.
   D) most people admire and respect officers of the law.

3. Which of the following sentences is the best introduction to the material in the next paragraph?
   A) Police officers should not be worried if they do not fit the stereotypes.
   B) The amount of responsibility that comes with being a police officer can be overwhelming.
   C) Police officers must possess a number of varied characteristics in order to be successful as representatives of the law.
   D) The question of whether someone should pursue police work can be answered by knowing oneself.

4. Which of the following choices suggests that officers of the law must possess strong moral character?
   A) NO CHANGE
   B) as innocent until they are proven guilty
   C) as though they are their closest friends
   D) without regard for the concerns of others

5.
- A) NO CHANGE
- B) which begins
- C) that begin
- D) that begins

6.
- A) NO CHANGE
- B) evaluations, they are intended
- C) evaluations, being intended
- D) evaluations—these are intended

7.
- A) NO CHANGE
- B) its
- C) his or her
- D) the

8.
- A) NO CHANGE
- B) his or her agencies
- C) their agencies
- D) their agency's

9.
- A) NO CHANGE
- B) self-defense, firearms, emergency response, and first aid,
- C) self-defense, firearms, emergency, response and first aid,
- D) self-defense, firearms emergency, response, and first aid,

10.
- A) NO CHANGE
- B) investigate reported crimes, gather and protecting evidence, conduct interviews, and solve crimes
- C) investigating reported crimes, gathering and protecting evidence, conducting interviews, and solving crimes
- D) investigation reported crimes, to gather and protect evidence, to conduct interview, and solving crimes

The writer is considering whether or not to add the following sentence:

According to the United States Bureau of Labor Statistics, this promotion is a valuable one: in 2012, the median pay for detectives was nearly $20,000 more than the median pay for uniformed officers of the law.

11. Would this be an appropriate sentence to add at this point?
    A) Yes, because it provides more information about the work of detectives and their motivation for doing it.
    B) Yes, because it provides more information about the difference between uniformed officers and detectives.
    C) No, because it distracts the reader from the main point of the passage.
    D) No, because the reader does not know how much uniformed police officers usually make.

Bioluminescence

(12) Adaptations, features that develop over centuries of natural selection, allow the animals to function more effectively in their environments and can be found in many species. Sometimes these adaptations are physical: the giraffe's long neck allows it to reach food in the highest trees, and the camel's hump allows it to survive for days in an arid environment. Other adaptations, like bioluminescence, are chemical.

Bioluminescence, the ability to create light, is an adaptation that is most present in animals that live in primarily dark environments like the ocean. It is caused by a chemical reaction in the animal's body, which allows the animal to fulfill a particular need. Like other types of adaptations, bioluminescence serves a different function in each species that displays the ability; however, for the most part, these functions can be divided into three categories: (13) protection, hunting, and reproduction.

For many ocean-dwelling, bioluminescent creatures, the ability to create light serves a defensive function. The vampire squid, for example, uses the light to stun and confuse its predators. Unlike other squid, which may emit a dark liquid to confuse predators, the vampire squid has adapted to a deep ocean environment— where light is limited and dark liquid has no effect. As a result, the vampire squid instead emits (14) a glowing goo, which (15) surprises their predators and distracts them while the squid escapes capture.

Bioluminescence serves other defensive purposes as well. Some species, like the hatchet fish, use their own light to create a sort of camouflage: (16) when a predator is swimming, below, a lit underbelly allows the prey to swim along unnoticed blending in with the light from above. Misdirection is also a common application of bioluminescence. Some animals, like the brittle star, can detach lit body parts and leave (17) them behind in order to draw predators away from themselves. (18) Other animals use their bioluminescent abilities differently.

On the head of an anglerfish, for example, is a long barb that lights up at the tip. The fish uses this light to lure smaller fish directly into its mouth. (19) In addition, bioluminescent animals may use their natural spotlight to seek out prey in dark places; still others use their light to surprise, disorient, and capture their meals.

Finally, some animals, like the firefly and some types of underwater crustaceans, use bioluminescence in their mating practices. Female syllid fireworms, for example, luminesce while swimming in circles in order to attract males of their species. (21)

12.
- A) NO CHANGE
- B) Many species display adaptations, features that develop over centuries of natural selection, which allow the animals to function more effectively in their environments.
- C) Adaptations are features that develop over centuries of natural selection, which allow the animals to function more effectively in their environments, and can be found in many species.
- D) Developing over centuries of natural selection, animals have adaptations that allow them to function more effectively in their environments and can be found in many species.

13.
- A) NO CHANGE
- B) for protection, to hunt, and reproduction.
- C) protecting, to hunt, and reproducing.
- D) for protection, hunting, and to reproduce.

14. Which of the following is most appropriate considering the tone and purpose of the passage?
- A) a bright, nasty gunk
- B) a secretion of organic, bioluminescent matter
- C) the brightest, weirdest goop you ever saw
- D) a glowing goo

15.
- A) NO CHANGE
- B) surprises its predators and distracts it
- C) surprise their predators and distracts them
- D) surprises its predator and distracts it

16.
- A) NO CHANGE
- B) when a predator is swimming below, a lit underbelly allows the prey to swim along unnoticed, blending in with the light from above.
- C) when a predator is swimming below a lit underbelly allows the prey to swim along unnoticed, blending in, with the light from above.
- D) when a predator is swimming below, a lit underbelly, allows the prey to swim along unnoticed, blending in, with the light from above.

17.
- A) NO CHANGE
- B) it behind in order to draw predators away from itself.
- C) them behind in order to draw predators away from itself.
- D) it behind in order to draw predators away from themselves.

18. Which choice provides the best transition between the previous paragraph and this one?
- A) NO CHANGE
- B) There are myriad reasons that an animal might use bioluminescence, and protection is just one of them.
- C) While many creatures create light for defensive purposes, not all do: some animals, instead, use bioluminescence to find and capture prey.
- D) If an animal is hungry, it might use bioluminescence to find its food.

19. At this point, the writer wants to add an additional detail about animals that use bioluminescence to hunt. Considering the tone and purpose of the passage, which of the following choices is most effective?
   A) Even some sharks light up to attract prey.
   B) If you ever have an opportunity to go deep- sea diving, you should take advantage of it and hope that you get to see an anglerfish in action.
   C) The anglerfish may look scary, but it won't eat anything as large as a human.
   D) These creatures are fascinating to watch in action.

20. The best placement for the underlined sentence (19) is
   A) where it is now.
   B) at the beginning of this paragraph.
   C) at the end of the second paragraph.
   D) after the first sentence of the fourth paragraph.

21. At this point the writer wants to add a concluding sentence. Considering the tone and purpose of the passage, which choice is most appropriate?
   A) Despite its initial intrigue, bioluminescence is far more common and less interesting than one might assume.
   B) In conclusion, bioluminescence is an essential adaptation for many animal species, and we would be irresponsible to ignore it.
   C) Bioluminescent species are some of the most fascinating animals on our planet, so it is essential that we consider committing time and resources to preserving their natural habitats.
   D) With its commonality among species and its variety of applications, bioluminescence is a fascinating topic that can enliven our senses and spark our curiosities about the natural world.

The Expert

Dr. Martin Kemp sat at his computer (22) examining emails.

(23) Some he responded to quickly, while marking others for later, still others he deleted immediately. Then he came across an email from someone named Peter. The subject read: *Leonardo?*

Another loony, Kemp thought. (24) He scoffed a little but clicking to open the message anyway. He received these emails fairly regularly, two or three times a week most weeks, and he had yet to come across an inquiry that even gave him pause. (25) As Professor Emeritus of Art History at Oxford University, Kemp was a da Vinci expert, and he regularly received notes from people thinking they had come across a lost work of the great artist.

(26) Then he opened the image.

A feeling of utter astonishment fell over Kemp. He put down his coffee, stopped shuffling papers, and stared at the high-resolution image on his screen.

He moved his chair (27) closer to his desk, and attempting to get a better look at the striking portrait. He looked at it in its full form for a number of minutes before zooming in to get a better view. The detail work was magnificent, and the portrait seemed to have a life about it. (28) *Uncanny*, Kemp thought. He decided to respond to the inquiry: he would travel to Zurich, at no fee to the owner of the piece, to (29) eyeball the work in person.

Outside of his vault in Zurich, Peter Silverman slowly pulled the mysterious portrait out of its protective envelope. He could not believe he was finally here. When he first lost the auction of the portrait almost a decade before, he thought he would never see it again. Now, he held it in his gloved hands, discussing its potential origins with one of the world's leading experts. He laid the portrait down carefully in front of Martin Kemp and waited for the (30) connoisseur's expert opinion.

Kemp stared silently down at the piece. A rush of energy rolled over him, a feeling he would later have trouble describing in words. He only knew that this portrait was special, unlike any of the works he had evaluated before. (31) The subject of the portrait, a young woman, appeared compose d and thoughtful, as one who was living in a world that required her to act, by today's standards, well beyond her age. Her eyes had been drawn to show her vitality, and her hair seemed to respond naturally to the pressure of the headdress that hugged her head. These details... Kemp thought to himself, trailing off. (32)

22.
- A) NO CHANGE
- B) sifting through
- C) scrutinizing
- D) straining

23.
- A) NO CHANGE
- B) Some he responded to quickly, others he marked for later, and still others he deleted immediately.
- C) Some he would respond to quickly, and others he marked for later, still others he would delete.
- D) Some he is responding to quickly, others he would mark for later, still others he deletes immediately.

24.
- A) NO CHANGE
- B) He scoffed a little and clicking to open the message anyway.
- C) He scoffed a little but clicked to open the message anyway.
- D) He scoffs a little but clicking to open the message anyway.

25. Which choice provides the most relevant detail about Dr. Kemp?
- A) NO CHANGE
- B) As a lover of Leonardo da Vinci's work, Dr. Kemp was shocked by how often people sent him emails claiming to have found an undiscovered work by the great artist.
- C) Dr. Kemp had viewed a number of da Vinci's works at museums around the world, and he found them to be every bit as magnificent as the artist's reputation would suggest.
- D) Dr. Kemp is a professor and a lover of da Vinci's works.

26. The writer wants to add the following sentence about Dr. Kemp's skepticism toward the contents of the email:

He had no reason to believe this one was any different.

Where should this sentence should be placed?
- A) at the beginning of the paragraph
- B) after the first sentence
- C) after the second sentence
- D) after the third sentence

312 Practice Test #1

27.
- A) NO CHANGE
- B) closer to his desk, attempting
- C) closer to his desk as though
- D) closer to his desk; next he was attempting

28. Which choice best expresses Dr. Kemp's cautious interest in the image?
- A) NO CHANGE
- B) *That's weird*
- C) *It must be a da Vinci*
- D) *Stellar*

29.
- A) NO CHANGE
- B) inspect
- C) display
- D) contemplate

30.
- A) NO CHANGE
- B) connoisseur's opinion
- C) educated connoisseur's opinion
- D) educated connoisseur's expert opinion

31.
- A) NO CHANGE
- B) A young woman, the subject of the portrait, appearing composed and thoughtful, as one living in a world, by today's standards, that required her to act well beyond her age.
- C) The subject of the portrait, a young woman who was living, by today's standards, in a world that required her to act well beyond her age, appeared composed and thoughtful.
- D) Composed and thoughtful, a young woman, the subject of the portrait, appearing composed and thoughtful, was living in a world that required her to act well beyond her age by today's standards.

32. To conclude, the writer wants to add a sentence that will make the reader want to do further research about Kemp's discovery. Which choice accomplishes this goal?
- A) In that moment, Dr. Kent decided that the work was, indeed, a work of the great artist Leonardo da Vinci.
- B) He was impressed by the level of sophistication, but he was sure that this was not, after all, a work of the great artist Leonardo da Vinci.
- C) He concluded in that moment that only a highly sophisticated forger could produce such a convincing piece of work.
- D) He could not know by that time, of course, whether the portrait was actually the work of the great da Vinci, but he knew he wanted to investigate further.

Food Trucks

Across the United States, a new trend in dining has taken (33) hold. Cities like Austin, Portland, San Francisco, and Seattle are seeing a significant increase in one particular type of dining establishment—the food truck. Though the modern food truck phenomenon is still in (34) it's prime, mobile dining is in no way (35) a unique, novel idea: precursors to the modern food truck can be traced back as far as the 1800s.

The earliest predecessors to the modern food truck (36) was actually not trucks; in fact, they were not motorized at all. (37) Push carts were some of the earliest vehicles for mobile food distribution and were popular in urban areas like New York City, where workers needed access to quick, cheap lunches. (38) Instead, while these carts were mobile, (39) they were not always available when they were most needed.

In the late 1800s, two new inventions marked important milestones in the development of the modern food truck. In 1866, Charles Goodnight created the first (40) chuck wagon and a covered wagon that served as a mobile kitchen for cowmen who were herding cattle northward for sale. The cooks, or "cookies," who traveled with the cowmen would wake early and prepare meals of beans, dried meats, and biscuits using the tools and ingredients on the chuck wagon. (41) Similarly, in 1872, a food vendor named Walter Scott conceived of the lunch wagon, from which he would serve sandwiches, coffee, and desserts to journalists outside a Providence, Rhode Island, newspaper office.

[1] In the 1900s, mobile dining took even newer forms, as the invention of motorized transportation began to transform the industry. [2] Ice cream trucks followed in the 1950s, serving children and adults alike cold treats on hot summer afternoons. [3] In the 1960s, large food service trucks called roach coaches began to pop up near densely In some places, whole streets or even neighborhoods are devoted to hosting these food trucks, (46) so they are easier than ever to access.

(47) populated urban areas, often serving cheap meals from grungy kitchens. (42)

(43)

(44) In recent years, the food truck industry has transformed the mobile dining experience from one of convenience to one of excitement. Today, city dwellers and tourists (45) will have flocked to food trucks not only for ease and affordability, but also for unique foods, new flavors, and fun experiences.

33.
- A) NO CHANGE
- B) hold in cities
- C) hold of cities
- D) hold, cities

34.
- A) NO CHANGE
- B) its
- C) its'
- D) it is

35.
   A) NO CHANGE
   B) a new or novel idea
   C) a novel idea
   D) a uniquely novel idea

36.
   A) NO CHANGE
   B) were
   C) are
   D) is

37.
   A) NO CHANGE
   B) Push carts were some of the earliest vehicles for mobile food distribution, popular in urban areas where workers needed access to quick, cheap lunches like New York City.
   C) Popular in urban areas like New York City, some of the earliest vehicles for mobile food distribution were push carts, which were located wherever workers needed access to quick, cheap lunches.
   D) Some of the earliest vehicles were push carts for food distribution, popular in urban areas, like New York, where workers needed quick, cheap lunches in the city.

38.
   A) NO CHANGE
   B) However,
   C) As a result,
   D) Therefore,

39. Given that all the choices are true, which of the following would be most effective in highlighting one of the major differences between the push cart and the modern food truck?
   A) No change
   B) they sometimes stayed in one place for long periods of time.
   C) they were not equipped with the tools necessary to prepare the food.
   D) they often had the same people working in them all the time.

40.
   A) NO CHANGE
   B) chuck wagon, and a covered wagon
   C) chuck wagon, a covered wagon
   D) chuck wagon; a covered wagon

41. If the writer were to delete the preceding sentence, the paragraph would primarily lose
   A) details about how cooks on the cattle trails came to be called cookies.
   B) a transition between two points in the paragraph.
   C) details about how the cooks made food on the chuck wagons.
   D) information about the meaning of the phrase *mobile kitchen*.

42. The writer is considering whether or not to delete the words *cheap* and *grungy* from the preceding sentence. Should the writer make these deletions?
    A) Yes, because the words distract from the main idea of the sentence.
    B) Yes, because the words are offensive to people who like food trucks.
    C) No, because the words provide insight into the origin of the term *roach coach*.
    D) No, because the words provide more information about early food trucks.

43. Upon reviewing the previous paragraph and realizing that some information had been left out, the writer composes the following sentence:

During the World War II era, mobile canteens popped up near army bases to serve quick, easy meals to the troops.

The most logical placement for this sentence would be
    A) before sentence 1.
    B) before sentence 2.
    C) before sentence 3.
    D) after sentence 3.

44.
    A) NO CHANGE
    B) Consequently,
    C) Therefore,
    D) In conclusion,

45.
    A) NO CHANGE
    B) are flocking
    C) have flocked
    D) have been flocking

46. Which of the following choices would provide an ending most consistent with the statement made in the first sentence of the paragraph?
    A) NO CHANGE
    B) so you rarely run out of delicious options.
    C) but sometimes these areas can be busy.
    D) and people travel from all over the city, sometimes even farther, to try what they're offering.

47. Suppose the writer had intended to write an essay on the historical development of the modern food truck. Would this essay successfully fulfill that goal?
    A) Yes, because it provides detailed information about the inventor who designed the first food truck.
    B) Yes, because it provides a brief overview of the trends and innovations that preceded the modern food truck.
    C) No, because it is primarily a descriptive essay about the modern food truck trend and its followers.
    D) No, because it focuses primarily on the differences between modern food trucks and older forms of mobile food distribution.

The Grand Canyon

The Grand Canyon is a landmark (48) who's enormity cannot truly be under- stood until it is experienced. The canyon, which was formed by millions of years of erosion by the Colorado River, is over one mile deep, nearly twenty miles wide, and over 250 miles long. It is located in northern Arizona and falls primarily inside Grand Canyon National Park, which (49) bisects the Kaibab National Forest. Adjacent to the park (50) is three Indian reservations—the Hualapai, the Kaibab Paiute, and the Navajo. (51) Management of this enormous landmark is achieved through the cooperation of many different groups. The tribal nations that (52) would reside in the area work alongside governmental (53) organizations, like the National Park Service to ensure that the lands are protected and tourists are kept (54) safe and free from harm.

[1] (55) Consequently, the Grand Canyon is one of the most popular tourist attractions in the world, (56) drawing upwards of five million visitors every year. [2] People come from all over the world to see the massive landmark, so activities and attractions are abundant. [3] Outdoor activities (57) like hiking, rafting, and camping, are popular, especially during the cooler months of spring and autumn. [4] Other activities like airplane and helicopter flyovers allow visitors a (58) broader perspective of the canyon.

(59)

Most activities at the Grand Canyon, however, are extremely limited by the weather, which varies significantly based on season and time of day. During the summer months, temperatures inside the canyon can reach above one hundred degrees

(60) Fahrenheit; during winter months, the temperature can drop below zero degrees. Even daytime and nighttime temperatures can vary substantially, so it is important for visitors to follow weather forecasts and pack carefully.

48.
- A) NO CHANGE
- B) of which its
- C) where
- D) whose

49. Which of the following alternatives to the underlined portion would be LEAST acceptable?
- A) separates
- B) crosses
- C) intersects
- D) cuts across

50.
- A) NO CHANGE
- B) are
- C) were
- D) exists

51. The writer is considering deleting the following phrase from the preceding sentence, ending the sentence with a period after the word *reservations*: the Hualapai, the Kaibab Paiute, and the Navajo

If the writer were to make this deletion, the paragraph would primarily lose
- A) information about the background of the Native American people who work in the canyon.
- B) details about people who control the land surrounding the Grand Canyon.
- C) insight into the history of the Grand Canyon.
- D) nothing because the information is irrelevant.

52.
- A) NO CHANGE
- B) had resided
- C) are residing
- D) reside

53.
- A) NO CHANGE
- B) organizations—like the National Park Service,
- C) organizations, like the National Park Service,
- D) organizations like the National Park Service,

54.
- A) NO CHANGE
- B) safe.
- C) safe and out of harm's way.
- D) safe and avoid injury.

55.
- A) NO CHANGE
- B) In fact,
- C) Nevertheless,
- D) Therefore,

56. Given that all of the following choices are true, which would most effectively support the claim made earlier in the sentence?
- A) No change
- B) even though most of its visitors don't stay long.
- C) though it is still surpassed in popularity by the Eiffel Tower.
- D) making its upkeep a difficult job.

57.
- A) NO CHANGE
- B) like, hiking, rafting, and camping
- C) like, hiking, rafting and camping,
- D) like hiking, rafting, and camping

58. Which of the following is the best placement for the underlined word?
    A) where it is now
    B) after the word *other*
    C) after the word *like*
    D) after the word *allow*

59. The writer is considering adding the following true statement to the preceding paragraph:

Visitors can even walk over and look down at the canyon from the Grand Canyon SkyWalk, a transparent bridge that juts out in a horseshoe shape from one side of the canyon.

This sentence would most logically be placed
    A) before sentence 1.
    B) after sentence 1.
    C) after sentence 2.
    D) after sentence 4.

60. Which of the following alternatives to the underlined portion would NOT be acceptable?
    A) Fahrenheit, and during
    B) Fahrenheit, during
    C) Fahrenheit, whereas during
    D) Fahrenheit, but during

The Essay

Topic: Driving Age: Is Sixteen Too Young?

Passage 1: The Case for Teen Drivers by Riya Sidana

A recent spate of articles appearing in major publications are raising the question of whether states should change the driving age for teens, raising it by one or even two years. The proposals cite statistics about the risks of impulsive, distractible, inexperienced drivers on the road harming themselves and others. Unfortunately, these proposals fail to account for the hardships the change might impose on parents and teens in some families. For instance, some teens provide income by working a part-time job that they might need a car for. Furthermore, the proposals completely overlook other, potentially more useful solutions to the issue.

Teens are indeed inexperienced and impulsive decision makers, and car accidents are the number one cause of death for teens, but raising the driving age will not automatically instill more experience and stronger decision-making. Solutions such as graduated licensing and improved driver's education courses have reduced teen fatalities and road accidents in states that have implemented them, such as New Jersey and Connecticut. These states employ changing requirements for teen drivers that are stricter and harsher for younger drivers and more relaxed as drivers grow more competent. In addition to greater penalties, increasing the amount of supervised driving time and limiting the number of passengers a teen can carry help to gradually improve that teen's skills on the road.

Before eliminating a beloved rite of passage for American teens, inconveniencing families, and demonstrating to teens that that they cannot be trusted, states should seek to address dangers and problems with solutions that have been proven to work.

Passage 2: Raising the Driving Age by Thomas Maddow

In 2010, 33 percent of deaths of teens aged sixteen to nineteen were caused by motor vehicle crashes.

Talking on a phone can double the likelihood of an accident, and more than 56 percent of teens admit to using a cell phone while driving.

Of all these groups, sixteen-year-olds have higher crash rates than any other age.

These are just a few of the statistics that demonstrate the need for serious consideration of the age at which we allow our teens to drive. The driving age should be legally raised to seventeen or even eighteen, giving teens time to develop a stronger ability to make responsible choices on the road, avoid the pressures of showing off dangerously for friends, and gain a greater understanding of the responsibilities of a driver. While teens understandably long for the freedom of the road and feel that another year of waiting may be impossible to bear, many other industrialized nations impose an older driving age, and it is the responsibility of adults and lawmakers to do what is best for teens—despite their protests.

Prompt

The author of passage 1 argues that rather than changing the driving age, states should add limitations and rules for younger drivers. The writer of passage 2 suggests that the correct course is to raise the driving age.

In your response, analyze both texts. Write a persuasive essay explaining which side is more convincing, using examples from each text to support your argument.

Mathematics

Directions: Read the problem carefully, and choose the best answer.

1. Classify the number $\frac{13}{14}$.
    A) Irrational
    B) Imaginary
    C) Rational
    D) Integer
    E) Complex

2. If $16^{x+10} = 8^{3x}$, what is the value of x?
    A) 0.5
    B) 2
    C) 4
    D) 5
    E) 8

3. If $j = 4$, what is the value of $2(j-4)^4 - j + \frac{1}{2}j$?
   A) 0
   B) –2
   C) 2
   D) 4
   E) 32

4. Simplify: $(-7 + 2i) - 2(4 - 3i)$
   A) $-15 - 4i$
   B) $-15 - i$
   C) $-15 + 5i$
   D) $-15 + 8i$
   E) $-15 - 8i$

5. Simplify: $(4.71 \times 10^3) - (2.98 \times 10^2)$
   A) 1.73×10
   B) 4.412×10^2
   C) 1.73×10^3
   D) -14.038×10^5
   E) 4.412×10^3

6. A restaurant offers burritos on a corn or a flour tortilla, 5 types of meat, 6 types of cheese, and 3 different toppings. When ordering, customers can choose 1 type of tortilla, 1 meat, and 1 cheese. They can then add any of the 3 toppings. How many different burrito combinations are possible?
   A) 180
   B) 330
   C) 480
   D) 660
   E) 1620

7. The average speed of cars on a highway (s) is inversely proportional to the number of cars on the road (n). If a car drives at 65 mph when there are 250 cars on the road, how fast will a car drive when there are 325 cars on the road?
   A) 50 mph
   B) 55 mph
   C) 60 mph
   D) 85 mph
   E) 87 mph

8. If $\triangle ABD \sim \triangle DEF$ and the similarity ratio is $3:4$, what is the measure of DE if $AB = 12$?
   A) 6
   B) 9
   C) 12
   D) 16
   E) 96

9. Simplify: $(1.2 \times 10^{-3})(1.13 \times 10^{-4})$
    A) 1.356×10^{-12}
    B) 1.356×10^{-7}
    C) 1.356×10^{-1}
    D) 1.356×10
    E) 1.356×10^{12}

10. The pie graph below shows how a state's government plans to spend its annual budget of $3 billion. How much more money does the state plan to spend on infrastructure than education?

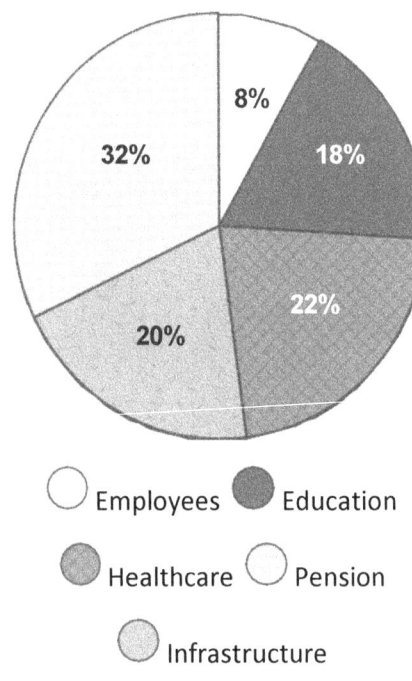

    A) $60,000,000
    B) $120,000,000
    C) $300,000,000
    D) $540,000,000
    E) $600,000,000

11. Which of the following is equivalent to $z^3(z+2)^2 - 4z^3 + 2$?
    A) 2
    B) $z^5 + 4z^4 + 4z^3 + 2$
    C) $z^6 + 4z^3 + 2$
    D) $z^5 + 4z^4 + 2$
    E) $z^5 + 4z^3 + 6$

12. Which of the following is equivalent to $54z^4 + 18z^3 + 3z + 3$?
    A) $18z^4 + 6z^3 + z + 1$
    B) $3z(18z^3 + 6z^2 + 1)$
    C) $3(18z^4 + 6z^3 + z + 1)$
    D) $72z^7 + 3z$
    E) $54(z^4 + 18z^3 + 3z + 3)$

13. Which of the following represents a linear equation?
    A) $\sqrt[3]{y} = x$
    B) $\sqrt[3]{x} = y$
    C) $\sqrt[3]{y} = x^2$
    D) $y = \sqrt[6]{x^3}$
    E) $y = \sqrt[3]{x^3}$

14. Simplify: $\frac{7.2 \times 10^6}{1.6 \times 10^{-3}}$
    A) 4.5×10^{-9}
    B) 4.5×10^{-3}
    C) 4.5×10^{-2}
    D) 4.5×10^3
    E) 4.5×10^9

15. Line a and line b are perpendicular and intersect at the point $(-100, 100)$. If $(-95, 115)$ is a point on line b, which of the following could be a point on line a?
    A) $(-112, -104)$
    B) $(-112, 104)$
    C) $(-100, -95)$
    D) $(-95, 115)$
    E) $(104, 168)$

16. Which of the following has the greatest value?
    A) $20 - (-20)$
    B) $-16 - 17 + 31$
    C) $18 - 15 + 27$
    D) $-20 + 10 + 10$
    E) $-4(3)(-2)$

17. Which of the following is a solution of the given equation?

    $$4(m + 4)^2 - 4m^2 + 20 = 276$$

    A) 3
    B) 4
    C) 6
    D) 12
    E) 24

18. Which of the following is the y-intercept of the given equation?

$$7y - 42x + 7 = 0$$

  A) (0, 1)
  B) (6, 0)
  C) (0, −1)
  D) (−1, 0)
  E) (0, 7)

19. Fifteen DVDs are to be arranged on a shelf. Four of the DVDs are horror films, six are comedies, and five are science fiction. In how many ways can the DVDs be arranged if DVDs of the same genre must be placed together?
  A) 1800
  B) 2,073,600
  C) 6,220,800
  D) 12,441,600
  E) 131,216,200

20. The coordinates of point A are (7, 12) and the coordinates of point C are (− 3, 10). If C is the midpoint of AB, what are the coordinates of point B?
  A) (− 13, 8)
  B) (− 13, 11)
  C) (2, 11)
  D) (2, 14)
  E) (17, 14)

21. Which of the following is not a negative value?
  A) $(-3)(-1)(2)(-1)$
  B) $14 - 7 + (-7)$
  C) $7 - 10 + (-8)$
  D) $-5(-2)(-3)$
  E) $-10 - (-8)$

22. What is the x-intercept of the given equation?

$$10x + 10y = 10$$

  A) (1, 0)
  B) (0, 1)
  C) (0, 0)
  D) (1, 1)
  E) (10, 10)

23. A company interviewed 21 applicants for a recent opening. Of these applicants, 7 wore blue and 6 wore white, while 5 applicants wore both blue and white. What is the number of applicants who wore neither blue nor white?
   A) 1
   B) 6
   C) 8
   D) 12
   E) 13

24. A high school cross country team sent 25 percent of its runners to a regional competition. Of these, 10 percent won medals. If 2 runners earned medals, how many members does the cross country team have?
   A) 8
   B) 10
   C) 80
   D) 125
   E) 1250

25. What is the slope of the graph below?

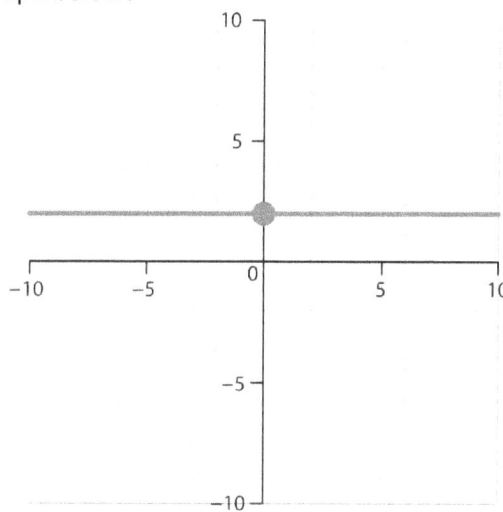

   A) ∞
   B) Nonexistent
   C) 0
   D) 1
   E) 4

26. What is the value of z in the following system?
$$z - 2x = 14$$
$$2z - 6x = 18$$

   A) −7
   B) −2
   C) 3
   D) 5
   E) 24

27. 50 shares of a financial stock and 10 shares of an auto stock are valued at $1,300. If 10 shares of the financial stock and 10 shares of the auto stock are valued at $500, what is the value of 50 shares of the auto stock?
- A) $30
- B) $20
- C) $1300
- D) $1500
- E) $1800

28. A pair of 6-sided dice is rolled 10 times. What is the probability that in exactly 3 of those rolls, the sum of the dice will be 5?
- A) 0.14%
- B) 7.2%
- C) 11.1%
- D) 30%
- E) 60%

29. Which inequality is represented by the following graph?

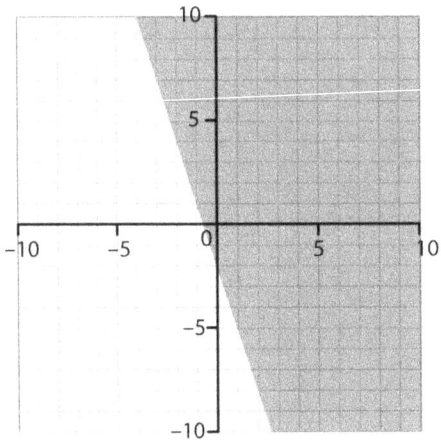

- A) $y \geq -3x - 2$
- B) $y \geq 3x - 2$
- C) $y > -3x - 2$
- D) $y \leq -3x - 2$
- E) $y > -3x + 2$

30. Cone A is similar to cone B with a scale factor of $3:4$. If the volume of cone A is 54π, what is the volume of cone B?
- A) 72π
- B) 128π
- C) 162π
- D) 216π
- E) 378π

31. What are the roots of the function $f(x) = 4x^2 - 6x + 7$?
   A) $\{\frac{3+i\sqrt{19}}{4}, \frac{3-i\sqrt{19}}{4}\}$
   B) $\{0, 2\}$
   C) $\{\frac{6+\sqrt{-76}}{4}, \frac{(6-\sqrt{-76})}{4}\}$
   D) $\{\frac{3+i\sqrt{-5}}{4}, \frac{3-i\sqrt{-5}}{4}\}$
   E) $\{\frac{3+\sqrt{19}}{4}, \frac{3-\sqrt{19}}{4}\}$

32. Convert 8 pounds, 8 ounces to kilograms to the nearest tenth of a kilogram.
   A) 3.9 kilograms
   B) 4.1 kilograms
   C) 17.6 kilograms
   D) 18.7 kilograms
   E) 19.36 kilograms

33. Which of the angles in the figure below are congruent?

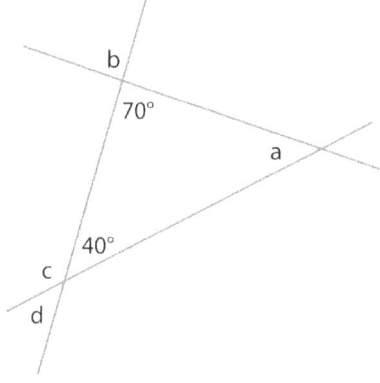

   A) *a* and *d*
   B) *b* and *d*
   C) *a* and *b*
   D) *c* and *b*
   E) *c* and *a*

34. Which statement about the following set is true?

$$\{60, 5, 18, 20, 37, 37, 11, 90, 72\}$$

   A) The median and the mean are equal.
   B) The mean is less than the mode.
   C) The mode is greater than the median.
   D) The median is less than the mean.
   E) The mode and the mean are equal.

35. Which of the following is the solution set to the given inequality?

$$2x + 4 \geq 5(x - 4) - 3(x - 4)$$

A) $(-\infty, \infty)$
B) $(-\infty, 6.5]$
C) $[6.5, -\infty)$
D) $(-\infty, 6.5) \cup (6.5, \infty)$
E) ∅

36. Which of the following is a solution to the inequality $2x + y \leq -10$?

A) $(0, 0)$
B) $(10, 2)$
C) $(10, 10)$
D) $(-10, -10)$
E) $(0, 10)$

37. What is the total number of 6-digit numbers in which each individual digit is less than 3 or greater than 6?

A) 38,880
B) 46,656
C) 80,452
D) 101,370
E) 279,936

38. What are the roots of the equation $y = 16x^3 - 48x^2$?

A) $\{\frac{3+i\sqrt{5}}{2}, \frac{3-i\sqrt{5}}{2}\}$
B) {0, 3, –3}
C) {0, 3i, –3i}
D) {0, 3}
E) {0}

39. What is the maximum value of the function $f(x) = 3sin(x - 2) + 1$?

A) 1
B) 3
C) 4
D) 6
E) 7

40. Which of the following could be the perimeter of a triangle with two sides that measure 13 and 5?

A) 24.5
B) 26.5
C) 36
D) 37
E) 37.5

41. In a theater, there are 4500 lower-level seats and 2000 upper-level seats. What is the ratio of lower-level seats to total seats?

  A) $\frac{4}{9}$

  B) $\frac{4}{13}$

  C) $\frac{9}{13}$

  D) $\frac{9}{4}$

  E) $\frac{13}{9}$

42. What is the axis of symmetry for the given parabola?

$$y = -2(x+3)^2 + 5$$

  A) $y = 3$
  B) $x = -3$
  C) $y = -3$
  D) $x = 3$
  E) $x = 5$

43. What is the solution set for the inequality $2x^2 - 4x - 6 < 0$?
  A) $(-1, 3)$
  B) $(-\infty, \infty)$
  C) $\emptyset$
  D) $(-\infty, -1) \cup (3, \infty)$
  E) $(-1, \infty)$

44. The mean of 13 numbers is 30. The mean of 8 of these numbers is 42. What is the mean of the other 5 numbers?
  A) 5.5
  B) 10.8
  C) 16.4
  D) 21.2
  E) 30.0

45. Which of the following are the vertical asymptotes of the given function?

$$f(x) = \frac{x^3 - 16x}{-4x^2 + 4x + 24}$$

  A) $x = -4$ and $x = 4$
  B) $x = -3$ and $x = 2$
  C) $x = -2$ and $x = 3$
  D) $x = 0$ and $x = 4$
  E) $x = 0$ and $x = 2$

46. The regular octagon below is inscribed within a circle. What is the approximate difference between $arc\widehat{HB}$ and $arc\widehat{CF}$?

A) 45°
B) 90°
C) 137°
D) 320°
E) 540°

47. If the length of a rectangle is increased by 40% and its width is decreased by 40%, what is the effect on the rectangle's area?
   A) The area is the same.
   B) It increases by 16%.
   C) It increases by 20%.
   D) It decreases by 16%.
   E) It decreases by 20%.

48. Which of the following is a solution to the given function?

$$cos\ x - sin\ x = -1$$

A) 0
B) $\frac{\pi}{4}$
C) $\frac{\pi}{3}$
D) $\frac{\pi}{2}$
E) $\frac{3\pi}{2}$

49. Allison used $2\frac{1}{2}$ cups of flour to make a cake, and $\frac{3}{4}$ cup of flour to make a pie. If she started with 4 cups of flour, how many cups of flour does she have left?

   A) $\frac{3}{4}$
   B) 1
   C) $\frac{5}{4}$
   D) $\frac{5}{2}$
   E) $\frac{13}{4}$

50. In the diagram, $\overline{BD}$ is a diameter of circle O. If $AB = 55°$ and $BC = 85°$, what is the measure of angle DMC?

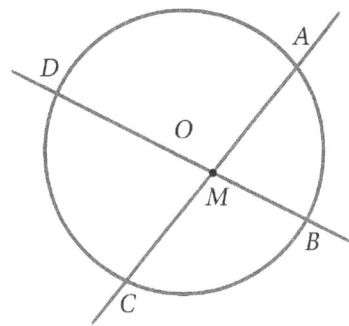

   A) 55°
   B) 70°
   C) 75°
   D) 80°
   E) 82.5°

51. What are the real zero(s) of the following polynomial?

$$2n^2 + 2n - 12 = 0$$

   A) $\{-3, 2\}$
   B) $\{2\}$
   C) $\{2, 0\}$
   D) $\{2, 4\}$
   E) There are no real zeros of n.

52. What is the greatest number of complex roots a 17th degree polynomial can have?
   A) 8
   B) 15
   C) 16
   D) $16i$
   E) 17

Practice Test #1

53. A bag contains 6 blue, 8 silver, and 4 green marbles. Two marbles are drawn from the bag. What is the probability that the second marble drawn will be green if replacement is not allowed?
    A) $\frac{2}{51}$
    B) $\frac{2}{9}$
    C) $\frac{4}{17}$
    D) $\frac{11}{17}$
    E) $\frac{7}{9}$

54. Which of the following is the vertical asymptote of the function $f(x) = \frac{x+4}{-2x-6}$?
    A) $x = -6$
    B) $x = -3$
    C) $y = -2$
    D) $y = \frac{1}{2}$
    E) $x = 3$

55. A cube is inscribed in a sphere such that each vertex on the cube touches the sphere. If the volume of the sphere is 972π cm^3, what is the approximate volume of the cube in cubic centimeters?
    A) 9
    B) 104
    C) 927
    D) 1125
    E) 1729

Science

Directions: Read the question carefully, and choose the best answer.

1. A chemical reaction occurs when one or more reactants undergoes a chemical change to produce new substances called products. The reaction is described in a chemical equation with the reactants on the left, the products on the right, and an arrow in the middle. Five types of chemical reactions are shown in the following table.

Type of Reaction	General Formula
Synthesis	$A + B \rightarrow C$
Decomposition	$A \rightarrow B + C$
Single displacement	$AB + C \rightarrow A + BC$
Double displacement	$AB + CD \rightarrow AC + BD$
Combustion	$C_xH_yO_z + O_2 \rightarrow CO_2 + H_2O$

332   Practice Test #1

Based on the information in the table, which of the following is a decomposition reaction?
- A) $2Na + Cl_2 \rightarrow 2NaCl$
- B) $Zn + 2HCl \rightarrow ZnCl_2 + H_2$
- C) $CH_4 + 2O_2 \rightarrow CO_2 + 2H_2O$
- D) $H_2CO_3 \rightarrow H_2O + CO_2$

Question 2 is based on the following passage:

Water moves across cell membranes through the process of osmosis. The concentration of solute inside and outside a cell will determine which way water moves across the membrane. Water molecules will move down their concentration gradient, meaning they will move from areas of high concentration to areas of low concentration. In other words, water will flow into the cell when the solute concentration in the cell is higher than the environment. The reverse is also true—water will flow out of the cell when the solute concentration is lower in the cell than in the surrounding environment.

2. A certain prokaryotic organism typically lives in a 10 percent saline concentration environment. Which of the following environments would cause the organism to lose mass due to osmosis?
- A) A solution of pure water
- B) A solution of 5 percent saline concentration
- C) A solution of 10 percent saline concentration
- D) A solution of 20 percent saline concentration

3. Which planet orbits closest to Earth?
- A) Mercury
- B) Venus
- C) Jupiter
- D) Saturn

Question 4 is based on the following passage:

Electrical charge can be positive (+), negative (−), or neutral. Objects that are both positive or both negative will repel each other. Objects that have opposing positive and negative charges will be attracted to each other. Neutral objects will not be affected by either positive or negative objects.

4. Two negative charges are held at a distance of 1 meter from each other. What will the charges do when they are released?
- A) Remain at rest
- B) Move closer together
- C) Move farther apart
- D) Move together in the same direction

5. A phylogenetic tree is a diagram that shows the evolutionary relationship between species based on their genetic and phenotypic similarities. Each node, where a branch starts, represents the most recent common ancestor shared by the species on the branches extending from that node.

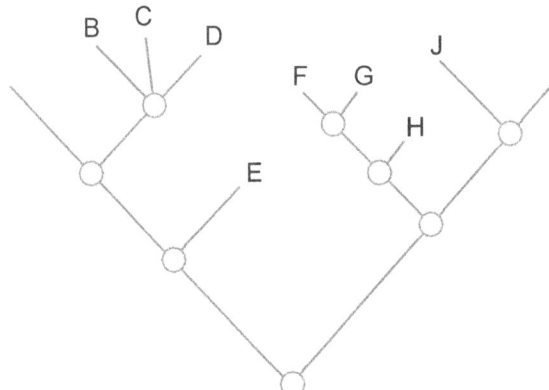

Which nodes represent common ancestors shared by species *H* and *K*?
- A) 1 and 2
- B) 2 and 3
- C) 3 and 4
- D) 4 and 5

Questions 6 and 7 refer to the following passage.

A scientist designs an experiment to test the hypothesis that exposure to more sunlight will increase the growth rate of elodea, a type of aquatic plant. The scientist has accumulated data from previous experiments that identify the average growth rate of elodea exposed to natural sunlight in the wild.

In the experiment setup, there are three tanks housing ten elodea each. Tank A is positioned in front of a window to receive natural sunlight similar to what elodea are exposed to; tank B is positioned in front of the same window but has an additional sunlight-replicating lamp affixed to it; and tank C is positioned in a dark corner with no exposure to natural sunlight.

6. When setting up the preceding experiment, the scientist has the option of using a separate water filter for each of the three tanks or using a single filtration system that attaches all three and affects them simultaneously. Which of the following filter setups makes a more valid experiment and why?
- A) Separate filters for each of the three tanks, because this ensures a higher quality of water for each tank
- B) One filtration system for all three tanks, because this makes filtration a controlled variable
- C) One filtration system for all three tanks, because this reduces the workload for the researcher
- D) Separate filters for each of the three tanks, because this adds another variable to be tested and analyzed for inclusion in the experiment's results

7. Which of the following is the control group in the preceding experiment?
- A) Tank A
- B) Tank B
- C) Tank C
- D) There is no control group in this experiment.

8. Which of the following is NOT a typical property of metals?
    A) Metals have low densities.
    B) Metals are malleable.
    C) Metals are good conductors of electricity and heat.
    D) Metals in solid state consist of ordered structures with tightly packed atoms.

Question 9 is based on the following passage:

Weathering is the breaking down of rocks, minerals, and organic materials. Weathering can be either mechanical or chemical. Mechanical weathering occurs when a material is physically torn apart. Chemical weathering occurs when a chemical reaction causes the material to decompose, forming new materials in the process.

9. Which action is an example of mechanical weathering?
    A) Calcium carbonate reacts with water to form a cave.
    B) An iron gate rusts.
    C) Tree roots grow under the foundation of a house and cause cracks.
    D) Bananas turn brown after they are peeled.

10. Which of the following is NOT present in an animal cell?
    A) Nucleus
    B) Mitochondria
    C) Cytoplasm
    D) Cell wall

11. Which of the following describes a physical change?
    A) Water becomes ice.
    B) Batter is baked into a cake.
    C) An iron fence rusts.
    D) A firecracker explodes.

Questions 12 and 13 refer to the following passage and figure.

Gastric lipase is an enzyme that breaks down fat produced by cells that line the stomach. α-amylase is an enzyme produced in the pancreas that helps break down starches into simple sugars. It is released into the small intestine.

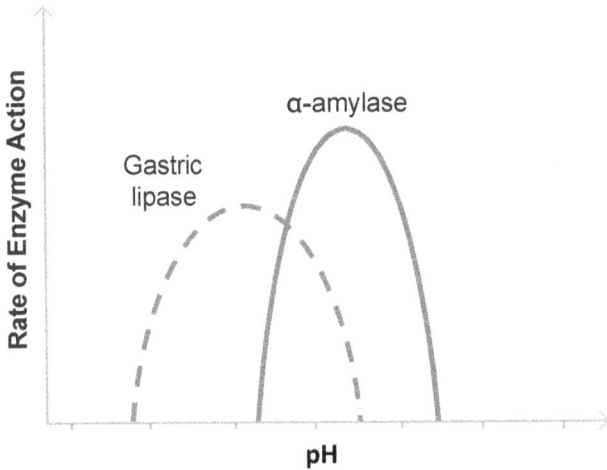

12. The small intestine has a pH higher than 7. According to the graph, what will happen to the activity of gastric lipase when it enters the small intestine?
    A) Its activity will increase.
    B) Its activity will remain the same.
    C) Its activity will increase initially, then decrease.
    D) Its activity will decrease.

13. According to the preceding graph, what is the optimal pH level for α-amylase?
    A) 4
    B) 6
    C) 7
    D) 9

14. Entropy is often described as a measure of randomness or chaos in a system. It can also be thought of as the number of possible configurations, or microstates, within a system. Increasing the number of possible microstates in a system will increase the chaos or randomness of a system: with increasing possible configurations, it is less likely that molecules will be in a particular microstate. This principle explains why gases spontaneously expand: molecules have more possible arrangements when they have more space to move around.

Systems will favor processes that create more possible configurations for the molecules in the system. Entropy will increase when temperature, volume, or the number of molecules in the system increases.

Which of the following changes will increase the entropy of the system?
    A) splitting water to form hydrogen gas and oxygen gas
    B) freezing gaseous carbon dioxide to form dry ice
    C) using a piston to compress the air in a cylinder
    D) condensing water from the atmosphere on a cold glass surface

15. How long does it take the Earth to rotate on its axis?
    A) One hour
    B) One day
    C) One month
    D) One year

16. As a gas giant, the planet Jupiter has a much lower density than terrestrial planets. Earth has a density of 5.51 grams per cubic centimeter, but Jupiter's density is only 1.33 grams per cubic centimeter. The largest planet in the solar system, Jupiter has a radius of 71,492 kilometers, a remarkable size more than ten times that of Earth. By volume, more than 1,300 Earths would fit within Jupiter. Jupiter has a solid core and a gaseous atmosphere that transitions slowly into a liquid state with no definable lower boundary.

Which of the following planets is most similar to Jupiter?

	Planet	Density (grams per cm^3)	Radius (miles)
A)	Neptune	1.6	24,746
B)	Mercury	5.4	1516
C)	Mars	3.9	3396
D)	Venus	5.2	6051

17. When Earth moves between the Moon and the Sun, it is called a
    A) Solar eclipse
    B) Lunar eclipse
    C) Black hole
    D) Supernova

18. Which of the following scenarios accurately describes primary succession?
    A) The ground is scorched by a lava flow; later the establishment of lichens begins on the volcanic rock, leading to the eventual formation of soils.
    B) A meadow is destroyed by a flood; eventually small grasses begin to grow again to begin establishing a healthy meadow ecosystem.
    C) A fire destroys a section of a forest; once the ashes clear, small animals begin making their homes within the area.
    D) A farmer overuses the land causing all the minerals and nutrients in the soil to be used up. Some leftover grass seeds in the soil begin to sprout, repopulating the land.

Questions 19 and 20 refer to the following graph.

19. Which of the salts on the preceding solubility curve graph has the greatest solubility at 50°C?
    A) Na_2SO_4
    B) $NaCl$
    C) $Ba(NO_3)_2$
    D) Na_2HAsO_4

20. At what temperature is the highest mass of NaCl soluble in 100 grams of water?
    A) 0°C
    B) 40°C
    C) 80°C
    D) 100°C

21. An experiment was conducted to study the effect of temperature on the survival rate of a fish species. The study included five populations, each held for ten days at a different temperature. The number of individuals in each population was recorded after five days and after ten days. The results are shown in the following table.

Temperature	Survival Rate		
	Day 1	Day 5	Day 10
15°C	100%	94%	80%
20°C	100%	96%	94%
25°C	100%	84%	73%
30°C	100%	81%	58%
35°C	100%	72%	41%

Which of the following statements is supported by the observations recorded in the table?
A) The population held at 30°C had the lowest survival rate after ten days.
B) Of the five populations, only the one held at 35°C had a survival rate of less than 50 percent after ten days.
C) After ten days, the survival rate of the population held at 30°C was half the survival rate of the population held at 15°C.
D) The survival rate after five days was lowest for the population held at 30°C.

22. A scientist discovers a new species of snail that lives in the ocean. He tested the ability of this species to handle heat by measuring its growth rate as he increased the temperature of the water. He also tested two different concentrations of salt to determine which type of marine environment the snail would be best suited for. Which of the following is the dependent variable in the experiment described above?
A) Salt concentration
B) Temperature
C) Growth rate
D) Number of snails

23. Each cell organelle performs a specific task within a cell. The genetic material, which contains the code needed to produce proteins, is held in the nucleus. Ribosomes produce proteins that are processed and transported by the Golgi apparatus. In plant cells, chloroplasts transform the sun's energy into sugar; in both plants and animals, mitochondria transform sugar into the energy-rich molecule ATP. Waste products from all these processes are stored in vacuoles.

Which of the following cells would likely contain a higher than normal number of mitochondria?
A) Muscle cell
B) Skin cell
C) Egg
D) Red blood cell

Questions 24 – 27 refer to the following passage and graph.

A survivorship curve shows the percentage of individuals in a population who survive over time. Type I species produce a small number of offspring and care closely for them. Type III species produce large numbers of offspring but do little or no caretaking for their young. Type II species show a balance between number of offspring and caretaking.

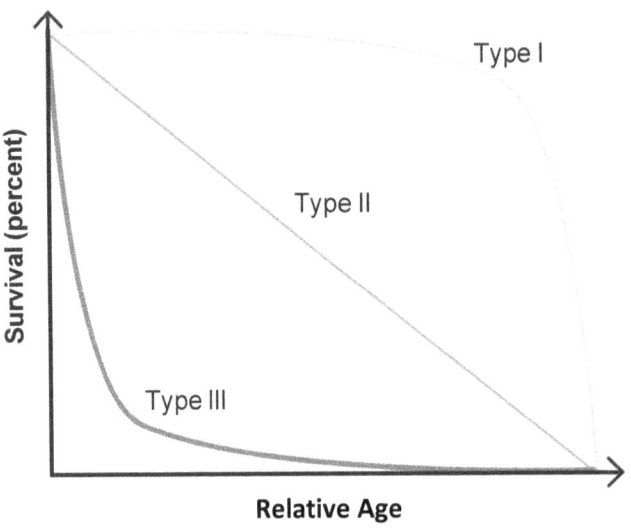

24. Which survivorship curve would describe mice?
    A) Type I
    B) Type II
    C) Type III
    D) There is not enough information to answer the question.

25. Which survivorship curve would describe humans?
    A) Type I
    B) Type II
    C) Type III
    D) There is not enough information to answer the question.

26. Which survivorship curve would describe oak trees?
    A) Type I
    B) Type II
    C) Type III
    D) There is not enough information to answer the question.

27. Which survivorship curve would describe ducks?
    A) Type I
    B) Type II
    C) Type III
    D) There is not enough information to answer the question.

28. What type of energy is stored in the bond between hydrogen and oxygen in water (H_2O)?
    A) Mechanical
    B) Chemical
    C) Nuclear
    D) Electric

29. Which of the following aquatic biomes are located where freshwater streams empty into the ocean?
    A) Wetlands
    B) Coral reef
    C) Estuaries
    D) Littoral

30. Why do some photosynthetic structures, like leaves, appear green?
    A) The epidermis of the leaf absorbs red and blue light.
    B) The epidermis of the leaf absorbs green light.
    C) The chlorophyll of the leaf absorbs red and blue light.
    D) The chlorophyll of the leaf absorbs green light.

31. A system is the part of the universe where an actual process takes place or where observations are made; the rest of the universe is the surroundings.

There are three types of systems. An open system allows the exchange of energy or matter between the system and its surrounding. In a closed system, only exchange of energy between the system and its surroundings is possible; exchange of matter is not possible. Finally, in an isolated system there is no exchange of energy or matter between the system and its surroundings.

Which of the following is a closed system?
    A) A glass of water at room temperature
    B) A balloon filled with warm water
    C) An insulated container filled with ice water
    D) An uncovered pot of boiling water on the stove

32. Activation energy is the energy required for a chemical reaction to occur. If the activation energy for a reaction is too high, a reaction may not proceed or may proceed only at a very slow rate. The activation energy can be modified by the addition of a catalyst. A catalyst is a compound that lowers the activation energy of a reaction by changing the mechanism of the reaction to one with a lower activation energy. This process will increase the rate of the chemical reaction.

A catalyst increases a reaction rate by doing which of the following?
    A) Increasing the activation energy
    B) Increasing the concentration of the reactants
    C) Changing the type of energy required to move the reaction forward
    D) Changing the reaction mechanism

33. Displacement (d) is a measure of how far an object has moved from its starting point, usually given in meters (m). Velocity (v) is the distance covered by an object over a given period of time, usually given in meters per second (m/s). The change in velocity over time is called acceleration (a) and is measured in meters per second squared (m/s^2). Distance, velocity, time, and acceleration are related through the following formulas:

$$d = \frac{1}{2} at^2 + v_i t$$

$$v_f = v_i + at$$

A race car accelerates from 0 meters per second to 4 meters per second in 8 seconds. What is the race car's acceleration?
- A) 1 m/s^2
- B) 2 m/s^2
- C) 4 m/s^2
- D) 8 m/s^2

Use the following table to answer questions 34 and 35.

Planet	Mass	Acceleration Due to Gravity (g)
Mercury	3.18×10^{23}	3.59
Earth	5.98×10^{24}	9.81
Mars	6.42×10^{23}	3.77
Jupiter	1.90×10^{27}	25.95
Neptune	1.03×10^{26}	14.07

34. Free fall is a type of motion in which the only force acting on an object is gravity. The velocity of an object in free fall is described as the equation $v = gt$, where v is velocity, g is the acceleration due to gravity, and t is time.

On which planet would an object reach the highest speed after being in free fall for three seconds?
- A) Earth
- B) Mars
- C) Jupiter
- D) Neptune

35. Weight (W) is defined as the force exerted on an object by gravity. It is equal to the acceleration due to gravity (g) times the object's mass (m): $W = ga$.

On Earth, objects A and B have the same mass and weight. If object B is moved to Mars, which of the following statements is true?
- A) Object A now has a greater mass and weight.
- B) Object B now has a greater mass and weight.
- C) Both objects have the same mass, but object A now has the greater weight.
- D) Both objects have the same mass, but object B now has the greater weight.

Questions 36 and 37 refer to the following passage.

In a chemical reaction, it is only the number of electrons in an atom that changes—the nucleus remains unaffected. Conversely, in a nuclear reaction, changes occur in an atom's nucleus, affecting the number of protons, neutrons, or both. In a nuclear reaction, unstable atoms called radioisotopes spontaneously emit particles and energy.

The time it takes for substances to decay varies widely—some radioisotopes decay completely in only a few seconds, whereas others decay over millions of years. The time it takes for half of a sample to decay is that substance's half-life (h or $t_{\frac{1}{2}}$). The equation for half-life is written as

$$A = A_0 \left(\frac{1}{2}\right)^{\frac{t}{h}}$$

where A is the final amount, A_0 is the initial amount, t is the time, and h is the half-life.

36. Which of the following is the best description of radioactive decay?
    A) The absorption of energy by an atom's nucleus
    B) The movement of electrons into an atom's nucleus
    C) The release of particles by the atom's nucleus
    D) The sharing of electrons between atoms

37. The half-life of iodine-131 is eight days. How much of a 120-gram sample of iodine-131 will remain after twenty-four days?
    A) 0 grams
    B) 15 grams
    C) 30 grams
    D) 60 grams

38. Which of the following is composed only of members of the same species?
    A) Ecosystem
    B) Community
    C) Biome
    D) Population

39. In 1897, J.J. Thomson discovered the existence of electrons. Thomson incorporated the electron into a new model of the atom. He proposed that the atom had a spherical shape with a uniformly distributed positive charge. The electrons, which made up only a small portion of the atom's mass, were uniformly embedded in the positive mass. This model is also called the plum pudding model.

Ernest Rutherford built on Thomson's model of the atom by introducing the concept of the nucleus. From his experiments, Rutherford concluded that an atom is not just empty space with electrons distributed inside it. Instead, an atom has a positively charged nucleus that contains most of its mass.

Which of the following changes did Ernest Rutherford make to the plum pudding model of the atom?
- A) Rutherford claimed that an atom was composed of both positively and negatively charged particles.
- B) Rutherford claimed that the positive charge of the atom was contained in a small area at the center of the atom.
- C) Rutherford claimed that the nucleus of an atom contained both positive and neutral particles.
- D) Rutherford claimed that the mass of an atom was contained mostly in the electrons.

40. A barnacle is attached to the outside of the whale to collect and consume particulate matter as the whale moves through the ocean. The barnacle benefits, while the whale is unaffected. The phenomenon described is an example of
- A) predation
- B) commensalism
- C) mutualism
- D) parasitism

41. A team of ecologists tested the effect of parenting in a species of bird for a period of five years. For this particular bird species, both males and females cared for the young. During their research, the ecologists transferred chicks between sites to manufacture small broods of chicks (three to four), normal broods (five to six), and large broods (seven to eight). The researchers then measured the percentage of male and female parent birds that survived the winter. The data is represented in the graph.

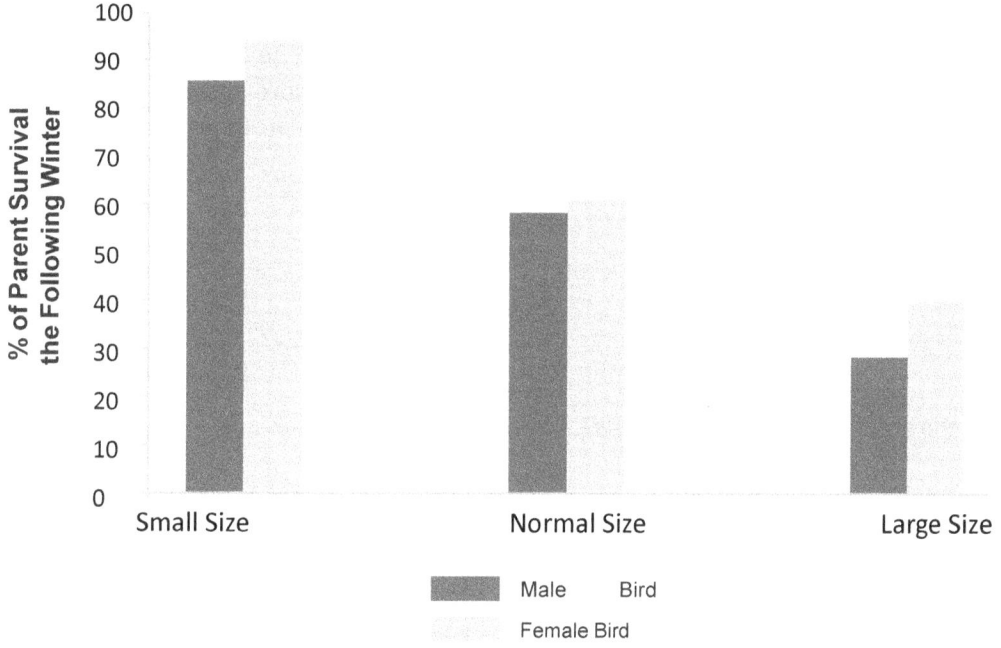

Which of the following conclusions would be accurate based on the data represented in the preceding graph?
- A) There is an apparent negative correlation between brood (nesting) size and parental survival.
- B) The chicks in the smaller nests received more food than those in the larger nest sites. This allowed them more weight gain and a better chance of surviving the winter.
- C) The survival rate of the female birds is more drastically affected by the larger nest sizes than the male birds.
- D) The survival rate of the male birds increased by 50 percent at the larger nest sizes than the smaller nest sizes.

42. Thermal conductors are substances that easily absorb and release heat. Diamond is a good thermal conductor, as are many metals. Thermal insulators do not absorb or release heat easily and are used to prevent heat transfer. Air, for example, is a good insulator. Materials that trap air, such as feathers and foams, are commonly used as insulators.

A rubber ball, a metal ball, and a wooden ball are placed in the same pot of boiling water. Which ball will have the highest temperature?
- A) The wooden ball will have the highest temperature.
- B) The rubber ball will have the highest temperature.
- C) The metal ball will have the highest temperature.
- D) All three balls will have the same temperature.

Questions 43 – 49 refer to the following passage and the periodic table on page 175.

All matter is composed of atoms. Atoms, in turn, are made up of subatomic particles. Protons, which are positive, and neutrons, which are negative, form the nucleus of the atom. Negative particles called electrons orbit the nucleus. All atoms of the same element have the same number of protons, which is that element's atomic number. On the periodic table, an element's atomic number is written above the element's symbol.

A neutral atom will have an equal number of protons and electrons. When a neutral atom loses or gains electrons, it gains or loses charge accordingly, forming an ion. An ion with more protons than electrons has a positive charge and is called a cation. An ion with more electrons than protons has a negative charge and is considered an anion.

43. Which of the following ions has eleven protons and ten electrons?
    A) Na^+
    B) Ca
    C) Na
    D) Na^-

44. Which ion has the greatest number of protons?
    A) Mg^{2+}
    B) Br^-
    C) Na^+
    D) N^{3-}

45. Which of the following groups on the periodic table will typically adopt a charge of +1 when forming ionic compounds?
    A) Alkaline earth metals
    B) Lanthanides
    C) Actinides
    D) Alkali metals

46. Which element is a metalloid?
    A) Rubidium
    B) Vanadium
    C) Antimony
    D) Iodine

47. An atom of oxygen (O) has eight protons. How many electrons does a neutral atom of oxygen have?
    A) Two
    B) Four
    C) Six
    D) Eight

48. Which of the following determines the atomic number of an atom?
    A) The number of electrons orbiting the nucleus
    B) The number of protons in the nucleus
    C) The number of protons and neutrons in the nucleus
    D) The number of protons and electrons in the atom

49. Which element has chemical properties most similar to sulfur?
   A) Fluorine
   B) Argon
   C) Phosphorus
   D) Oxygen

50. Most cell organelles are membrane-bound structures, and each performs an important cellular process. The nucleus, for instance, is a spherical structure that houses an organism's genetic information. The Golgi apparatus collects, packages, and distributes the proteins produced by ribosomes, which are found either free in the cytoplasm or attached to the endoplasmic reticulum. The Krebs cycle and electron transport chain are carried out in various parts of mitochondria; therefore, much of the energy-producing metabolism of a cell takes place in these organelles. Chloroplasts are plant organelles; the reactions of photosynthesis are catalyzed in these compartments. Vacuoles are also typically found in plant cells; these organelles hold water, waste, and other important molecules.

Seeds store proteins for use by the young growing plant. Which organelle would you expect to store these proteins?
   A) Rough endoplasmic reticulum
   B) Golgi apparatus
   C) Vacuole
   D) Chloroplast

Use the following passage and the diagram to answer questions 51 and 52.

The circulatory system includes two closed loops. In the pulmonary loop, deoxygenated blood leaves the heart and travels to the lungs, where it loses carbon dioxide and becomes rich in oxygen. The oxygenated blood then returns to the heart, which pumps it through the systemic loop. The systemic loop delivers oxygen to the rest of the body and returns deoxygenated blood to the heart.

51. Which blood vessel(s) carry oxygenated blood?
    A) superior vena cava
    B) inferior vena cava
    C) pulmonary artery
    D) pulmonary veins

52. What is the role of the aorta?
    A) to carry oxygenated blood from the heart to the body
    B) to carry deoxygenated blood from the body to the heart
    C) to carry oxygenated blood from the lungs to the heart
    D) to transport blood within the heart

Questions 53 and 54 refer to the diagram below. This diagram shows the carbon cycle, which is the movement of carbon throughout the atmosphere, biosphere (plants and animals), hydro- sphere (oceans), and lithosphere (ground).

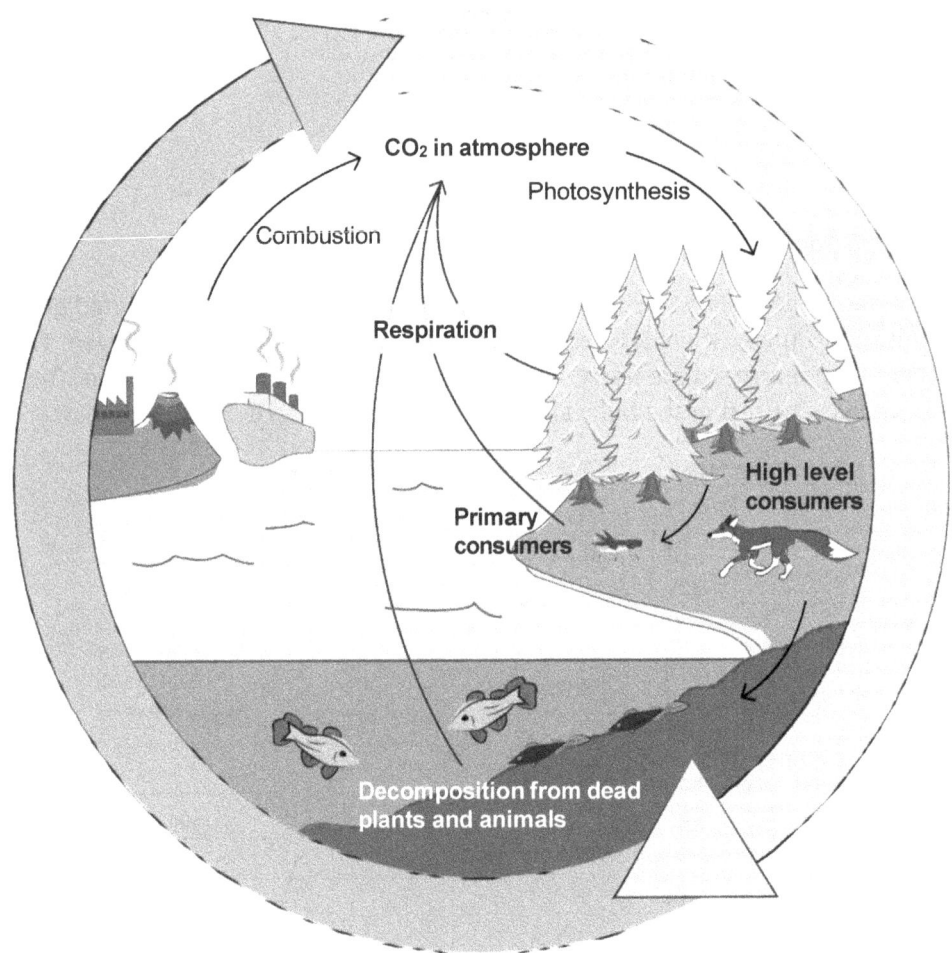

53. Which of the following decreases the amount of carbon in the atmosphere?
    A) burning fossil fuels
    B) photosynthesis
    C) deforestation
    D) animal respiration

54. Which of the following is NOT a natural carbon reservoir in the carbon cycle?
    A) the oceans
    B) the soil
    C) the buildings
    D) the atmosphere

55. Three types of plate boundaries occur where tectonic plates meet. At a convergent plate boundary two tectonic plates move toward each other and collide, forming a mountain or a deep sea trench. At a divergent plate boundary, also called a spreading center or rift zone, the two plates are moving apart. This process creates rifts or valleys. At a transform plate boundary, the two plates are sliding past each other, causing a great deal of friction and a large buildup of energy that may be released in the form of an earthquake.

Which type of plate boundary is shown in the following diagram?

    A) Convergent plate boundary
    B) Divergent plate boundary
    C) Transform plate boundary
    D) No plate boundaries are shown

56. A solution consists of a solute and a solvent. The solute is the substance that is dissolved, and the solvent is the substance that dissolves the solute. The solubility of a solution is the maximum amount of solute that will dissolve in a specific quantity of solvent at a specified temperature. The graph below shows the solubilities of solid, liquid, and gas solutes as pressure increases.

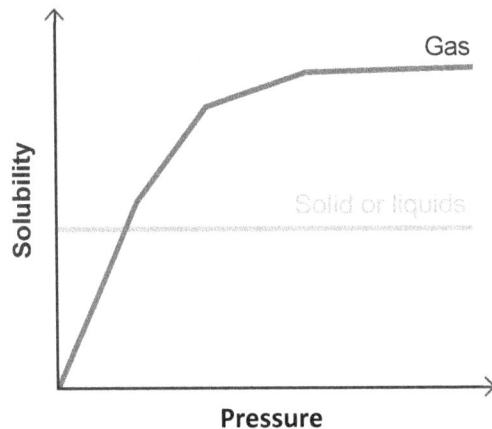

Which of the following would increase in solubility as pressure increases when it is dissolved in liquid water?
- A) solid salt
- B) carbon dioxide gas
- C) liquid ethanol
- D) solid water

Questions 57 and 58 refer to the passage and chart below.

Biomes are vast geographical areas of certain climates that share similar ecosystems with flora and fauna. Biomes are defined based on the area's temperature, rainfall, and dominant vegetation. Five biomes are described in the table below.

Biome	Temperature	Rainfall	Vegetation
tropical rainforest	hot year-round	high	dense community of diverse tree species
desert	hot during day; cold at night	low	moderately diverse community of drought-tolerant grasses and shrubs
temperate forest	mild summer; cold winter	moderate	dense community of diverse deciduous tree species
temperate grassland	warm summer; mild winter	moderate	moderately diverse community of grasses
tundra	mild summer; cold winter	low	sparse community of low-diversity grasses

57. The Atacama region of Chile is one of the driest areas in the world and is home to over 500 species of drought-tolerant vegetation. According to the table, what type of biome is the Atacama?
    A) desert
    B) temperate forest
    C) temperate grassland
    D) tundra

58. The Amazon River basin region of Brazil has some of the highest global rainfall rates, with hot temperatures year-round, and is densely forested. Many researchers argue it has the most biodiversity anywhere on the planet. According to the table, what type of biome is the Amazon?
    A) tropical rainforest
    B) temperate forest
    C) temperate grassland
    D) tundra

59. A chemical process changes the chemical composition of the reactants. These processes can be endothermic or exothermic. An endothermic process absorbs energy in the form of heat, while an exothermic process releases energy from the system into the environment. The diagrams below show the relative energy of the reactants and products during endothermic versus exothermic processes.

Which of the following is an endothermic process?
- A) Boiling water
- B) Burning wood
- C) Slicing a cake
- D) Nuclear fission in a bomb

60. The process of photosynthesis includes two parts: the light-dependent reactions and light-independent reactions. The light-dependent reactions create energy in the form of ATP and NADPH. These molecules are then used in the Calvin cycle, which is light independent. The Calvin cycle produces carbohydrates, specifically glucose ($C_6H_{12}O_6$). The balanced chemical equation for photosynthesis is shown below:

$$6CO_2 + 6H_2O \rightarrow C_6H_{12}O_6 + 6O_2$$

Which molecule is produced during the Calvin cycle?
- A) Carbon dioxide
- B) Glucose
- C) Water
- D) ATP

Social Studies

Read the question carefully, and choose the best answer.

Questions 1 and 2 are based on a political cartoon published in 1904. It shows President Theodore Roosevelt tiptoeing barefoot through the Caribbean Sea, dragging the US Navy along with him. He carries a "big stick," and the title reads "The Big Stick in the Caribbean Sea."

1. This political cartoon best represents what aspect of Theodore Roosevelt's presidential policies?
   A) His reputation as a "trust buster" in his battle against Big Business
   B) His goal to "speak softly and carry a big stick" in enforcing the Monroe Doctrine in Latin America
   C) His belief in national conservation efforts and a National Parks system
   D) His declaration that he felt as "fit as bull moose" after an assassination attempt on his life

2. What does the political cartoon imply about Theodore Roosevelt and the US Navy's involvement in Latin America at that time?
   A) Roosevelt and the US Navy tried to police Latin America while diplomatically tiptoeing there.
   B) Roosevelt and the US Navy felt smaller or inferior to Latin American governments.
   C) Roosevelt and the US Navy believed they had no role as leaders in Latin American diplomacy.
   D) Roosevelt and the US Navy did not care about the entire region.

3. What advantage did the colonists have in the American Revolution?
   A) Vast financial wealth
   B) Superior weaponry
   C) Strong leadership and knowledge of the terrain
   D) A professional military and access to mercenaries

4. Following the collapse of the Western Roman Empire, what was the status of serfs in Europe?
   A) Serfs, while bound to the land on the manors where they lived and forced to farm for the lords, were not enslaved, nor were they forced to fight for lords. Rather, they were to be protected.
   B) Serfs were agricultural slaves expected to farm the land on manors in order to support lords.
   C) Serfs were peasants on manors, expected to farm the land for lords but also able to farm their own land; they were free to leave manors if they wished but rarely did due to unsafe conditions.
   D) Serfs were agricultural slaves who were also expected to fight for lords when called upon for defense.

Questions 5 – 7 are based on the following text from the Bill of Rights. The Bill of Rights was added to the Constitution in 1789 as a political compromise. Proponents of the Bill of Rights wanted to ensure that the Constitution remained a living document that could be amended. The Bill of Rights comprises the first ten amendments to the Constitution, the foundational governing document of the United States of America.

The Bill of Rights

Amendment I

Congress shall make no law respecting an establishment of religion, or prohibiting the free exercise thereof; or abridging the freedom of speech, or of the press; or the right of the people peaceably to assemble, and to petition the government for a redress of grievances.

Amendment II

A well regulated militia, being necessary to the security of a free state, the right of the people to keep and bear arms, shall not be infringed.

Amendment III

No soldier shall, in time of peace be quartered in any house, without the consent of the owner, nor in time of war, but in a manner to be prescribed by law.

Amendment IV

The right of the people to be secure in their persons, houses, papers, and effects, against unreasonable searches and seizures, shall not be violated, and no warrants shall issue, but upon probable cause, supported by oath or affirmation, and particularly describing the place to be searched, and the persons or things to be seized.

Amendment V

No person shall be held to answer for a capital, or otherwise infamous crime, unless on a presentment or indictment of a grand jury, except in cases arising in the land or naval forces, or in the militia, when in actual service in time of war or public danger; nor shall any person be subject for the same offense to be twice put in jeopardy of life or limb; nor shall be compelled in any criminal case to be a witness against himself, nor be deprived of life, liberty, or property, without due process of law; nor shall private property be taken for public use, without just compensation.

Amendment VI

In all criminal prosecutions, the accused shall enjoy the right to a speedy and public trial, by an impartial jury of the state and district wherein the crime shall have been committed, which district shall have been previously ascertained by law, and to be informed of the nature and cause of the accusation; to be confronted with the witnesses against him; to have compulsory process for obtaining witnesses in his favor, and to have the assistance of counsel for his defense.

Amendment VII

In suits at common law, where the value in controversy shall exceed twenty dollars, the right of trial by jury shall be preserved, and no fact tried by a jury, shall be otherwise reexamined in any court of the United States, than according to the rules of the common law.

Amendment VIII

Excessive bail shall not be required, nor excessive fines imposed, nor cruel and unusual punishments inflicted.

Amendment IX

The enumeration in the Constitution, of certain rights, shall not be construed to deny or disparage others retained by the people.

Amendment X

The powers not delegated to the United States by the Constitution, nor prohibited by it to the states, are reserved to the states respectively, or to the people.

5. Which of the following is NOT an amendment discussed in the Bill of Rights?
 A) An amendment banning the quartering of soldiers
 B) An amendment abolishing slavery
 C) An amendment that disallows unlawful search and seizures
 D) An amendment that ensures the right to a speedy and public trial

6. Freedom of religion is protected by the
 A) First Amendment
 B) Second Amendment
 C) Eighth Amendment
 D) Tenth Amendment

7. The text indicates that the Second Amendment is sometimes colloquially referred to as what?
 A) The right to a trial by jury
 B) The right to freedom of speech
 C) The right to protection from unreasonable searches and seizures
 D) The right to bear arms

8. In the production possibility curve below, economic growth would be indicated if the curve moved

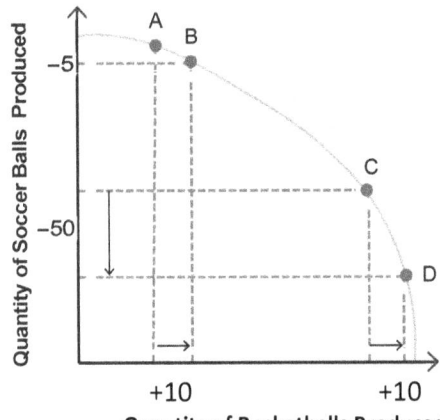

A) from point C to point A.
B) from point A to point B.
C) from point A to point D.
D) from point D to point C.

Questions 9 and 10 are based on the map of OPEC, the Organization of Petroleum Exporting Countries.

OPEC Countries

Algeria	Iran	Libya	Saudi Arabia
Ecuador	Iraq	Nigeria	United Arab Emirates
Indonesia	Kuwait	Quatar	Venezuela

9. What conclusion can be drawn from the information and map above?
A) OPEC only includes a few countries, so it is probably not very powerful.
B) The Middle East and North Africa are important to world gasoline prices.
C) Most OPEC countries are poor because they are in the developing world.
D) There is less petroleum in South America than there is in Africa.

10. The United States is one of the world's biggest oil consumers. Looking at the map, and knowing that the United States is a top consumer of oil, what might readers conclude about the United States' relationship with OPEC and its gas prices?
    A) The United States—like many other oil-consuming nations—likely depends on OPEC to set global oil prices even though it is not part of OPEC or the price-setting process.
    B) The United States is part of OPEC, so it likely controls the price-setting process for oil.
    C) The United States is not part of OPEC, so it likely does need to worry about OPEC's price-setting process.
    D) The United States and OPEC must be enemies.

11. Immigration to the United States, particularly from famine-hit Ireland, increased in the nineteenth century. What was one widespread response?
    A) The nativist movement, which promoted the rights of Native Americans
    B) The "Know-Nothing" movement, a nativist, anti-immigrant, anti-Catholic society
    C) The "Know-Nothing" movement, a nativist, anti-immigrant, anti- Protestant society
    D) The privileging of Chinese immigrants over white Irish immigrants

12. Following the collapse of the Ottoman Empire after the First World War, European countries took control of the Middle East, establishing protectorates according to arbitrary boundaries and installing rulers in accordance with European strategic interests. What effect has this had on the Middle East in the twentieth and twenty-first centuries?
    A) The Middle East has not been greatly affected.
    B) Illegitimate national borders and rulers have led to instability in the region.
    C) Better governance, thanks to the protectorates, improved stability following the decline of the Ottoman Empire in the region.
    D) European investment in strategic resources supported long-term political stability in the Middle East.

Questions 13 – 15 are based on the following excerpt from Jefferson Davis' speech explaining his retirement from the US Senate to join Mississippi as it seceded from the United States. He would go on to become the president of the Confederacy.

It has been a conviction of pressing necessity, it has been a belief that we are to be deprived in the Union of the rights which our fathers bequeathed to us, which has brought Mississippi into her present decision.

She has heard proclaimed the theory that all men are created free and equal, and this made the basis of an attack upon her social institutions; and the sacred Declaration of Independence has been invoked to maintain the position of the equality of the races. That Declaration of Independence is to be construed by the circumstances and purposes for which it was made. The communities were declaring their independence...that there was no divine right to rule; that no man inherited the right to govern; that there were no classes by which power and place descended to families, but that all stations were equally within the grasp of the body-politic.

These were the great principles they announced; these were the purposes for which they made their declaration... They have no reference to the slave; else, how happened it that among the items of arraignment made against George III was that he endeavored to do just what the North has been endeavoring of late to do—to stir up insurrection among our slaves? Had the Declaration announced that negroes were free and equal, how was the prince to be arraigned for stirring up insurrection among them?

...When our Constitution was formed, the same idea was rendered more palpable, for there we find provision made for that very class of persons as property; they were not put upon the footing of equality with white men...but, so far as representation was concerned, were discriminated against as a lower caste, only to be represented in the numerical proportion of three-fifths.

– Jefferson Davis, *On Retiring from the Senate*,

U.S. Congress, Senate, Congressional Globe, 36th Congress, 2nd Session, p. 487.

13. How does Jefferson Davis use American history to justify slavery?
    A) He argues that the Declaration of Independence asserted *political* equality rather than *racial* equality. He believed that no men (presumably no white men) had the right to rule over others (presumably other white men).
    B) He reminds the Senate of the Three-Fifths Compromise, in which the states agreed that to count a state's population, slaves would count as three-fifths of a person (although they could not vote).
    C) He reminds the Senate that King George III was accused of inciting rebellion among slaves to weaken the Revolution.
    D) All of the above

14. How does Jefferson Davis describe the society of Mississippi?
    A) Mississippi believed that all men were free and equal.
    B) Mississippi's social institutions were based on the premise that all men were NOT free and equal.
    C) Mississippi's social institutions were based on freedom and equality for all people, women and men.
    D) Mississippi did not support the Declaration of Independence.

15. Read the following sentence from the speech:

It has been a conviction of pressing necessity, it has been a belief that we are to be deprived in the Union of the rights which our fathers bequeathed to us, which has brought Mississippi into her present decision.

Given how Jefferson Davis develops the text that follows this sentence, which of the following BEST explains the specific rights that Mississippi fears it will lose under the Union?
    A) The right to secede from the Union
    B) The right to make its own laws
    C) The right to legally enslave black people
    D) The right to trade internationally

16. The Bill of Rights was added to the Constitution
    A) In response to the Supreme Court's ruling in *Marbury v. Madison*.
    B) By the first Congress immediately after ratification.
    C) By Congress slowly over the first twenty years of the nation's existence.
    D) Through George Washington's signature before he left office.

17. Which clause of the Constitution best supports the idea of the rule of law?
    A) The Supremacy Clause
    B) The Elastic Clause
    C) The Advise and Consent Clause
    D) The Due Process Clause

18. When the president vetoes a bill, he or she is effectively
    A) sending it back to conference committee.
    B) rejecting one part of the bill.
    C) rejecting the whole bill.
    D) declaring the bill unconstitutional.

19. Which of the following is NOT a basic factor of production?
    A) Labor
    B) Land
    C) Consumers
    D) Capital

20. How did Cesar Chavez and the United Farm Workers impact Hispanic Americans?
    A) They supported Mexicans who wanted to join the Bracero program and become guest workers in the United States.
    B) They supported Mexican American agricultural workers in California and the Southwest and provided a foundation for later advocacy groups working for Hispanic Americans.
    C) They worked on behalf of Texas farmers to coordinate agreements with agricultural workers from Mexico.
    D) They worked on behalf of the California state government to negotiate temporary worker agreements with Mexico.

21. Which of the following was a major difference between British and French colonization of the Americas?
    A) French colonists tended to be single men who intermarried with local residents, while British colonists brought their entire families to settle permanently, forming insular communities.
    B) British colonists tended to be single men who intermarried with local residents, while French colonists brought their entire families to settle permanently, forming insular communities.
    C) French colonists were more likely to form alliances with Native American tribes, while the British shunned them.
    D) British colonists had more economic interests in the Americas than the French did.

22. Boston, New York, Philadelphia, Baltimore, and Washington, D.C., as geographically close urban areas, form a(n)
    A) urban realm.
    B) world city.
    C) megalopolis.
    D) transition zone.

Practice Test #1   359

23. How did the US government break down tribal bonds and weaken Native American societies?
    A) Through policies of assimilation
    B) By forcing Native American children to go to white schools and reject their cultures
    C) By forcing Native Americans to move onto reservations
    D) All of the above

Questions 24 – 28 are based on this diagram depicting the separation of powers of the three branches of US government: the legislative branch, executive branch, and judicial branch.

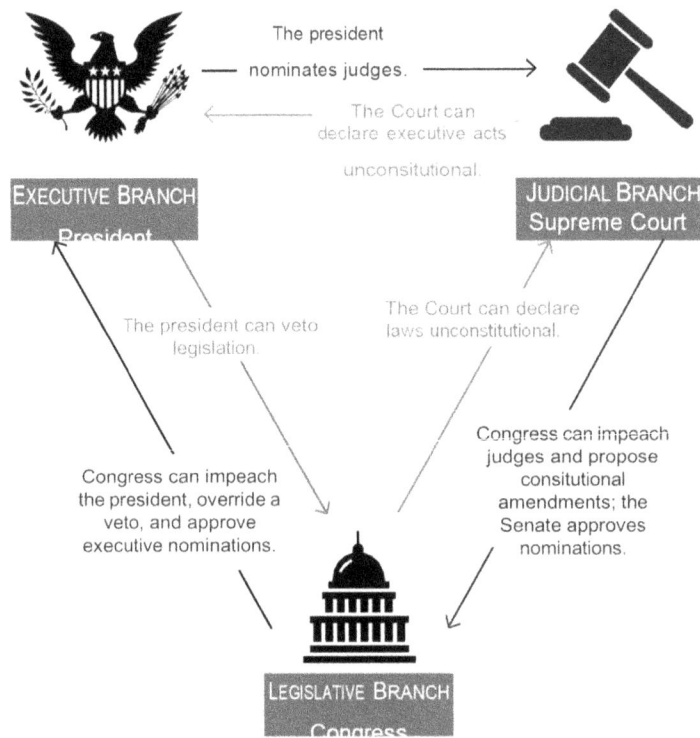

24. According to the diagram, what are the responsibilities of the judicial branch?
    A) Create the laws
    B) Veto the laws
    C) Interpret the laws
    D) Enforce the laws

25. Who has impeachment power over the president?
    A) District Courts
    B) Courts of Appeals
    C) Supreme Court
    D) Congress

26. Which entity can declare laws unconstitutional?
    A) The House
    B) The Senate
    C) The Supreme Court
    D) The president

27. Which entity can veto laws?
    A) Congress
    B) The president
    C) Courts of appeals
    D) The Supreme Court

28. According to the diagram, what are the responsibilities of the legislative branch?
    A) Create the laws
    B) Veto the laws
    C) Interpret the laws
    D) Enforce the laws

29. According to the map below, which city is located at approximately 39°N, 126°E?

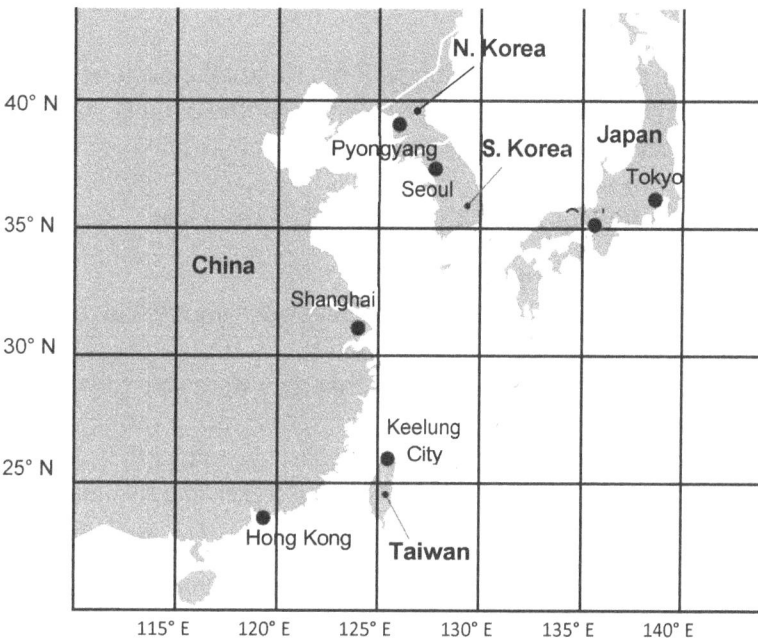

    A) Tokyo
    B) Keelung
    C) Pyongyang
    D) Hong Kong

30. Which of the following best explains the impact of the Watergate scandal on the United States?
    A) President Nixon was impeached.
    B) President Nixon declined to seek a second term of office.
    C) Americans lost faith in the federal government.
    D) Americans began supporting third party candidates more.

31. The United States remained relatively neutral in international conflicts for much of its early history. Which of the following conflicts is considered to be its first major assertion of international power overseas?
    A) The Spanish-American War
    B) The First World War
    C) The Texan Revolution
    D) The War of 1812

32. According to the law of demand, when the price of cucumbers increases, which of the following should happen?
    A) The quantity of cucumbers demanded increases.
    B) The quantity of cucumbers demanded falls.
    C) The demand for cucumbers falls.
    D) The demand for cucumbers increases.

33. Which of the following is the most common critique of the Electoral College system?
    A) A president can be elected without winning the majority of the popular vote.
    B) It threatens the two-party system.
    C) It gives too much power to small states.
    D) Electors have too often voted for candidates not listed on the ballot.

34. Why did Rome evolve into an empire from a republic?
    A) It was able to conquer so much land that it would have been impossible to maintain the Republic in its original form.
    B) The patricians of Rome amassed so much wealth that they were able to take over the Senate and establish an empire.
    C) Hannibal was able to overthrow the Senate and establish an empire in its place.
    D) The wealthy patricians of the Senate became corrupt, disregarding the interests of the plebeians who then supported Julius Caesar's coup.

35. How was the Mandate of Heaven an important concept in early Chinese history?
    A) It taught that the people in the area that became China were divinely fated to unite as one culture.
    B) It taught that the emperor had a divine mandate to rule the people in what would become China.
    C) It taught that China was a divinely important world power, meant to become a global leader.
    D) It taught that the emperor was a divine servant of the people of in the area that would become China.

Questions 36 and 37 are based on an editorial cartoon published in the Philadelphia Press in 1898. It is entitled "Ten Thousand Miles from Tip to Tip." It depicts an American eagle hovering over the globe with its wings extended from Puerto Rico to the Philippines. Below this larger eagle is a smaller eagle with a wingspan that extends from the East Coast to the Mississippi River. This smaller illustration is labeled with a different date: 1798.

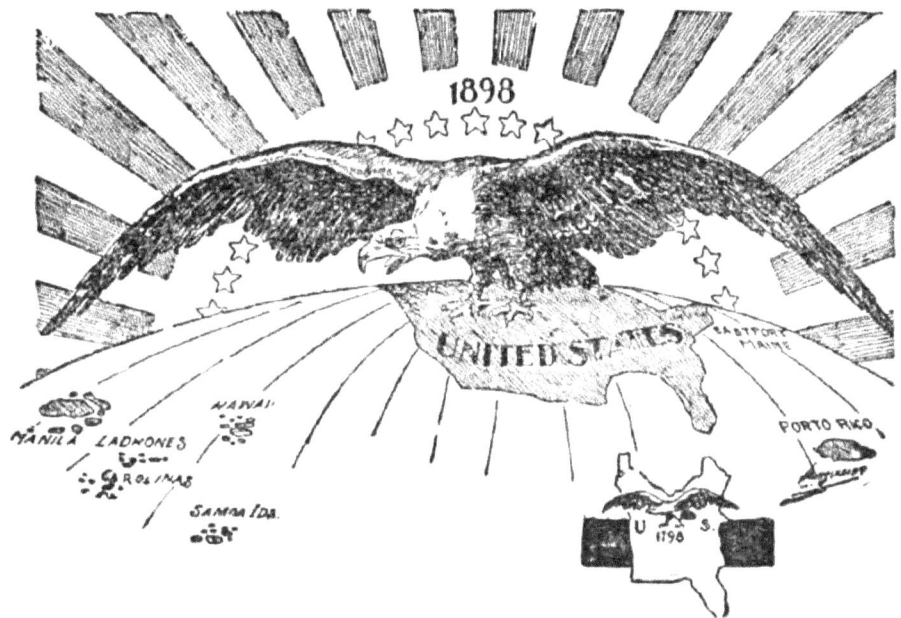

Ten thousand miles from tip to tip.—Philadelphia Press.

36. The widespread wings of the American eagle in this cartoon best represent
    A) the wide reach of American imperialism at the turn of the century.
    B) the threat of the German military's reach during World War I.
    C) the unstable nature of the United States' land claims following the Spanish-American War.
    D) the failure of the United States in its display of manifest destiny.

37. Why did the cartoonist juxtapose the larger eagle (labeled 1898) with a smaller eagle (labeled 1798)?
    A) To illustrate how much the United States has declined in 100 years
    B) To illustrate how far the United States has expanded in 100 years
    C) To illustrate that the United States was much better off in 1798
    D) To illustrate that the United States is much less powerful in 1898

38. Which of the following is a nonrenewable resource?
    A) Coal
    B) Wind
    C) Plants
    D) Fish

39. Constitutional amendments have been proposed to make abortion illegal, to ban same-sex marriage, and to prohibit flag burning. What can be deduced from these movements?
    A) It is easy to amend the Constitution.
    B) People sometimes disagree with Supreme Court decisions.
    C) Some people believe that the Constitution is outdated.
    D) Americans tend to avoid complicated social issues.

40. The executive can check the legislative branch by doing which of the following?
    A) The president can remove members of Congress.
    B) The president selects the Speaker of the House.
    C) The president can pocket veto laws passed by Congress.
    D) The president can line-item veto laws passed by Congress.

41. At the Constitutional Convention, what did small states and large states disagree about?
    A) The creation of an executive branch
    B) The federal power to tax
    C) The method of electing Senators
    D) Representation in the legislature

42. The United States entered WWI largely because of which of the following?
    A) The Zimmerman Telegram
    B) The rise of Nazi Germany
    C) The assassination of Franz Ferdinand
    D) The attack on the *Lusitania*

43. What was the significance of the Voting Rights Act of 1965?
    A) It gave African Americans the right to vote in the segregated states.
    B) It gave Americans under the age of twenty-one the right to vote.
    C) It ended segregation in voting.
    D) It ended restrictions that prevented African Americans from voting in many states with histories of institutionalized racism.

44. Which of the following is the best example of a public good?
    A) Tickets to a popular concert
    B) Electricity
    C) An energy bar
    D) A newspaper subscription

45. Which of the following best describes the motivation for Protestant reformers?
    A) Protestants, including Martin Luther, originally sought to develop a new form of Christianity separate from the Catholic Church.
    B) Protestants like Martin Luther were unhappy with the teachings of the Church, including papal indulgences and corruption in the Church, and originally sought reform.
    C) Protestants were initially influenced by European political leaders, who used them to limit the power of the Church.
    D) Protestants, including Martin Luther, originally sought to topple the Catholic Church, believing it to have become too corrupt.

46. The price of the type of tomatoes used in ketchup drops dramatically. At the same time, the price of mustard, a substitute for ketchup, increases. What impact will these two events have on the supply and price of ketchup?
   A) Price falls, but quantity is hard to determine.
   B) Price rises, but quantity is hard to determine.
   C) Price is hard to determine, but quantity rises.
   D) Price is hard to determine, but quantity falls.

Questions 47 – 49 are based on a photo of a sign that was created during the apartheid in South Africa. The sign reads: FOR USE BY WHITE PERSONS: THESE PUBLIC PREMISES AND THE AMENITIES HAVE BEEN RESERVED FOR THE EXCLUSIVE USE OF WHITE PERSONS. *The statement is by order of the Provincial Secretary. The sign includes the same message in Afrikaans, a derived form of Dutch used in South Africa.*

47. The content of the sign sheds light on the fact that apartheid in South Africa was similar to Jim Crow segregation in the American South in what way?
   A) Both separated public premises according to race.
   B) Both separated public premises according to first language.
   C) Both separated public premises according to class.
   D) Both separated public premises according to gender.

48. The statement tells us what about apartheid in South Africa?
   A) It promoted racial integration.
   B) It promoted social stability.
   C) It promoted racial diversity.
   D) It promoted racial segregation.

49. What can be inferred from the inclusion of two languages on the sign?
    A) Most South Africans spoke English, and it was probably the official language of South Africa.
    B) Only Afrikaans and English were recognized as major languages in South Africa at the time.
    C) The provincial secretary did not want the message to be disseminated to more than one group.
    D) People of color were the only intended audience of this sign.

Questions 50 and 51 are based on a photograph of a domestic standoff between protesters and military police in Arlington, Virginia, in the late 1960s. A female protester extends a flower to a military police officer who is armed and holding his baton. Another protester holds a sign that states: "Free...Leaders Jailed For Aiding Anti-War GIs." Other military police officers hold their batons tightly as they stand like a barrier in front of the young protesters.

50. This photo likely depicts what domestic conflict during the 1960s?
    A) Student protests over the Vietnam War
    B) Civil Rights protests in the streets of the South
    C) Feminist marches on Washington, D.C.
    D) The Black Power movement

51. The photo likely indicates that this event was
    A) violent in character, with a call for peace.
    B) peaceful in character, with the threat of military force.
    C) violent in character, with the threat of military force.
    D) generally peaceful in nature, with a few noticeable acts of violence.

52. Which of the following best explains the economic impact on Germany following the First World War?
   A) Overspeculation on German farmland caused the market to crash.
   B) The Great Depression and wartime reparations mandated by the Treaty of Versailles caused inflation to skyrocket, plunging the German economy into crisis.
   C) Germans were forced to pay extra taxes to cover reparations, and due to high prices, many could not afford to do so.
   D) The Reichsmark was removed from circulation and replaced with the dollar as a means of punishment, forcing many Germans into poverty.

Questions 53 – 57 are based on a 2018 Electoral College map of the current breakdown of Electoral College votes per state. The number of Electoral College votes depicted on each state corresponds to that state's number of members in Congress. Every state has two senators. Each state also has at least one congressional representative. A state's number of representatives is determined by its population, not territorial size. For instance, Wyoming has two senators and one representative, so it has three Electoral College votes.

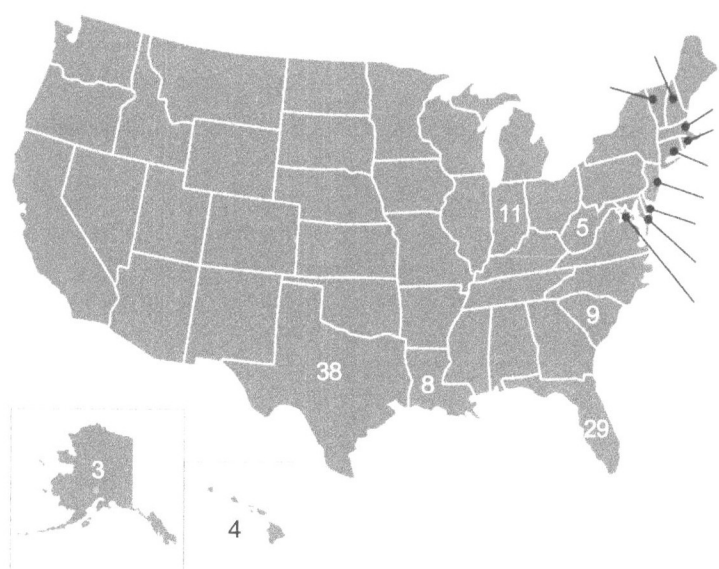

53. Since the electoral map shows that Montana only has three electoral votes, it can be assumed that Montana is a state with
   A) a small amount of territory with a small population to match it.
   B) a large amount of territory with a large population to match it.
   C) a large amount of territory but a small population.
   D) a small amount of territory but a large population.

54. How many US representatives does Texas have?
   A) 29
   B) 36
   C) 38
   D) 55

55. Since the electoral map shows that New Jersey has a total of fourteen electoral votes, it can be assumed that New Jersey is a state with
    A) a large amount of territory with a large population to match it.
    B) a small amount of territory with a small population to match it.
    C) a large amount of territory but a small population.
    D) a small amount of territory but a large population.

56. According to the map, which state has a larger population: Texas or California?
    A) Texas
    B) California
    C) They have the same population.
    D) The map does not provide enough information to determine which state has a larger population.

57. According to the map, what is the LEAST populous part of the United States?
    A) The East Coast
    B) The West Coast
    C) The South, including Texas and Florida
    D) The Great Plains and Rocky Mountain states

58. Why was the Mayflower Compact an important contribution to the foundation of American government?
    A) It provided for equal treatment of all Christians under the law.
    B) It was the first treaty between European settlers (the Pilgrims) and Native Americans.
    C) It laid out terms for government with the consent of the governed.
    D) It allowed people of all faiths to practice their religions freely under the law.

59. During the colonization of the Americas, the triangular trade across the Atlantic developed, and Africans suffered greatly; however, Africans still developed forms of resistance. Which of the following events or phenomena is an example of African resistance to slavery during this period?
    A) The Maroon communities
    B) The Seminole Wars
    C) The Underground Railroad
    D) The Ghost Dance movement

60. The Mexican-American War resulted in which of the following gains for the United States?
    A) Territory south of the Rio Grande
    B) The Southwest and California
    C) Oregon and Washington State
    D) Western land including Idaho

Answer Explanations

Language Arts: Reading Comprehension

1. A: This detail is not stated in the passage.

2. B: In the first paragraph, the author writes, "But what's the best way to get an accurate reading? The answer depends on the situation." She then goes on to describe various options and their applications.

3. B: The author indicates that "[t]he most common way people measure body temperature is orally" but that "[t]here are many situations [...] when measuring temperature orally isn't an option." She then goes on to describe these situations in the second and third paragraphs.

4. A: The second paragraph of the passage states that "[u]sing the rectum also has the added benefit of providing a much more accurate reading than other locations can provide."

5. A: The final paragraph states that "agitated patients...won't be able to sit still long enough for an accurate reading." The reader can infer that an agitated patient is a patient who is visibly upset, annoyed, or uncomfortable.

6. B: The author writes that "[j]azz music was played by and for a more expressive and freed populace than the United States had previously seen." In addition to "the emergence of the flapper[,]" the 1920s saw "the explosion of African American art and culture now known as the Harlem Renaissance."

7. A: The author writes that "[j]azz music was played by and for a more expressive and freed populace than the United States had previously seen." In addition to "the emergence of the flapper," the 1920s saw "the explosion of African American art and culture now known as the Harlem Renaissance."

8. C: The author opens the passage saying, "In recent decades, jazz has been associated with New Orleans and festivals like Mardi Gras, but in the 1920s, jazz was a booming trend whose influence reached into many aspects of American culture." He then goes on to elaborate on what these movements were.

9. B: At the end of the first paragraph, the author writes, "Ella Fitzgerald, for example, moved from Virginia to New York City to begin her much-lauded singing career, and jazz pioneer Louis Armstrong got his big break in Chicago."

10. C: The author writes that "[j]azz music was played by and for a more expressive and freed populace than the United States had previously seen." In addition to "the emergence of the flapper[,]" the 1920s saw "the explosion of African American art and culture now known as the Harlem Renaissance."

11. A: The author describes the steps for making coffee in chronological order.

12. D: This choice lists the steps for brewing coffee in the same order as the passage.

13. B: The writer uses the first person, showing his or her opinion, to recommend a French press as the best way to brew coffee.

14. D: This passage is a step-by-step explanation of how to brew a cup of coffee.

15. D: The passage mentions several times that decisions about things like water minerals, ground size, and steep time will depend on the preference of the coffee drinker.

16. A: The passage as a whole describes from start to finish how to make a cup of coffee the drinker will enjoy.

17. D: According to the passage, "the flu is...relatively difficult to contract," and "[w]hile many people who contract the virus will recover, many others will not."

18. A: This choice addresses all of the main ideas of the passage: the flu is potentially deadly, highly infectious, and difficult to contain due to viral shedding.

19. C: The second paragraph states that the flu is "relatively difficult to contract" because it "can only be transmitted when individuals come into direct contact with bodily fluids of people infected with the flu or when they are exposed to expelled aerosol particles[.]"

20. A: The author uses the term measures to describe the steps that people to take to prevent the spreading of the influenza virus.

21. C: The final paragraph of the passage states that viral shedding is "the process by which the body releases viruses that have been successfully reproducing during the infection."

22. A: The second paragraph of the passage states that "the virus can be contained with fairly simple health measures like hand washing and face masks."

23. A: This choice describes the order of Julia's actions that matches chronological order of the passage.

24. B: The passage describes how Julia had an exhausting morning, and it can be assumed that when "she'd had enough" she decided to go home.

25. C: Whether it was irresponsible for Julia to leave work is a matter of opinion. Some readers may agree, and others may disagree. The other statements are facts that can be proven from the passage.

26. B: The phrase "set a course for home" is an idiom that means to head in a certain direction, so Julia is planning to go home.

27. D: The passage emphasizes that Julia is tired, so she's most likely going to drive home and go to sleep.

28. A: The author writes that "[t]here's another class of symbiosis that is controversial among scientists" and goes on to say that "many scientists claim the relationships currently described as commensal are just mutualistic or parasitic in ways that haven't been discovered yet." This implies that scientists debate about the topic of commensalism.

29. B: The author writes that "[a]s these communities have evolved, the species in them have developed complex, long-term interspecies interactions known as symbiotic relationships." She then goes on to describe the different types of symbiotic relationships that exist.

30. D: The author writes, "Often, relationships described as commensal include one species that feeds on another species' leftovers; remoras, for instance, will attach themselves to sharks and eat the food particles they leave behind.

It might seem like the shark gets nothing from the relationship, but a closer look will show that sharks in fact benefit from remoras, which clean the sharks' skin and remove parasites."

31. C: The author writes, "A relationship where one individual benefits and the other is harmed is known as parasitism."

32. A: The author writes, "But is it possible for two species to interact and for one to remain completely unaffected?... In fact, many scientists claim that relationships currently described as commensal are just mutualistic or parasitic in ways that haven't been discovered yet."

33. D: The author writes, "The bacteria, fungi, insects, plants, and animals that live together in a habitat have evolved to share a pool of limited resources...As these communities have evolved, the species in them have developed complex, long-term interspecies interactions known as symbiotic relationships."

34. A: The author states that "popcorn continued to rule the snack food kingdom until the rise in popularity of home televisions during the 1950s" when the industry saw a "decline in sales" as a result of the changing pastimes of the American people.

35. B: The author states, "For the Aztec people who called the caves home, popcorn (or *momochitl*) played an important role in society, both as a food staple and in ceremonies." This implies that the Aztec people popped popcorn both for special occasions ("in ceremonies") and for regular consumption ("as a food staple").

36. C: In the opening paragraph the author writes, "But popcorn isn't just for fun—it's also a multimillion-dollar-a-year industry with a long and fascinating history." The author then goes on to illustrate the history of popcorn from the ancient Aztecs, to early twentieth century America, to the present day.

37. C: The author writes, "The popcorn industry flourished during the Great Depression when it was advertised as a wholesome and economical food."

38. A: This statement summarizes the entire passage, including the brief history of popcorn in ancient cultures and the growth in the popularity of popcorn in America.

39. C: The author writes, "However, it wasn't until microwave popcorn became commercially available in 1981 that at-home popcorn consumption began to grow exponentially. With the wide availability of microwaves in the United States, popcorn also began popping up in offices and hotel rooms."

40. B: The author writes that "many human communities want answers about the current status and future of Arctic marine mammals, including... indigenous people whose traditional ways of subsistence are intertwined with the fate of species such as ice seals, narwhals, walruses, and polar bears." This implies that the survival of these groups depends on the survival of these animal species.

41. A: The author writes, "The Arctic Sea ice cover...naturally grows in the fall and winter and melts during the spring and summer every year. But over the past decades, the melt season has grown longer and the average extent of Arctic Sea ice has diminished."

42. D: The author writes that "the melt season has grown longer and the average extent of Arctic Sea ice has diminished, changing the game for many Arctic marine mammals."

43. D: The author quotes one scientist as saying, "mainly, just continuing daily coverage is what's important for the long-term monitoring of habitat changes."

44. D: The author writes that "there are many unknowns...about how their fragile habitat will evolve in a warming world." This implies that the habitat is at risk due to the changes in the earth's temperature.

Answer Explanations

45. D: This excerpt implies that the survival of Arctic species is in jeopardy as a result of longer melting seasons and decreased sea ice extent.

46. D: The author writes, "Using daily sea ice concentration data from the satellite record, he [Stern] calculated changes in the dates of the beginning of the melt season in spring and the start of the fall freeze-up from 1979 to 2013. He found that, in all regions but one, the melt season had grown longer (mostly by five to ten weeks, and by twenty weeks in one region)."

47. A: The author states that, unlike other Arctic species, "in the case of Arctic whales, the changes in sea ice might benefit their populations, at least in the short term: the loss and earlier retreat of sea ice opens up new habitats and, in some areas of the Arctic, has also led to an increase in food production and the length of their feeding season."

48. C: The author indicates that the "earlier retreat of sea ice opens up new habitats," implying the retreat of sea ice is its recession due to melting.

49. D: The author indicates that "monitoring" the "daily coverage" of sea ice is necessary to understanding how the expansion and recession of sea ice will shape habitats over time.

50. C: The graph indicates that Arctic ice extent was 8,000,000 sq. km in 1979 but is only around 2,000,000 sq. km today.

Language Arts: Writing

Grammar

1. A: The two commas correctly set off the adjectival phrase *especially those in the public eye*, which describes the noun *careers*.

2. A: Earlier in the paragraph, the author says that careers such as law enforcement "lend themselves to controversy and caricatures." The phrase *crooked cops and detectives with donuts* supports these claims.

3. C: This is a good introduction to the paragraph. The paragraph goes on to specifically describe a few of the characteristics someone needs in order to be a successful police officer.

4. A: If an officer treats others with "sincere care and unwavering equity," it suggests that the officer has a strong moral character.

5. B: The singular noun *series* agrees with the singular verb *begins*. Also, the relative pronoun *which* is correctly used here: the opening phrase *To become...requirements* can stand on its own as a sentence. This means that the phrase beginning with *which* is not needed to complete the thought.

6. A: The relative pronoun *which* is correctly used here: the opening phrase *After meeting...evaluations* can stand on its own as a sentence. Also, the plural noun *evaluations* agrees with the plural verb *are*.

7. C: The possessive pronouns *his* and *her* agree with the antecedent *each candidate*, which is singular.

8. A: The possessive pronouns *his* and *her* agree with the antecedent *an applicant*, which is singular. Also, *agency's* correctly uses an apostrophe and *s* to show possession.

9. B: All four commas appear in the correct places, including the serial comma that precedes the word *and*.

10. C: All verbs in the series parallel one another grammatically: *investigating, gathering, protecting, conducting,* and *solving*.

11. C: Adding this sentence distracts the reader from the passage's two main focuses: the requirements for becoming a police officer and a police officer's many duties.

12. B: This choice is well constructed. The reader is able to keep good track of the connections between the main subject, *adaptations*, and each piece of information the author gives about this subject.

13. A: The series of three nouns, *protection, hunting,* and *reproduction,* is correctly punctuated. Parallel construction allows the phrase to read smoothly.

14. D: This phrase is appropriate to the passage's tone and purpose. It is short, yet it provides a vivid, accurate description of the substance that the squid emits.

15. D: The singular verb *surprises* agrees with the singular noun *goo*. Also, the singular possessive pronoun *its* agrees with the singular noun phrase *the vampire squid*. Finally, the singular noun *predator* agrees with the singular object pronoun *it* in *distracts it*.

16. B: Both commas are correctly placed.

17. A: The plural pronoun *them* agrees with the plural noun *parts*. Also, the plural reflexive pronoun *themselves* agrees with the plural noun *animals*.

18. C: This sentence provides an effective transition because it mentions the topic of the previous paragraph, protection, as well as the fifth paragraph's topic, hunting.

19. A: This is the only choice that mentions a second fish, the shark, that uses bioluminescence to hunt.

20. A: This paragraph's main topic is ways that creatures use bioluminescence to hunt.

21. D: This sentence effectively sums up the passage in an enthusiastic manner that makes readers feel glad to have read it.

22. B: This phrase accurately describes what Dr. Kemp is doing with his many emails: glancing at them and quickly deciding how to deal with each.

23. B: This sentence's three past-tense verbs agree with one another. The author uses parallel structure effectively.

24. C: The two past-tense verbs, *scoffed* and *clicked,* agree.

25. A: It makes good sense that people who need guidance on da Vinci's work would write to Dr. Kemp, an expert on the artist.

26. D: The phrase *this one* refers to *these emails* in the third sentence. Dr. Kemp does not think this email will be any different from the many other emails he has received from loonies.

27. B: This sentence is succinct and grammatical. It describes Kemp's action and tells why he does what he does.

28. A: The adjective *uncanny* shows that Kemp is awed by the mysterious image.

29. B: The verb *inspect* shows exactly what Kemp plans to do when he sees the artwork in person.

30. B: *Connoisseur's expert opinion* is redundant, so it is correct to delete either *connoisseur* or *expert*.

Answer Explanations

31. A: This sentence is well constructed and correctly punctuated. It reads smoothly and its meaning is clear.

32. D: This choice encourages readers to do further research because Kemp himself wants to investigate further.

33. A: Since the second sentence is already so long, it is probably best not to combine the two.

34. B: The singular neuter possessive pronoun *its* agrees with its singular neuter antecedent, *phenomenon*.

35. C: Using just one adjective, *novel*, saves the phrase from being redundant.

36. B: The plural verb *were* agrees with the plural noun *predecessors*.

37. A: The writer used parallel construction, correctly placed phrases, and correct punctuation to write this sentence. It flows smoothly, making it easy to understand.

38. B: The adverb *however* makes good sense here. It paves the way for the author to say something negative about push carts that contrasts with their positive qualities.

39. C: This clause effectively points out a major difference between the push cart and the modern food truck: a food truck features a full kitchen in miniature, while the push cart did not.

40. C: This construction correctly conveys the idea that a chuck wagon was a covered wagon that served as a kitchen.

41. D: The sentence provides detailed information on the meaning of *mobile kitchen*.

42. C: These trucks were apparently called roach coaches because their grungy kitchens attracted bugs.

43. B: This placement fits with the paragraph's chronological order.

44. A: The adverbial phrase *in recent years* makes good sense here. It fits in with the phrase *a new trend*, which appears earlier in the passage.

45. B: The progressive verb tense in *are flocking* makes good sense here. The author is describing events that are happening in the present day.

46. D: This description jives with the first sentence in that they both show people's excitement about the new food trucks.

47. B: As well as giving details about today's food trucks, the essay describes push carts, chuck wagons, roach coaches, and other food-purveying vehicles of the past.

48. D: The phrase *a landmark whose enormity* is grammatical and makes good sense in the sentence.

49. A: By itself, the verb *separates* asks the question, "Separates what from what?"

50. B: The plural verb *are* agrees with the plural noun *reservations*.

51. B: The next paragraph says that members of these three groups help to manage the landmark.

52. D: The present-tense verb *reside* agrees with the present-tense verbs in the rest of the essay.

53. C: Two commas correctly frame the phrase *like the National Park Service*.

54. B: Since *safe* and *free from harm* have similar meanings, using just one of them is sufficient. Using both would be redundant.

55. B: In paragraph 2, the writer says that park managers "ensure that the lands are protected and tourists are kept safe." At the beginning of paragraph 3, it makes good sense to use the transitional phrase *in fact* to introduce the idea that the Grand Canyon attracts millions of tourists per year.

56. A: The beginning of the sentence claims that "the Grand Canyon is one of the most popular tourist attractions in the world." Supplying the figure "upwards of five million visitors every year" is an effective way to support this claim.

57. D: This choice is correctly punctuated. The two commas appear in the right spots.

58. A: The phrase *a broader perspective of the canyon* makes good sense in the sentence.

59. D: The phrase *can even* suggests that walking on the SkyWalk is the most amazing activity of all. Thus it makes good sense to list it last.

60. B: This choice creates a comma splice.

The Essay

The argument over whether or not to raise the driving age is not simple, with arguments and statistics supporting both sides. The two passages given both offer compelling reasons why their argument is more correct; however, passage 1 by Riya Sidana offers a more complete argument that addresses a broad audience and includes clear evidence and explanation.

Thomas Maddow's article begins with clear statistics that support his argument, stating them directly and starkly; however, the statistics are missing any context that can help the reader understand how they fit into a larger picture. Sidana, on the other hand, fleshes out her argument that there are better ways to address the issues Maddow lists. She says that "solutions such as graduated licensing and improved driver's education courses have reduced teen fatalities," giving clear examples of how the issues can be addressed without raising the driver's age. By addressing the issues themselves, she makes her argument more complex and complete.

Additionally, Sidana mentions New Jersey and Connecticut to provide specific examples of states that have already done what she suggests. She says these states "employ changing requirements" and that "increasing the amount of supervised driving time and limiting the number of passengers" also helps improve teens' driving skills. In contrast, Maddow calls for action from like-minded adults, citing their responsibilities, but not explaining how the changes will help. Sidana's explanations are more persuasive because they provide more detail.

Finally, Sidana's argument seems to be addressed to a broader audience, both teens who believe they should have the freedom to drive and parents or lawmakers charged with making the changes suggested. Sidana acknowledges the problem rather than dismissing it, but also acknowledges the difficulties that might be faced by families and teens, mentioning that a teen "may provide income." Her language paints teens as potentially responsible, helpful members of the family, but does not deny that they are "inexperienced and impulsive decision makers." By describing both sides impartially, Sidana widens her audience and allows both sides to agree to a compromise.

Because she addresses both sides fairly, makes a more complex argument, and supports it with evidence, Sidana's argument is simply more effective than Maddow's, despite his clear, straightforward statistics. Passage 1 does a better job of persuading its audience.

Mathematics

1. C: $\frac{13}{14}$ is rational number because it can be written as a fraction.

2. E: Rewrite the bases so they are the same, then set the exponents equal and solve.
$$16^{x+1} = 8^{3x}$$
$$(2^4)^{x+10} = (2^3)^{3x}$$
$$2^{(4x+40)} = 2^{9x}$$
$$4x + 40 = 9x$$
$$x = \mathbf{8}$$

3. B: Plug 4 in for j and simplify.
$$2(j-4)^4 - j + \frac{1}{2}j$$
$$2(4-4)^4 - 4 + \frac{1}{2}(4) = \mathbf{-2}$$

4. D: Distribute the negative 2 and combine like terms.
$$(-7 + 2i) - 2(4 - 3i)$$
$$= -7 + 2i - 8 + 6i$$
$$= \mathbf{-15 + 8i}$$

5. E: Make the exponents the same and subtract the digit parts of each term.
$$(4.71 \times 10^3) - (2.98 \times 10^2)$$
$$4.71 \times 10 \times 10^2 = 47.1 \times 10^2$$
$$47.1 - 2.98 = 44.12$$
$$44.12 \times 10^2 = \mathbf{4.412 \times 10^3}$$

6. C: Use the fundamental counting principle. Each topping has two possible choices (yes or no).
$$2(5)(6)(2)(2)(2) = \mathbf{480}$$

7. A: Use the formula for inversely proportional relationships to find k and then solve for s.
$$sn = k$$
$$(65)(250) = k$$
$$k = 16{,}250$$
$$s(325) = 16{,}250$$
$$s = \mathbf{50}$$

Answer Explanations

8. D: Set up a proportion and solve.

$$\frac{AB}{DE} = \frac{3}{4}$$

$$\frac{12}{DE} = \frac{3}{4}$$

$$3(DE) = 48$$

$$\mathbf{DE = 16}$$

9. B: Multiply the digits and add the exponents.

$$(1.2 \times 10^{-3})(1.13 \times 10^{-4})$$

$$1.2 \times 1.13 = 1.356$$

$$-3 + (-4) = -7$$

$$\mathbf{1.356 \times 10^{-7}}$$

10. A: Find the amount the state will spend on infrastructure and education, and then find the difference.

$$infrastructure = 0.2(3,000,000,000) = 600,000,000$$

$$education = 0.18(3,000,000,000) = 540,000,000$$

$$600,000,000 - 540,000,000 = \mathbf{\$60,000,000}$$

11. D: Simplify using PEMDAS.

$$z^3(z+2)^2 - 4z^3 + 2$$

$$z^3(z^2 + 4z + 4) - 4z^3 + 2$$

$$z^5 + 4z^4 + 4z^3 - 4z^3 + 2$$

$$\mathbf{z^5 + 4z^4 + 2}$$

12. C: Factor the expression using the greatest common factor of 3.

$$54z^4 + 18z^3 + 3z + 3 = 3(18z^4 + 6z^3 + z + 1)$$

13. E: Solve each equation for y and find the equation with a power of 1.

$$\sqrt[3]{y} = x \rightarrow y = x^3$$

$$\sqrt[3]{x} = y \rightarrow y = \sqrt[3]{x}$$

$$\sqrt[3]{y} = x^2 \rightarrow y = x^6$$

$$y = \sqrt[6]{x^3} \rightarrow y = x^2$$

$$y = \sqrt[3]{x^3} \rightarrow y = x$$

Answer Explanations

14. E: Divide the digits and subtract the exponents.

$$\frac{7.2 \times 10^6}{1.6 \times 10^{-3}}$$

$$7.2 \div 1.6 = 4.5$$

$$6 - (-3) = 9$$

$$\mathbf{4.5 \times 10^9}$$

15. B: Find the slope of line b, take the negative reciprocal to find the slope of a, and test each point. Find the slope of line b using the two given points:

$$(x_1, y_1) = (-100, 100)$$
$$(x_2, y_2) = (-95, 115)$$
$$m_b = \frac{115 - 100}{-95 - (-100)} = \frac{15}{5} = 3$$

The slope of line a is the negative reciprocal of the slope of line b:

$$m_a = -\frac{1}{3}$$

Use the point-slope formula to create an equation for line a and test each point in the equation. If the point makes both sides of the equation equal then it is a point on the line.

$$y - y_1 = m(x - x_1)$$
$$y - 100 = -\frac{1}{3}(x + 100)$$

Choice A:

$$-104 - 100 = -\frac{1}{3}(-112 + 100)$$
$$-204 = 4$$

Choice B:

$$104 - 100 = -\frac{1}{3}(-112 + 100)$$
$$4 = 4$$

Choice C:

$$-95 - 100 = -\frac{1}{3}(-100 + 100)$$
$$-195 = 0$$

Choice D:

$$115 - 100 = -\frac{1}{3}(-95 + 100)$$
$$15 = -\frac{5}{3}$$

Choice E:

$$168 - 100 = -\frac{1}{3}(104 + 100)$$

$$68 = -68$$

16. A: Evaluate to find the greatest value.

$$20 - (-20) = \mathbf{40}$$
$$-16 - 17 + 31 = -2$$
$$18 - 15 + 27 = 30$$
$$-20 + 10 + 10 = 0$$
$$-4(3)(-2) = 24$$

17. C: Plug each value into the equation.

$$4(3 + 4)^2 - 4(3)^2 + 20 = 180 \neq 276$$
$$4(4 + 4)^2 - 4(3)^2 + 20 = 240 \neq 276$$
$$4(6 + 4)^2 - 4(6)^2 + 20 = 276$$
$$4(12 + 4)^2 - 4(12)^2 + 20 = 468 \neq 276$$
$$4(24 + 4)^2 - 4(24)^2 + 20 = 852 \neq 276$$

18. C: Plug 0 in for x and solve for y.

$$7y - 42x + 7 = 0$$
$$7y - 42(0) + 7 = 0$$
$$y = -1$$

The y-intercept is at $(0, -1)$.

19. D: Use the fundamental counting principle to determine how many ways the DVDs can be arranged within each category and how many ways the 3 categories can be arranged.

$$ways\ to\ arrange\ horror = 4! = 24$$
$$ways\ to\ arrange\ comedies = 6! = 720$$
$$ways\ to\ arrange\ science\ fiction = 5! = 120$$
$$ways\ to\ arrange\ categories = 3! = 6$$
$$(24)(720)(120)(6) = \mathbf{12,441,600}$$

20. A: Use the midpoint formula to find point B.

$$M_x : \frac{7+x}{2} = -3$$

$$x = -13$$

$$M_y = \frac{12+y}{2} = 10$$

$$y = 8$$

$$B = (-13, 8)$$

21. B: Evaluate to find the non-negative value.

$$(-3)(-1)(2)(-1) = -6$$

$$14 - 7 + (-7) = \mathbf{0}$$

$$7 - 10 + (-8) = -11$$

$$-5(-2)(-3) = -30$$

$$-10 - (-8) = -2$$

22. A: Plug 0 in for y and solve for x.

$$10x + 10y = 10$$

$$10x + 10(0) = 10$$

$$x = 1$$

The x-intercept is at $(\mathbf{1, 0})$.

23. E: Set up an equation to find the number of people wearing neither white nor blue. Subtract the number of people wearing both colors so they are not counted twice.

$$21 = 7 + 6 + neither - 5$$

$$neither = \mathbf{13}$$

24. C: Work backwards to find the number of runners in the competition (c) and then the number of runners on the team (r).

$$\frac{2}{c} = \frac{10}{100}$$

$$c = 20$$

$$\frac{20}{r} = \frac{25}{100}$$

$$r = \mathbf{80}$$

25. C: The slope of a horizontal line is always 0.

26. E: Solve the system using substitution.

$$z - 2x = 14 \rightarrow z = 2x + 14$$
$$2z - 6x = 18$$
$$2(2x + 14) - 6x = 18$$
$$4x + 28 - 6x = 18$$
$$-2x = -10$$
$$x = 5$$
$$z - 2(5) = 14$$
$$\mathbf{z = 24}$$

27. D: Set up a system of equations and solve using elimination.

f = the cost of a financial stock

a = the cost of an auto stock

$$50f + 10a = 1300$$
$$10f + 10a = 500$$
$$50f + 10a = 1300$$
$$\underline{+ \;\; -50f - 50a = -2500}$$
$$-40a = -1200$$
$$a = 30$$
$$50(30) = \mathbf{1500}$$

28. B: Use the equation for Bernoulli trials (binomial distribution).

$$P = nCr(p^r)(q^{n-r})$$
$$n = 10$$
$$r = 3$$
$$p = \frac{4}{36} = \frac{1}{9}$$
$$q = \frac{8}{9}$$
$$P = 10C3 \left(\frac{1}{9}\right)^3 \left(\frac{8}{9}\right)^7 = 0.072 = 7.2\%$$

29. A: Eliminate answer choices that don't match the graph.

B) The graph has a negative slope while this inequality has a positive slope.

C) The line on the graph is solid, so the inequality should include the "or equal to" symbol.

D) The shading is above the line, meaning the inequality should be "y is greater than."

Answer Explanations

E) The y-intercept is –2, not 2.

30. B: Set up a proportion. Cube the scale factor when calculating volume.

$$\frac{54\pi}{x} = \frac{3^3}{4^3}$$

$$x = \mathbf{128\pi}$$

31. A: Use the quadratic formula.

$$f(x) = 4x^2 - 6x + 7$$

$$x = \frac{-(-6) \pm \sqrt{(-6)^2 - 4(4)7}}{2(4)}$$

$$x = \frac{3 \pm i\sqrt{19}}{4}$$

32. A: Multiply by the conversion factor to get from pounds to kilograms.

8 pounds, 8 ounces = 8.5 pounds

$$8.5 \text{ lb} \times \frac{1 \text{ kg}}{2.2 \text{ lb}} = \mathbf{3.9 \text{ kg}}$$

33. C: Find the measure of each angle.

$$m\angle a = 180 - (70 + 40) = 70°$$
$$m\angle b = 70°$$
$$m\angle c = 180 - 40 = 140°$$
$$m\angle d = 40°$$
$$\angle a \cong \angle b$$

34. D: $\{5, 11, 18, 20, \mathbf{37}, 37, 60, 72, 90\}$

$$median = 37$$
$$mode = 37$$
$$mean = \frac{60 + 5 + 18 + 20 + 37 + 37 + 11 + 90 + 72}{9} = 38.89$$

The median is less than the mean.

35. A: Simplify the inequality.

$$2x + 4 \geq 5x - 20 - 3x + 12$$
$$2x + 4 \geq 2x - 8$$
$$4 \geq -8$$

Since the inequality is always true, the solution is all real numbers, $(-\infty, \infty)$.

36. D: Plug in each set of values and determine if the inequality is true.

$2(0) + 0 \leq -10$ FALSE

$2(10) + 2 \leq -10$ FALSE

$2(10) + 10 \leq -10$ FALSE

$2(-10) + (-10) \leq -10$ TRUE

$2(0) + 10 \leq -10$ FALSE

37. A: There are six digits that can be used to make up the 6-digit number: 0, 1, 2, 7, 8, and 9. However, 0 cannot be used for the first digit. Use the fundamental counting principle:

$$(5)(6)(6)(6)(6)(6) = \mathbf{38,880}$$

38. D: Factor the equation and set each factor equal to 0.

$$y = 16x^3 - 48x^2$$
$$16x^2(x - 3) = 0$$
$$\mathbf{x = 0 \text{ and } x = 3}$$

39. C: This sine function has an amplitude of 3 and has been shifted up 1, so it has a maximum value of 4.

40. B: Use the triangle inequality theorem to find the possible values for the third side, then calculate the possible perimeters.

$$13 - 5 < s < 13 + 5$$
$$8 < s < 18$$
$$13 + 5 + 8 < P < 13 + 5 + 18$$
$$26 < P < 36$$

26.5 is the only answer choice in this range.

41. C:

$$\text{total seats} = 4{,}500 + 2{,}000$$
$$\frac{\text{lower seats}}{\text{all seats}} = \frac{4{,}500}{6{,}500} = \frac{9}{13}$$

42. B: The axis of symmetry will be a vertical line that runs through the vertex, which is the point $(-3, 5)$. The line of symmetry is $x = -3$.

43. A: Use the zeros of the function to find the intervals where it is less than 0.

$$2x^2 - 4x - 6 = 0$$
$$(2x - 6)(x + 1) = 0$$
$$x = 3 \text{ and } x = -1$$
$$(-\infty, -1) \to 2x^2 - 4x - 6 > 0$$
$$(-1, 3) \to 2x^2 - 4x - 6 < 0$$
$$(3, \infty) \to 2x^2 - 4x - 6 > 0$$

The function is less than 0 on the interval $(-1, 3)$.

44. B: Find the sum of the 13 numbers whose mean is 30.

$$13 \times 30 = 390$$

Find the sum of the 8 numbers whose mean is 42.

$$8 \times 42 = 336$$

Find the sum and mean of the remaining 5 numbers.

$$390 - 336 = 54$$
$$\frac{54}{5} = \mathbf{10.8}$$

45. C: Make sure there are no factors that cancel, and then set the denominator equal to 0.

$$\frac{x^3 - 16x}{-4x^2 + 4x = 24} = \frac{x(x^2 - 16)}{-4(x^2 - x - 6)} = \frac{x(x + 4)(x - 4)}{-4(x - 3)(x + 2)}$$

The graph has no holes.

$$-4(x - 3)(x + 2) = 0$$
$$x = 3 \text{ and } x = -2$$

46. A: Find the measure of each arc and then find the difference in the two segments.

$$each\ arc = \frac{360°}{8} = 45°$$

The difference between CF and HB is one arc, or **45°**.

47. D: Use the formula for the area of a rectangle to find the increase in its size.

$$A = lw$$
$$A = (1.4l)(0.6w)$$
$$A = 0.84lw$$

The new area will be 84% of the original area, a decrease of **16%**.

48. D: Plug each value into the function and evaluate.

$$\cos 0 - \sin 0 = 1 \neq -1$$

$$\cos\frac{\pi}{4} - \sin\frac{\pi}{4} = \frac{1}{2} - \frac{\sqrt{3}}{2} \neq -1$$

$$\cos\frac{\pi}{3} - \sin\frac{\pi}{3} = \frac{1-\sqrt{3}}{2} \neq -1$$

$$\cos\frac{\pi}{2} - \sin\frac{\pi}{2} = \mathbf{-1}$$

$$\cos\frac{3\pi}{2} - \sin\frac{3\pi}{2} = 1 \neq -1$$

49. A: Add the fractions and subtract the result from the amount of flour Allison started with.

$$2\frac{1}{2} + \frac{3}{4} = \frac{5}{2} + \frac{3}{4} = \frac{10}{4} + \frac{3}{4} = \frac{13}{4}$$

$$4 - \frac{13}{4} = \frac{16}{4} - \frac{13}{4} = \mathbf{\frac{3}{4}}$$

50. C: Find $m\angle DMC$ by averaging the lengths of $\widehat{DC}$ and $\widehat{AB}$.

$$\widehat{AB} = 55°$$

$$\widehat{DC} = 180° - 85° = 95°$$

$$m\angle DMC = \frac{55 + 95}{2} = \mathbf{75°}$$

51. A: Factor the trinomial and set each factor equal to 0.

$$2n^2 + 2n - 12 = 0$$

$$2(n^2 + n - 6) = 0$$

$$2(n + 3)(n - 2) = 0$$

$$\boldsymbol{n = -3} \text{ and } \boldsymbol{n = 2}$$

52. C: Complex solutions always come in pairs. Therefore, the number of possible complex solutions is the greatest *even* number equal to or less than the power of the polynomial. A 17th degree polynomial can have at most **16** complex roots.

53. B: Find the probability that the second marble will be green if the first marble is blue, silver, or green, and then add these probabilities together.

P(first blue and second green) =

$$P(first\ blue\ and\ second\ green) = P(blue) \times P(green|first\ blue) = \frac{6}{18} \times \frac{4}{17} = \frac{4}{51}$$

$$P(first\ silver\ and\ second\ green) = P(silver) \times P(green|first\ silver) = \frac{8}{18} \times \frac{4}{17} = \frac{16}{153}$$

$$P(first\ green\ and\ second\ green) = P(green) \times P(green|first\ green) = \frac{4}{18} \times \frac{3}{17} = \frac{2}{51}$$

$$P(second\ green) = \frac{4}{51} + \frac{16}{153} + \frac{2}{51} = \frac{2}{9}$$

54. B: Find where the denominator equals 0.

$$-2x - 6 = 0$$
$$x = -3$$

55. D: Use the formula for the volume of a sphere to find its radius.

$$V = \frac{4}{3}\pi r^3$$
$$972\pi = \frac{4}{3}\pi r^3$$
$$r = 9$$

Use the super Pythagorean theorem to find the side of the cube.

$$d^2 = a^2 + b^2 + c^2$$
$$18^2 = 3s^2$$
$$s \approx 10.4$$

Use the length of the side to find the volume of the cube.

$$V = s^3$$
$$V \approx (10.4)^3$$
$$\mathbf{V \approx 1125}$$

Science

1. D: This is a decomposition reaction in which a single reactant produces two products.

2. D: Increasing the solution to 20 percent solute concentration would cause water to flow out of the cell, causing its mass to decrease.

3. B: Venus's orbit is closest to Earth and is the second planet from the sun.

4. C: Objects with the same charge will repel each other, so two negative charges will move farther apart.

5. B:

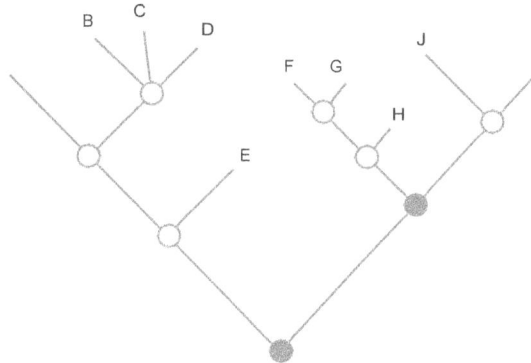

The two marked nodes (2 and 3) are common ancestors shared by species *H* and *K*. The branch containing species *H* diverges from the branch containing species *K* at the second node.

6. B: Using one filtration system for all three tanks keeps the water quality across all three tanks constant and eliminates experimental bias for this variable.

7. A: Tank A is the control group because the sunlight variable is unchanged from the sunlight the elodea are exposed to in their natural environment.

8. A: Because metals tend to consist of ordered, tightly packed atoms, their densities are typically high (not low).

9. C: The tree root is breaking up the rocks and minerals that form the foundation of the house without changing their chemical composition. The other choices are examples of chemical weathering.

10. D: The cell wall is the structure that gives plant cells their rigidity.

11. A: When water changes form, it does not change the chemical composition of the substance. Once water becomes ice, the ice can easily turn back into water.

12. D: From the graph, it is clear that the activity of gastric protease drops off completely at a pH around 7. Entering the small intestine with a pH greater than 7 would cause the enzyme reactivity to decrease or stop completely.

13. C: The highest point on the graph for α-amylase is its optimal pH level because that is where it is the most reactive. According to this graph, that level is a pH of 7.

14. A: Splitting a single water molecule to form two molecules ($H_2O \rightarrow H_2 + O_2$) increases the number of molecules in the system, increasing entropy.

The other choices decrease entropy by decreasing temperature or volume.

15. B: Earth takes approximately twenty-four hours to rotate on its axis.

16. A: Neptune, like Jupiter, has a low density and a large radius.

17. B: A lunar eclipse is when Earth moves between the moon and the sun.

18. A: Primary succession can only occur on newly exposed earth that was not previously inhabited by living things. Often this new land is the result of lava flows or glacial movement.

Answer Explanations

19. D: The solubility for Na_2HAsO_4 at 50°C is around 55 grams per 100 grams of water. This is the highest for the solutes listed on the graph.

20. D: At 100°C about 40 grams of NaCl is soluble. The solubility of NaCl decreases with a decrease in temperature.

21. B: At day 10, the population held at 35°C had a survival rate of 41 percent, which is less than 50 percent. All the other population have a survival rate greater than 50 percent.

22. C: The growth rate is the variable that is dependent on the changes to water temperature and concentration of salt in the water.

23. A: Muscle cells use ATP to create muscle contractions, so they need high numbers of mitochondria to produce the needed ATP.

24. C: Mice produce large numbers of offspring but do little or no caretaking for their young.

25. A: Humans produce a small number of offspring and care closely for them.

26. C: Oak trees produce large numbers of offspring but do no caretaking for their young.

27. B: Ducks have a moderate number of offspring and provide some care for them.

28. B: Chemical energy is stored in the bonds between atoms.

29. C: Estuaries are found at the boundary of ocean and stream biomes and are very ecologically productive areas.

30. C: Light passes through the epidermis and strikes the pigment chlorophyll, which absorbs the wavelengths of light that humans see as red and blue and reflects the wavelengths of light that the human eye perceives as green.

31. B: A closed system allows exchange of energy but not matter with its surroundings. Matter (water) cannot enter or leave the balloon, but energy in the form of heat can penetrate the balloon. Choices A and D are open systems, and choice C is an isolated system.

32. D: A catalyst reduces the activation energy by creating an alternative reaction mechanism for the reaction.

33. A: Plug the variables into the appropriate formula and solve for acceleration.

$$v_f = v_i + at$$
$$4\ m/s = 0 + a(8\ s)$$
$$a = \frac{4\ m/s}{8\ s}$$
$$a = \frac{1}{2}\ m/s^2$$

34. C: The acceleration due to gravity is highest on Jupiter, so the object's speed would increase at the greatest rate on Jupiter.

35. C: The mass of an object is constant. The weight of an object depends on the force of gravity that the object experiences. The gravity on the surface of Mars is less than Earth's, so object B will have the same mass but a smaller weight.

36. C: During radioactive decay, an atom's nucleus emits particles and energy, which changes the composition of the atom's nucleus.

37. B: Use the half-life equation:
$$A = A_0 \left(\frac{1}{2}\right)^{\frac{t}{h}}$$
$$A = 120 \frac{1}{2}^{\frac{24}{8}} = 120 \times \frac{1}{2}^3 = 120 \times \frac{1}{8} = 15$$

38. D: A population is all the members of the same species in a given area.

39. B: Ernest Rutherford introduced the concept of the nucleus, which he claimed contained the positive charge of the atom and most of its mass.

40. B: In a commensal relationship, one species benefits with no impact on the other.

41. A: From the data on the graph, there is a clear correlation between increased size of bird nest and parent mortality.

42. C: The material that transfers heat the best will have the highest temperature. Wood and rubber are insulators, and metal is a conductor; therefore, the metal will have the highest temperature.

43. A: The element with the atomic number 11 (for eleven protons) is sodium. If it has one more proton than electron ($11 - 10 = 1$), it has a charge of +1. This cation is written as Na^+.

44. B: Br^- is element number 35, which means it has thirty-five protons. Mg^{2+} has twelve, Na^+ has eleven, and $N3^-$ has seven.

45. D: By losing one electron and thereby adopting a +1 charge, alkali metals achieve a noble gas electron configuration, making them more stable.

46. C: Antimony is a metalloid. Rubidium is a metal, vanadium is a transition metal, and iodine is a halogen.

47. D: For the atom to be neutral, it must have the same number of protons and electrons. If oxygen has eight protons, then a neutral atom of oxygen must have eight electrons.

48. B: Atomic number is defined as the total number of protons in the nucleus of an atom.

49. D: Oxygen is in the same group as sulfur and is also a nonmetal.

50. C: Vacuoles are large organelles found in plant cells and some animal cells. They store water, waste, and compounds that are needed for specialized tasks, including proteins.

51. D: The pulmonary veins carry oxygenated blood from the lungs to the heart.

52. A: The aorta carries oxygenated blood from the heart to the body.

53 B: During photosynthesis, plants use carbon dioxide (CO_2) from the air to produce sugars. Burning fossil fuels, deforestation, and animal respiration all add CO_2 to the atmosphere.

54 C: Structures and buildings can contain carbon but are not natural carbon reservoirs. The oceans, soil, and atmosphere all store carbon.

55. B: At a divergent plate boundary, the plates are moving away from each other forming a trench or valley.

Answer Explanations

56. B: The graph shows that the solubility of gases increases with an increase in pressure. Because carbon dioxide (CO_2) is a gas, its solubility in water increases with pressure. The solubility of liquids and solids remains the same when pressure increases.

57. A: Deserts are biomes with low rainfall that are home to a moderately diverse community of drought- tolerant grasses and shrubs.

58. A: Tropical rainforests are biomes characterized by high temperatures, high rainfall, biodiversity, and dense forests.

59. A: Boiling water is an endothermic process that absorbs energy, such that the product (water vapor) has more energy than the reactant (liquid water). Burning wood and nuclear fission are both exothermic reactions that release energy in the form of heat and light. Slicing a cake does not produce a change in the chemical composition of the cake, and thus does not use or release energy.

60. B: The Calvin cycle is the set of reactions during photosynthesis in which ATP is used to convert CO_2 and water to sugar.

Social Studies

1. B: One of Roosevelt's famous quotes about US diplomacy in Latin America was that his goal was to "speak softly and carry a big stick" as he reinforced US influence in Latin America: the Roosevelt Corollary of the Monroe Doctrine. The phrase "The Big Stick in the Caribbean" is even included on the cartoon. He is also tiptoeing with a club, or a "big stick."

2. A: This is the best answer because it accounts for all the symbolism embedded in the political cartoon. Roosevelt, a president who invoked the power of the Monroe Doctrine, believed that the United States should police Latin America using diplomatic influence, with the threat of military force. The larger-than-life, giant depiction of Roosevelt conveys a sense of power and authority in the region. The US Navy is also smaller than him, but also towed and controlled by him. He is carrying a "big stick" to symbolize his assertive power, but he is also tiptoeing around the coast of the region in order not to disrupt relationships too much.

3. C: The colonial military did have strong leaders, and an intimate knowledge of the terrain, many having been born there.

4. A: Serfs were not slaves, but they were not entirely free as they were bound to the lord's land and had to farm it. However, the lord was obligated to protect them, and they were not expected to fight.

5. B: The Thirteenth Amendment, which abolished slavery, was not added until after the Civil War.

6. A: The First Amendment, which also protects freedom of speech, protects freedom of religion.

7. D: Some Americans quote the Second Amendment to protect their "right to bear arms," which is justified by the Bill of Rights as being "necessary for the security of a free state."

8. C: Economic growth is shown by an overall outward shift in the production possibility curve, as would happen if A moved to D.

9. B: Since most OPEC countries are located in the Middle East and North Africa, those regions are important in determining world gasoline prices.

10. A: Although the United States has been trying to be more independent when it comes to energy in recent years, it is still very dependent on OPEC's price-setting process for oil and gas. The United States is not part of OPEC, as the map shows, but it is still a top oil consumer. This means it has to work with OPEC in order to navigate its oil dependency.

11. B: The Know-Nothings were an underground nativist and anti- immigrant group.

12. B: Borders did not account for history or ethnic groups; installed rulers did not necessarily have legitimacy in the eyes of the people, leading to political instability and violence.

13. D: Davis referred to all these points in his speech.

14. B: Davis justifies his departure based upon the right of Mississippi as a state to maintain a society based on the premise that all men were *not* free and equal.

15. C: Davis asserts that Mississippi has the right to maintain slavery, since "the theory that all men are created free and equal, and this made the basis of an attack upon her social institutions."

16. B: Including the Bill of Rights in the Constitution was a condition of ratification for several states.

17. A: The Supremacy Clause declares the Constitution the highest law in the land. The only way to change the Constitution is through the amendment process; no individual has authority higher than the Constitution.

18. C: A veto is a formal rejection of a bill by the president. The only way for a vetoed bill to become a law is through a two-thirds vote in both houses of Congress.

19. C: Consumers provide the demand for products. They do not play a role in production.

20. B: Cesar Chavez and the UFW advocated for the rights of Mexican and Mexican American farmworkers in the United States, who were often disadvantaged. The activism of the UFW set a precedent for later advocacy in support of Hispanic Americans.

21. A: French colonists were generally single men seeking profit; if they stayed, they were more likely than the British to intermarry.

22. C: A megalopolis is a large urban area formed by the close proximity of multiple urban centers. These five cities are sometimes called the "BosWash megalopolis."

23. D: All of the above are true.

24. C: According to the diagram, the judicial branch interprets the laws that are created by Congress and enforced by the executive branch.

25. D: As the diagram illustrates, Congress is the only governmental entity that is able to impeach the president.

26. C: The president can veto laws, but that's not the same as declaring them unconstitutional; that power belongs to the Supreme Court.

27. B: The president can veto laws passed by Congress.

28. A: According to the diagram, the legislative branch creates laws.

29. C: Pyongyang is located at approximately 39°N, 126°E.

30. C: Watergate destroyed many Americans' trust in the government, which had already been weakened after the turbulent 1960s and the Vietnam War.

Answer Explanations

31. A: The United States was the aggressor in the Spanish-American War—it was never definitively proven that the *Maine* was actually attacked by Spain. Furthermore, the war was fought in several different theaters worldwide.

32. B: The law of demand states that, holding all else constant, an increase in price causes a fall in demand.

33. A: As the American political system has moved closer to a direct democracy, many people feel that the Electoral College is anachronistic. They believe the president should be the candidate who wins the majority vote of the people.

34. D: Caesar, with the support of dissatisfied Romans, took over the weak and corrupt Senate.

35. B: The Mandate of Heaven legitimized imperial governance.

36. A: In 1898, the United States was at its peak as an imperial state. Following the Spanish-American War, the empire had grown to include enclaves in the Caribbean and the Pacific. The wide-reaching wings of the eagle convey a sense of not only protection, but expansion.

37. B: The smaller eagle (labeled 1798) protects a smaller United States. But the larger eagle (labeled 1898) protects an entire American empire. The message here is that the United States has expanded dramatically into a global empire in as little as 100 years.

38. A: Coal is a finite resource. It is an organic rock formed over millions of years.

39. B: Each of these amendments was proposed either after a Supreme Court decision or in anticipation of one. For example, in 1973 the Supreme Court determined in *Roe v. Wade* that abortions are legal. Now, the only way to change that would be through a new decision or constitutional amendment.

40. C: If a bill arrives at the president's desk within ten days of the end of the term, he or she can cause the bill to fail simply by doing nothing. This is called a pocket veto.

41. D: Small states wanted equal apportionment of representation in the legislature, while large states wanted proportional representation.

42. A: The Zimmerman Telegram, a German offer to assist Mexico in attacking the U.S., forced the United States to enter WWI, following a series of other German provocations.

43. D: The Voting Rights Act abolished discriminatory restrictions that prevented African Americans from exercising their right to vote.

44. B: When one person turns on the lights in their house, it does not prevent anyone else from turning on their own lights.

45. B: Martin Luther and his followers opposed corruption in the Church and wanted changes.

46. C: Price cannot be determined from the information given; however, the lowered tomato price will increase the supply of ketchup, and the higher mustard price will increase the demand for ketchup. Together, these will increase the overall supply of ketchup.

47. A: The apartheid in South Africa and the Jim Crow segregation laws in the United States were very similar: they both banned blacks and other people of color from entering white spaces in public. These spaces were typically labeled with signs like the one above.

48. D: The phrase "reserved for the exclusive use of white persons" signals that this sign is mostly about separation by race, or racial segregation.

49. B: The inclusion of two languages on the sign shows that South Africa had more than one widely spoken language. During apartheid, the government only recognized Afrikaans and English as official languages, even though many South Africans spoke other languages such as Zulu and Xhosa. After apartheid, the government recognized eleven official languages, more accurately reflecting the population of the country.

50. A: The "anti-war" sign and the youthful characteristics of the protesters indicate that it is likely a student protest. The casual clothes and acts of nonviolent protest contextualize the photograph in the late 1960s, during the era of the Vietnam War.

51. B: The protest, as depicted in this photo, is generally peaceful/non-violent, as symbolized by the extension of the flower toward military forces, but there is also the imposing presence/force of the military police who form a phalanx in front of the protesters.

52. B: The main factors in post-WWI German economic collapse are all addressed here.

53. C: According to the map, Montana is one of the largest states but has the lowest number of electoral votes. With only three votes, it is evident that Montana has just one US representative (and two senators). This is the lowest number a state can have, which means that Montana must have a small population.

54. B: This correct answer subtracts the proper number of US senators (two) from the total number of electoral votes in Texas to arrive at the correct number of US representatives: thirty-six.

55. D: This answer correctly notes New Jersey's small territorial size and also accounts for the fact that New Jersey has a similar number of electoral college votes as physically larger states like North Carolina.

56. B: According to the map, California has fifty-five Electoral College votes, while Texas has thirty-eight. California therefore must have a larger population, because it has fifty-three US representatives, whereas Texas only has thirty-six. US representatives are determined based on a state's population. Electoral College votes are determined by adding the number of a state's US representatives to its senators. Every state has two senators.

57. D: Most of the states in the Great Plains and Rocky Mountain region have quite small Electoral College votes. Several states in the northern Great Plains and Rocky Mountain region have only three Electoral College votes, meaning they only have one US representative and therefore have very small populations.

58 C: As a governing document, the Mayflower Compact was notable in that it provided for governance with the consent of the governed, a departure from British rule.

59. A: Maroon communities were communities of escaped slaves throughout the Americas.

60. B: Following the war, the United States took control of the Southwest (today, Arizona, New Mexico, and adjacent areas), as well as California.

Answer Explanations

Practice Test #2

To reduce paper usage, and to provide users with an online testing experience, the second practice test is found on our online resource page. Follow the link below or scan the QR code for the SECOND HiSET practice test:

acceptedinc.com/hiset-online-resources

Dear HiSET test taker,

Great job completing this study guide. The hard work and effort you put into your test preparation will help you succeed on your upcoming HiSET exam. Thank you for letting us be a part of your education journey!

We have other study guides and products that you may find useful. Search for us on Amazon.com or let us know what you are looking for. We offer a wide variety of study guides that cover a multitude of subjects.

If you would like to share your success stories with us, or if you have a suggestion, comment, or concern, please send us an email at support@triviumtestprep.com.

Thanks again for choosing us!
Happy Testing
Accepted, Inc. Team

www.ingramcontent.com/pod-product-compliance
Lightning Source LLC
Chambersburg PA
CBHW080329170426
43194CB00014B/2506